Contemporary Germany:
Politics and Culture

About the Book and Editors

Contemporary Germany: Politics and Culture
edited by Charles Burdick, Hans-Adolf Jacobsen, and Winfried Kudszus

A joint effort by American, German, and English scholars, this volume focuses on Germany since 1945, mainly on the Federal Republic of Germany and to a lesser extent on the German Democratic Republic. The first part, edited by Charles Burdick and Hans-Adolf Jacobsen, contains chapters on history, political structures, and economic developments. The second part, edited by Winfried Kudszus, discusses literature, film, and art, with the literary chapters covering the entirety of German letters, in which Austrian and Swiss German writings play an important role. The two parts provide a background for post-1945 developments by covering history and literature, respectively, from 1871 to 1945.

The publication of this volume follows the tricentennial of German immigration to the U.S. With the cross-disciplinary information they have assembled, representing a wide range of perspectives and approaches, the authors offer new insights into the growing field of German studies and shed light on divergent views of contemporary Germany.

Charles Burdick is professor and past chairman of the Department of History at San Jose University, where he specializes in twentieth-century history. **Hans-Adolf Jacobsen,** chairman of the Department of Political Science at the University of Bonn, is the author of numerous books on German politics. **Winfried Kudszus,** professor of German at the University of California at Berkeley, has published extensively on German literature.

Published in cooperation with the University of Bonn,
the University of California, Berkeley,
and the National Endowment for the Humanities

Contemporary Germany: Politics and Culture

edited by Charles Burdick,
Hans-Adolf Jacobsen, and
Winfried Kudszus

Westview Press / Boulder and London

Copyright © 1984 by Charles B. Burdick, Hans-Adolf Jacobsen, and Winfried Kudszus

Published in 1984 in the United States of America by
  Westview Press, Inc.
  5500 Central Avenue
  Boulder, Colorado 80301
  Frederick A. Praeger, Publisher

Library of Congress Cataloging in Publication Data
Main entry under title:
Contemporary Germany.
  Includes index.
  1. Germany (West)—Politics and government—Addresses, essays, lectures. 2. Germany (West)—Economic conditions—Addresses, essays, lectures. 3. Germany—Politics and government—20th century—Addresses, essays, lectures. 4. German literature—20th century—History and criticism—Addresses, essays, lectures. 5. Arts—Germany—Addresses, essays, lectures. I. Burdick, Charles Burton, 1927– . II. Jacobsen, Hans-Adolf, 1925– . III. Kudszus, Winfried, 1941– .
DD259.4.C67   1984   943.087   83-5825
ISBN 0-86531-443-8
ISBN 0-86531-449-7 (pbk.)

Printed and bound in the United States of America

Contents

Photographs

Preface

This volume, a joint effort by American, German, and English scholars, consists entirely of original contributions. It focuses on Germany since 1945, mainly on the Federal Republic of Germany and to a lesser extent on the German Democratic Republic.

The first part of the volume, edited by Charles Burdick and Hans-Adolf Jacobsen, contains chapters on history, political structures, and economic developments. Translations of Chapters 2, 3, 5, and 7 were provided by Richard Straus.

The second part of the volume, edited by Winfried Kudszus, contains chapters on literature, film, and art. In the literary chapters, Austrian and Swiss German writings play an important role. Translations of Chapters 15 and 17 were provided by Francis M. Sharp, who also contributed to the translation of Chapter 14.

The two parts provide a background for post-1945 developments by discussing history and literature, respectively, from 1871–1945. Issues, trends, and countercurrents appear in a broad context, spanning more than a century.

The publication of this volume follows the tricentennial of German immigration to the United States; the book is aimed at American readers concerned with German studies. It is a cross-disciplinary work designed to fill a gap in this growing field of area studies. Contributions were obtained from noted scholars who reflect a wide range of perspectives and approaches that shed light on divergent views of contemporary Germany.

The editors wish to extend their appreciation to all whose scholarly contributions enhanced this volume and to our two translators. For their help in the preparation of the manuscript, the editors' particular appreciation goes to Lynn Arts at Westview Press, to Dorothea Jacobsen and Dagmar Grope in Bonn, to Elaine Straus in Washington, and to Irmgard Mehmedbasich in Berkeley. For the expert work on the index and on bibliographical matters, they wish to thank Lisa Whicker in Berkeley. Leroy L. Miller in Washington and Victor Udwin in Berkeley provided valuable research assistance, and Johanna Mayer in Palo Alto gave generous counsel.

A special word of thanks goes to Richard Straus, whose editorial consulting and astute advice were indispensable throughout the preparation of the book. We are also grateful for Frederick Praeger's extraordinary contribution in giving the book its final shape, both in substance and in detail. Last, but not least, the editors wish to express their appreciation for the generous financial assistance made available by the National Endowment for the Humanities, the University of Bonn, and the University of California, Berkeley.

Charles Burdick   *Hans-Adolf Jacobsen*   *Winfried Kudszus*
San Jose   *Bonn*   *Berkeley*

Literary Credits

The editors would like to thank the following publishers and individuals for granting permission for reproduction and translation of material that appears in Part 2 of this book:

Page 247: "The Two," by Hugo von Hofmannsthal, translated by Walter Kaufmann in Kaufmann, *Twenty German Poets,* New York: Random House, 1962; pp. 174-75. Used by permission of Hazel D. Kaufmann.

Pages 252/53: "The Panther," by Rainer Maria Rilke, translated by C. F. MacIntyre in MacIntyre, *Rainer Maria Rilke: 50 Selected Poems,* Berkeley: University of California Press, 1947; p. 63. © 1940, renewed 1968 by C. F. MacIntyre. Used by permission.

Page 256: "World's End," by Jakob van Hoddis, translated by J. M. Ritchie in Paul Raabe, ed., *The Era of German Expressionism,* Woodstock, New York: The Overlook Press, 1974; pp. 44-45. Translation © Calder & Boyars, 1974. Original © Verlags AG "Die Arche," Zürich, 1958. Used by permission.

Page 257: Excerpts from "Songs," by Gottfried Benn, translated by Francis M. Sharp for this volume; © for original held by Ernst Klett–J. G. Cotta'sche Buchhandlung Nachfolger GmbH, Stuttgart. Used by permission.

Pages 258-59: "Grodek," by Georg Trakl, translated by Francis M. Sharp in Sharp, *The Poet's Madness: A Reading of Georg Trakl,* Ithaca: Cornell University Press, 1981; p. 188. © 1981 by Cornell University Press. Used by permission of the publisher.

Page 261: Excerpt from "Caravan," by Hugo Ball. © for original (identical with translation) held by Verlags AG "Die Arche," Zürich. Used by permission.

Pages 292-93: "Daily behind the barracks . . . ," by Ruth Klüger, translated by Sander Gilman. © Ruth Klüger. Used by permission.

Page 307: Excerpt from Peter Handke, *Kaspar and Other Plays,* translated by Michael Roloff. Used by permission from Farrar, Straus & Giroux, Inc., New York.

Page 340: Excerpt from "Inventory," by Günter Eich, translated by Francis M. Sharp for this volume. © for original held by Suhrkamp Verlag, Frankfurt. Used by permission.

Page 341: Excerpt from "Above all I experience bottles . . . ," by Gottfried Benn, translated by Francis M. Sharp for this volume. © for original held by Ernst Klett–J. G. Cotta'sche Buchhandlung Nachfolger GmbH, Stuttgart. Used by permission.

Page 341: Excerpt from "I have often asked myself . . . ," by Gottfried Benn, translated by Francis M. Sharp for this volume. © for original held by Ernst Klett–J.G. Cotta'sche Buchhandlung Nachfolger GmbH, Stuttgart. Used by permission.

Page 342: "Thread Suns," by Paul Celan, translated by Michael Hamburger. © for translation, Michael Hamburger, 1980. © for original held by Suhrkamp Verlag, Frankfurt. Used by permission.

PART ONE

□

Historical Background, Politics, and Economy

JAMES J. SHEEHAN

1

German Politics, 1871–1933

Nations are so much a part of our modern world that we tend to see them as natural phenomena, the historically necessary expression of a people's political identity. We readily assume that the lines on the map *must* run the way they do because they describe deeply rooted ethnic, cultural, and linguistic communities. Nowhere is this the case. There is something artificial, contingent, even accidental about practically every nation-state. From Iberia to the Russian steppes, from Scandinavia to Sicily, cartographers' lines have been drawn in response to particular historical circumstances, dynastic alliances, political agreements, and most frequently, the outcome of military conflicts. Why should Catalonia be part of Spain, while Portugal is not? Why should Nice be a French city, while Brussels is not? On what ethnic or linguistic community do states like the Netherlands and Switzerland depend? Similar questions can be asked about almost every state in modern Europe. Most historians do not ask such questions because most national history is written by and for those who finally succeeded in imposing their model of how the nation should look. Consciously or unconsciously, this winners' history presents the nation as the inevitable product of a natural historical process. Power over a nation's present and future has always involved the power to shape the picture of its past.

These general considerations are important to bear in mind when we consider the German Empire, proclaimed by the princes of its member states in the Hall of Mirrors at Versailles in January 1871. This Reich was, its historians have told us again and again, the ultimate realization of the Germans' longing for political unity. After decades of delays and disappointments, the political genius of Bismarck used the power of the Prussian state to achieve the will of the *Volk*. In reality, however, the Reich proclaimed in 1871 was a very imperfect expression of the German national community. The new nation *excluded* millions of German-speaking people living in Austria and Switzerland and in islands of ethnicity scattered across Eastern Europe. Moreover, the Reich *included* a French minority in the west, a small number of Danes in the north, and almost two and a half million Poles in the east. Even among its German-speaking citizens, there were many who did not acknowledge the Reich as their fatherland. Prussian conservatives and Bavarian Catholics, particularists in Hanover and Saxony—these groups and many others viewed the new nation with dislike and distrust. And of course there were millions more who took little interest in the princes' proclamation. In the crowded tenements of German cities and the crude dwellings of peasant villages, men and women had other things to worry about. To these members of the *Volk* the unfolding national pageant seemed to have little immediate significance.

We must be aware from the outset, therefore, that the date with which our story begins marked the formation of the German Reich as a sovereign state, but not as a political community. Such a community could not be proclaimed, nor could it be won on the battlefield. It had to emerge, slowly and unevenly, from a complex process of institutional and cultural development. In this sense, 1871 marks the beginning, not the end, of German nation-building.

Integration and Conflict in the Kaiserreich, 1871–1914

"The great questions of our time will not be decided with speeches and proclamations—that was the great error of 1848–1849—they will be decided with blood and iron." With these famous words, spoken to a shocked audience of liberal parliamentarians in September 1862, Otto von Bismarck began his career as Prussian minister president. Bismarck and his audience knew that "the great questions of our time" had to do with Germany's political future, with the problem of nationhood and the long-standing contest for leadership between Prussia and Austria. And in questions like this, Bismarck's insistence on the priority of force is difficult to dispute. The shape of the German nation, like that of almost every major state, was determined by blood and iron. Without the Prussian victories, over Denmark in 1864, Austria in 1866, and France in 1870, the Reich would not have come into existence. But force is a necessary, not a sufficient basis for nationhood. Once the blood has been spilled and the iron's work is done, words—speeches and proclamations—become important once again, to praise the victors and conciliate the vanquished, to dignify power and legitimate its use. Of this fact, Bismarck, for all his bluster and violent rhetoric, was acutely aware. No sooner had the military victories been achieved than he moved to create a set of institutions through which Prussia's conquests could be transformed into a stable order.

A convinced royalist and Prussian patriot, Bismarck hoped to strengthen the position of his king and state by linking them to the forces of popular representation and German nationalism. To do this he designed a constitution that rested on a complicated set of balances, between national unity and federal power and between monarchical authority and parliamentary participation. At the center of the imperial system was the king of Prussia, who, as German emperor, commanded the armed forces in time of war, represented the nation abroad, and appointed the chancellor, the Reich's only constitutionally designated executive officer. The other key central institution was the national parliament, the Reichstag, which was composed of 397 delegates elected by all adult males. The Reichstag could not appoint or dismiss the chancellor, but its control over the budget gave it significant influence over the government, as did its right to approve all national legislation. In 1871, however, no one knew just how significant either the chancellor or the Reichstag would be. The obvious functions of government—law enforcement, education, religious policy—remained the prerogatives of the states, which retained their own representative institutions and bureaucratic apparatus. The states all had access to national power through the Bundesrat (the Federal Council), which shared legislative power with the Reichstag. Because of its control over the largest Bundesrat delegation, Prussia was able to exercise an effective veto over any constitutional changes and had a dominant position in the Bundesrat's deliberations.[1]

The most extraordinary and in the long run the most consequential element in the new constitution was the Reichstag's democratic suffrage. Bismarck, who was in no sense a democrat by conviction, had introduced this suffrage because he believed that the majority of Germans were patriotic, monarchical, and willing to follow the lead of their social superiors. He expected the masses of the *Volk* to be much more willing to support his policies than those propertied and educated elites that had given him so much trouble during his first years in politics.[2] In fact, the democratic suffrage did not promote a politics based on deference. On the contrary, electoral democracy brought into the central arena of German politics social forces that became increasingly difficult to control. Within a few years, Bismarck was looking for ways to bypass the Reichstag; by the end of his long career he was toying with the idea of a coup d'etat that would enable him to reestablish the imperial system on a more stable basis.

The following figures provide some idea of how the "participation revolution" transformed German public life between the formation of the Reich and World War I: In the first imperial election of 1871, the German electorate numbered 7.65 million, of whom 3.88 million (50.8 percent) actually went to the polls; forty-one years later, in the last prewar election (1912), the number of eligible voters had doubled, while the number of those voting had risen to 12.2 million, an extraordinary 84.5 percent of the electorate. Data like these have meaning only if we think about the institutional and attitudinal changes they reflect: the growth of political parties and interest groups, the emergence of a mass press and other forms of communication, the expansion of government, and the increasing relevance of politics for people's everyday lives. And of course these developments were themselves part of larger social and cultural transformations, economic development and industrialization, demographic growth and social mobility, improvements in popular education, and a weakening of certain kinds of local loyalties and identifications. The growth of a mass electorate, therefore, is at once cause and reflection of a much deeper and more complex process of integration, a process that helped to create a sense of national identity, which had been confined to a minority of the population when the Reich was founded in 1871.

The same forces that created a national social and political system also generated new sources of conflict and discontent. This was the painful irony of German public life after 1871: The more Germans became part of a single community, the more reasons they found to break into separate groups, each defined in opposition to another. Economic developments, for example, created powerful bonds within the Reich, such as an extensive transportation network and national markets for commodities, capital, and labor. But economic growth also produced deep social conflicts, among regions, between city and countryside, and of course between capital and labor. Similarly, the mass press made people more aware of their national identity at the same time that it fed their special interests and political antagonisms. The democratic suffrage was also an integrating as well as a fragmenting force: When they voted, an extraordinarily large percentage of the adult male population acted together, involved at the same time and in the same way in a powerful rite of participation. The most manifest outcome of this ritual, however, was the articulation of cleavages throughout state and society.

Perhaps the quickest way to survey some of the divisions within imperial Germany is to consider the major political parties. During the early years of the new nation, from 1867 to 1878, the liberals were the strongest and most influential political force in German public life. In the Reichstag they were divided into two major parties, the National Liberals and the Progressives, the former more supportive of Bismarck, the latter more critical. Both liberal parties, however, backed key aspects of government policy during this formative period. They provided the parliamentary base for the economic, social, and judicial legislation that consolidated the Reich and laid the groundwork for its further integration. By the end of the 1870s, the alliance between Bismarck and the liberals had deteriorated; at the same time, they had begun to lose electoral ground to new political forces, both on the right and on the left. In 1874 the two liberal parties had had a majority in the Reichstag, as well as in most important state and local parliaments. By the turn of the century they had been reduced to an embattled minority, internally divided and cut off from a large section of the population.

The Free Conservatives were as close to a governmental party as existed in imperial Germany. Essentially a party of notables—great landowners, top-ranking civil servants, wealthy entrepreneurs—the Free Conservatives paid little attention to political organizations or electoral campaigns; their parliamentary positions depended on social prestige and local influence. Not surprisingly, the democratization of German politics significantly undermined their power: By 1912 there were just over a dozen of them left in the Reichstag. The Conservative party had a more complicated and significant history. Led by those Prussian landowners conventionally called "Junkers," the Conservatives were at first uncertain whether or not they wanted to participate in the Reich. Their primary loyalty was to Prussia, not the new Germany. Moreover, as defenders of hierarchy and privilege, they recoiled from Bismarck's democratic suffrage. Eventually, however, the Conservatives did become engaged in German politics, even though their geographical base remained in Prussia and their antipathy to democracy continued. In the 1890s, at a time when their social and economic positions seemed in serious jeopardy, the Junkers tried to broaden the basis of their party's support by working with and through the Agrarian League, the Bund der Landwirte, which engaged in intense popular agitation and sought to appeal to a broad cross-section of farmers, craftsmen, and small proprietors. The Bund der Landwirte, together with several similar right-wing organizations in the 1890s, propagated an unsavory blend of anti-Semitism, antimodernism, and antisocialism that anticipated fascist programs after 1918. Even with the Bund's support, however, the Conservatives remained a small minority: In 1912 they received less than 10 percent of the vote and elected only forty-three delegates.

By far the most stable feature of the German political landscape was the Center party, which managed to return between ninety and one hundred delegates in every election between 1874 and 1912; it held more than seventy districts without interruption throughout this period. The main source of the Center's persistence was its affiliation with the institutions of the German Catholic church, which had been mobilized for electoral purposes by the anti-Catholic campaigns waged by Bismarck and his liberal allies during the early 1870s. Over time, the Center had had to become engaged in a variety of political and social issues; in some regions its religious appeal began to be less important than other aspects of its program. Nonetheless, it remained a confessional party, which could hold together its various discordant elements only by common allegiance to—and dependence upon—the church.

As impressive as the Center's stability was the dramatic growth of social democracy. In 1871 the Social Democrats were internally divided, organizationally weak, and consistently harassed by the government. They were able to elect only two delegates with 124,000 votes. Thereafter their strength steadily increased, despite the repressive measures taken against them between 1878 and 1890. By 1912, one out of three German voters cast his ballot for the Socialists; their delegation of 110 members was the largest in the Reichstag. In contrast to the other parties, the Social Democratic party (SPD) did not have nonpolitical institutions on which it could depend. Its leaders lacked the local connections and social prestige that assisted both liberals and conservatives; nor could they count on the dense network of institutions available to the representatives of political Catholicism. The Social Democrats' strength had to rest on their own institutional base, clubs, local party groups, and eventually trade unions. By 1912, the SPD was a model of modern political organization, not only in Germany but throughout Europe.

After Bismarck's break with the liberals in 1878, the imperial government was unable to build a solid parliamentary foundation for its policies. Despite a few temporary successes, most notably by Bismarck in 1887 and by Bernhard von Bülow in 1907, governmental majorities always collapsed under the weight of their divergent economic interests and political values. Normally, chancellors were forced to build a series of ad hoc alliances, which changed from issue to issue. This became increasingly difficult as the Reichstag's composition shifted to the left. By the time Theobald von Bethmann-Hollweg was named chancellor in 1909, it was nearly impossible for the government to chart a coherent political course. All along the political spectrum, contemporaries complained about a lack of direction in both foreign and domestic affairs. The bright promise of the new nation so lyrically celebrated in 1871 had given way to the darkest fears about present drift and future danger.

These fears were felt most strongly by those who benefited most from the existing social and political order. The Junkers, despite their narrow social base, played a disproportionately large role in the Prussian bureaucracy and the officer corps. Their political and social values had been adopted by some industrialists and bankers, who invested in landed

TABLE 1
Reichstag Elections of 1871, 1890, 1912
(Total vote in millions)

Party	1871			1890			1912		
	Total vote	(%)	Seats	Total vote	(%)	Seats	Total vote	(%)	Seats
Conservative	0.549	(14.1)	57	0.895	(12.4)	73	1.126	(9.2)	43
Free Cons.	0.346	(8.9)	37	0.482	(6.7)	20	0.367	(3)	14
National Liberals	1.171	(30.1)	125	1.178	(16.3)	42	1.663	(13.6)	45
Left Liberals[1]	0.361	(9.3)	47	1.308	(18)	76	1.497	(12.3)	42
Center	0.724	(18.6)	63	1.342	(18.6)	106	1.997	(16.4)	91
Social Democrats	0.124	(3.2)	2	1.427	(19.7)	35	4.25	(34.8)	110
Anti-Semites, etc.				0.048	(.7)	5	0.3	(2.5)	10
Particularists[2]	0.253	(6.6)	20	0.475	(6.3)	38	0.706	(5.7)	33
Others	0.079	(2)	1	0.075	(1)	2	0.301	(2.5)	9
Total (% of eligible)	3.888	(51)	382[3]	7.229	(71.6)	397	12.2	(84.9)	397

[1]Includes the Fortschrittspartei and its various successors plus the Volkspartei.

[2]Includes the Guelphs, Danes, Poles, and the French from Alsace-Lorraine.

[3]Alsace-Lorraine did not elect delegates until 1874.

property, sent their sons into fashionable regiments, and married their daughters to the scions of prominent aristocratic families. Businessmen who profited from Germany's economic prosperity, academicians who enjoyed great social prestige, civil servants who ran the complex machinery of government—all these groups worried about the threat of social and political upheaval. They disagreed among themselves about what should be done but agreed that their power, privilege, and wealth were endangered by the weakness of the government and the strength of its democratic opponents.

In the years before the war, we can also find signs of discontent within all the major political parties, whose members frequently seemed restless and uncertain about their political commitments. Liberal voters often lacked any institutional connection to their party; only a minority of them were enthusiastic about the party's programs; most seemed to have voted liberal because they disliked the other alternatives. The Conservatives' constituency was threatened by radical right-wing parties and by the Social Democrats, who began to make some inroads among farm workers. Despite the stability of its Reichstag delegation, the Center party's position within the Catholic electorate was steadily declining. And even the Social Democrats' success was shadowed by the deep animosities within the party caused by those who believed (not without reason) that the leaders had abandoned their programmatic commitment to a radical transformation of the political and social system.

With anxieties among the elites and a variety of discontents at the grass roots, the German Reich in 1914 seems to have been a deeply flawed and fragile regime. But few regimes are so flawed and fragile that they simply collapse; regimes usually continue until they are replaced by something else, often after a long and painful struggle. If war had not come in 1914, what might that something else have been? It is difficult to believe that a revolution from the left could have occurred in the foreseeable future: The potential leaders of such a revolution were few in number, their potential support slender and dispersed, the forces against them formidable. Nor does it seem likely that there would have been a revolution from the right, an authoritarian coup to alter the Reichstag suffrage and repress dissent. Of course there were some Germans who would have been delighted by such a coup, but they were isolated and without influence. It is possible that the regime might have reformed itself from within, working in a peaceful way to soften social inequalities and remove the barriers to a parliamentary system. But the reformist alternative also seems unlikely when we consider how divided the reformers were among themselves and how resolute their enemies would have become, especially in a bastion of reaction like eastern Prussia.

The weakness of these alternatives suggests that many, perhaps most, Germans were willing to live with the status quo. However angry they may have been at particular policies, however frustrated by the Reich's injustices and inequalities, however eager for change, few on either the left or right were willing and able to run the risks any radical transformation would inevitably have involved. Most regimes rest upon a similar base: Few governments are intensely loved, many last because the alternatives seem unattainable or undesirable. Had there been no world war, the Reich, I suspect, could have continued to live with its difficulties and discontents, no more or less doomed to internal destruction than its counterparts throughout most of Western and Central Europe.

The origins of the war that destroyed the Kaiserreich have been studied more intensely than almost any other problem in modern German history. Since the publication of Fritz Fischer's monumental studies in the early 1960s, scholars have focused on two overlapping sets of questions. First, what was Germany's responsibility for the war? Was Germany, as Fischer and his followers claimed, the principal aggressor in 1914? Or was the war a product of misunderstandings and miscalculations to which all the major powers contributed? Second, what was the relationship between the war and German domestic politics? Did German statesmen decide to fight because they hoped a victory would enable them to preserve the social and political order? Or was their decision based on a diplomatic calculus that operated independently of its political setting? Despite an extraordinary amount of research on these issues, I think it is fair to say that they remain unresolved. Neither the Fischer school nor its opponents have been able to provide definitive answers to questions about Germany's responsibility for the war or the role of domestic politics in diplomatic calculations. The same documents that Fischer believed "proved" German culpability were interpreted quite differently by his critics, who then came up with equally authentic pieces of evidence to support their own case. Considering the tangle of difficulties and disagreements that surrounded this entire matter, we can do no more than briefly sketch the main lines of German foreign policy between the formation of the Reich and the outbreak of war.

As Bismarck himself recognized, the creation of a unified Germany fundamentally altered the European balance of power. The presence of a great nation in the heart of Europe increased the chances of a conflict that could embrace the entire continent. Bismarck feared that if a European war did come, Germany would have to fight enemies in both the east and west, "a nightmare coalition" against which his nation's power could not prevail. The best way to avoid such a coalition, he believed, was to keep France diplomatically isolated. To do this Germany had to have agreements with both the great eastern states, Russia and

Austria. But when Bismarck made overtures to the governments in Vienna and St. Petersburg, he found each eager for a German alliance— against the other. Throughout his tenure in office, Bismarck managed to keep lines open to both the eastern powers, although as time went on this required ever more elaborate and fragile diplomatic arrangements. It seems very likely that even if Bismarck had not been forced to resign in 1890, Germany would have had to choose between the two. In any case, shortly after Bismarck's dismissal, his successor did not renew Germany's treaty with Russia. Two years later, the Russians signed an agreement with the French. Bismarck's nightmare had become a reality.

Policymakers in Berlin hoped that they could counter the Franco-Russian combination by drawing Britain into an alliance with the Reich. Throughout the 1890s, a number of British and German statesmen labored to create an alliance between their nations, which they viewed as natural partners, the one dominating the continent, the other the sea. Both sides must bear part of the blame for the failure of these efforts, but a major share of the responsibility must rest with those German leaders who insisted that Germany should become a world power, with a great fleet and a colonial empire. Such ambitions, loudly proclaimed in Berlin by the kaiser and many of his major advisers, were viewed in London as a direct challenge to Britain's position in the world. By the turn of the century, therefore, the best opportunities for an Anglo-German alliance had passed. Within a few years, Britain began to make agreements with Germany's rivals, first with France, then in 1907 with Russia.

By 1907, international relations in Europe had been reduced to an unhealthy dualism. Britain, France, and Russia were tied together by a series of economic, political, and military agreements. Germany was formally allied to Austria and Italy, although it was by no means clear that Germany could count on the Italians' support in the event of military conflict. From 1910 on, all the powers expanded their armies and poured an increasing amount of their resources into preparing for war. Modern armies were of unprecedented size and technological complexity; modern wars, most experts believed, would be decided with great speed. As a result, strategists had coordinated their military plans with their nation's allies, tightening the political bonds among them and further narrowing the diplomats' room to maneuver. Nowhere was the unhealthy influence of the military more apparent than in Germany, where the officer corps enjoyed enormous prestige and political power, both in the councils of government and in the kaiser's entourage.

In 1912 and 1913, the political climate was poisoned by a number of conflicts in southeastern Europe, precisely the area in which the antagonism between Russia and Austria was most intense. The final crisis began in June 1914, when a group of South Slav terrorists, trained and armed by the Serbian Secret Service, assassinated the heir to the Austrian throne, Archduke Franz Ferdinand. The Austrians decided to use the murder as an excuse to humiliate the Serbs and thus remove a source of attraction for the restless Slavic minority within the Austrian empire. After receiving assurances of support from Berlin, the Austrians pressed a series of punitive measures against the Serbs, even when it seemed probable that Russia would come to Serbia's aid. By the time it had become obvious that neither side would back down, both alliance systems had become engaged and no one seemed willing or able to stop the outbreak of full-scale war.

Since we know what is coming, we watch the events of 1914 with horrified fascination. Like the characters in some ancient tragedy, the statesmen move relentlessly toward their own destruction, each step taking them closer to a conflagration that will engulf their world. Why did it happen? There is no doubt that the decisions taken in Berlin were crucial. Each of the powers could have stopped the war, but Germany could have done so more quickly and easily than most. Why did German statesmen not try to moderate the demands of their Austrian allies? Could it be that they wanted war in 1914? One thing seems clear: Few German leaders wanted the war they eventually got. But most were willing to risk a war, certainly against the Serbs, if necessary against the Russians, perhaps against the French. This risk seemed worth taking, not simply to support the Reich's only reliable partner but also to achieve greater mobility and flexibility on the international scene. When Chancellor Bethmann-Hollweg saw that the stakes were much higher than he had thought, he made some ineffective and perhaps insincere efforts to slow things down. The generals, however, brushed aside such last-minute interference. They had their own plans for a victory and their own timetable for achieving it.

What about the domestic scene? Was one motive for war the desire to escape the endemic crisis that seemed to grip the imperial political order? Did Bethmann-Hollweg hope that victory would bring greater flexibility to political life at home as well as abroad? The voluminous documentary records of this period do not provide answers to these questions. The few references to domestic politics that the documents contain reflect statesmen's concerns about war's political dangers rather than its potential advantages. It is difficult, therefore, to prove a case for domestic motivations. It is, however, also difficult to believe that there were no links between Germany's domestic situation and the horrendous miscalculations its leaders made in the summer of 1914. After all, the same men who made the decisions leading to war had been struggling to find a way out of the Reich's domestic doldrums.

That sense of inflexibility and decline so oppressive in Germany's foreign affairs had obvious analogues at home; the atmosphere of crisis and the longing to escape, so prevalent throughout Europe in the years before 1914, had both diplomatic and domestic sources.

The Collapse of the Kaiserreich and the Victory of the Moderate Alternative, 1914–1923

The declaration of war in the summer of 1914 produced an outburst of national enthusiasm that seemed to banish the discontents and close the cleavages within the imperial order. Catholics and Protestants, Social Democrats and liberals, workers and employers, all stood together in what they were convinced was a war to defend their nation against aggression. In those exciting August Days, as the troops marched west through flower-strewn streets, the German cause seemed just and victory certain. By Christmas the war for which the generals had prepared was over, but to their great surprise no one had won. From the English Channel to the Swiss frontier a jagged line of trenches took shape, scarring the landscape and marking out the ground over which millions would fight and die through four terrible years. As the war dragged on, the national cohesion of the August Days evaporated. Old antagonisms reappeared, new enmities were born. By 1917, the alternatives so dimly visible three years earlier had taken much clearer shape: On the left, the Independent Social Democrats had split off from the majority SPD and were demanding an immediate peace with radical change at home; on the right, the small but well-connected Fatherland party included many who favored the introduction of an authoritarian government that could purchase its legitimacy with the fruits of German victory; and in between a group of moderates, drawn from the liberal, Center, and majority Socialist parties, began to press for restricted war aims and limited reforms. From the summer of 1917 until the final collapse of the war effort a year later, the extremes of right and left reciprocally reinforced the other: As the left's demands grew louder, the right's call for victory became more urgent, and this conflict in turn made the need for peace and revolution seem yet more pressing. In a fashion that foreshadowed the shape of postwar politics, the moderates, who desperately tried to set a course between the extremes of left and right, were paralyzed by their own indecision and in the end were overtaken by events.

In September 1918 the German High Command finally recognized that victory was beyond its grasp. The U-boats had not been able to cut Britain off from its supplies or to stop the arrival of fresh U.S. troops; the spring offensives had failed; at home, food and supplies were running low while at the front, military discipline was beginning to weaken. In a sudden reversal of their position, therefore, the generals called upon the government to create a parliamentary regime that could set about making peace. Almost overnight, the moderates found themselves about to take power. But as the negotiations to end the fighting dragged on into early November, the floodgates of popular anger and war-weariness finally broke open. Beginning in the fleet anchored at Kiel and spreading more or less spontaneously throughout the Reich, revolutionary upheavals swept away the representatives of the old order with surprising speed. Garrisons surrendered and monarchs fled as the red flag was raised over public buildings from Hamburg to Munich. In the meantime, with an armistice finally at hand, the moderate leaders in Berlin declared a republic, with a caretaker government headed by Friedrich Ebert, a Social Democrat.

Ebert's position was extraordinarily difficult. He was the head of a government that did not exist—the last chancellor of a fallen empire, the first chancellor of a republic without a constitution. Neither the old governmental apparatus nor the revolutionary masses recognized the legitimacy of his rule. The tasks he faced were enormous: to restore order, make peace, and establish a new regime and to accomplish all this as swiftly as possible.

Ebert's path out of this thicket of difficulties involved some of the most fateful and controversial decisions in modern German history. Instead of allying with the left and trying to draw support from the revolutionary forces around him, Ebert struck a series of bargains with the representatives of the old regime. These agreements, some formal, some tacit or implied, joined Ebert's moderates with the established elites against the left. In late 1918 and early 1919, bands of armed volunteers, the so-called Freikorps, organized by and for the government, fought a bloody series of engagements against the revolutionaries. By the spring of 1919, when the constitutional convention gathered at Weimar finished drafting the legal basis for the new republic, the German revolution was over, many of its leaders were dead or in prison, the last red flag had been torn from its staff. The moderates apparently had won.[3] The republic was theirs. But the price of victory was high: The counterrevolutionary terror had permanently alienated a number of potentially democratic groups from the new regime, and a number of democracy's opponents remained in positions of power in the army, the civil service, and the economy.

Was Ebert's path the only one he could have taken? Was his alliance with the right forced upon him by events? Probably not; there is some evidence that the revolutionary movement was not, as Ebert feared, the German counterpart of Lenin's Bolsheviks, bent upon a total transformation of the social and political order. Many revolutionaries could have been used to defend parliamentary democracy. Furthermore, in his eagerness to ally himself with the forces of order, Ebert gave away too much and thereby let slip opportunities for reform that would not come again. It is difficult to quarrel with the remark of one moderate leader that "from 1918 to the Kapp Putsch (1920) politics were fluid and in this time the worst mistakes were made."[4] But it should also be noted that the choices open to Ebert are much clearer in retrospect than they were at the time. A man of order, who had made his career by working his way up through the organizational hierarchy of the Social Democratic party, Ebert hated revolution like the plague. The Russian model was fresh and powerful, its relevance to his own situation difficult to dismiss. Ebert's decisions are surely regrettable, but considering the circumstances and the man, they are certainly understandable.

From 1919 until the end of 1923 the Weimar Republic was in a state of chronic crisis. In June 1919 the victorious Western powers imposed upon Germany the Treaty of Versailles, a harsh settlement seen by the overwhelming majority of Germans as vindictive and unfair. Not only did the treaty seem to place the blame for the war on Germany and its allies, it also burdened them with paying reparations to compensate the victors for the damages caused by Germany's alleged aggression. The reparations question made it more difficult for the Republic to deal with the economic upheavals that came in the aftermath of the defeat. Unwise taxation policies, enormous government spending, the material costs of the war, and the losses in territory and resources demanded by the Allies at Versailles combined to make a restoration of normal economic activity extremely difficult. Inflation, which had steadily eroded the value of the German mark throughout the war, threatened to destroy the monetary basis of economic life. Patriotic frustrations and socio-economic discontents helped to perpetuate the climate of violence that had been one of the war's most unfortunate legacies. The Freikorps, organized to save the Republic from the revolution, soon became a source of antirepublican activity. In 1920 government leaders were forced to flee when a Freikorps battalion marched on Berlin and briefly installed a right-wing official named Wolfgang Kapp as head of state. For the next three years, Freikorps members and other right-wing fanatics engaged in sporadic acts of violence against the regime, murdering government leaders and preparing armed revolts.

In 1923 the problems facing the Republic came to a head. When Germany failed to make a reparations payment, French and Belgian troops occupied the Ruhr, the key center of industrial power in western Germany. The government responded by calling upon its citizens to resist the invaders with a general strike that had to be supported by printing more money and thus aggravated further the already perilous economic situation. By the summer of 1923, hyperinflation had drained all value from the currency; in November a newspaper cost 50 billion marks. Powerless to defend itself against its foreign enemies and unable to provide the basis of a stable economic life, the Republic was obviously vulnerable to attack from its internal opponents. Separatists were at work in the Rhineland. In Saxony and Thuringia, Communists were preparing for the long-awaited revolution of the German proletariat. In Bavaria, a right-wing state government tolerated a variety of antirepublican groups including a newly prominent party called the National Socialists under the leadership of Adolf Hitler. It seemed that the moderate settlement of 1919 was about to unravel.

We cannot follow in detail how the Republic survived in 1923, but two points need to be emphasized, if only to contrast the outcome of this crisis with the destruction of the Republic ten years later. In the first place, during the darkest days of 1923 the regime was fortunate enough to find someone prepared to take vigorous action in its defense. Gustav Stresemann, formerly a National Liberal and now a member of the German People's party, became chancellor in August. Although a nationalist and monarchist by conviction, Stresemann had come to realize that for all its faults, the Republic offered Germany the best hope for a strong and stable government. In the months after taking office, he attempted to conciliate the Western powers and thus relieve the pressure on Germany from abroad; he reformed the currency, abandoning the worthless mark and issuing the rentenmark, whose value was guaranteed by the nation's property; and he acted against the regime's internal opposition.

Stresemann succeeded in 1923 not simply because of his own skill and resolution but also because of the weakness of his enemies. Despite the widespread frustration many Germans felt, despite their anger at the dictated peace of 1919, and despite their deep social and economic discontent, the alternatives to the existing order were dispersed and divided. The Communists, who had the support of important elements within the industrial work force, were always a minority and could never have taken power, either legally or by force. On the right, the Republic's enemies were more numerous but also more divided. There were scores of radical parties spread across the land, foci of opposition and potential violence, but none of them was strong enough to be the basis for a government. The German Nationalist People's party, the heir to the imperialist Conservatives, was hostile to the Republic but ambivalent about how to combat it. Some Nationalists were prepared to tolerate and even justify radical right-wing violence; others believed they should express their opposition within the confines of the law. In his few months as chancellor Stresemann took full advantage of his opponents' weakness. He moved swiftly against the Communists and thereby quieted the fears of the more moderate elements within the right wing. As a result he managed to isolate the radical right: When Hitler tried to lead his National Socialists in a putsch against the Republic, he was quite easily repressed by a handful of Bavarian state policemen.

By the end of 1923, the moderate Republic had apparently survived its most difficult test. Stresemann, who left the chancellorship to become foreign minister in November, labored to provide a more stable basis for Germany's international position, negotiated the evacuation of foreign troops from German soil, and achieved a more reasonable schedule of reparation payments. After the currency reforms the economy picked up again, production increased, and a measure of prosperity returned. Most important, the political violence that had marked the Republic's early years virtually ceased. The Freikorps were either disbanded or forced underground. The Nazis, divided and uncertain in the wake of their failed putsch, polled less than 3 percent of the total vote in the Reichstag elections of December 1924.

Given all these signs of renewed economic vitality and political stability, it is not surprising that observers spoke of a new Germany, which had managed to put behind it the travails of the postwar era: "Germany," wrote a well-informed American journalist in 1928, "after years of tribulation and suffering has staged one of the most remarkable comebacks as well as conversions in history and has taken her place among the truly democratic and liberal states of the world."[5]

The Destruction of German Democracy and the Rise of National Socialism, 1923–1933

In the lives of nations as in the lives of individuals, time is often the most precious commodity. If the Weimar Republic had had time to build upon its achievements, to consolidate its hold on German institutions, and to capture the loyalties of its citizens, the years from 1919 to 1923 might have come to seem like the unhappy prelude to a new and stable order. In fact, of course, the Republic was not granted the gift of time; by 1929 it was again plunged into a new series of crises from which it would not be able to recover. From our perspective, it is the years of relative stability from 1923 to 1929 that seem like an aberration, a false calm between the agonies of birth and death.

It is clear enough in retrospect that the Republic was never as strong as its most optimistic observers believed, even during its period of apparent prosperity and stability. By the end of the 1920s the economy

TABLE 2

Reichstag Elections of 1928
(Total vote in millions)

Party	Total vote (%)		Seats
National Socialists	.810	(2.6)	12
DNVP	4.38	(14.2)	73
DVP	2.67	(8.7)	45
DDP	1.5	(4.9)	25
Regional and Special Interest Parties	4.298	(13.7)	51
Center	3.712	(12.1)	62
BVP	.945	(3)	16
Social Democrats	9.15	(29.8)	153
Communists	3.26	(10.6)	54
Total	30.75	(74.6)	491

had managed to reach prewar levels of production and welfare, but structural weaknesses (especially in banking and finance) and deep-seated inequalities and imbalances remained. On the political front, the Republic's most virulent enemies were in disarray, but the regime was still viewed skeptically by a number of key groups in German society. The officer corps, elements within the civil service and judiciary, and the academic elite all had grave reservations about democracy. That these reservations were shared by a dangerously large proportion of the population was indicated in 1925 by the election of Paul von Hindenburg to succeed Friedrich Ebert as president of the Republic. Hindenburg, a Prussian Junker and career officer, had been one of the first heroes of World War I and had commanded the German armies until the fall of 1918. Seventy-eight years old at the time of his election, Hindenburg was a man without political skills or experience, the captive symbol of his supporters' longing for the lost authority of the Kaiserreich.

The results of the elections of 1928 provide another perspective from which we can observe the weakness behind the facade of republican stability. Although the Social Democrats were the big winners in 1928, the impressive number of Communist voters suggests the continued hostility toward the regime felt by many working people. The Republic's supporters must have been delighted by the shrinkage of radical right-wing groups like Hitler's Nazis, whose tiny parliamentary faction was isolated and easy to ignore. But it was also clear in 1928 that widespread uncertainty remained among voters on the center-right of the political spectrum. The two republican successors to the old liberal parties, the German People's party (DVP) and the Democratic party (DDP), had not been able to consolidate their constituencies. Many of those who had once voted for these parties had moved from one group to another and in 1928 were spread across a variety of regional, single-issue, or special interest groups. After 1930 many of these voters would end up in the Nazi camp.

In 1928 there were also some changes within the leadership of the political parties that would have unhappy consequences for the Republic's future. First of all, there was a shift to the right in the DVP, which began to move away from the moderate policies favored by Stresemann, whose death in 1929 deprived the Republic of one of its most effective leaders. There was also a shift to the right in the ruling circles of the Catholic Center party. During the early stages of the Republic, the Center had been one of the most effective pillars of the Weimar regime; in 1928, however, the election of Ludwig Kaas as party chairman signaled a weakening of the party's commitment to democracy. Finally, in 1928 Alfred Hugenberg became the leader of the German National People's party (DNVP). A longtime enemy of the Republic, Hugenberg was obsessed with the peril of communism, whose evil influence he saw at work in every policy he deplored. He soon became a prime mover behind a coalition of right-wing groups formed in 1929 to fight against the Young Plan, Stresemann's last scheme for a more favorable reparations program.

The arrival of the Great Depression brought all of the Republic's weaknesses to the surface. Beginning with the collapse of the New York stock market in October 1929, the worldwide economic crisis swiftly destroyed the prosperity Germans had just begun to enjoy. The banking system failed to provide capital for investment; production plummeted; real income dropped sharply. Most dramatically, unemployment cut deeply into the German economy: By 1932 more than 40 percent of the German work force was without a job. Young people, the last to be hired and usually the first to be let go, faced an apparently hopeless future. And although manual workers suffered most, unemployment had also begun to affect white-collar employees. No one felt safe.

The economic crisis was attended by a rebirth of political extremism. On the left, the Communists gained support from those who viewed the depression as the final crisis of capitalism, the prelude to the European revolution that some had been predicting since 1917. Radicalism on the left encouraged, and was in turn encouraged by, the growth of radicalism on the right. Among the various fascist organizations that sprang to life again in 1929 and 1930, none had greater vitality and organizational energy than the National Socialists. The economic

TABLE 3

Reichstag Elections of 1930
(Total vote in millions)

Party	Total vote (%)		Seats
National Socialists	6.409	(13.3)	107
DNVP	2.458	(7)	41
DVP	1.578	(4.5)	30
DDP	1.322	(3.8)	20
Regional and Special Interest Parties	5.088	(4.4)	72
Center	4.127	(11.5)	68
BVP	1.059	(3)	19
Social Democrats	8.577	(24.5)	143
Communists	4.592	(13.1)	77
Total	34.97	(81.4)	577

crisis enabled people like Hitler to charge their usual opponents—Jews, Communists, and republicans—with new crimes against the German *Volk*. Whereas the left saw the Depression as the death throes of Western capitalism, the radical right saw it as one more example of the Jewish-Communist-internationalist plot to humiliate and destroy Germany.

The story of the moderate republicans' response to these attacks from left and right is one of the most depressing features of this bleak historical epoch. The government of Social Democrat Herman Müller, which had been formed on the basis of the elections of 1928, rested on a moderate majority in the Reichstag. There was no need to hold new elections until 1932. Unfortunately, however, the government did not stand firm; despite the manifest signs of political crisis, the coalition collapsed in 1930 when its Socialist and liberal members could not agree on the question of unemployment insurance. To replace Chancellor Müller, President von Hindenberg chose Heinrich Brüning, a member of the Center party, who tried to form a right-of-center government. In the summer of 1930, when the Reichstag did not accept Brüning's economic program, the chancellor responded with one of the most monumental errors in modern political history: He dissolved the Reichstag and called for new elections, confident that his own moderate and conservative allies would win a safe majority. The figures in Table 3 show just how badly Brüning miscalculated the electorate's temper.

Following the elections of 1930, parliament's authority steadily declined. More and more, Chancellor Brüning became dependent on the presidential power of decree in order to govern. In the halls of the Reichstag and in the streets of German towns and cities, Communists and Nazis demanded an end to the Weimar system. In the officer corps, the bureaucracy, the landed and industrial elites, men began to wonder if the current dangers did not provide the opportunity to destroy the bankrupt Republic and create a system in which their power and interests might once again predominate.

Considering the Republic's structural weaknesses, the unusual severity of the German depression, and the potential for political conflict within German society, it is not difficult to explain the collapse of parliamentary government after 1930. Although certainly not inevitable, the failure of German democracy was part of a European-wide pattern that can be found throughout the interwar period. The perplexing question about the German case is not why the Weimar regime collapsed, but rather why National Socialism became its heir. In answering this question the experience of other European states is much less helpful. Of course the Nazis bore a family resemblance to fascist parties in the rest of Europe, but nowhere was there a movement or a regime with the same blend of dynamism and ambition, energy and aggression. In these respects, Nazism was unique.

In our effort to understand the character and appeals of Nazism, it is difficult not to make too much of Hitler himself. When he is on the stage, our eyes are drawn to him as to some particularly powerful actor; our fascination with him tempts us to reduce Nazism to a problem of biography. One thing is certain: Without Hitler, Nazism could never have come to power and could not have created the regime that it did. There was no one else in the movement with his peculiar skills and instincts, no one who could match his energy and sense of mission. But although these qualities were a necessary cause of Nazism's success, they are not sufficient to explain where Nazism came from and what it accomplished. For all his qualities, Hitler was not the magician he is sometimes said to have been, that evil genius able to bewitch an innocent people and lead them to their doom. Nazism succeeded not because Hitler tricked people into believing what *he* wanted; it succeeded because he was able to tell them in especially powerful and effective ways what *they* wanted to hear and what they already believed. We are inclined, I think, to overrate the creative effects of political agitation. Most often, the propagandist's success involves the affirmation or clarification of existing beliefs, not the imposition of new ones.

To understand Hitler's appeal, therefore, we must see his program in the light of existing political values and traditions. We must also carefully distinguish among the different groups to which Hitler's message was directed. One way to divide these groups is by a distinction Hitler

himself always insisted upon, the distinction between what he called
"members" and "supporters," between those with a deep, lasting commitment to Nazism and those who simply voted for the party without
further involvement in its activities. Since Hitler believed that he would
have to take power legally, he knew that a hard core of members would
not be enough; he would need a mass base of supporters to help him
acquire and legitimate his authority. This insight, which separated Hitler
from the violent putschists on the radical right, was itself an important
prerequisite for the Nazis' ultimate triumph.

From its formation in 1919 until the election of 1930, the party's
ability to attract electoral support was very limited. As we saw, in the
elections of 1928 Hitler got only 810,000 votes, significantly fewer than
several ephemeral parties that have since been forgotten. But even when
his mass appeal was faint, Hitler did retain a hard core of members,
energetic and talented men totally committed to the Führer and his
ideals. The Nazi program during these years was a hodgepodge of themes
long current on the radical right: anti-Semitism, racial nationalism,
anticommunism, and a diffuse set of social appeals to farmers, craftsmen,
and other "independent" proprietors. Hitler himself seems to have had
little interest in the socioeconomic aspects of the program. He cared
about foreign policy and race (in his mind two facets of the same
problem) and was quite ready to jettison any social or economic appeals
that might stand in the way of his success.

Two key events link the embattled minority of 1928 with the mass
movement of 1930. The first was Hitler's participation in Hugenberg's
anti–Young Plan coalition, which gave the Nazis badly needed funds
and also a kind of respectability they had previously lacked. As they
watched Hitler stand with the well-tailored leaders of the German right,
some people were prepared to overlook his radical past and his violent
rhetoric and to see him merely as an energetic and outspoken advocate
of traditional values—patriotism, anticommunism, conventional morality. The second linking event was the Depression and its attendant
radicalization of public life. This brought into the Nazis' ranks a flood
of new members, many of them young, frustrated, and ready to follow
someone who promised a national rebirth, a new social order, and
unlimited personal opportunity. University students especially, the sons
and daughters of the propertied and educated elites, threw themselves
into political activity on the Nazis' behalf. It was, therefore, not without
some justification that Hitler could claim to represent the future, the
party of youth, the most vigorous defender of patriotic values, the best
defense against the red peril. This combination of traditional values
and youthful dynamism drew many voters from the right and center
to Hitler's movement in 1930 and seemed to establish the Nazis as the

only effective alternative to the Communists. In the elections of 1932, this trend continued as voters deserted both the decaying liberal parties and the newly formed special interest groups for the Nazis.

Despite the vigor of their organization and the impressive growth in their mass support, the Nazis' rise to power was by no means inevitable. The labor movement, unhappily divided between Communists and Social Democrats, held onto its supporters, as did the two Catholic parties. There was even some indication that the Nazis' support may have peaked: In the elections of November 1932 their total vote was 2 million, less than it had been in the elections held four months earlier, and their share of the electorate declined from 37.4 to 33.1 percent. Some of these losses may have been due to marginal voters who simply did not show up at the polls in November (the total national vote declined from 36.88 to 35.47 million), but some Nazi voters evidently turned to the DNVP, which gained almost 800,000. Perhaps the voters whom Hitler had briefly gathered under his banner had once again begun to shift their allegiances, as they had done so often in the preceding decade.

In the weeks following the November election a group of men around President Hindenburg set out to destroy the Weimar regime and replace it with an authoritarian government under their own control. These conspirators wanted to use Hitler for their own purposes. Army officers, landowners, civil servants, industrialists—they were confident that they could control the upstart leader of the Nazi rabble. He would be their "drummer," attracting the masses whose support they needed. In a series of complex negotiations, Hitler managed to hold out for the chancellorship in a cabinet almost totally controlled by his would-be allies. "We have him hemmed in," one of the conspirators is reported to have said when Hitler became the last chancellor of the republic on January 30, 1933. On January 31, Hugenberg provided a much more apt summary of the situation: "Yesterday I committed the biggest blunder of my life. I allied myself with the biggest demagogue in the history of the world."[6]

Conclusion: 1871–1933, a German *Sonderweg?*

The story a historian has to tell is shaped by where he begins and ends. These two points inevitably determine both the trajectory of the explanation and the content of the narrative. Beginnings and ends, therefore, are filled with assumptions and implications that are too easily overlooked as we rush into the story itself. This is especially apparent in the dates assigned for this chapter: 1871, the official proclamation of the Kaiserreich, and 1933, the year of Hitler's appointment as the last chancellor of the Republic. What are the lines of continuity that link these two dates? Was the progression from Bismarck to Hitler unavoidable, woven into the fabric of German history by forces impossible to change? Was 1933 the necessary destination toward which historical forces had to move? Or, as some have claimed, was January 30, 1933, an unfortunate accident, the unforeseeable consequence of the Depression, the work of a small group of men who suddenly seized power while no one was looking? A great deal of what has been written about German history turns on how one addresses these issues of continuity and circumstance, inevitability and accident.

Inseparable from the question of continuity is the problem of German peculiarity. If Hitler was the inevitable product of German history then Germans must have followed a unique path, a *Sonderweg,* toward disgrace and degradation. Every stop along this path, every political movement and cultural achievement helps to explain the terrible journey to Nazism. On the other hand, the more circumstantial Nazism's success can be made to appear, the easier it is to see the German experience as part of European history, sharing the same problems, facing similar difficulties, contributing to the same cultural enterprise as other European countries.

Obviously a chapter as brief and schematic as this one cannot possibly resolve these questions of continuity and peculiarity. But I hope it will be clear that I believe the answers are most likely to be found between the extremes of inevitability and accident, uniqueness and universality. It is as foolish to suppose that Hitler was the logical outcome of a uniquely German past as it is to believe that Nazism was a European phenomenon that came to power in Germany merely because of a peculiar set of circumstances. To understand Hitler we must carefully examine the German traditions upon which his success was based. But we must deny ourselves the reassuring illusion that what he represented was uniquely and necessarily German. The story of German politics from 1871 to 1933 is significant not just for Germans, but for all of us.

Notes

1. In 1871 the Reich was composed of the following states (with their number of votes in the Bundesrat): Prussia (17), Bavaria (6), Saxony (4), Württemberg (4), Baden (3), Hesse (3), Mecklenburg-Schwerin (2), Braunschweig (2), Mecklenburg-Strelitz, and Sachsen-Weimar-Eisenach, Oldenburg, Sachsen-Meiningen, Sachsen-Altenburg, Sachsen-Koburg-Gotha, Anhalt, Schwarzburg-Rudolstadt, Schwarzburg-Sondershausen, Waldeck, Reuss ältere Linie, Reuss jüngere Linie, Schaumburg-Lippe, Lippe, Lübeck, Bremen, and Hamburg (1 each). Alsace-

Lorraine, the area annexed from France, was originally a protectorate (*Schutz-gebiet*); in 1911 it was given representation in the Bundesrat with three votes.

2. The Prussian Parliament, with which Bismarck was engaged in a bitter conflict between 1862 and 1866, was elected according to the so-called three-class system that greatly advantaged the wealthier elements in society. Prussia retained this system until the end of the Reich in 1918.

3. In 1919 the German parties had reconstituted themselves as follows: The two conservative parties, together with some National Liberals and other right-wing groups, became the German National People's party (DNVP). Most National Liberals joined the German People's party (DVP), most left-liberals the Democratic party (DDP). The Center retained its name and character but its Bavarian wing was reconstituted as the Bavarian People's party (BVP). The Social Democrats had split in 1917 when the antiwar wing formed the Independent Social Democratic party; in the early 1920s most independents either rejoined the majority SPD or joined the Communist party (KPD), formed in December 1918.

4. Rudolf Hilferding to Karl Kautsky, September 1933, quoted in E. Kolb, *Die Arbeiterräte in der deutschen Innenpolitik, 1918–1919* (Düsseldorf, 1962), p. 7.

5. Raymond Leslie Buell, quoted in S. William Halperin, *Germany Tried Democracy. A Political History of the Reich from 1918 to 1933* (New York, 1946), p. 362.

6. Quoted in Richard F. Hamilton, *Who Voted for Hitler?* (Princeton, N.J., 1982), p. 240.

Readings

Craig, Gordon A. *Germany, 1866–1945.* New York: Oxford University Press, 1978.

Hamilton, Richard. *Who Voted for Hitler?* Princeton, N.J.: Princeton University Press, 1982.

Nicholls, Anthony J. *Weimar and the Rise of Hitler.* New York: St. Martin's Press, 1979.

Sheehan, James J. (ed.). *Imperial Germany.* New York: New Viewpoints, 1976.

HANS-ADOLF JACOBSEN

2

The Third Reich, 1933–1945: A Sketch

The rise and fall of the Third Reich between 1933 and 1945, with all its far-reaching consequences for Germany, Europe, and the world, can be comprehended only in the context of the major changes in the international system after World War I, and through understanding other historical events. Foremost among these was the failure of the postwar democratic experiment in Germany. The Weimar Republic was troubled from its outset by the perception that the Versailles Treaty of 1919 discriminated against Germany. It was weakened by numerous political and economic crises, particularly by severe unemployment and disastrous inflation; it was burdened by traditional national-conservative ideologies; and its development was limited because its true democratic supporters remained a minority. The demise of the Republic in the early 1930s was hastened by antiparliamentary attitudes and activities, by its system of multiple political parties, by unmistakable weaknesses in its constitution, and by personal intrigues among its elite.

The level of expectation that then existed in German society must be added to these factors. In the last nominally free Reichstag elections in March 1933, although barely 44 percent of the voters chose the National Socialist German Workers Party (NSDAP, the Nazi Party) headed by Adolf Hitler, it thereby became the largest single party. This result may have been an expression of a mood of political crisis and a certain mass psychosis in the spirit of a "national revolution." Yet most of these voters did not intend to provide a mandate for terror, genocide, and the conduct of total war. Their hope was rather to reach such goals as a rescue from poverty, "work and bread," restoration of "honor," chances for professional advancement, security for the family farm, or other social benefits. It is probable that very few Germans had read *Mein Kampf.* Even those who had done so and had more or less understood it would, under the circumstances, have been doubtful that a program so difficult to comprehend could be put into practice by the Reich chancellor. The events of 1933 were, therefore, attempts at radical surgery in response to all the negative experiences since 1919.

We must also consider another important aspect: A theme of under-estimation runs through the entire history of the Third Reich. Hitler and his cohorts wanted to achieve power legally but did not want to use this power legally. Their constant emphasis on the desire for peace and hints that National Socialism was not meant for export for a long time misled people both at home and abroad about their real aims. It is now clear that the National Socialist leadership consistently pursued its programmatic goals once they had been clearly articulated. Diverse reasons caused it to deviate from its route now and then but it always returned to the set course.

These explanations are not intended to excuse or trivialize the behavior of the German people in this fateful period of German history. Caught up in the slogans and successes of the "rise" of a greater Germany—which often appeared to compensate for the excesses of the regime—intoxicated by the fanfare of victory in the early stages of the war, and permanently manipulated by centrally controlled mass media, most Germans recognized only too late to what extent the National Socialist leadership had disappointed the people's expectations, betrayed their ideals, disregarded their values, and recklessly gambled with their lives. In view of what we now know about what really happened during this period, it is clear that because the people were both subject and object of this process, they must bear some share of responsibility for it.

Program Development (1919–1933)

The rise of National Socialism from its beginnings until the government of "national awakening" was established in 1933 was the result of all these phenomena as well as of the efforts of Adolf Hitler. Hitler was born in 1898 in Braunau am Inn, a small town in Austria. He mobilized and tightly organized a party of cadres that became a mass movement. He also devised brilliant tactics that used legitimate methods to achieve his goals. The "Führer's" eclectic view of the world developed during his stay in Vienna from 1908 to 1914. His experiences at the front during World War I and his prejudiced analysis of his environment at the end of the war had come together by 1919—the year the National Socialist Party was founded—to form the radical ideological concept that was expressed in the party program of February 24, 1920. At the same time this program reflected the protest of rather primitive nationalistic groups against the collapse of the Reich in 1918 and the subsequent disintegration of the internal structure of the Republic.

Instinctively, Hitler had found seductive points of reference for the unscrupulous agitation he initiated in 1919: The Versailles Treaty, Jews, Communists, and the "criminals of November" were, in a grotesque distortion of facts, held solely responsible for the catastrophe of 1918 and its consequences. He saw them as "destructive" elements of society opposed to the constructive counterforces that were to mobilize for the Reich's renewed ascent. The German people, "shaken awake," "defeated," and "mistreated" by the Allies, were finally to find their long-awaited instrument of revenge in the NSDAP.

At its helm, however, stood the man whose closest collaborators—especially Hermann Göring, Rudolf Hess, Josef Goebbels, Heinrich Himmler, the provincial party leaders, and later Martin Bormann—constantly knew how to further his "myth." Hitler himself, by use of the "Führer" principle (the principle of the infallible leader), was able to exact absolute obedience from his followers. Clearly, once the domestic goals had been achieved, the same struggle would have to be transferred to the arena of international relations. The German people, especially their youth, were to be reeducated; new emphases were needed: virtue, a simple lifestyle, sacrifice, and the readiness to bear arms.

The National Socialist leadership assumed, beginning in the 1920s, that war was a legitimate, inevitable tool of its policies. Since the party leadership held this view of war, it logically expected to realize its goals by the use of armed force. This concept was based on an extreme form of social Darwinism, the natural law of the rights of the stronger, of survival, of the permanent selection of the "fittest," and of the disintegration of everything that is decaying or brittle. War, entered into in the interest of the "best race," was to prove the superiority of the Nordic race; it was simultaneously the "highest expression of the life force" of a people and the sole chance of the nation's survival inasmuch as the world provided nothing more than an "unrestricted arena for the testing of forces." This permanent struggle for realization of the historic claim of a "racially more worthy" people to mastery of the world was, however, not restricted to an exclusive aristocratic elite but included every member of the so-called "racial blood nobility" (*völkischer Blutadel*) in a broad social equalization of all classes. It was important, therefore, to create a spirit of community, if necessary by force and terror, but preferably by manipulated consent (plebiscites). It was the task of a great statesman, according to Hitler's *Mein Kampf,* to exercise and train his people for an unlimited war so that thereafter, according to all "human reason," the nation's future could be "legitimately" secured ("pax Germanica"). Until that day there could be no appreciable difference between war and peace.

The most fundamental task of the movement, however, was to fulfill the National Socialist aspiration to obtain adequate territory for the nation (*NS-Raumpolitik*). Proceeding from the basic axiom that conditions of landownership were not "values for eternity" but were subject to "constant change," to its myth of force, its mysticism of blood and soil, and its unilateral interpretation of geopolitics, the National Socialist Party demanded the forceful conquest of *Lebensraum,* land for settlement. If they could accomplish this, the Nazis thought they could be absolutely certain of being able to safeguard the existence of the German people and guarantee their economic independence. All they needed was sufficient land to gather in all Germans and guarantee their military security. They postulated this as the only way to devise a settlement policy that would deal with the awkward disproportion between population and land. This policy was considered morally justified because only such an exalted goal could compensate for the inevitable losses in blood and treasure necessitated by a war to achieve it. The revisionist policies of the Weimar regimes were contemptuously rejected: The future of the German Reich could be assured only when at least 500,000 square kilometers of Eastern Europe had been annexed to create a "new homestead" for millions of German farmers. The acquisition of land was naturally tied to the use of military force. As Hitler stated: "To forge this sword is the task of the domestic political leadership of our people; to safeguard the work of the sword and to find comrades in arms is the task of those responsible for its foreign policy." Included in this task were efforts to coax Italy and Great Britain into an alliance.

The leaders of the National Socialist movement constantly reiterated that for them the struggle for a racial "new order" in Europe was indissolubly tied to the ideological war of destruction against Marxism and its "manipulators." Here their ideology absorbed certain traditions of the German middle class, especially those of the reactionary ethnic societies (*Völkische Verbände*). The Nazi ideologists characterized their struggle as the sole "total counterthrust" to the idea of communism. This was a war to the bitter end, a life or death struggle in which they intended to engage the "enemy of the world" (*Weltfeind*). No quarter could be given. They would fight relentlessly using every last ounce of their physical and mental resources. After the conquest of *Lebensraum* "racially foreign elements" were to be isolated or in short order "totally removed." The world was sick. It suffered from a "cancerous growth," the Jews, and Bolshevism was its most virulent form. This cancer had to be excised, for only then would Germany and Europe recover. In the peculiar logic of the Nazi propagandists, it was perfectly reasonable to employ the most "inhumane" and "unfair" means in the struggle against the "corruptors of the world." Any measure was justified to break the power of the racial enemy because victory would guarantee Germany's salvation.

The National Socialist "Führer" State

Beginning in the 1920s, Hitler wanted to sweep away those forces in the Reich that he had accused of destroying the nation economically, ruining the farmers, pauperizing the middle class, and creating an army of millions of unemployed. He reached the first stage on the road toward this goal on January 30, 1933, the day he assumed power as chancellor of Germany. The elderly president of the Reich, Paul von Hindenburg, had called upon him, the leader of the largest single group in the parliament (Reichstag), to be the new chancellor in the expectation that he would overcome the crisis in the republic. Von Hindenburg was persuaded by his conservative advisers to put aside all misgivings about this "Bohemian corporal." In the months that followed, Hitler and his cohorts demonstrated how intolerantly they intended to act—in keeping with their own previous statements—in order totally to absorb Germany in their grasp, to form it in their image, and to rule it. As a first measure, they unhesitatingly used the Reichstag fire of February 27, 1933, to remove the basic guarantees provided by the German constitution; to initiate the persecution of the Communists, including the immediate outlawing of the German Communist Party; and to arrest political opponents. The proclamation for the "Protection of the People and the State" of February 28, 1933, not only indefinitely revoked the most important basic rights of the Weimar constitution—including the inviolability of the freedom of the individual and the right of free speech—but also made it possible summarily to remove the governments of the provinces (*Länder*). One after another, Hitler replaced the conservative members of his new cabinet, who had begun their cooperative role in the government believing that they could tame the leader of 1.4 million National Socialists, with compliant party members. He governed through a small group of cronies, all leaders of regional, local, or national party organizations or of the quasi-military Storm Troopers (SA). He enforced the continuing state of martial law through emergency proclamations and regulations for which he provided an administrative cover. In addition, he established so-called reeducation camps, which soon became infamous as concentration camps.

In the spring and summer of 1933 a mass exodus of German intellectuals, writers, and artists threatened and persecuted by the regime began. One political action speedily followed another. They were accompanied by spectacular demonstrations such as the "Day of Potsdam" (March 21) on which the synthesis between the traditions of Prussianism and the "national uprising" was proclaimed, a most effective exercise in mass psychology. Another spectacular event was the burning of books considered "un-German." In early March, Hitler carried out the subordination of the *Länder* to the centrally established policies and changed their governmental structure by the appointment of Reich commissars, later known as Reich governors. By these steps, the *Länder* were reduced to administrative units; the power in them was held by the regional party chieftains (*Gauleiter*). On March 24, 1933, the Reichstag gave up its own powers by voting for the so-called Enabling Act; 441 deputies voted in favor and only the 94 deputies of the Social Democratic Party voted against the measure. The separation of power between the legislative and executive branches of the government was thus removed, and the Reich government could now pass unconstitutional legislation. Beginning with the manipulated elections of November 1933, the Reichstag was reduced to deputies of the NSDAP who rubberstamped legislation, mere extras acclaiming Hitler's speeches. A similar development took place in the cabinet: For the Führer, it too was only a stage setting. He used it as the arena in which to justify his political decisions. After the cabinet members had been compelled to take an oath of personal loyalty to Hitler in October 1934, their constitutionally mandated individual responsibility ceased. They had been reduced to the position of top civil servants and like all other civil servants were subject to orders. Moreover, the law for the Reestablishment of the Professional Civil Service of April 7, 1933, provided Hitler with the legal tool for the removal of politically or racially objectionable civil servants.

In place of the dissolved labor unions, the German Labor Front under Robert Ley was established in May 1933. This organization, which in the mid-1930s had approximately 20 million members, combined both worker and employer groups in one organization in an effort to remove traditional concepts of class struggle and so to further the creation of a unified National Socialist society (*NS-Volksgemeinschaft*). The associations of various agrarian interest groups were shortly thereafter similarly integrated into the Reich Agricultural Organization (*Reichsnährstand*). With the enactment of the laws of July 14 and December 1, 1933, against the establishment of new political parties and for the Establishment of the Unity of Party and State, the dictatorship of a single party was created—the other parties had either been prohibited (SPD, the Social Democratic Party) or had dissolved themselves. Thus the first phase of the total subordination (*Gleichschaltung*) of all bodies with political power was essentially completed. It constituted the effective completion of the National Socialist government's decision to integrate previously autonomous public and social institutions under its rule and to make them uniform. Many of them had eased the effort by timely assimilation.

By the summer of 1934, the second phase of total subordination had followed. It rigorously excluded or limited the power of rival factions within the party itself (e.g., the assassination of one of the highest party leaders, SA Chief Ernst Röhm, and other unpopular party opponents; and the reduction of the power of the Storm Troopers). On the very day of von Hindenburg's death, August 2, 1934, the offices of Reich president and Reich chancellor were combined in Hitler and the armed forces of the Reich swore an oath of "unconditional obedience" to the new head of state. With this step, Hitler became not only the absolute leader of state and party but also the commander-in-chief of the armed forces, which he designated as the "sole bearer of arms" of the nation. His deputy, Rudolf Hess, had early in 1934 used the radio to accept the loyalty oath of nearly a million political leaders, leaders of the Hitler Youth, and of the compulsory Labor Service. All had sworn that "Adolf Hitler is Germany and Germany is Adolf Hitler. Whoever takes an oath to Hitler, takes an oath to Germany."

Meanwhile, Heinrich Himmler succeeded in strengthening his influence in the nucleus of power by assuming all police security functions and accelerating the establishment of the "Protective Service" known as the SS. In 1937 he was appointed head of the German police, reporting directly to Hitler. Arbitrary power could now be freely exercised.

All this took place at a time of general economic recovery during which the use of skillful financing and public works employment (*inter alia,* the construction of superhighways and the arms buildup) improved the economic situation in Germany and reduced unemployment from 6 to 4 million. This recovery contributed to the stabilization of the regime as much as the plebiscites ordered by the National Socialist leadership, in which more than 90 percent of the population approved basic domestic and foreign policy decisions. These plebiscites were designed to make clear abroad that accusations of arbitrary rule and the use of force were unfounded and that the regime had the full support of the people.

The third phase of subordination of all organizations and offices was concluded in February 1938, when Hitler entrusted the remaining two instruments of state power to party cronies. He made Joachim von Ribbentrop foreign minister in place of von Neurath; he dismissed Reich War Minister Werner von Blomberg and Army Commander-in-Chief Colonel General Freiherr von Fritsch. Their replacements were General Wilhelm Keitel, who became the head Commanding Officer of the High Command of the Armed Forces (OKW), and Colonel General von

Brauchitsch, who was appointed Commander of the Army. By these actions Hitler excluded any remaining leaders who might have restrained him and those who had expressed concern about his increasingly radical course of political action.

Without doubt, the Führer state in its National Socialist version was first of all the work of Adolf Hitler. This self-taught individual and man of unlimited willpower who, with his power of persuasiveness, attested and experienced by many observers, was able to amaze experts, obtain the admiration of critics, and transform unbelievers into unquestioning disciples, knew how to govern with near-totalitarian power. To achieve this, he used decentralized, at times competing, apparatuses of power: police terror units, a nationalistic revolutionary ideology that served to integrate diverse elements of society, and modern technology. For a long time he permitted a certain amount of freedom to the churches, the army, and the economy. Once he had assumed the role of charismatic leader, however, it became clear that he alone manifested the will of the nation, for he alone knew what the nation should be demanding.

Initially Hitler operated successfully in the international arena. His early demands for the German Reich were those his predecessors had already made known abroad. The tactic of one-sided accusations and unilateral measures, combined with the constant reiteration of the promise that the revolution brought about by National Socialism was strictly limited to the area of the Reich or to Germans, made it difficult to recognize his true intentions; most of all, it prevented a clear differentiation between the moderate and the extravagant, between the justified and the unjustifiable. Hitler was always able to appear as the injured, misunderstood, disappointed national politician who only wanted what was best for his own people, with no desire to violate the rights of other nations. His political successes helped him to demonstrate this attitude and to draw strength and confidence for the next step on the road to achievement of his final goals. But these same successes also became his downfall: They formed the beginning of the end because they subjected him to no controls as his far-ranging imagination carried him further and further from a realistic sense of the people's attitude and of the environment in which he operated. In the end he became the victim of his own ever more extravagant wishful thinking. The world, which, with minor exceptions, he knew only from hearsay and from personally selected publications and films, had to be as he imagined it. As was the case with many dictators throughout history, he cynically despised people and, with all his pretense of acting for the "well-being of society" as he interpreted it, saw the highest value first and foremost in himself.

Even though he was marked by a naked hunger for power and an unfettered drive for conquest, he was obsessed by a "historic mission" to become the great benefactor of the world. To him it seemed as if Divine Providence had selected him for this purpose; he saw as proof of this the failure of all attempts on his life. A few months before he seized power, he proclaimed at the top of his voice in a campaign speech: "We have chosen our goal and shall defend it fanatically, without reservations, even into the grave!" And a few years earlier he had postulated that "Germany will become a world power or it will not exist at all." At least as far as he personally was concerned, these prophecies certainly held true.

Even though the National Socialist leadership remained determined to establish a modern, mobile, national mass society, it recognized after a few years that criticism of its policies had not diminished in Germany, not even within its own ranks. The spread of its ideology was not as extensive as the leaders had wished. There were too many nominal members, too many opportunists, and too many who professed 150 percent of their loyalty. Numerous civil servants and eminent conservatives remained distinctly detached from the "national revolution" and displayed the condescending air of experts who know that they are needed. Most of them had made their accommodation with the new situation and would not support it actively. The campaign against the churches, the persecution of the Jews, concentration camps, and the economic austerity measures that had become necessary—all the numerous interventions by the government—did nothing to strengthen the consensus between the population and the regime. Critical observers drew the conclusion in 1935 that the German people were by no means securely anchored in National Socialism and that many Germans were willing to listen to opposing views. The cohesive power of National Socialism, which acted more emotionally than rationally, achieved some breadth within the population but failed to achieve much depth.

It was not possible to achieve the triumph of the regime solely by the use of systematic ideological training, even though it included enforced intellectual conformity, numerous promises, and the "Strength through Joy" movement (which provided systematic recreation through party-sponsored competitive sports events) and yearly party conventions for the demonstration of national unity. The Nazis tried everything to create a unified and obedient nation, all in an environment of economic recovery and widespread coercion, but it was not enough. Successes in foreign policy became a brilliant and supplemental means of strengthening the myth of the Führer and securing the regime's hold. These successes were constantly reiterated by the powerful National Socialist propaganda machine. In boastful annual reviews it pointed to the magnificent achievements of the Third Reich, to the altered role of Germany in world politics, to its might and strength—all thanks to National Socialism. It is clear that numerous foreign visitors were impressed by "the German people's will to live" and by the many achievements of National Socialism. Although Hitler had demanded in the 1920s that the goals of his domestic policy had to be realized as a precondition for an active foreign policy, he now increasingly used foreign policy to consolidate his domestic power. Nevertheless, it is necessary to note that after six years of "national reconstruction," the Führer state still could not claim a thoroughly politicized and indoctrinated society, nor had its ideology alienated the people from their previous beliefs.

Images of the Enemy

In the meantime, the National Socialist rulers methodically propagated certain images of the enemy, to each of which they assigned special functions. Continuing the assumptions held in the 1920s, they elevated the ruthless fight against Bolshevism to a central theme in domestic and foreign policy. Even though the effectiveness of the "Antikomintern" central office (a coordinating office to fight international communism founded in Berlin in 1933–1934) remained insignificant, domestic propaganda along these lines achieved great success. By incessantly pointing to the threat of the "Bolshevik enemy," it facilitated the terrorist activities of the Secret State Police (Gestapo) and the party against the opposition in Germany. Himmler and his deputy, Reinhardt Heydrich, by controlling the SS, gained easy access to tools of enforcement; they also controlled the concentration camps so as to execute their own program. The criticism of the Communist model was also intended to demonstrate the dangers from which Hitler had saved the German people. A consequence of this policy was the systematic poisoning of German-Soviet relations and a reshaping of the people's consciousness about friends and enemies. This propaganda, which used every method of modern mass communication to bring about mental corruption, prepared the soil for the concept of "*Untermensch*" (human beings of lesser value), which was translated into action in World War II with such frightful consequences.

In terms of Germany's posture in the international arena, such a propaganda campaign also had notable advantages. On the one hand, it offered a "moral formula" for cooperation with other states without giving the impression that the Reich was pursuing its own goals in power politics. On the other hand, it created a convenient platform from which the Berlin leadership could demand participation in major policy decisions, especially in Europe. For a long time many foreign political leaders believed that National Socialist Germany was an important stronghold against Bolshevism.

Even more important was the concurrent unremitting fight against "Jewry" (*Judentum*). The National Socialist leadership believed that fanatical anti-Semitism followed by aggressive action was required by its national as well as international interests. The founders of the NSDAP had unmistakably stated in their party program that only persons of German blood, regardless of religion, could be members of the "national community" (*Volksgenossen*). At the center of their absurd image of the enemy was the "racial enemy," whose elimination was seen as a "service to humanity." That such a goal did not stop with theory but was translated into practice in an inhuman policy was demonstrated in the years from 1933 to 1945, when the pre-1933 program was made reality, initially by small steps and later with increasing rapidity and thoroughness.

In the first phase of the National Socialist persecution of the Jews, to which the approximately 500,000 Jews in the Reich were subjected, it was the goal of all regulations and ordinances to ensure the "civic death" of the hated enemy. It began with brutal riots, boycotts of businesses and stores, arrests and incarcerations in concentration camps, the exclusion of numerous Jews from public life, and the "Aryanization" of Jewish middle-class enterprises. Jewish citizens were isolated and deprived of the normal protections of the law. The Nuremberg laws proclaimed in mid-September 1935 for the "Protection of German Blood and German Honor" reduced Jews to second-class citizens without rights, while Reich citizens of "German or related blood" were designated as the true holders of full political rights. Marriage and sexual intercourse between Jews and non-Jews were prohibited. The subsequent administrative regulations under the Reich Citizen Law stipulated who was to be regarded as a Jew. With these steps the National Socialist leadership annulled the emancipation of the Jews that had taken place in the nineteenth century. The doctrine of the equality of all human beings was replaced by a cynical doctrine of human "inequality and differentiation created by the laws of nature." Simultaneously, the regional party leader of Franconia, Julius Streicher, in his sensationalist weekly *Der Stürmer* appealed to the most primitive instincts of the German people with the slogan, "The Jews are our Disaster!"

In the early years, more radical measures were not taken because the National Socialist leadership apparently believed it had to be concerned about its domestic and foreign political image. Initially it wished to overcome the "danger zone" of possible international isolation or insufficient military preparedness. As soon as Hitler was satisfied that his rule was secure, preparations for war and anti-Jewish measures were expanded. The year 1938 was marked by heightened economic difficulties for Jews: Over 4,000 enterprises were "Aryanized," partly through forced sales and partly through sordid extortion. The marking of passports with a stamped red "J" and the order that Jews had to add the first names Israel (for males), and Sarah (for females) to their given names was a further form of discrimination. The occasion for even harsher treatment was provided by an event that took place in November 1938. A young man named Grynspan, in retaliation for anti-semitic excesses in the Reich, shot and killed an official of the German Embassy in Paris. The violent pogrom initiated in the wake of this event by Goebbels and other Nazi leaders became known as the *Reichskristallnacht* (the night of the crystal, because of all the windows of Jewish shops and offices that were smashed) and led to the destruction of more than 7,000 businesses and 200 synagogues. More than 20,000 Jews were arrested and sent to concentration camps. Insofar as a determination could be made, 91 Jews were murdered; many more committed suicide. National Socialist officialdom now moved against the Jews with relentless brutality. Pitiless interference in their cultural life, confiscation of their property, and restrictions on travel all limited their personal freedom. Additionally, they were required to pay an "atonement" fee of over 1 billion marks. The pressure to emigrate accompanied by simultaneous economic piracy increased so much that at the outbreak of war in 1939 the number of Jews (by Nazi definition) had sunk below 200,000.

The Road to War (1933–1939)

The goals of the National Socialists were largely fixed and the general direction of their policies was established. This, however, does not mean that the leadership had worked out concrete plans with dates, phases, and alternatives: It had somewhat deliberately rejected the predetermination of specific methods for the stabilization and expansion of power, and its decisions were not absolutely logical or consistent with the outline of their program. Particularly in the initial and development phases of the Third Reich, many decisions were taken because of elements of perceived expedience; because of the need to experiment; and in an effort, in light of the power politics of Europe, to find better ways to achieve long-range goals one step at a time. It was important also to gradually accustom public opinion to changed circumstances. The foreign policy successes of the National Socialists contributed to effecting the unity of people and leadership, but this situation changed during the course of the war, when Hitler confronted the armed forces with insuperable tasks and when confidence in the genius of the Führer began to wane.

Within a few days after he assumed power, Hitler told his immediate circle about his decision to change conditions in the Reich completely, to eliminate every opponent, to revive the armed resolve of the German people, and to force a revision in the Versailles Treaty. At the same time he wanted to find allies abroad; if and when he could, additional export opportunities or preferably new *Lebensraum* in the East would be obtained. The latter would have to be rigorously Germanized.

At first, however, he initiated a grandiose strategy to absolve himself in advance from any blame for future actions. With the support of the minister for propaganda, Josef Goebbels, Hitler and his colleagues constantly repeated the German Reich's "sincere desire for peace." At the same time, Hitler's apparatus systematically prepared Germany militarily, economically, organizationally, and mentally for war, without permitting this firmly established goal to penetrate fully into the consciousness of the German people. Goebbels later explained this tactic by pointing out that the National Socialists always had to proceed according to the power and resources available to them at any given moment. In 1933 they could not have undertaken what they tackled in 1934 or later because the people would not have gone along with them; they were not adequately prepared. It was necessary to achieve their goals in phases.

To these phases belong the first decisive measures in foreign and military policy that were designed to guarantee Germany freedom of action and military sovereignty to make new alliances possible. They included the German withdrawal from the League of Nations (1933); a nonaggression pact with Poland (1934); the return of the Saar territory to Germany and the introduction of universal military service (1935); and the reoccupation of the demilitarized zone of the Rhineland by German armed forces (1936). They also included Hitler's success in breaking up the alliance of World War I victors by concluding a German-British naval treaty in 1935. New alliances became possible, paving the way for the formation of the so-called Berlin-Rome-Tokyo Axis in 1936–1937. All of these successes raised the prestige of the Führer and the Reich at home and abroad, as did German achievements at the 1936 Olympics in Berlin. At the beginning of 1937, Hitler was able to announce that Germany had again become a major European power, even a world power. Thereafter he became more daring, authorizing the use of German military contingents to support General Franco in the Spanish Civil War and flagrantly threatening war against other countries. He hoped all the while that Great Britain would grant him a "free hand" in Eastern Europe. In a position paper connected with the Four-Year Plan, he demanded as early as 1936 that the German armed forces be prepared for warfare in four years and that the German economy be placed on a war footing. Thereafter the NS leadership had a more pervasive influence on German industry and demanded that it speed up supplying the Reich with raw materials needed for war.

In the spring of 1938, the invasion of Austria by German troops and the subsequent annexation (*Anschluss*) of that country to the German Reich brought about national intoxication. The widely publicized slogan "one People, one Reich, one Führer" was enthusiastically accepted without concern for its real background. Hitler, who was hailed as superior to Bismarck because he was able to create the long-sought Greater German Reich without the use of "blood and iron," now decided that Czechoslovakia would be the next object of his policy of conquest. In November 1937, he had confidentially made this intention known to an intimate group of advisers. As ignition he employed the Sudeten German Party led by Konrad Henlein. The Sudeten territory was a narrow crescent of land along the western, northern, and eastern borders of Bohemia, settled by German-speaking people. The party made increasingly radical demands for greater autonomy on the government in Prague. The imminent threat of war was averted at the last moment by the conclusion of the Munich accords of September 29, 1938, to which Germany, Great Britain, France, and Italy—but not the Soviet Union—were signatories. Czechoslovakia had to surrender the Sudeten territory to Germany.

The National Socialist leadership, however, was not satisfied with this victory. To representatives of the press, Hitler now revealed that for years circumstances had forced him to speak of peace. In the long run, however, this was dangerous because it could lead to a seductive pacifism. It was now essential to motivate the German people for war. It was the task of the press to make clear that the leadership was acting absolutely properly and that there were foreign policy problems that could be resolved only by force.

It would undoubtedly be erroneous to divide National Socialist foreign policy from 1933 to 1939 into a revisionist and an expansionist period. Rather there was a phase of covert preparation for aggression to 1937, a period of open expansionism using the threat of force beginning in 1938, and the initiation of war in 1939. War was probably seen as a way out of the national bankruptcy that resulted from rising arms expenditures and increasing public debt.

The decisive turn toward war began when the Germans entered Prague, the capital of Czechosolvakia, in March 1939 and occupied Bohemia and Moravia. Not satisfied with this success, Hitler turned his entire attention to Poland. From 1935 on he had sought to win Warsaw for a joint fight against the Soviet Union: He had to abandon this plan early in 1939 because the leaders of Poland had no intention of permitting themselves to be made tools of a Nazi policy of aggression. On March 21, 1939, Hitler made suggestions for a solution to the questions of Danzig and the Polish Corridor. The Poles refused. Ten days later Great Britain issued a declaration guaranteeing the territorial integrity of Poland, having finally decided to stop the expansion policy of the National Socialists. Hitler thereupon renounced the Anglo-German Naval Agreement and on April 28 renounced the German-Polish Nonaggression Pact. Less than a month later, on May 22, he concluded a military alliance with Italy ("The Pact of Steel"). Previously he had swallowed the Memel territory, a strip of land adjoining East Prussia at the north that had originally been settled by German-speaking people.

During this time Hitler had intensified his diplomatic activities in Moscow—in competition with the Western powers—in order to obtain a free hand in Poland. Stalin's price for not resisting Hitler's initiative was a Soviet sphere of influence in the Baltic, in Eastern Poland, and in the Moldavian area of eastern Romania. Hitler was willing to pay it, and on August 23, 1939, the spectacular nonaggression pact between Germany and the Soviet Union was concluded. A secret protocol annexed to the treaty delineated their mutual spheres of interest in Eastern Europe. For a temporary advantage Germany delivered the eastern part of Central Europe to Communism. In early August, after Hitler had definitely decided to attack Poland, German-Polish relations became increasingly testy. The excesses of Poles against ethnic Germans provided a welcome excuse for forceful intervention.

The conclusion of the Polish-British Mutual Assistance Pact of August 25, 1939, and Italy's declaration that it was unprepared for war led once more to a postponement of the attack and an attempt by Berlin to isolate Poland from the Western powers. But on August 31, 1939, Hitler gave the order for attack after he had deliberately prevented further German-Polish negotiations and after Poland, completely failing to recognize its hopeless military position, had ordered the mobilization of its armed forces on August 30.

In contrast to the psychological situation in 1914, the outbreak of World War II evoked not enthusiasm but skepticism and generally gloomy resignation among the German people. It found the German armed services in the midst of rearmament that had quickly, perhaps precipitately, spread to all parts of the armed forces but lacked all depth, both in materiel and personnel. Germany could hardly boast a completed instrument of war, even if its advantage over the Western powers in the production of modern weapons and in the number of trained soldiers (increased from 100,000 to 1,000,000 between 1933 and 1939) was in its favor. Of the generally accepted requirement of four months' supply of equipment of all types, about one-quarter was available; anti-aircraft ammunition and bombs were sufficient for three months, while fuel availability from reserves and current production would last at most through four months of warfare. In addition, the General Staff of the army had made operational preparations only for an offensive against Poland.

Between 1933 and 1939, the National Socialists' education program and systematic training in party and state organizations and in the armed forces sought to instill the ideal of the fighting man. It was the leadership's intention to indoctrinate all classes of the population with what became known as National Socialism's "laws of deportment." In doing so, the leadership sought and found ties to some of the metaphysical attributes of the Kaiser's Reich and even of the Weimar Republic. They could link up with the ideology of the militant societies and connect with the nationalistic/patriotic message that had been part of the traditional educational inventory. The catalogue of military virtues— obedience, loyalty, courage, discipline, the heroic ideal—was to become the standard of values for the nation, an "armed community" consisting of a leader and his followers. Social differences were to be removed through the wearing of uniforms and the introduction of command structures. Songs and symbols, poems and novels glorified war. The idea of immortality started to play a major role in literature. The military spirit of permanent readiness to attack was to penetrate the lifestyle of the citizenry and to strengthen their awareness that the "sacred treasures" of the nation could be preserved only by war.

Based on this reversion to Spartan and Prussian ideals—including physical heroism, the dedication of the individual to the greater good, the love of fighting as the first moral duty, and the readiness to die a hero's death—curricula were developed at various training institutions for the National Socialist elite. The barrackslike environment also served to promote physical training and military discipline. Appropriate texts embedded in the youngsters the traditions of German militarism. The purpose of this effort was twofold: It was intended to prepare young people for the "battle for this world," for dominance over others and thereby to inculcate in them the missionary spirit of the Nordic race; they also were to become instruments to stabilize and secure the social and political system. Conditioned to blind obedience, they would provide a permanent control mechanism. Although only the rudimentary beginnings of this thorough, far-reaching goal of education could be translated into reality because of basically different historical predispositions, the time factor, and the resistance engendered by frictions and rivalries between organizations, it was nevertheless undoubtedly decisive for the attitude of many Germans. This attempt at psychological manipulation had some disastrous effects, as was demonstrated by

German behavior during their occupations of various countries, in the persecution and extermination of Jews, and in the attitudes toward other peoples. In the years from 1941 to 1944 the Nazis attempted to portray the war as an ideological-racial struggle with the dynamics provided by a fanatical pursuit of victory. This meant that an extremely thorough educational system had to be organized in the armed forces. The soldiers were indoctrinated in the party ideology. The officers became prophets of the NS *Weltanschauung;* they became political soldiers. Still, success remained elusive. In many cases the basic values of German nationalism and the traditional military spirit proved to be stronger than the new indoctrination.

The Fight for World Hegemony (1939–1943)

The course of military operations from 1939 to 1942 made clear that the Nazi leadership was conducting a regionally limited war in specific campaigns, a war that could be regarded as a continuation of its policies by different means. Its propaganda called the war a "just" defensive or preventive action. Later the rulers proclaimed the "Freedom Fight of Greater Germany." The soldiers at the front and the people at home were to form one unit determined to victoriously conclude this "fateful struggle for Europe," in "unshakable confidence in a glorious future, and in complete faith in the Führer" as "guarantor of victory." The initial goal of the war was the military defeat and partition of Poland, the strategic securing of the northern flank through the occupation of Denmark and Norway, and the elimination of France and Great Britain as power factors on the European continent. Three days after the start of German military operations against Poland, war was declared against Germany by Britain, the Commonwealth, and France. Italy remained a nonbelligerent, and the United States declared its armed neutrality. The Western powers, in spite of Hitler's solemn promises that he had no interest in the West, were determined to stand by their alliances. The nonaggression pact between Germany and the Soviet Union did not motivate the Allies to change their policy. The time was past when they were willing to accept *faits accomplis.* They failed, however, to follow up with offensive operations; they lacked will and apparently were not prepared. As a result, German leadership gained valuable time and concluded the campaign against Poland victoriously within a few weeks. When the Red Army moved into eastern Poland on September 17, 1939, under the pretense of protecting the Byelorussian and Ukrainian populations, the fate of Poland was sealed—but still there was no immediate reaction on the part of the Western powers, although Hitler had expected it.

After the fourth partition of Poland had been agreed upon between Germany and the Soviet Union on September 28, 1939, Hitler left the future of western Poland in suspense. By proclamation he first separated purely Polish territories and established the so-called "incorporated Eastern territories" (the Reich territories of West Prussia and Posen) and then grouped the remainder under the title of the Government General for the Occupied Polish Territories. He hoped to be able to use the latter to bargain in future peace negotiations with Great Britain, but British determination to resist stiffened in spite of Hitler's victorious campaign against France. In early June a frustrated Hitler renamed the Government General as an annexed territory and in the fall he actually incorporated it into the Reich.

While the Polish campaign was still under way, Hitler decided to force a decisive battle with France and Great Britain by a ruthless violation of the neutrality of the Netherlands, Belgium, and Luxembourg. Political developments in Scandinavia (the Soviet-Finnish War of the winter of 1939-1940) motivated him to secure the strategic northern flank. On April 9, 1940, German troops occupied Denmark and landed in Norway: Hitler's action took place only hours before a similar action planned by the Allies. Thus Hitler obtained an exit on the Atlantic for the conduct of the war at sea and also ensured continued availability of Swedish iron ore. The shifting battles in Scandinavia ended with a German victory in June 1940.

The offensive in the West finally began on May 10, 1940, under strategic conditions favorable to Germany, and resulted in a military victory hardly deemed possible. The Allied rout was mitigated by the successful British-French evacuation of forces that had retreated to the beach at Dunkirk; the British forces had been driven from the continent. In the woods at Compiègne, site of the German surrender after World War I, representatives of France signed the fairly moderate German conditions to end hostilities. The armistice became effective when France also signed a corresponding pact with Italy, which had entered the war on the side of Germany on June 10, 1940. Vichy France, not occupied by Germany, remained dependent on and allied with Germany under the leadership of Marshal Pétain. Only Great Britain, which on May 10, 1940, had entrusted its fate to the resolute leadership of Winston Churchill, would not give up the fight.

By the summer of 1940, Hitler had gone from one political success to another since 1933 and had now been victorious in three military campaigns. He had reached the apex of his career, and his predictions once more had been proved correct. The opponents had collapsed in the shortest of time. He had thereby apparently reached his mid-term political goal. In his mind, it was tied to his concept of a "second act" of the war of 1914–1918, which this time would end with a German victory. It was in character for him to believe that this part of the war was a "restitution" for those whose lives had been sacrificed in World War I.

Until this time Hitler had conducted his foreign policy like a sleep-walker, relying on his instinct for perfect timing. It appeared that he was able to conduct a war with similar ease thanks to his "intuition." The territory of National Socialist authority now extended from the northern tip of Norway to the Spanish border and was secured by the world's most effective armed forces. The only question that remained was how to get Britain to knuckle under. After Churchill had rejected Hitler's offer of peace on June 19, 1940, Germany made preparations to carry the fight to this last remaining enemy by land, by sea, and in the air.

At the same time Hitler concerned himself with the idea of a "grand coalition." Beginning in 1936, Joachim von Ribbentrop, who became foreign minister in 1938, had attempted to bring about a globe-girdling alliance with Japan. This alliance was to direct its efforts first (1936–1937) against the Soviet Union and later (1938–1939) against Great Britain. In the summer of 1940, the task was different: It was to prevent the entry of the United States into the current conflict and any future confrontation between the United States and Japan. Only a strong, decisive stand on the part of Germany, Italy, and Japan could act as a powerful and effective deterrent against the United States. In the treaty signed by the Axis powers on September 27, 1940, Germany and Italy agreed to recognize Japan's leading role in Greater Asia. Japan did the same for the "new order" in Europe under the leadership of Germany and Italy. This triangular political relationship never developed into a clear community of interest and even less into a community of joint action. It ended by being an "alliance without backbone." Germany was unable to persuade Japan to undertake an active role in the Far East. Moreover, the reactions of both Roosevelt and Churchill made clear that threats would deter neither the Americans nor the British from resisting aggression.

The air battle for Britain developed into a German defeat and eliminated the most important precondition for the success of the planned invasion of Britain (Operation Sealion). At the same time the German High Command started preparations for an attack against the Soviet Union (Operation Barbarossa). Interestingly, Hitler was still toying with the idea of including the Soviet Union, in addition to Vichy France, Spain, and Portugal, in a continental anti-British alliance, thereby expanding his envisioned global political triangle into a bloc of major powers so strong that resistance to it would be futile.

When Soviet Foreign Minister Molotov came to Berlin in November 1940, Hitler made a major effort to interest the Soviet Union in what should be done with all the valuable properties of a bankrupt Britain. Wouldn't the Soviet Union be interested in inheriting Britain's treasures in India and the Middle East? But Molotov relentlessly insisted on dealing with the Soviet interests in Finland, Bulgaria, and the various straits. The demands made by the Soviet Union in return for joining the three-power alliance made it apparent that an agreement to delineate relative spheres of interest between these two countries, both bent on expansion, was impossible then and would be in the future. They also removed any doubts Hitler may have had that his intention to defeat the Soviet Union in a quick military campaign was the only correct solution to his current and future problems. The conclusion of the Soviet-Yugoslav Friendship treaty on April 5, 1941, a few days after an anti-German coup in Belgrade, reinforced his decision. Only the sword could control what had already been won, conquer the desired territories, and create the basis for the restructuring of Europe, but before taking such action, Hitler believed it was necessary to secure his own southeastern flank. In the Balkan campaign of April and May 1941, Greece and Yugoslavia were defeated in quick moves and Crete was occupied. Hungary, Romania, Slovakia, Bulgaria, and eventually Croatia had in the meantime joined the three-power pact, and Hitler decided to support the Italians after their reverses in the Balkans and in Libya. He remained convinced, however, that he could achieve the desired hegemony in Europe only through a defeat of the Soviet Union.

The National Socialist leadership had made a crucial mistake in its choice of means to terminate the war after hostilities ended in the west in the summer and fall of 1940. This was the turning point of World War II. After their triumph in the west, Hitler and his advisers apparently believed they could translate even their most extravagant foreign policy goals into reality by military means. In this way they brought about their own downfall. By trying to carry out their wild plans they also forged an alliance of the three greatest world and sea powers: Great Britain, the Soviet Union, and the United States. In spite of the differences among them, these three countries formed a staunch wartime alliance that collapsed only when the German Reich had unconditionally surrendered in 1945 and after Soviet Communism had extended its power to the Elbe.

Here we need to devote a few lines to an explanation of German military tactics. A fairly novel and particularly effective method of warfare used from September 1939 to May 1941 was the so-called *Blitzkrieg,* a sudden surprise attack along a single front directed toward a specific objective and using the full mobility and firepower of all weapons in a combined tank-air operation. It was designed to bring about a swift defeat of the enemy. In contrast to later campaigns, the objective of the *Blitzkrieg* was the destruction of the enemy's forces rather than the conquest of foreign territory. The unusually short campaigns had the advantage of avoiding long battles, which involved large amounts of equipment and the resultant burden on the civilian population at home. They also constituted a defensive measure against economic alliances, potentially threatening to Germany's raw materials position. By tying them into a whole series of diplomatic peace offers, Germany sought to shift the moral responsibility for continued destruction of human lives to the enemy. Moreover, the *Blitzkrieg* concept corresponded realistically to the production capacity of the German defense industry. It also dispelled early widespread doubts about final victory, caused a general silencing of criticism of the Nazi system, and strengthened the growing identification of large parts of the population with Hitler as the nation's captain and with his partially revealed war goals.

The definitive qualitative change in the conduct of the war occurred with the German surprise attack on the Soviet Union in June 1941, in which it was joined in short order by Finland, Romania, Hungary, Slovakia, and Italy. Germany's leaders justified the attack as a "preventive action." The first indication of this change had been in measures directed toward ethnic annihilation in 1939–1940 in Poland, which were, however, kept secret from the public or at least obscured. The increasing radicalization of the war was marked by simultaneous operations on several fronts, conquest of large territories, economic exploitation of occupied areas, efforts at autarky, the destruction of ideological opponents, and rule by terror by German special units behind the lines. To an increasing extent, the war now also attracted the participation of representatives of Germany's economic establishment, who became profit-hungry beneficiaries and unscrupulous stooges.

When the German offensive came to a halt at the gates of Moscow and Leningrad in November 1941, the *Blitzkrieg* had failed for the first time. Among the main reasons for the failure was the German inability to appreciate the importance of the vast extent of Soviet territory and of the enemy's indomitable will to resist. They simply misjudged the Soviet Union's personnel and materiel strengths. It is, of course, true that even a military victory in 1941 and the conquest of Moscow would hardly have turned the war in favor of Germany. The Soviet Union had by no means exhausted its capacities, as later military operations proved again and again. The determining factor, rather, lay not only in Hitler's desire to destroy the opponent's military potential but also in his refusal to abandon his far-reaching political plans. In light of the insane National Socialist war goals in the east—exploitation, domination, and suppression of the Soviet Union—any yielding, any accommodation with the enemy, seemed unacceptable. Thus Hitler not only misused and betrayed the "ideals" of his German soldiers, but also those of many volunteers (Spanish, French, Flemish, Walloon, Norwegian, Danish, Croatian, Slovene, Dutch, and Swiss) who thought they were fighting on the side of the Axis for a "better order" in Europe.

Another fateful miscalculation was made by Hitler in December 1941, after the Japanese attack on the U.S. fleet at Pearl Harbor, when he and Mussolini declared war on the United States. The European conflict thereby became a global confrontation. In 1939 Hitler had pointed with pride to his "diplomatic triumph" that made it possible for Germany to fight on only one front at a time, but now the multiple-front war had become reality. Goebbels was later to remark that such a war had "never been won by the Reich." The Allied resolve received important impetus from the first defeats of the German armed forces at Moscow and Leningrad, for now their reputation of invincibility had been lost. Perhaps Hitler himself began to have doubts: At the height of the first great military crisis, in November 1941, he intimated that perhaps a negotiated peace settlement would be necessary because the opposing groups could not defeat one another. But a few weeks later he seemed confident that in 1942 he could force victory. He ordered an attack on the Soviet southern sector; Leningrad was to be taken in the north so as to finally link the German and Finnish forces. By conquering the remainder of the Ukraine, the Caucasus, and the Donets Basin he hoped to capture control of all the resources of the Soviet Union's war economy and in this way finally destroy the enemy's remaining defensive strength.

The German attack was successful from June to September 1942, but the two major German armies were deflected from their original coordinated objectives. One army group planted the German flag on Mt. Elbrus and advanced through the highest range of the Caucasus to within 20 kilometers of Sukhumi, while units of another army group infested the western and northern portions of the city of Stalingrad, but this was as far as their momentum would carry them.

The same scenario applied in North Africa. German units had supported Italian forces since early 1942, but in late June 1942 the offensive operations had to be halted 100 kilometers west of Alexandria. On October 23, 1942, the British began their counteroffensive. The German and Italian divisions were too weak to stop it. When additional strong Allied forces under General Eisenhower landed to the rear of the German Afrika Korps in Algeria and Morocco on November 7 and 8, 1942, the Axis powers soon found themselves in a hopeless two-front war. In mid-May 1943 the last remnants of these forces capitulated.

Thereafter Africa was held by the Allies; they had fought for and obtained the base for the final thrust into the "soft underbelly" of the Axis.

At the same time, the British and U.S. air forces increased their attacks on German bases, industrial centers, and cities. At the end of January 1943 the U.S. Army Air Corps made its first daylight raid over German soil without fighter protection, and in June the Allies began the "Combined Bomber Offensive" decided on at the Casablanca Conference. While the U.S. Army Air Corps conducted daylight precision bombardments, the Royal Air Force started area bombardments at night. These superior bomber and fighter units were based not only in the British Isles but also in southern Italy and so were able to move on the Reich from two directions and to reach any point they wanted to attack.

Meanwhile the Soviets had recognized the German weaknesses at the front along the Don River and had carefully prepared a pincer operation. On November 19–20, 1942, the Red Army counterattacked with strong forces both north and south of Stalingrad and encircled the German 6th Army within five days. On Hitler's orders, these troops attempted to defend all their positions, hoping for relief from outside the encirclement and for supplies by air. The first failed and the second were totally insufficient. The crushing superiority of the Soviets forced the surrender of the 6th Army at the end of January 1943. Two months later the successful operation of German submarines in the Atlantic caused such heavy losses that the Allies seriously considered giving up their convoy supply system. But new Allied weapons brought about the collapse of German submarine warfare in April–May 1943.

Europe's "New Racial Order"

Hitler and his closest followers postulated a "new racial order" on the continent under National Socialist leadership. Had they succeeded in this endeavor, the German sphere of influence might have extended from the Arctic Ocean in the north to the Mediterranean in the south, from the Atlantic in the west to the Urals in the east. A permanent rural population would have been settled in these mountains, armed to defend itself and to deter surprise attacks from Asian enemies. In the event of a German victory, such a hegemony might have existed in close international harmony with the Latin states of Italy, France, Spain, and Portugal which would have maintained their ostensible independence, albeit with a dependence on Germany, especially economically. The same situation might also have applied to Finland, Turkey, and some of the Balkan states. In northern and central Europe, however, the area that in Hitler's view, was the home of the

"Nordic master race" that would rule the new "Greater German Reich of the German Nation" in the nucleus of Europe—here only German dominance could be considered. No true national independence would have been permitted among the privileged "Germanic" peoples who were to be incorporated into the Reich by ideological subordination and subjugation to German military protection.

The future "Greater Germanic Reich with Berlin as a giant world capital called 'Germania'"—a fantasy undoubtedly based on the idea of a universal Holy Roman Empire of the German Nation in a National Socialist format—was to be an unblockadeable, autarkic economic empire that would be superior to the Anglo-Saxon world economic system and, together with Japanese hegemony in Asia, would even trump the United States. Law and the constitution would be embodied only in the "will of the Führer." In this new "Germanic federation," where more than 600,000 ethnic Germans from abroad had already been resettled by 1943, new Germanic residents would be able to acquire a "Greater Germanic Reich citizenship" with specific political and economic rights, a status that would transcend normal citizenship privileges.

In this Reich, in which adherence to the authoritarian Führer principle was to be assumed, all "racial enemies" were to be eliminated as the final logical sequence of anti-Semitic ideology. Those of "lesser value," the sick and crippled, were to be exterminated through euthanasia. Between 1939 and 1941 some 70,000 mentally and physically handicapped persons were killed by gassing. Those who contributed to the discomfort of the regime (political opponents and Eastern European peoples) were either to be deported to concentration camps where, *inter alia,* they could—and did—serve as guinea pigs for "progressive" scientists or to be resettled in Siberia. Gypsies were to be exterminated—they were sent to concentration camps in large numbers. The remainder of the "foreign peoples" (subhumans) of Eastern Europe would be reduced to serfdom in the style of extremist imperialist colonialism. As early as 1943, the National Socialist leadership initiated vigorous measures to prevent the presence of "damaging" influences from "alien population policies" in the so-called German settlement area.

The broad expanses of Russia could serve the SS armies—now the "true" bearers of the nation's arms—as an exercise area for "maneuvers with live ammunition." Christianity was to be replaced by the rules of the Order of the SS, while functionaries of all party organizations were to replace the traditional or economically privileged upper classes. They were expected to live according to the precepts of the "magnificent model," imbued by a "new moral code," married to specially bred "superwomen," thus able to represent the spirit and posture of the Nordic elite, the so-called master race. War heroes would, as their highest reward, be allowed to practice bigamy, thus ensuring an increase in the "Germanic population." Victory by warfare was to be succeeded by the "victory of the child."

The most extreme expression of this planned and partly initiated "new racial order" was the physical elimination of the "world enemy": the Jews. Beginning with the outbreak of World War II, National Socialist policy regarding Jews became increasingly radical. When the "fight for national existence" against the external enemy required the complete concentration of all forces for the conduct of war, the pressure at home on the Jews was sharply increased. Initially there was no unified concept as to their fate and that of the millions of Jews who had fallen into German hands in the newly conquered territories of Eastern Europe and those who lived in the countries allied with Germany, but it soon became clear that draconian measures similar to those used in Germany would be employed to exclude the Jews from society, deprive them of property, and expel them. Himmler and Heydrich established a tight network of police and SD (security service) units, which, beginning in Poland, were entrusted with the tasks of deportation and the creation of ghettoes. As early as the fall of 1939 the first mass killings on the way to these ghettoes began in Poland.

For a time in 1940, the National Socialist leadership considered the possibility of resettling about 4 million Jews on the island of Madagascar. This plan, however, was short lived. With the German surprise attack on the Soviet Union in 1941, the fight against "Jewry" increased in intensity and cruelty. This could be seen in the deportation of Jews under the cover name of "planned allocation of labor" and actual genocide in former Soviet territory. At the same time, the policy of discrimination against Jews in the Reich increased in severity. By a police regulation of September 1, 1941, Jews who were six years old or older could not appear in public without wearing the distinctive yellow badge consisting of the Star of David with the word *"Jude"* (Jew) in its center. This was followed by prohibitions against leaving the place of residence without permission of the local police, against the use of any form of public transportation, against subscriptions to newspapers, against obtaining ration cards for tobacco products, against the keeping of pets, and against the use of barber or beauty shops. All electrical appliances had to be surrendered.

It is quite probable that the Nazi leadership decided during the second half of 1941, in strict secrecy, systematically to exterminate all European Jews. At the so-called Wannsee Conference of January 20, 1942, the administrative regulations of the "final solution" were established in detail, probably under Hitler's direct orders. The acts of extermination, bureaucratically prepared and technocratically executed under the direction of Adolf Eichmann, used mass executions and mass gassings at camps in Kulmhof, Auschwitz, Belzec, Sobibor, Treblinka, and Lublin-Maydanek—to mention only the most important. They caused some 4 to 6 million deaths. It is true, however, that the extent and the importance of the holocaust was known at the time only to a minority in Germany. There were undoubtedly hundreds of individuals who helped the persecuted and tormented, but indifference, a retreat into privacy, inadequate solidarity with fellow human beings, lack of civic courage, fear of persecution, and daily concern for the lives of family members at the front characterized the actions and inactions of the German population. This shameful behavior is, no doubt, also traceable to the carefully structured constant manipulation of the National Socialist mass media, which most people failed to see through. Today it is clear that the Nazis' extermination of the Jews resulted less from improvisations to meet a wartime situation but rather that it was the final step of a program established in the 1920s. The core of National Socialism's program was the determination to fight "Jewry" as part of a "historic mission" and to destroy it out of fear that it would destroy them.

The German Resistance

The beginnings of German opposition to National Socialism, its ideology, and its claim to unlimited authority go back to 1931 after the NSDAP had become the second largest party in the Reichstag as a result of the 1930 elections. People with strong religious convictions feared from the outset that a National Socialist regime would threaten morality, Christianity, and culture. In 1932, conservative politicians with strong nationalistic beliefs castigated the destructive effects of National Socialist party policies, the attitude of National Socialism toward religion, and the planned degrading of the state into a protector for the breeding of the Aryan race.

There is ample evidence that the leading Social Democrats had no illusions about the goals and methods of the National Socialists. All of them were initially excluded from any further role in public life; many were arrested and placed in "protective custody" in prisons and concentration camps for several years. Even so, the Gestapo was unable to break their resistance. If they were released, they cooperated tirelessly on plans for a revolt in concert with other circles and opposition groups until they were arrested again.

The first opposition activities were initiated by the left, which had vigorously resisted the National Socialists during the Weimar Republic. Although the Communists and the Social Democrats often moved in different directions, both agitated underground. They organized resistance in cells and in factories, they flooded Germany with illegal brochures, they warned and predicted but were unable appreciably to slow the process of mental seduction going on within Germany. Meanwhile, the Gestapo wove its net ever tighter so that there remained little room for secret activities. Nevertheless, the Social Democrats particularly, under the most difficult conditions, built a "silent reserve" of cadres for use in the hour of liberation. Courageous individuals who spoke up for human dignity got as little hearing as the warnings of numerous German politicians in exile. Most of their words were lost in the intoxication of national enthusiasm. The stormy development of the German Reich sucked many a critic or skeptic into its wake; only a few saw through the empty phrases of "spiritual awakening" and the new "national revolution."

The two major Christian denominations—Catholic and Protestant—did not recognize the true nature of National Socialism for several years. The open fight of the National Socialist Party for the "De-Religionization of Public Life" was in reality a cover for a fight against all Christian ideas and opened the eyes of many believers. It led to protest actions, declarations and sermons against this false Nazi doctrine, against anti-Semitism, and against the deification of the head of state. The fight against the churches reached its climax in 1937 when the Gestapo arrested numerous ministers of religion and had them condemned. Many of the representatives of the churches courageously stood up for the freedom of their message and for its spirit, but words alone could not keep the demon at bay.

A number of courageous and insightful Germans who felt concerned for the fate of Germany had turned away from Hitler. They realized that weapons of the spirit were inadequate to fight the arbitrary exercise of power, injustice, and terror. Only an armed revolt or uprising could bring about a major change in the existing conditions. But for such an action, the participation of those who bore the nation's arms would be required. At that time, Colonel General von Fritsch headed the army and the chief of the Army General Staff was General Ludwig Beck. Associated with them were men who viewed their military task not only as the application of their military expertise but also as a duty to people and country, particularly as they understood how the political-military system worked. By the end of 1937 they had to recognize that Hitler did not intend to use the armed forces exclusively for defensive purposes but had built them up to conduct wars of aggression. This was an arrogant, reckless game designed to push not only the armed forces but also the nation and all of Europe into the abyss.

When the warnings of the chief of the General Staff went unheeded by the top leadership, General Beck saw no way out but to resign his post. Under the circumstances, he was unwilling to take responsibility for a war unleashed by Hitler. His successor, General Franz Halder, together with some others who shared his views, made preparations to arrest Hitler at the start of the attack on Czechoslovakia and to try him before a court of law. This action, planned in August–September 1938, was the first attempt at a coup backed by small German opposition groups that were absolutely determined to remove the National Socialist system. They were not only concerned with the prevention of war but also sought a European pacification directed toward the reestablishment of human dignity both between nations and within the nation itself. The complaisance of the Western powers probably was a significant factor in the failure of their plan. At the Munich Conference they supported Germany's demands, thereby removing the psychological basis of any action against Hitler. To conduct a coup against the "great European statesman" would have been senseless; the majority of the German people would have rejected it.

But the opposition groups, particularly those around General Beck and Carl Goerdeler, the former lord mayor of Leipzig, continued to urge action, tailored to each possibility and situation, both at home and abroad. They even sent warnings to other governments that the National Socialist ruler would take further action by the use of force, but their messages fell on unreceptive ground. After Hitler's prestige had been further enhanced by the Polish campaign in the fall of 1939, a few of the conspirators made the first plan to assassinate the dictator in order to prevent the limited war from expanding into a worldwide conflagration. But these plans were squelched by the hesitance of some generals.

Most of the officers who were aware of the intended action refused to participate because they considered an assassination contrary to the tradition of the officer corps. Most of all, there was no suitable successor readily available, and the younger officer corps had to be considered unreliable in view of Hitler's successes. The mood inside Germany was not propitious for such an act. Some of the military conspirators also hoped that after a military success in the West the army could improve its position within the state and then reject Hitler's most extreme demands. There can be no doubt that the officers had a real problem of conscience. They faced the difficulty of choosing between their moral sense of responsibility and their military sense of obedience. It is hard to judge the true depth of their dilemma without firsthand knowledge of the social, cultural, and military indoctrination that shaped their thinking.

After the German military successes in the north and west in 1940, small groups of opponents struggled vainly against the exuberance of victory among the German people and the concomitant attrition of ethical values. Only with the increasing number of defeats on all fronts after 1941 were they able to regain some ground and win adherents to their cause. While some of them, through intermediaries in Sweden, Switzerland, and the United States, sought to define circumstances under which the Allies might negotiate a peaceful solution with a new German government, others desperately sought to convince senior and high-ranking officers of the armed forces that a coup was necessary. Both efforts were unsuccessful. The Western powers had become victims of their own war propaganda and were skeptical about contact with the German opposition. As for most German generals, some were prepared to act when ordered to do so, others were prepared to give orders after someone had acted.

Unlike the resistance in France and various similar movements in Europe during World War II, the conspiracy in Germany took place in great secrecy. Here there could be no guerrilla war; rather there was a collection of ideas and writings preparing for a single stroke. Completely on their own, ignored by the Allies, subject to denunciation at home, constantly threatened by the terror organs of the police system, some rather heterogeneous groups dared the most extreme action. Beginning in 1942, members of the military attempted on five occasions to remove Hitler. There were courageous individual acts like the attempt of the Scholls, students at the University of Munich, to use pamphlets to stimulate a more widespread underground propaganda campaign. Many people decided on the so-called "emigration within," which furnished a sort of refuge for their outraged consciences. Others used international connections to inform allies and neutrals of possible surprise attacks. As time went by, however, all efforts concentrated on measures leading to the removal of the dictator and his system. The extraordinary factor distinguishing the German opposition from resistance movements in the countries occupied by Germany was that any action in Germany would run counter to the feelings of the majority of the population.

Anyone concerned with the moral and ethical motives of the German resistance groups becomes deeply aware of their "spirit of freedom" and their "revolt of conscience." The reform movement, as parts of it became justifiably known, did not seek merely a revolution but a renewal of the national commonwealth with responsibility for the restoration of the traditions and culture of the German people. In this it was fully aware that it was urgent to bring about political developments that would move Germany and other countries away from the concept of the nation-state toward a continent-wide economic area and eventual integration into a world economy. This same spirit was also evident in the drafts of the Kreisau Circle, a resistance group that upheld the idea of a legal system that would punish those who violated it.

The increasing exasperation and the moral resentment against the demonic nature and the crimes of National Socialist totalitarianism, the deep feeling of responsibility for the people and the country, the desire for the restoration of traditional values, and finally, the feeling of duty to preserve Germany from total ruination and to call a halt to Hitler's disastrous policies in World War II—these were the forces that motivated the actions of the German opposition. Their last great attempt to avert the catastrophe failed on July 20, 1944, when the attempted assassination of Hitler by Colonel Count Stauffenberg misfired. The resultant maelstrom of persecutions involved thousands, many of whom were shot or hanged. Nevertheless, as a symbol, the German resistance had been victorious.

The Collapse (1944–1945)

After the fortunes of war had turned against Germany—after the battles of El Alamein, Tunis, Morocco, and Stalingrad and those of Midway and Guadalcanal in the Pacific and after the failure of German submarine warfare in the Atlantic in 1942–1943—National Socialist Germany continued to fight the war for the sake of war itself. Since the anti-Hitler coalition controlled 75 percent of the world's personnel and material resources, the war could not be won. Moreover, the German war economy was collapsing.

Reich Minister Albert Speer achieved some successes in the armament industry and war economy during the years 1942–1945 through the application of great organizational skill, efficient methods, and the total mobilization of German and foreign workers. These policies were accompanied by the exploitation of the occupied territories. Yet nothing could change the fact that, even without the increased Allied bombardment, German arms production at its height in July 1944 could not have been increased by more than 20–30 percent. At that point, arms production would have exhausted the raw materials available. Inasmuch as Hitler's political actions had far exceeded German military and economic resources and the multi-front war had led from defeat to defeat, a fanatic faith in the final victory of a totalitarian ideology was supposed to substitute for the missing power.

After day and night Allied strategic bomber raids, the storming of "Fortress Europe" began in 1943: From the east came the Red Army, in the southeast German forces were attacked by Yugoslav and Greek partisans, and the British and U.S. forces moved from the south via Sicily and Italy. Germany was still willing but barely able to defend the resultant front of approximately 15,000 kilometers, from the North Cape via the "Atlantic Wall" in France to Italy and the Aegean and north again through the Soviet Union to Murmansk. But now it was just a question of how long the available forces could stand up to the expected attacks in the various theaters of war as well as to the bombardment—even though Goebbels had proclaimed "total war."

The attack on the "bulwark" that German propaganda had pictured as impregnable began at its Achilles heel. On July 10, 1943, under cover of their unchallenged fleet, the Allies landed in Sicily while heavy bombardment destroyed the Italian will to fight. Under the pressure of obvious Allied successes, the Fascist regime in Italy collapsed within a few days. In early September, British and U.S. troops crossed the straits from Sicily to the southern tip of Italy; four weeks later they had reached the line from Foggia to Naples. By the end of the year they had broken through the defenses on the Sangro River and had reached the monastery at Monte Casino.

Meanwhile Hitler executed plans to disarm the Italian forces in order to prevent their wholesale surrender to the enemy. A large part of the army fell into German hands, but the Italian fleet escaped at the last minute from La Spezia to Malta. Mussolini, who had been arrested on July 25, 1943, and was then freed from Gran Sasso by a special SS commando group, proclaimed a new Socialist Republic of Italy on September 18, but it led only a shadow existence in northern Italy until the end of the war. The new royal government of Italy, however, declared war on Germany; the former ally had become a new enemy.

While Yugoslav partisans under Marshal Tito placed more and more pressure on the German occupation forces in that country, the Soviets went on the attack after the failure of the last German offensive at Kursk in June 1943. As early as January of that year, the Soviet forces had restored the land connection to the hard-pressed city of Leningrad. Once on the attack, Soviet forces were able to achieve a breakthrough along the entire front of 1000 kilometers, advancing about 300 kilometers. The approximately 5.1 million Soviet soldiers faced about 3 million Germans; the Soviets also commanded a materiel superiority, with two to three times as much equipment as the German forces.

In 1944 the Red Army resumed its westward advance along the entire front from Lapland to the Black Sea. Its divisions had reached Poland and the eastern borders of Czechoslovakia and Romania when, under the cover of immense sea and air forces, the allies carried out the long-awaited landing in Normandy on June 6. This was followed by a second invasion in the south of France on August 15. The attack by the British-U.S.-Canadian and French expeditionary armies, supported by partisan groups and the French resistance, broke through the German lines within a few weeks. In August Paris was liberated, as were Toulon and Marseilles in southern France.

In a headlong advance, the Allied armies reached the German border at Aachen in October 1944. The overwhelming offensives of the anti-Hitler coalition, the systematic bombardment and destruction of German transportation, communication, and production centers, the devastating attacks on cities and the countryside by the British and American air forces—all these events announced the coming end of the war. Impressed by Allied military successes, Romania, Finland, Bulgaria, and Hungary one by one ended hostilities and turned against Germany. German troops, under the most difficult of conditions, continued their steady withdrawal.

The agony of the German Reich began in the fall of 1944, accompanied by an ever-increasing movement of the population from east to west. At the same time, Hitler sought to achieve the impossible by throwing children and old men (the *Volkssturm*) into battle. Instead of using his last remaining forces for defense in the east, he ordered the Ardennes offensive (Battle of the Bulge) on December 16, 1944, in the vain hope that the German armed forces could repeat what they had achieved in 1940. The effort failed within a few weeks.

On January 12, 1945, Soviet troops moved from the bridgehead at Baranow toward Berlin. A few weeks later Allied troops crossed the Rhine along a broad front. At the end of April the advance parties met at the Elbe. Now Hitler removed himself from all responsibility by committing suicide. On May 7, 1945, his successor, Grand Admiral Dönitz, had to sign the document of unconditional surrender.

From 1943 onward, whatever Hitler did or ordered to be done can be characterized neither as the conduct of war nor as politics. In many ways he simply tried to apply the methods of the National Socialist struggle for power in the 1920s in the military arena. Fanatic slogans ("Victory or Extinction!"), propaganda and indoctrination, the "Führer's Powers of Suggestion," the unconditional defense of improvised fortifications, and the new "V" rockets were supposed to help him master the numerous crises and to find new methods for final victory. They were supposed to work until one of the accursed enemies became too tired to continue the fight. The final consequence of this mad enterprise was his order for Germany to self-destruct. Hitler had staked everything on a single card and lost. He now blamed the German people for the catastrophe. They had not proved themselves worthy of him; since the people were weak, they deserved extinction—the future would belong to the "stronger people of the East."

In May 1945 Soviet, U.S., British, Canadian, and French troops occupied a Reich whose entire institutional structure had collapsed. Legislative, judicial, and executive authority was assumed by the Allied commanders. With these events, the Third Reich, intended to be the apex of German history, fell to its lowest depth. Germany had suffered its worst political and military defeat. Inasmuch as the policies of the years from 1933 to 1945 had been carried out with the tools of terror and inhumanity, the German people emerged from the war with a huge historical mortgage to burden the conscience of future generations.

Readings

V. R. Berghahn. "The Third Reich 1933–1945," in *Modern Germany: Society, Economy and Politics in the Twentieth Century.* New York: Cambridge University Press, 1982, pp. 129–176.

Karl Dietrich Bracher, *The German Dictatorship. The Origins, Structure, and Effect of National Socialism.* New York: Praeger Publishers, 1970.

K. D. Bracher, M. Funke, and H.-A. Jacobsen, *Nationalsozialistische Diktatur, 1933–1945.* Düsseldorf: Droste Verlag, 1983.

Andreas Hillgruber. *Germany and the Two World Wars.* Cambridge, Mass., and London: Harvard University Press, 1981.

Eberhard Jäckel. *Hitlers Weltanschauung: A Blueprint for Power.* Middletown, Conn.: Wesleyan University Press, 1972.

Robert Lewis Koehl. *The Black Corps. The Structure and Power Struggles of the Nazi SS.* Madison: University of Wisconsin Press, 1983.

Eugen Kogon, *The Theory and Practice of Hell.* New York: Octagon, 1972.

HANS-ADOLF JACOBSEN

3

The Division of Germany

The period many Germans had intended to be the apex of German history (1933–1945) was in reality the cause, largely self-inflicted, of its fall into a deep abyss and of Germany's departure from the scene as a major world power. The year 1945 marks not only the end of "Greater Germany" but also the beginning of new processes on the world's political stage. The democratic powers and the Soviet Union had been challenged by the policies of imperial conquest that the Japanese, Fascist, and National Socialist alliance had simultaneously embarked on and that had been shattered. As a result, the old multilateral system of European states, which up to that time had been at the center of the world, lost its importance. At the same time colonial possessions were either lost through the efforts of independence or liberation movements or at least placed in jeopardy. Of the seven great world powers prior to the outbreak of World War II, only two emerged as real victors following the intensive application of all of their material and personnel resources: the United States and the Soviet Union. The resultant bipolar balance shifted the centers of world power to Washington and Moscow. Concurrently the ground was being prepared for the diffusion and neutralization of their power by the new nations of the Third World.

It is clear today that the representatives of the anti-Hitler coalition of 1941–1945 did not, by any means, have identical ideas of the new order they wanted to see created after the end of the war. Great Britain, France, and the United States had fought primarily for the universal principle of democracy and had planned to leave decisions about the structure of their respective social systems to the liberated peoples of Europe themselves. The Soviet Union, on the other hand, made use of favorable historic developments to extend its Marxist-Leninist system through revolutionary methods in Europe, the Near East, and East Asia.

Simultaneously, it protected its own empire by securing a strategic buffer zone.

The years of bloody conflict did not, as many had hoped, lead to a peaceful world under the watchful eye of the world's policemen (the United States, the Soviet Union, Great Britain, France, and China). Instead, the war led to a disclosure of antagonisms that existed between the former allies in their economic, ideological, and power-political goals. These differences lay openly exposed, thereby underscoring the provisional nature of the peace that had been achieved.

It is true that in 1945 fifty nations joined the United Nations, which was founded as an instrument of collective security. However, unlike the situation in 1918, there was no prior agreement on the status quo. Even though the United States and the Soviet Union, each in its own way, professed a belief in "progress," in the "unity" of humanity, and in the individual's right to freedom, welfare, and happiness, the practical application of power in Eastern and Western Europe soon made clear the principal differences between a free society based on the rule of law and a communist system.

The competitive struggle between the two political blocs divided by the Iron Curtain increased from year to year, permeated by an "either-or" characterization. Every step taken by one side was interpreted by the other as a challenge, as a danger to its own security, as a conspiracy against or a subversion of its own national interests. The atmosphere of the postwar negotiations was poisoned and full of distrust. Because of the ideological division between East and West, the world could no longer be understood by applying the same yardsticks.

The atomic age dawned at the same time. Possession of the new, nearly apocalyptic atomic weapons carried with it the possibility of world domination and became the decisive characteristic of a major power, of true sovereignty, and of the possession of modern armed forces. The law of reciprocal action was applied to the arms race of the 1950s and 1960s and led to the precarious "balance of terror" (the atomic stalemate) that overshadows the existence of all peoples to this day.

The fate of Germany after 1945 must be seen against the background just sketched and evaluated in its light. There were several reasons for the division of the German Reich, and to some extent of Europe, which found its most visible representation in the creation of two German states with different social systems. First, it was the consequence of the lunatic attempt to "order" the European continent according to the racial principles of National Socialism. The war loosed upon the world in 1939 by those wielding power in the National Socialist regime led in 1941 to that "strange alliance" whose superiority ensured military victory over the aggressor. The meeting of the Allied forces at the Elbe in 1945 symbolized not only the total collapse of the "Thousand Year Reich" but also the start of the Cold War. The Germans, however, had squandered the unity of their country as it had existed within the 1937 boundaries.

Beyond these factors, the division of Germany was the immediate result of the decisions made in 1944 on behalf of the Big Three (Roosevelt, Churchill, and Stalin) by the European Advisory Commission through its determination of various military zones of occupation and of the establishment of a joint administration for Berlin. During the period of military occupation, Germany was to be governed in unity by an Allied Control Council (consisting of three, later four, military supreme commanders). This was conceived as a temporary, limited transition solution. At the Yalta Conference in 1945 this decision was supplemented by the creation of a French occupation zone carved from the two Western zones of occupation. But the split among the victorious coalition resulted in a definitive division of the former Reich along the present German-German border. The plans for a division that had been discussed at the Tehran and Yalta summit meetings during World War II played no noticeable role in bringing about this result. Stalin, who had long appeared sympathetic to Roosevelt's suggestion for a division of Germany into five parts, declared in May 1945, much to the surprise of his allies, that although the Soviet Union celebrated the victory it did not intend to fragment or destroy Germany.

Even at the Potsdam Conference (July 30–August 2, 1945), at which the victorious powers established certain principles for demilitarization, for restitution for the losses suffered by victims of Nazi persecution, and for denazification, decartelization, and democratization, Germany was treated as an economic unit, although two economic spheres, one in the Western zones and one in the Eastern zone, were recognized. No unanimity was achieved on the question of reparations, but certain important, in part temporary, territorial decisions were made: Austria was to be restored as an independent republic, Berlin was to be jointly governed, and subject to definitive decisions, the city of Königsberg (now Kaliningrad) and surrounding territory were to be handed over to the Soviet Union. The territories of Germany lying east of the rivers Oder and Neisse were to be placed under Polish administration pending a definitive determination of Poland's western boundaries in a peace treaty. Additionally, it was decided to transfer the German population residing in these territories and in Poland, Czechoslovakia, and Hungary in an "orderly and humane" fashion to Germany. The latter was, however, no more than a good intention, for evacuation, flight, death, and expulsion were the fate of millions of Germans in the months following the collapse of the Third Reich.

The de facto division of Germany was, finally, the consequence of the policies of the Allies and the Soviet Union from 1945 to 1949. In retrospect it may perhaps be viewed as a strategy of move and countermove without placing the responsibility on one side or the other. In place of the envisaged joint control and neutralization of Germany, there developed the gradual assimilation of the occupied areas to the political, economic, and ideological principles of the occupying powers. This started in local communities and in numerous economic areas. It continued in the creation of new political parties on the county and *Länder* level, at the first political elections (1946 in Hessen, Baden-Württemberg, and Bavaria) and in the deliberations on the *Länder* constitutions. Even though the four victorious powers had constituted the Allied Control Council, which assumed control on August 30, 1945, as the supreme administrative organ in Germany during the occupation period (and had determined that all of its decisions required unanimity), East and West proceeded to govern with different priorities, initiatives, and tempos, bringing about a fusion of Western occupation zones and new administrative structures for the areas of occupation. Both sides claimed that their actions were motivated by those of the other. Meanwhile, Control Council Law No. 46 of February 1947 had formally dissolved the State of Prussia as the "supporter of militarism and reactionary ideas in Germany."

The increasing tensions between the occupying powers over the future development of Germany and the question of reparations caused the U.S. and British authorities to combine their zones in 1947 in order to meet the requirements of the Potsdam Agreement through a unified economic area. France did not adhere to this policy until the spring of 1949, when it had to recognize that its intention to decentralize and weaken Germany to the greatest possible extent could not be realized in light of the East-West conflict.

In the view of the Western powers, the Soviet policy of creating faits accomplis (land reform, forced unification of the Communist and Socialist parties in 1946 into a new Socialist Unity party (SED), reparations demands on the Western zones, and so on) made the creation of a single national government illusory. As a result, they agreed with the Benelux countries at the London Conference in the spring of 1948 to establish an independent German state. This decision was welcomed in the summer of that year by the German representatives who had meanwhile been elected on the *Länder* level. The new German leaders in the Western zones had early on supported Allied policy. The majority of them supported Germany's orientation toward the West and were as opposed to a neutralist stance as to a possible orientation to the East. They simultaneously participated singlemindedly in the democratic reconstruction of local communities and *Länder*.

The Four-Power Administration collapsed when the Soviet supreme commander, Marshal V. D. Sokolovski, left the meeting of the Allied Control Council on March 20, 1948, in protest against the intention of the Western powers to establish a single authority in their zones of occupation. The 1948 currency reform carried out in the three Western zones provided the Soviet Union with an excuse for blockading Berlin in order to bring the former capital totally into its domain. But the determination of the Allied troops and the willingness of the population to make sacrifices for the assertion of its rights finally caused the Soviet Union to back down. On May 4, 1949, an agreement ending the blockade was arranged through the United Nations. The division of Berlin into Eastern and Western zones took place during the blockade period, at the end of 1948. A few months later, in 1949, the Federal Republic of Germany was created by the acceptance of its Basic Law and by free elections to the first German parliament (Bundestag). The reaction of the Communist leadership was not long in coming. The Movement for a People's Congress, which had been created to ensure general social and political conformity in the Soviet occupation zone, led to the formation of the German Democratic Republic. Both German states immediately claimed to be the sole "legal" German state and to represent all Germany (see p. 204).

The final, decisive cause of the division of Germany can therefore be found in the unbridgeable differences, both in ideology and in power structure, between the former allies as well as in their contrasting economic policies and their differing interpretations of the Potsdam Agreement. If the strategy of 1945–1949, in which Germany was the object of policy, is analyzed, it may be summarized as follows: The Cold War that broke out in this period was an international interaction of power; reciprocal actions resulted that had to lead to an extreme step. In 1949 this took the form of the de facto division of Germany and the inclusion of the newly sovereign parts into the respective power blocs. Since then the question of German unity and the resolution of this problem has been one of the basic conflicts in European and world politics, which was not defused until the 1970s by a modus vivendi embodied in an agreement between the two German states.

Readings

Eschenburg, T. *Jahre der Besatung 1945–1949. Geschichte der Bundesrepublik Deutschland,* Bd. 1. Stuttgart-Wiesbaden: Deutsche Verlagsanstalt-Brockhaus, 1983.

Feis, Herbert. *From Trust to Terror, The Onset of the Cold War, 1945–1950.* New York: Norton, 1970.

Fritsch-Bournazel, Renata. *Die Sowjetunion und die deutsche Teilung. Die sowjetische Deutschlandpolitik, 1945–1979.* Opladen: Westdeutscher Verlag, 1979.

Gimbel, John. *The American Occupation of Germany; Politics and the Military.* Stanford: Stanford University Press, 1968.

Smith, Jean, ed. *The Papers of General Lucius D. Clay: Germany 1945–1949.* 2 vols. Bloomington: Indiana University Press, 1977.

KARL HARDACH

IN COLLABORATION WITH
HANS-JOACHIM LANDMESSER AND ULRICH NOCKEN

4

Germany Under Western Occupation, 1945–1949

With the unconditional capitulation of Germany on May 8, 1945, the Reich government ceased to exist, the German economy collapsed to a large extent, and responsibility for it fell to the victorious Allies. Germany and its capital, Berlin, were divided into separate zones of occupation in which the respective military commanders had full executive power and responsibility. The Potsdam Conference in July–August 1945 confirmed the division, placing about one-quarter of Germany's territory in the east under Polish and Soviet administration pending a final peace treaty. For the remaining occupation zones, at least, the economic unity of Germany was upheld by the Potsdam agreements, which provided for the establishment of a central administration for finance, communication, transport, foreign trade, and industry. However, due to increasing discord among the occupying powers, these provisions were never put into effect. As a consequence, each of the four zones developed its own bureaucracy and differing policies at an early stage.

At Potsdam there had been agreement only on the general policy goals of demilitarization, denazification, administrative decentralization, economic deconcentration, and industrial disarmament. These general principles were translated into practice according to the greatly differing national goals and ideologies of the occupying powers. Conflicts over the realization of these goals extended deep within the governments of the Western Allies. Disputes over postwar planning in the United States— the most powerful nation militarily and economically—had especially important consequences for Germany.

Until 1944, U.S. planning for the immediate postwar era took place in the State Department, where a moderate version of the later Potsdam

66

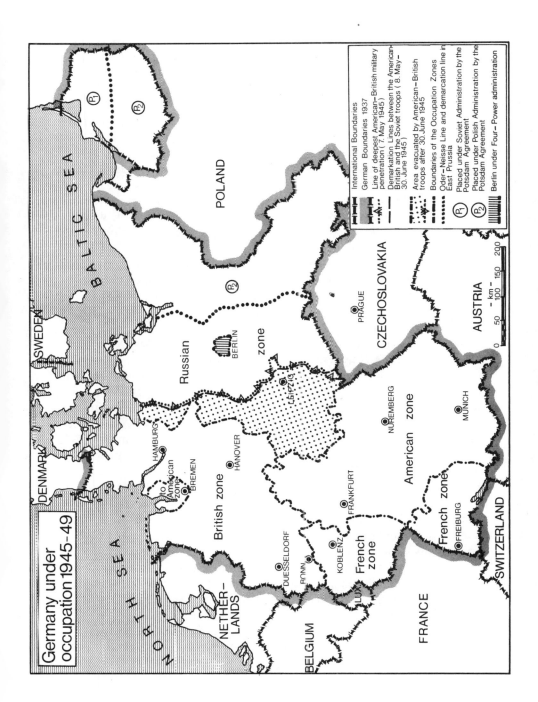

Germany under occupation 1945–49

Legend:

- International Boundaries
- German Boundaries 1937
- Line of deepest American–British military penetration (7 May 1945)
- Demarcation Lines between the American–British and the Soviet troops (8 May–30 June 1945)
- Area evacuated by American–British troops after 30 June 1945
- Boundaries of the Occupation Zones
- Oder–Neisse Line and demarcation line in East Prussia
- ⓟ₁ Placed under Soviet Administration by the Potsdam Agreement
- ⓟ₂ Placed under Polish Administration by the Potsdam Agreement
- Berlin under Four–Power administration

SWEDEN

DENMARK

BALTIC SEA

NORTH SEA

NETHER–LANDS

BELGIUM

LUX

FRANCE

SWITZERLAND

AUSTRIA

CZECHOSLOVAKIA

POLAND

British zone

American zone

French zone

Russian zone

ⓟ₁

ⓟ₂

ⓟ₃

BERLIN

HAMBURG

BREMEN

to American zone

HANOVER

LEIPZIG

NUREMBERG

MUNICH

FRANKFURT

KOBLENZ

BONN

DUESSELDORF

FREIBURG

PRAGUE

0   50   100   150   200
– km –

principles was drawn up. Only industrial plants producing purely military goods were to be dismantled, reparation deliveries were to be quite limited in size and time, and Germany was to be given the chance to reintegrate itself as an accepted member in the world economy. The State Department, supported by the War Department, tried to hold to these principles, but it suffered a serious setback when Secretary of the Treasury Henry Morgenthau actively intervened in the postwar planning. He believed that a peaceful Germany was an impossibility and that the Germans had an ineradicable tendency to aggression, domination, lack of conscience, automatic submission to authority, and sadism. Thus he developed plans to ensure that the Germans should never again be a threat. Although his department had no obvious authority or competence in this field, he used his personal relationship with Roosevelt, who also favored a hard line toward Germany, to gain official sanction for the plan that came to bear his name.

The Morgenthau Plan extended far beyond limited industrial disarmament to advocate large-scale destruction of industry, in effect reducing Germany to an agrarian nation. Not only would this eliminate the danger of continued German aggression, it would also, according to Morgenthau, have the beneficial effect of removing German competition from the world market for industrial goods. At the Quebec conference in September 1944, Morgenthau was able to win general acceptance of his proposals from Roosevelt and Churchill, even though the latter disliked the whole concept. The War and State departments continued their opposition to the Morgenthau Plan, but the final official directive to the U.S. occupation authorities in April and May 1945 incorporated many, later embarrassing, elements of this extremist position.

This directive, which remained in effect for two years, made it the official aim of the U.S. government not to let the German standard of living rise above that of its neighbors. Furthermore, the military authorities were forbidden to take any action that would contribute to strengthening the German economy. Although the Morgenthau Plan had a negative influence in the early postwar years, the War and State departments took their cue from a provision in the directive that allowed the U.S. military to intervene in order to prevent unrest and epidemics among occupied Germans. Interpreting this paragraph to justify their actions, the military administration began to modify the nature of the directive in practice almost as soon as it had been issued.

Nevertheless, "Morgenthauism" died hard. One reason for this was that the Soviets and, to a lesser degree, the French also favored a policy of permanently weakening Germany through reparations and dismantling. The Americans accepted the proposition that the German standard of living should be reduced to the average European level in the hope that a common Four-Power administration of Germany would evolve. As it turned out, the standard that was approved was equivalent to the level in Germany in 1932, the nadir of the Great Depression. The Level-of-Industry Plan of March 1946 for implementing the Potsdam formula called for large-scale dismantling of German industry in order to reduce industrial capacity to about 50–55 percent of the 1946 level. Some industries, like steel, basic chemicals, and heavy engineering, were to be hit even harder; others, like the production of oceangoing ships, aircraft, ball bearings, and heavy machine tools, were totally forbidden; only a few consumer goods and the construction industries were to be free of restrictions.

Increasingly the varying interests of the powers, and especially those of the Western Allies and the Soviets, collided and frustrated any further efforts toward a collaborative policy of all Allied victors toward Germany. In May 1946 U.S. military authorities discontinued the shipment of dismantled plants to the Soviet Union because all efforts to create a united German economic administration had failed. With the failure of Four-Power cooperation, the pragmatic policy favored by U.S. military authorities and the State Department gradually gained the upper hand. The first and rather negative phase of occupation policy ended in late summer of 1946.

A revised Level-of-Industry Plan approved in August 1947 raised the allowed industrial capacity to 70–75 percent of the 1946 level. The new plan in effect repudiated the "strong Europe, weak Germany" concept underlying Morgenthauism and emphasized that a stable and productive Germany was necessary for an orderly and prosperous Europe. However, dismantling did not cease until 1951, after the protests of German workers had helped mobilize international support. The effects of dismantling on the German economy are difficult to gauge accurately, but various informed estimates conclude that by 1949 German industrial capacity had been lowered by 8 percent. The consequences for production, however, were much greater; for example, the removal of an important machine might cause a whole plant to lie idle for want of a replacement.

One justification for the dismantling policy was the direct elimination of German war-making capacity. In its extreme Morgenthau version, the policy would theoretically have removed all possibility for further German aggression. But if Germany, as even the harsh first Level-of-Industry Plan assumed, was to retain part of its industrial base, then the Western Allies were determined to break up the concentration of economic power in Germany. Since German big business and large landowners were widely believed to be at least partially responsible for conspiring to wage war, they were targeted by all the Allies for various degrees of punishment and loss of power. At the end of the war, the

Americans and British had planned a radical restructuring of agrarian property ownership by abolishing all large landholdings. But the large Junker estates were mostly located in the east, where the Soviets were pursuing their own radical policies, and the possibility for land reform was more limited in the Western zones. Even so, the end result was much less than might have been expected, given the earlier plans. As in other areas, a tough policy was proclaimed but its realization postponed: first because of fear that any sudden restructuring would worsen the critical food situation, and second because it was left to the new German political institutions to put the Allied goals into effect. These delays ultimately doomed any thorough reforms because the temporary survival of old structures tended to be cemented over time and especially because the German political authorities had no particular zeal for radical reforms.

A similar fate befell the efforts of the Western Allies to permanently reduce the concentration of economic power in industry. Here again basic differences in the policies followed by the various occupation authorities helped to limit any radical change. The smallest common denominator was deconcentration through the breakup of cartels and large companies in three branches: banking, chemicals, and heavy industry. In these sectors the major enterprises were split into a large number of successor firms, often with little regard for economic or technical rationality. As the shares in these new firms were generally redistributed to the original owners, in the long run there was a strong tendency toward reestablishing the old economic and technical ties. The decartelization measures were more effective because they were later reinforced by legislation passed by the Federal Republic.

The British aimed at more radical change in their zone by means of extensive nationalization measures, directed especially at heavy industry in the Ruhr. Although the active steps toward nationalization, such as the seizure of the coal and steel firms, were taken under the postwar British Labour government, it would be wrong to conclude that there was a dynamic, strongly directed effort to institute a copy of Labour socialism in Germany. It was rather part of the effort to punish the industrialists, to ensure future British security, and to improve the productive psychology of the Ruhr industry workers, who by 1946 were suffering from acute food shortages.

The U.S. government, which, with some justification, is seen as the defender of private enterprise in the postwar years, has often been given all the credit (or blame) for the failure of the British nationalization policy. This explanation has been shown to be much too simplistic. The War Department was generally politically conservative and thus adopted delaying tactics, hoping—correctly, as it turned out—that a democratic

Germany would choose the U.S. capitalist system as a model. In addition, one of its dominant motives throughout the occupation years was to avoid every socioeconomic experiment that might endanger the rapid recovery of Germany, thus prolonging the continued drain on the American taxpayer. The State Department, in contrast, not only accepted the idea of nationalization but even favored this policy within certain limits. Only reluctantly did it pressure the British into postponing the Ruhr coal mine nationalization, arguing that this step would fundamentally influence the future German economy as a whole; such a weighty decision should therefore be reserved for a democratically elected central German government, which meant indefinite postponement. The French also opposed the Ruhr nationalization schemes, fearing concentration of economic power in public hands as much as in private hands. Therefore it was only partly because of their financial dependence on the United States that the British finally agreed to the postponement.

Although the basic structure of ownership remained unchanged, the British made one lasting contribution to the democratization of German industrial relations by introducing codetermination on the parity principle in heavy industry. Under this system, which is still in effect in Germany today but does not exist in Great Britain, workers and stockholders send the same number of representatives to each company's board of supervisors. Although less than full industrial democracy, this system, which was later extended in a weaker form to other industries, has contributed to the relatively harmonious industrial relations for which Germany is internationally renowned and to the country's relatively rapid rise from the rubble and ashes of 1945.

In that year three problems were especially obvious to any Western visitor: the physical destruction in the urban areas, the breakdown of industrial production, and the catastrophic food situation. The latter problem was the dominant concern of most Germans until late 1948, when the U.S. military governor could finally report that the German people had enough to eat. Whereas the normal prewar diet had averaged 3,000 calories per person per day and even the Allied occupation government had taken 2,700 calories as its goal, the official rations available sank below 1,000 calories at times. By the end of 1945 only 12 percent of German children had the normal weight for their age and the average male adult in the U.S. zone weighed 112 lbs (51 kg). As a consequence of this malnutrition, the death rate, especially among the young and old, rose to catastrophic heights.

The food shortages were partly a result of the loss of the agrarian surplus areas in eastern Germany and of the decline in productivity due to the lack of fertilizers, farm machinery, and labor. In the early postwar stages, because of poor planning and the feeling that the Germans deserved to experience hard times, the U.S. military government did very little to improve the situation. In fact, many initial policies, like the restriction on fertilizer production and on distributing surplus food to the hungry population, tended to aggravate the problem. The Western Allies had retained the Reich bureaucracy that controlled food distribution, but it was not efficient and it lacked the draconian sanctions at the disposal of the Nazi regime. As a consequence, the population had to resort to illegal bartering and food procuring, which, although vital for the individual, was economically highly wasteful; it was time-consuming and detrimental to an efficient division of labor and occupational specialization. Germany also could not resort to its traditional system of supplementing its food supply by means of foreign trade. Not only did Germany lack the industrial production in the first years that might have made goods available for export, but the occupation authorities severely restricted German foreign trade. A serious disaster was avoided only when British and U.S. military authorities changed their policies and began large-scale food imports in 1947.

Next to quieting their worst hunger pains, Germans were most concerned about having at least a roof over their heads. The housing problem was especially acute; approximately one-half of all housing in western Germany had been damaged or destroyed. Herbert Hoover reported to President Truman in 1947 that the "housing situation is the worst that modern civilization has ever seen." In the three western zones, with 43.3 million inhabitants, there was an average of 1.8 persons per room. An additional reason for this housing shortage was the influx of approximately 6 million refugees and expellees from the east into the western zones. By 1950 the population was further swelled by more than 3 million additional refugees and returning prisoners of war. This almost totally dispossessed group of refugees experienced the greatest difficulties in finding housing, food, jobs, and social status. That their integration into the West German social, economic, and political system was accomplished without a great upheaval has been one of the least known yet extremely important success stories of the history of the Bonn Republic.

Given this huge population increase, the chances for revival of the German economy were not limited by a lack of labor. Its quality, however, was adversely affected by malnutrition, an unfavorable age and sex structure, and regional misallocation, i.e., a clustering in agricultural areas with considerable housing space but meager industrial employment opportunities. Ultimately this did not prove to be a great handicap, and in contrast to what many contemporary observers of the physical destruction had expected, capital (i.e., machines and plants) was not in short supply either. It is estimated that at the most, 17 percent of German industrial capacity was destroyed in the war. Even if one adds to this figure approximately 8 percent for the effects of dismantling for reparations and restitution, the capital stock in 1948 was still 11 percent higher in absolute terms and only 6 percent lower on a per capita basis than in 1936. This surprising result is explained by the fact that from 1936 until the end of the war a high rate of investment had persisted, which also meant that much of the existing capital stock was modern.

With both of these crucial factors of production in relatively abundant supply, the cause of the low production must be sought elsewhere. It was ultimately due to a series of bottlenecks and other restrictions that impeded recovery from the low early postwar levels. One basic reason for the slow industrial revival was Allied policy. Dismantling and the various controls on German production and on foreign and interzonal trade disrupted the existing economic ties in the highly complex and interdependent German industrial system. Compared with 1936, total industrial production in the Anglo-American zones reached a monthly average of 33 percent in 1946, 38 percent in 1947, and 47 percent in the first half of 1948. The shortage of important raw materials, partially due to the limitations on imports and the increasing breakdown of the system of fixed and regulated prices inherited from the Nazi era acted as a powerful brake on the forces of recovery. The unrealistic prices in the face of a huge repressed inflation only provided an incentive to hoard as much as possible any goods produced.

Even under these negative circumstances there was encouraging growth in the economy until the winter of 1946. This—the coldest winter in generations—revealed and worsened the most serious bottleneck to a further revival of the German economy: With the freezing of the waterways, transportation in Germany practically collapsed. This sector had been hardest hit by destruction, and as in the last phase of the war, it again disrupted the functioning of the German economy. By preventing delivery of the most vital industrial raw material, coal, it brought much of industrial activity to a standstill, not to mention the effect on the population of unheated rooms. This crisis of the whole economy continued into the spring of 1947 and as it was accompanied by serious food shortages, set off strikes, demonstrations, and unrest, especially in the Ruhr.

The economic crisis of the winter and spring of 1946–1947, combined with the increasingly chilly relations between the Soviet Union and the United States, provided the impetus for concerted action to stimulate German economic recovery. The institutional basis for this revival was set up with the creation of the Anglo-American Bizone in January 1947. The failure of the Moscow foreign ministers' conference in March–April

1947 can be seen as the turning point of the U.S. attitude toward German recovery and as the immediate origin of the Marshall Plan, outlined by the secretary of state in June 1947. A further step was the issuance of a new directive to the U.S. military authorities in July, which eliminated most vestiges of Morgenthauism. It officially directed the military governor to take positive steps to encourage the recovery of Germany so that it might contribute to a stable and prosperous Europe. The revised Level-of-Industry Plan drawn up in the following month reflected this changed attitude by loosening the tight controls on German industrial capacity.

Just as important as these major decisions was the pragmatic new economic policy followed in the bizone. All resources were now specifically mobilized to solve the bottlenecks in transport and coal production. The food supply also began to improve with the inflow of more imports, including Care packages after August 1947, and better administration of the food and agriculture programs. The effects of these changes were gradually reflected in the steady growth of industrial production after October 1947. Unfortunately, consumers noticed little of this improvement because an increasing proportion of output was hoarded. Currency reform as a prerequisite for normal exchange was overdue. But Four-Power wrangling over how this was to be achieved, Soviet delaying tactics, and increased mutual suspicions had caused continuous postponements. Finally on June 20, 1948, the three Western military authorities—France had decided to join at the last minute—introduced a new currency, the deutsche mark, into their zones. Partially in response to this move, the Soviet authorities stopped all surface traffic to Berlin four days later. The blockade, which was to last ten months, was countered by the Western allies' airlift of some 277,000 flights to bring all vital supplies to the beleaguered western part of the city. This action in effect sealed the breakdown of the victors' alliance, laying the basis for the process that culminated in the foundation of the Federal Republic of Germany in May 1949.

The currency reform, which can be regarded with some justification as an important prerequisite for the founding of the Bonn Republic, cannot, however, be given complete credit for creating the "economic miracle" of West German growth. This had already set in many months earlier. The reform did, however, ensure that this expansion continued. By helping to release the hoarded products, thus filling the shelves of the stores, and by laying the basis for calculating with real costs, prices, and profits, it broke down the still considerable structural barriers to further growth. If the currency reform had largely been based on a U.S. plan, credit must be given to Ludwig Erhard, the German director of the Economics Office, for forcing through complementary economic liberalization policies against strong Allied and domestic opposition, particularly from social democratic and trade union quarters. The extensive system of controls on prices and wages, which had been in effect since the early Hitler years, was thus largely eliminated. This gave market forces far wider scope and provided the framework for future German economic growth. Although successful in the long run, these policies did not, like a magic wand, solve all problems immediately, as superficial accounts and faulty memories often seem to suggest. Rising unemployment and prices accompanied by lagging wages resulted in strong social conflicts, and the success of these reforms remained in doubt for about two years. Only the Korean War boom of 1951 ensured sustained and rapid German growth.

Bottlenecks, due especially to the inadequate supplies of imported raw materials, continued to hamper recovery in the meantime. The lack of growth in foreign trade was one of the most serious problems facing the German economy before 1951, especially given the traditionally strong export orientation of German producers. It was in this area that the Marshall Plan made its greatest contribution to German recovery. Contrary to some opinions, the Marshall Plan was not designed primarily to aid German recovery. As its official title—European Recovery Program (ERP)—indicated, it was meant as general multilateral assistance for the reconstruction of war-ravaged Western Europe as a whole. Germany received only about 10 percent of the total funds distributed under its auspices; Great Britain and France received significantly more, and Italy and the Benelux countries were recipients of about the same amount as Germany.

The relative significance of the Marshall aid for Germany has recently been downgraded in some studies, but this should not detract from the great importance to Europe of this assistance. The generosity of U.S. aid can be seen in the fact that ERP funding made up 10 percent of the U.S. budget and 2.8 percent of U.S. gross national product (GNP); in comparison, today U.S. developmental aid to the Third World hovers around 0.27 percent of GNP. The ERP funds to Germany did not exceed 1.9 percent of German GNP during its existence. This relatively low figure does not do justice, however, to the effect of this aid in key areas such as the financing of industrial and infrastructure investments and of foreign imports. The so-called counterpart funds that were generated within Germany by ERP imports financed 8 percent of net industrial investments in the years 1949–1952. Theoretically these funds could also have been created by the central bank, but this was unlikely given the deep German fears of inflation. Economically even more important were the increased imports of raw materials and industrial goods that the Marshall Plan aid allowed. In 1949 almost one-half of

German imports were financed by U.S. funds. Although the first ERP deliveries did not reach Germany until the fall of 1948 and by the end of that year had only accounted for a relatively insignificant amount, their beneficial effects had already begun much earlier, as Germany's credit line for imports had been extended in anticipation of future ERP funds.

As far as Germany was concerned, the importance of the Marshall Plan went far beyond the purely economic effects of these aid payments. Basically the greatest achievement was that it reintegrated Germany into the international economic system. This was soon demonstrated when Germany joined such new international agencies and agreements as the Organization of European Economic Cooperation (OEEC), the General Agreement on Tariffs and Trade (GATT), and the European Payments Union (EPU). German membership in these organizations proved and further supported its international rehabilitation and the acceptance of the Federal Republic in the community of free Western nations.

Readings

Backer, John H. *Priming the German Economy; American Occupational Policies, 1945–1948.* Durham, N.C.: Duke University Press, 1971.

Balabkins, Nicholas. *Germany Under Direct Controls: Economic Aspects of Industrial Disarmament 1945–1948.* New Brunswick, N.J.: Rutgers University Press, 1964.

Gimbel, John. *The Origins of the Marshall Plan.* Stanford, Calif.: Stanford University Press, 1976.

Mayer, Herbert C. *German Recovery and the Marshall Plan 1948–1952.* Bonn: Atlantic Forum, 1969.

KLAUS VON BEYME

──────── **5** ────────

The Power Structure in the Federal Republic of Germany

The Political Structure

The constitution of the Federal Republic of Germany, called the Basic Law, was conceived as a provisional document. It deliberately avoided certain subjects (such as basic social rights, on which the two largest parties could not agree) because there was hope in 1948–1949 that a constitution for all of Germany might be enacted in the foreseeable future. The separate existence of the two German states during the Cold War and the inclusion of the separate parts of Germany in the economic and military alliance systems of West and East destroyed these hopes.

The constitution was designed to strengthen federalism. The occupying powers, especially the United States, intervened numerous times in the process of drafting the constitution. The role of the German president was kept deliberately weak because the experiences of the Weimar Republic suggested that competition between the president and the parliamentary majority should not be allowed to happen again. The dissolution of parliament was therefore tied to narrowly constructed rules. The stability of the government was to be safeguarded by a provision that the federal chancellor could be removed from office only by what has become known as a "constructive vote of no confidence." This meant that an official lack of confidence in the current head of government could take effect only if a new head of government was simultaneously elected.

In light of experience with the National Socialist dictatorship, the system was constructed with an exaggerated attention to the supremacy of law. For the first time in German history, the constitution became the supreme law of the land. Basic rights were protected without provision for exceptions, and all acts of the state were subject to judicial review. In this regard, the West German constitution emulated the American model. But it went beyond the model by creating a Federal Constitutional Court as a specialized guardian of the constitution with the task of resolving disputes between various governmental authorities as well as protecting the basic rights of citizens. In addition, the particularly German institution of a specialized judicial review of administrative decisions was created.

The primacy of parliament is reflected above all in the formal election of the head of government by parliament rather than in the mere parliamentary approval of the selection, as is the case in some other European parliamentary systems. In view of the severe reduction in the number of political parties (from 1961 to 1983 only three parties were represented in parliament), the elective function of parliament has shifted de facto to the largest party in the government and to the leaders of those parties that are participants in the formation of a governing coalition. To date no German party has formed a single-party government, although in 1957 the Christian Democrats had an absolute majority and could have done so.

In contrast to previous German systems, the training ground for anyone seeking a top position in the executive branch of the government now is clearly in parliament. Few ministers could hold their positions for very long without being members of a party and of parliament. This is true also at the *Länder,* or state, level.

The function of the German Bundestag (parliament) as an organ for the articulation of concerns and communication with the populace is somewhat less developed. The esteem in which parliament is held by the public and the media is lower than in other countries, in spite of efforts to make the debate livelier by introducing a British-style question hour and U.S.-style public hearings. In the parliament in Bonn no great value is attached to major debate. The working method of the German parliament has some similarity to that of the U.S. Congress, where the major work is done in committees. The ability of specific groups to articulate their views in parliament is limited, as is true in other countries, by the party's selection of candidates. Women are severely underrepresented (7–8 percent of the membership); workers as members are practically nonexistent (now and then there is one). Civil servants supply 40 percent of the membership, and lawyers have maintained their traditional dominance over other professions.

The Bundestag's legislative record, on the other hand, shows that it is a very industrious body. The high number of laws passed is, however, due partially to the fact that after the war substitute legislation was needed for a large number of laws that had originated in the Nazi

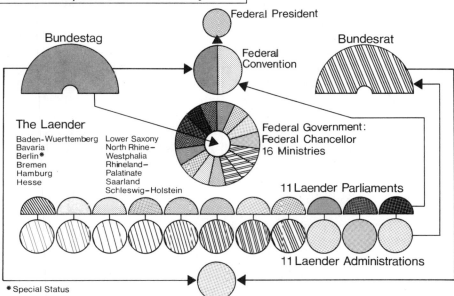

The Constitutional Branches of the Federal Republic of Germany

Federal President

Bundestag

Federal Convention

Bundesrat

The Laender

Baden-Wuerttemberg Lower Saxony
Bavaria   North Rhine–
Berlin*   Westphalia
Bremen   Rhineland–
Hamburg   Palatinate
Hesse   Saarland
                   Schleswig–Holstein

Federal Government:
Federal Chancellor
16 Ministries

11 Laender Parliaments

11 Laender Administrations

* Special Status

Federal Constitutional Court

Berlin—A Special Case. The London Agreement of 1944 provided for the occupation and joint administration of Greater Berlin by the four Allied Powers. Within the overall framework of the Four-Power responsibility for Berlin as a whole, the three Western Powers exercise sovereignty in the city's Western sectors. Hence, West Berlin is neither entirely integrated into the federation, nor governed by it.

The laws of the Federal Republic of Germany have since 1952 been adopted by and enforced in the Western sector of Berlin. This is done with the approval of the three Western Powers, without prejudice, however, to their prior rights and responsibilities. The Western sectors are also integrated in the economic and social system of the Federal Republic of Germany.

period. Fewer laws are passed by the *Länder;* the federal government is assuming an increasing amount of jurisdiction.

The Federal Council (Bundesrat) is, unlike the U.S. Senate, not a second chamber and therefore part of the parliament but a body of representatives of the *Länder* governments. The principle of equal representation of each of the *Länder,* as is the case in the U.S. Senate, was favored in 1948 by the Social Democratic party but was not accepted. The Christian Democrats persisted in the adoption of a graduated system of three to five representatives, which is less favorable to the smaller states than the U.S. system. This rather "bureaucratic" Federal Council is required to give its consent only to legislation that affects the division of powers between the federal government and the *Länder*—at the moment about 55 percent of all laws. In all other cases, it has only a delaying veto. Whenever the Christian Democrats are in opposition in the Bundestag they have been inclined to extend the number of laws requiring assent by the Bundesrat and have used the latter body as a method of obstructing government initiatives. More than two-thirds of all laws are introduced by the government, similar to the practice in other parliamentary democracies and in contrast to the separation of powers in effect in the United States. In terms of the percentage of laws actually enacted, the proportion of government-sponsored laws in contrast to private-member bills is even higher.

Conflicts between Bundestag and Bundesrat are resolved by a conference committee, based on the U.S. model, on which each of the two houses is represented equally. Although government and opposition frequently represent opposing positions on issues, there is considerable cooperation between them. Most laws are passed with the votes of both sides. The most controversial bills are distributive and participatory measures; the least amount of dissent surrounds regulatory and protective measures. In contrast to the U.S. Congress, there is a high level of party discipline in the Bundestag; in all parties 95 percent of the members will vote along party lines. This acceptance of party discipline has removed a previous difference between the two major parties, the cohesiveness of the Social Democrats and the fragmentation of the Christian Democrats into various wings. The behavior patterns of the parliamentary caucuses of the two parties have developed greater similarity, although the idea of German parties without an ideological base came to an end in 1969.

The parliament's function of exercising review over the execution of laws, which plays such an important role in the U.S. presidential system, has, in the opinion of German members of parliament, been insufficiently developed in the Bundestag. Investigative committees of the Bundestag do not have any quasi-judicial authority. Since the makeup of the

TABLE 1
Governments in the Federal Republic of Germany, 1949-1933

Start of government	Chancellor	Parties in the government	Reason for change
20. 9.1949	Adenauer (CDU)	CDU-CSU/FDP/DP	Election
20.10.1953	Adenauer II	CDU-CSU/FDP/DP/BHE	Election
24.10.1957	Adenauer III	CDU-CSU/FDP/DP	Election
14.11.1961	Adenauer IV	CDU-CSU/FDP	Voluntary Retirement
17.10.1963	Erhard (CDU)	CDU-CSU/FDF	Election
26.10.1965	Erhard II	CDU-CSU/FDP	Collapse of Coalition
1.12.1966	Kiesinger(CDU)	CDU-CSU/SPD	Election
21.10.1969	Brandt (SPD)	SPD/FDP	Parliament dissolved, election
15.12.1972	Brandt II	SPD/FDP	Voluntary Retirement
16. 5.1974	Schmidt (SPD)	SPD/FDP	Election
15.12.1976	Schmidt II	SPD/FDP	Election
15.11.1980	Schmidt III	SPD/FDP	Collapse of Coalition
1.10.1982	Kohl (CDU)	CDU-CSU/FDP	

committees reflects the makeup of the Bundestag, the representatives of the governing parties make up the majority on the committees. As a consequence of this factor and the high level of party discipline, the effects of the committees' actions are meager. It is more likely that a few low-level civil servants will be transferred from their posts than that a minister might be forced to resign. The ultimate weapon for control of the government, the vote of no confidence, has been used three times (unsuccessfully against Brandt in 1972, to topple Schmidt in 1982, and to force elections by Kohl in 1983). As a rule, a government stays in office for the entire four years between elections; only twice have heads of government resigned (Erhard in 1966 and Brandt in 1974). In neither case was the resignation brought about by parliamentary action.

In a parliamentary system such as exists in the Federal Republic, the parties serve as a more important tie between the government and the parliament than in a presidential system.

The division that traditionally existed in Germany between membership parties and parties that consist only of a nucleus of leaders no longer holds. The Social Democratic party still has more members than all other parties combined, but its lead in membership has become consistently smaller since the mid-1970s. For several years the Christian Democratic Union (CDU) and its Bavarian wing, the Christian Social Union (CSU), showed a higher level of increase. The trend toward "comradeship" in the development of voting patterns, which until 1972 tended to favor the Social Democratic party (SPD), can no longer be discerned in the development of its membership. In 1947 the SPD had 875,000 members, the largest number in the postwar period. By 1957, the year when its hopes had reached their lowest point and when the Christian Union parties achieved an absolute majority, its membership had fallen to the level of 1930, about 630,000. Between 1969 and 1974 a second wave of new members joined the party. It grew by nearly one-third, and in the mid-1970s passed the 1 million mark. Since that time it has appeared to stagnate (1981 membership was 998,000), and the party has become more reticent in the publication of membership figures.

The employment pattern of party members has also shown a marked change. It is true that the number of blue-collar workers voting for the Christian Democrats continues to decrease while the number of those voting for the SPD continues to grow. But because the percentage of blue-collar workers in the total work force is declining (in 1976 it was 42.6 percent) and the number of white-collar workers and civil servants in the parties, especially the SPD, has increased even more rapidly than the increase in their share of the work force, the percentage of blue-collar voters and party members has consistently fallen (in 1930 it was 59.5 percent; in 1952, 45 percent; and in 1981, 28 percent).

The increasing membership in all the parties has also caused a considerable change in their social structure. They can no longer depend on a homogeneous base of reliable members. The days are gone when solid subcultures adhered to specific parties, when many people belonged to a party from the cradle to the grave—from the Social Democratic day care center or the Catholic kindergarten to the crematorium closely associated with the Social Democratic party or to supreme unction—without ever venturing outside the circle of their own attitudes toward life. The Free Democratic party (FDP) always had the least to gain from such methods of membership recruitment, and its representatives are not as lackluster as their colleagues in the SPD or the Christian parties.

Traditional organizational ties still play a role in today's party membership. In the CDU, union members account for only 12 percent of the membership, as opposed to 38 percent in the SPD. On the other hand, one-third of the CDU members are active in church-related associations; a survey showed such association in only 2 percent of the SPD membership. The religious factor has, however, undergone some changes and shows marked differences between voters and party members. A 1976 survey showed that 34 percent of those voting for the SPD were Catholics, but only 26 percent of the party members belonged to the Catholic church. In the CDU, on the other hand, the number of party members belonging to the Catholic church (63 percent) exceeds the

TABLE 2

Election Results in the Federal Republic of Germany

Party	1949	1953	1957	1961	1965	1969	1972	1976	1980
Christian Democratic Union of Germany/Christian Social Union (CDU/CSU)	31.0	45.2	50.2	45.3	47.6	46.1	44.9	48.6	44.3
Social Democratic Party of Germany (SPD)	29.2	28.8	31.8	36.2	39.3	42.7	45.8	42.6	42.9
Free Democratic Party (SPD)	11.9	9.5	7.7	12.8	9.5	5.8	8.4	7.9	10.6
Communist Party of Germany (KPD) German Communist Party (DKP)	5.7	2.2					0.2	0.2	0.2
Bavarian Party (BP)	4.2	1.7	0.5			0.2			
German Party (DP)	4.0	3.2	3.4						
Center Party (Z)	3.1	0.8							
Association for Economic Reconstruction (WAV)	2.9								
German Conservative Party/German Rights Party (DKP/DRP) 1949; German Imperial Party (DRP) 1953-1961; National Democratic Party of Germany (NDP) since 1965	1.8	1.1	1.0	0.8	2.0	4.3	0.6	0.3	0.2
All-German Bloc/Bloc of Expellees and Disenfranchised (GB/BHE)		5.9	4.6						
German Peace Union (DFU) 1961-1965 Democratic Progressive Action (ADF) 1969				1.9	1.3	0.6			
The Green Party									1.5

number of Catholic voters (58 percent). The number of those professing
no religious belief is twice as high among SPD members as among SPD
voters (16 percent versus 8 percent).

The new social movements have recently had some impact on the
development of the German party system. The "cartel of three parties"
in parliament came to an end in the elections of March 1983. The
"green movement" for the first time jumped over the 5 percent hurdle
on a national level (in 1980 they had only 1.5 percent). The Green
Party defines itself as a party different from the rest of the established
parties: It tries to impose rotation on its deputies every two years and
limits the amount of money the parliamentarians are entitled to earn.
In spite of many conflicts with the old parties there are already signs
that the integration of the green movement into the political system
is making progress. Some of its leaders show increasing pragmatism
and are ready to compromise, whereas the ideologues still challenge the
majority principle underlying parliamentary democracy. The agenda of
the green movement has shifted in parliament: Their central issue used
to be atomic power stations. Even under the new government of Kohl
(CDU/CSU–FDP) it is likely that only those stations that had been
planned under previous administrations will be built. The central issue
has shifted to the peace movement. Deployment of Pershing II became
the central point of conflict. In this issue the green movement is not
completely isolated. Large parts of the SPD, in favor of deployment
under Schmidt's government until October 1982, moved into the camp
of the "freeze movement," opposing any additional deployment of missiles
on European soil.

There is relatively little talk of an end to parties in Germany. In
spite of competition from citizen action groups and public interest
groups, the parties have a strong institutionalized role, with formal
membership, party identification books, and state subsidies. There is
frequent mention of a process of turning the parties, which have
increasingly lost their character as free societal groupings, into instruments
of the state. The German parties receive 20–25 percent of their funds
for election campaigns from the state; the higher figure is granted during
election years. Additionally, state funds are channeled to party foundations for education and the training of cadres. Fund raising from
industry or from interest groups, which in the past had been well
organized in West Germany through the use of intermediary groups
known as conveyer organizations, has, however, continued. Even such
ideological parties as the SPD, which represent themselves as membership
parties, can today meet less than half their expenditures from membership
fees and contributions from their representatives.

The importance of factions within the German parties has also increased with the reintroduction of ideology into party platforms in 1969 (previously platforms had been pragmatic). Competition within the parties has become keener. The competitive struggle of the three parties represented in the Bundestag with other groupings has also taken on new importance. The environmental movement, based on numerous citizen action groups, is today the strongest challenge to the established parties. The Communists remain without importance; the Neofascists had in 1969 come close to winning the 5 percent of the votes needed to obtain representation in parliament, but they have since sunk to below 1 percent. The latent potential of both the right and the left, especially among young people, is, however, greater than the election results would indicate. Terrorism, antinuclear-power movements, squatting, and other forms of unconventional political behavior have increased in Germany in recent years and have in part attempted, as in other democracies, to undermine the legitimate role of the party system.

In former German systems of government, the executive branch and the administrative structure had a preponderance of power. The establishment of a true parliamentary system reduced but did not eliminate their dominant role.

According to the constitution (Article 65), the ministers of the government direct their areas of responsibility "independently and on their own responsibility" within the framework of policy guidance provided by the chancellor. Article 65 allows for competition among three principles: the principle of a dominant chancellor, the principle of departmental independence, and the principle of collegial decision. In the case of differences between ministers, decisions are to be made by the cabinet. In its effort to interpret the weight to be given to these various principles, the literature on the subject has frequently been influenced by actual leadership styles. During the Adenauer period, when a strong chancellor was in office, the authority to provide guidelines was subjected to restrictive interpretation; during the administration of Chancellor Erhard, whose leadership was weaker, it received a more expansive interpretation. During the latter's period in office, the debate over this authority threatened to become the functional equivalent of the discussion of the powers of the Reich president during the Weimar Republic.

The authority of the federal president relates not to the formulation of policy but solely to representative functions. He is not the supreme commander of the armed forces, a function assigned to the head of state in many parliamentary and presidential systems. This authority rests with the minister of defense in time of peace (Article 65a) and with the chancellor in time of war (Article 115b). The dictatorial powers held by the president under the Weimar constitution and the authority to declare an emergency and suspend the constitution were not included in the new constitution. The president's influence on the government and the administrative organs was deliberately reduced. The office may more correctly be consigned to the "dignified parts of the constitution."

In accordance with the federal structure of the Federal Republic of Germany there is no centralized, unified administrative apparatus. Many federal departments have no staff for the execution of their decisions but leave this function to the administrative organs in the *Länder,* which act on behalf of the federal government. There are no umbrella departments with tasks for different agencies, only specialized departments. Only the Foreign Service, the federal finance administration, the railroad, waterways and shipping, air traffic control, postal service, and, of course, the armed forces have their own administrative apparatus.

Compared with the Anglo-Saxon countries, Germany had long had a large number of civil servants. Since the end of World War II, however, the growth rates in civil service employment have become very similar.

For a time there were attempts to develop more planning in policy development. These failed when they encountered the egotism of the various ministers and of the coalition parties in the government, and the federal-state conflict. Beginning with the oil crisis of 1973, the lack of government financial resources appeared to make the planning of great new legislative programs impossible.

One of the most progressive aspects of German statehood is its federalism. The arbitrary drawing of *Länder* boundaries by the occupying powers was an encumbrance on German federalism. Only Bavaria and the Hanseatic cities were historical units. The *Länder* of Rhineland-Palatinate and North Rhine–Westphalia were artificial constructs. As there was no central governmental authority, actual power—to the extent that the occupying powers did not retain it—was in the hands of the *Länder* governments.

Federalist ideas after 1945 were dominated largely by the concept of a vertical division of authority. The *Länder* frequently saw themselves as governmental units separated from the federal government and jealously guarded their authority and financial resources. The political system established by the constitution did not satisfactorily cope with either state-federal cooperation or state-state cooperation, nor did it provide an adequate method for a joint solution of problems. Standards for cooperation as set forth in Article 29 (change of territorial boundaries), Article 107, Paragraph 2 (financial equalization between the states), and Article 35 (administrative and emergency assistance) were rare and insufficient in view of the flood of common problems.

As in the United States, there increasingly developed a form of cooperative federalism through voluntary cooperation among the *Länder* and informal cooperation. Federal-state committees and permanent institutions like the permanent Conference of Ministers of Education (essential because the most important authority of the German *Länder* remains the field of education) improved planning throughout the governmental structure.

As a result of the constitutional reform of 1969 and the creation of joint responsibilities under Article 91, a new method for the solution of problems was developed in the Federal Republic, which has for some time been discussed under the heading of "interlocking policy areas." Even before 1969, German federalism differed from other federal systems because its division was less along areas of responsibility than functionally along areas of authority. As a consequence, the bulk of legislative authority in financial and tax matters fell to the federal government; the *Länder* and communities had the major influence over the administration of laws and decisions on public expenditures, especially public investments. Article 91a of the constitution created joint responsibilities, with federal participation, in the following areas: expansion and new construction of universities, improvements in the regional economic structures, structural improvements in agriculture, and protection of the coastal areas.

In a number of areas, the constitutional reform is not sufficiently coordinated with other subsystems. Since *Länder* and communities are responsible for more than 80 percent of public investments, it is particularly disadvantageous that they do not need to be responsive to the requirements of a policy of economic stabilization. Only during a recession is there harmony between the goals of the federal government and those of the *Länder*.

The Federal Constitutional Court is, in comparison with the U.S. Supreme Court, which in some respects served as a model, a specialized court. It became the most important institution for the protection of the rule of law, in which a fundamental beginning was to be made after 1945. The authority of the Federal Constitutional Court goes beyond that of courts in similar systems of constitutional law. The U.S. Supreme Court, for example, is primarily a court of appeal from the decisions of lower courts. The judicial authority to interpret the constitution is far more decentralized in the United States because all courts, regardless of their level of authority, may make decisions on constitutionality. The German Federal Constitutional Court has sole authority for judicial determination of constitutionality; hence the danger of confrontation with other political authorities in the Federal Republic is considerably greater than in the United States, particularly as the U.S. system allows only concrete cases to be presented for decision.

Foreign commentators have called the Federal Constitutional Court, with its wide area of authority, the most original and most interesting institution in the West German constitutional system. But the court was not created solely for progressive reasons. The absence of a democratic tradition and the habit of giving greater emphasis to the state and its laws than to the political participation of the population combined with a desire to include stabilizing elements in the political system—a response to the trauma of Weimar.

As a result of the severe conflicts within the political system that began in 1969, the Federal Constitutional Court took on the important additional function of safeguarding the rights of minorities and the opposition, even during protracted periods of dominance by a majority, and of guaranteeing participation in the political process even by groups not belonging to the established parties. The court reaches far into the areas of authority of parliament and the executive branch, even though it is no substitute legislature, as its critics sometimes charge. In the United States, the Supreme Court has been able to avoid certain decisions by terming them political questions. From the point of view of European legal thought, the application of this doctrine occasionally appears to be arbitrary, as many legal conflicts are those concerned with new law, the right to legal protection rather than the legality of protection.

The Federal Constitutional Court is well aware of this divergence and has accepted another principle of U.S. constitutional law, the principle of judicial restraint. The court, therefore, refuses to check on the purpose and appropriateness of acts by other branches of government. The court has not interpreted the basic rights cited in the constitution as providing individuals with the right to demand specific performance by the state. The fact that there are relatively few references in the constitution to basic social rights supports this view. A support of such demands would necessarily have financial consequences and as a final result transfer to the court the establishment of budget priorities. As in the numerus clausus decision of 1972 (concerning requirements for admission to universities) the court as a rule has not saddled the executive branch with new financial obligations but has merely imposed the principle of equal treatment in the distribution of existing resources.

In 1972–1973 there appeared a change of attitudes, and judicial restraint appears to be increasingly absent. This lends support to the suspicion that the judges of the Federal Constitutional Court have an increasing interest in an active role in the political process and are moving toward judicial activism.

The Social Basis for the Political System

Internal social conflicts in the Federal Republic of Germany, an incomplete state, were fewer than in the previous undivided Germany. The brutal experiment that was practiced on the German population by Hitler and by the aftermath of his defeat, with its mass population movements and an unprecedented mixing of the population, left a partitioned Germany and a West German state that was socially relatively homogeneous. Aside from the small Danish minority in Schleswig, no non-German ethnic groups were living in the newly created country.

However, new conflicts became increasingly apparent in the 1970s. Four million foreign workers—more than 10 percent of the total work force, a percentage higher than in any country in Europe except Switzerland—resided in the Federal Republic. The recession that began in 1974 forced a stricter immigration policy. The percentage of unemployed among the foreign workers was disproportionately large, and differences between them and the German population led to new waves of xenophobia. The foreigners have so far not become an independent political force; their political participation is very limited. Their right to vote in local elections is, however, being discussed.

The 12 million expellees from former German eastern territories and from East European countries in which Germans had lived as minorities and in scattered settlements were integrated relatively quickly. They, and the 3.5 million who left the German Democratic Republic prior to the construction of the Wall in 1961, very soon turned from a social burden into a welcome pool of reserve labor, which after 1961 was increasingly maintained by the recruitment of foreign workers. The Equalization of Burdens Law of 1952, which made it possible to reintegrate those in the population who had suffered most from the ravages of war and which alleviated the unequal distribution of money and property, was an unprecedented redistribution measure in a capitalist economy and removed many bases of potential social conflict in the society.

Classes and groupings continue to exist in the population of the Federal Republic. A uniform middle-class society, which is often said to have been created, does not in fact exist. But class tensions are fewer than in former German societies. A large proportion of the formerly propertied class suffered losses from destruction and monetary devaluation, and the "economic miracle" of the reconstruction facilitated a degree of individual and collective social mobility unthinkable in any previous German society.

The homogenization of West German society was reflected in an unparalleled concentration of political forces, although there were nearly as many political parties in 1949 as there had been in the Weimar Republic. Even though the West German Basic Law was not ratified by a popular referendum, as had been the case with the Weimar Constitution, and even though it had been created with little popular participation, with the intervention of the Allies and a leading role by the party elite of the *Länder,* the opposition to the new regime was smaller than in previous German states. The latent fundamental opposition was greater, however, than was politically articulated in 1949. In the initial phase, the parties were licensed by the Allies, who sought to make a selection, particularly on the right of the political spectrum. The concentration and homogenization of the political forces stemmed from a number of different factors:

- The (Communist) left was discredited by the start of the Cold War and policies of *fait accompli* that the Soviet Union pursued in some areas in its occupation zone.
- The conflict between Catholics and Protestants was overcome by the formation of a single Christian party comprehending both. This took place much earlier than in other countries with more than one church (e.g., the Netherlands).
- Regional differences had been effectively removed and the population made into a homogeneous whole by the amputation of German territories and the mixing of the population. Regional parties were able to attract voters for the last time in the parliamentary elections of 1957 (Bavarian party, German party), but only the German party was able to gain representation, by means of a piggyback system worked out with the Christian Democratic Union.
- Agrarian interests were largely integrated into the Christian parties. Only in a few areas (northern Bavaria, northern Hessen, northern Württemberg) did the FDP have many rural adherents in the early days. The removal of the eastern territories of Germany from German control and the division of Germany eliminated any role for large landowners, and the traditional effort to bring the rural population into a conservative party was no longer a factor.
- The integration of the expellees took place much more rapidly than expected, thanks to the economic recovery and the mobilization of workers by such sociopolitical measures as the Equalization of Burdens Act. As early as 1957, the Expellees party was unable to reach the 5 percent minimum requirement for representation in the parliament, receiving only 4.6 percent of the vote.
- Extremist parties had increasingly fewer opportunities after they failed to receive from the Allies licenses allowing them to participate. The left was severely limited by controls and prohibitions even

before the formal prohibition of the Communist party in 1956. The developments in the German Democratic Republic were less than attractive to the majority of German citizens. Right-wing extremist groups were unable to thrive in a climate in which integration into the West was proceeding with relatively little friction.

The process of consolidation within these parties, solidly anchored in the system, advanced rapidly. The election of 1953 was occasionally cited as the "German election miracle." The three parties represented in parliament at that time received a total of 83.5 percent of the votes. The reasons for this consolidation are traceable primarily to the leveling of social disparities. The election law, with its rule that no party may receive representation in parliament unless it receives at least 5 percent of the votes, is of only subsidiary importance in comparison with these sociological changes.

Political attitudes in the Federal Republic appeared initially to be characterized by many remnants of the traditional authoritarian family structure and a lack of interest in politics. Participation was viewed as passive and formal, and politics was approached legalistically and in a confrontational manner. Early studies must be viewed with suspicion when they report little identification of the citizen with the state—as if such analyses could have compared nationalistic feelings for the rump state called the Federal Republic of Germany with those in other Western democracies. The emotional relationship to the state (that is, to the Federal Republic) and that to the nation (predominantly to a nation of German culture) diverged, even though the state made a major public relations effort to prevent the gap from becoming even greater. In light of the vagueness of the average citizen's hopes for the reunification of Germany, it is hardly surprising that people at best feel the existence of "subjective affinity" between the two parts of Germany and that in this field the identification is more intellectual than political.

U.S. surveys in the immediate postwar period showed that authoritarian attitudes were still strong. At that time, two-thirds of the population showed an aversion to party politics, and West German federalism appeared suspect. In the course of the 1950s, the increasing consolidation of the West German governmental system showed that political attitudes in the Federal Republic were subject to change. In comparison with other countries, the West Germans were well informed and demonstrated a high level of participation in conventional political behavior. The homogenization of the population also made rapid progress. The traditional differences between natives and expellees, men and women, Protestants and Catholics, became smaller. Even the adherents of the opposition parties did not judge the system as critically as is often the case in other countries. In periods of economic crisis (1966–1967 and 1973–1974) the majority of the West German population remained surprisingly optimistic about the ability of the system to solve its problems. In the 1970s satisfaction with the functioning of democracy was greatest in the Federal Republic among the nine nations of the European Community. The much maligned "lack of enthusiasm with the state" and the "crisis of legitimacy" cannot be substantiated for the Federal Republic when viewed in comparison with other states.

In the late 1970s, however, young people particularly began to show a certain estrangement from the political parties and a slight decrease in their interest in political participation. On the other hand, there was a growth in the trend toward unconventional political behavior (e.g., protest demonstrations) and toward participation in new, not yet firmly institutionalized forms of political action such as citizen initiatives. But even among young people, political participation is not the most highly prized value but is seen rather as a way to provide a shield behind which they can fulfill personal goals. In the long term, however, the interest in politics in the West German population has increased, and some observers see the Federal Republic as on the way toward a participatory political system as described by Gabriel Almond. In spite of this change in attitudes, a survey in 1978 showed more citizens proud of their economy than of their political system (40 percent versus 31 percent). The most threatening remnant of traditional political attitude patterns may be seen in attitudes toward the law. At a time when fear of terrorists and extremists was a major factor, more West German citizens were prepared to limit some of their political freedoms, such as the right to demonstrate, than was the case in other Western democracies. "Quiet" still seemed to take precedence over "freedom."

A consolidation of interest groups began to take place with the founding of the Federal Republic. The fragmentation traditionally inherent in a federal system led to more of a consolidation among private associations in Germany than is the case in the more centralized European states. The assistance of the state in the creation of associations and the trends toward "neocorporationism," under which the state with the help of the large corporations attempted to remove the causes for social conflict, also tended to support consolidation.

Hitler's brutal suppression of all freely organized groups, the impotence of the resistance movement, and the licensing policies of the Allies at the end of the war all contributed to the reestablishment of organizations representing (in addition to the traditional employer-worker relationship) different aspects of society and to a uniformity among them. Employees and expellees, who in the beginning were deliberately slowed by the occupying powers in their efforts at unification and in their political lobbying, quickly overcame the reduced influence that seemed to exist in 1948–1949, when the constitution was being drafted. Differences in status appeared to play a smaller role after 1949, so that the Union of Employees (DAG) did not achieve the same strength as the white-collar unions within the British TUC or as those of Scandinavia, which represent a competing labor organization to the national labor federations.

The loss of territory and the destruction of the basis of the political influence of the large landowners, especially in the Soviet occcupation zone and the eastern territories, also reduced the antagonism in agri-culture. The Reich Land Federation of the Weimar period, which was dominated largely by the large agricultural entrepreneurs from east of the Elbe and was closely tied to the politically conservative forces associated with the German National People's party (DNVP), did have important competition from organizations such as the Farmers Unions in western and southern Germany and the German Farmer (Deutsche Bauernschaft) as representatives of the smaller and middle-sized farms. The German Farmers Association (DBV), founded in 1948 in Munich, made possible an unprecedented uniformity of activity, even if a certain amount of domination by the larger enterprises of Lower Saxony and Westphalia is noticeable.

The internal organizational differences in the associations appear small for a medium-sized state. The trade union federation, which has only seventeen member unions, has a simpler structure than that of any other states but small ones like Luxembourg. The German Farmers Association has only fifteen member organizations even though it em-phasizes the German territorial boundaries that existed prior to the establishment of the Federal Republic. The level of participation in German organizations is high when compared with other countries. In the Employers Association (BDA) it lies at about 80 percent, in the Association of Industry (BDI) and the German Farmers Association at more than 90 percent. In the case of the trade unions, it would appear to equal the European average, with 39 percent. In most countries in which the level of participation is higher, it has been artificially raised either by organizational ties (as with the labor parties in Great Britain and Sweden) or through negative sanctions against nonmembership (such as the union shop in Great Britain or solidarity fees in Belgium). Because of the compulsory membership that had been instituted in the Third Reich and in the German Democratic Republic, the West German unions have decisively rejected any notion of forced union membership.

The organizations' power and financial might have often been admired and mistrusted abroad. Mistrust has occurred particularly in international organizations in which the German members supply a considerable portion of the financial resources and as a result exert some influence on the organizations' direction, especially in regional international organizations such as the European Trade Union Federation.

In contrast to the United States, the influence of interest groups does not so much take the form of paid lobbyists; rather, their representatives are included in the parliamentary bodies. The election law and the organization of the German Bundestag make it easier for organizations to exercise such influence. The dual list of candidates (one list for direct election and the other for proportional representation according to party affiliation) and the rank ordering of candidates on the party list make election of representatives of specific organizations a near-certainty. The ability to obtain expertise in parliament in this manner gives this process a positive value. Association executives, whose membership in the 1980–1983 parliament was slightly reduced, still appear to be the second largest group in parliament, immediately following the civil servants.

The relationship of specific representatives to associations is not always the result of their employment by the associations. The matter requires careful analysis. Ideologically motivated groups, such as those concerned with the environment, often receive the support of members of parliament even though these are in no way affiliated with the group lobbying for a specific policy. The proportion of representatives with a clear organizational affiliation rose in the 7th Bundestag (1972–1976) to 42.8 percent. An analysis of available figures shows that it is not members of the organizations representing the different classes of society—employers' organizations and trade unions—that seek most ardently to penetrate the parliamentary committees but those that represent status groups such as farmers', expellees', and certain social organizations.

The efforts of interest groups in a country with relatively infrequent changes in government cannot be concentrated solely on the placement of its representatives in the apparatus of the state. The main effort remains directed toward the daily decision-making process of the government and the administrators. The strong position of the chancellor in the parliamentary system and the increasing importance of the government and the administrators have from the beginning made the executive branch rather than legislative branch the preferred addressee of efforts at influence. The BDI, one of the most powerful associations in the country, has directed about 90 percent of its effort to ministries and government offices. Bundestag committees, by contrast, rarely play an independent role; most of the time they are the secondary addressee. Perhaps only the Finance Committee and the Commission of the European Community are important targets of lobbying efforts.

A new development is the extension of indirect articulation of interests through groups with ideological goals. Such promotional or public interest groups have, particularly in the United States, occasionally represented economic or status interests. What is new is the polarization of class or status conflicts apparently resulting not from business cycles but from the political threats felt by certain status groups.

If it appears that in the Federal Republic lobbying resources have been used more radically, it should be clear that this mere form is not a sign of increase in radicalism. The resources made available for a conflict have to be related to the goals they are designed to achieve. Traditional associations such as the German Farmers Association have long suffered from the untenable contradiction of their goals (defense of the family farm and a simultaneous desire for the benefits of working conditions and income achieved in industry). Such inconsistencies are increasingly being resolved, and even relatively radical measures often lead to a reduction in the acuteness of the conflict because they seem to be more suited than previously to the achievement of the supposed goals. But this is true also for the traditionalism of the underprivileged. The trade unions in the Federal Republic are today more aggressively oriented toward class conflict than was the case in the 1950s and early 1960s. But the gap between the class-war phases of older programs and the short-term goals that are to be realized through confrontation has become smaller as structural changes are proposed in terms of realizable parameters and with clearly stated timetables. These include such measures as codetermination in specific plants and in industrial sectors and extension of state ownership, rather than demands for a total socialization of industry.

Protests against the payment of taxes have not yet involved the radical methods that have been used in other countries, such as a call for a tax strike. The appropriate organization, the Federation of Tax Payers, was neither sufficiently homogeneous nor sufficiently influential for such militant actions. When it appeared at one point that some citizen initiative movements—especially those demonstrating against nuclear power plants—would not shy away from the use of force, the attempt of leftist, especially Marxist, groups to take advantage of these movements resulted in a moderation of their methods, because those leading the citizen initiatives quickly separated themselves from the leftist groups.

The more pronounced the confrontations arising in the Federal Republic have become, the more discussion has taken place of methods of institutionalizing their resolution. One of the most debated instruments of conflict resolution is "concerted action." Situated between the institutionalized labor and business councils that exist in the Mediterranean states and in the Netherlands and the looser advisory councils developed in Great Britain, concerted action has its closest parallel in the Harpsund conferences between the Swedish government and the most important associations of that country. Like these conferences, concerted action never went beyond an exchange of views without specific enforcement action. Concerted action's ability to direct economic action is, according to detailed research and contrary to popular assumption, relatively slight. Its function as a conflict-resolving and integrating method has been exaggerated, in part because of carefully harmonized press communiqués pretending a consensus. Measured against objective indicators, confrontations over distribution of income have increased in severity since the initiation of concerted action.

Policy Formulation and Implementation

Traditionally, Germany has provided strong direction to its political system through legislation. Precisely because of the existing political and social heterogeneity, previous governments in Germany adopted general governmental regulation in such policy areas as education, the military, labor, and welfare earlier than was the case in other large states. This was particularly true for the dominant German power in the second half of the nineteenth century, Prussia.

The dominant role of the military has been broken. It no longer has any influence on policy formulation. For the first time in German history, civilians who had never served in the armed forces have become ministers of defense. The supremacy of civilian political direction of the military has taken hold. When there was the least possibility that some individuals in the military might be sympathetic to right-wing extremists, decisive action was taken, particularly with regard to possible reaction abroad. The military is no longer a separate "state within the state," with its own loyalties and with an authoritarian tradition in conflict with democratic rules, as was still the case in the days of the Weimar Republic.

In its political system, the Federal Republic does not follow the traditional pattern of compensating for the lack of uniformity in living conditions by economic oversteering, certainly not in all sectors of activity. Because they are based on federalism and on a strong adherence to a free market economy with a widespread aversion to far-reaching planning of policies, the central institutions of the Federal Republic tended in the first two decades of its existence to understeering of the economy. The successes of the reconstruction phase, which had come about with hardly any planning, and the general aversion to oversteering as it had existed in the Nazi years and the occupation period and as it exists today in the German Democratic Republic, contributed to the growth of an ideology of nonplanning.

The proportion of the economy belonging to the state, already small, was reduced further under Chancellor Erhard. The state is therefore less able to steer the total economy than in other free market countries. In comparison with other Western democracies, planning is underdeveloped, and the federal structure tends to fragment planning in such areas as the economy and education. Decentralized directing institutions, increasingly independent of the government, have developed not only in constitutionally mandated bodies such as the Federal Constitutional Court and the Bundesrat but also in institutions belonging to various government departments such as the Federal (central) Bank and the Federal Labor Institute. The limits set on the capacity of the state to provide direction are the welcome results—from the point of view of strengthening the rule of law—of the strong institutionalized protection of basic rights and the security provided by the comprehensive authority of the Federal Administrative Court in relation to all the actions of the state. These measures make for limitations that are even greater than those in other Western democracies.

In spite of this partial understeering of the politico-economic system, its achievements have often been admired abroad. A comparison with other democracies shows the Federal Republic ahead in many indicators. In the development of industrial production, in hourly wages, and in the cost of living (see Table 3) the imbalances have been fewer than in other free market economies. The rise in hourly wages has not been absorbed by the effects of inflation, as has been the case elsewhere. In recent years, the rate of unemployment has been lower than in any country other than Austria, Sweden, and Switzerland. The Federal Republic has the highest level of currency reserves. The tax burden on citizens of the Federal Republic appears to be lower than that in other countries, except Switzerland and the United States (the latter provides less of a welfare state and substitutes private activities for those of the state in some areas). The public debt has increased in the 1970s and is slowly rising to the top of the various European countries; France and Italy rank ahead of the Federal Republic. Labor conflicts, measured in days of work lost due to strikes, have risen in the Federal Republic; labor is no longer as quiescent as in the first two decades of the republic's existence. Compared with other medium-sized or large Western democracies, however, the number of work days lost is still very small. The "German model," with its strict control of conflicts between interest groups, has been noted abroad with a mixture of criticism and secret admiration.

A comparison of budget expenditures with those of other highly developed industrial countries of the Western world is of limited use. A look at other federal states (Canada, Austria, Switzerland, the United States) shows that in all such systems the expenditures of the federal government in the field of education are small because the major costs are borne by the member states. In this field, critical popular literature

TABLE 3
Economic Indicators in International Comparison

	Federal Republic Germany	Belgium	Canada	France	Great Britain	Italy	Japan	Netherlands	Sweden	Switzerland	USA
(1) Industrial production 1981 (1975 = 100)	117	113	119	111	102	132	145	110	98	113	130
(2) Wages per hour 1981 (1975 = 100)	138	160	175	201	216	306	156	135	171	116	164
(3) Living Costs 1981 (1975 = 100)	129	144	168	181	219	258	145	142	181	118	167
(4) Percentage of unemployment (1981)	4,8	10,5	7,2	7,2	9,8	8,4	2,4	6,5	1,9	0,2	7,1
(5) Financial reserves in billion US dollars (1978)	54,0	8,3	3,2	32,8	19,0	18,7	28,3	11,1	4,4	13,8	29,1
(6) Public debts in DM per capita of the population (1977)	7500	15300	n.d.	3100	9800	6200	6800	10000	14100	8000	13700
increase (1975-1980) of public debts in %	82	111	n.d.	142	81	129	275	82	157	15	53
(7) Taxes and insurance fees in percent of GNP (1980)	38,4	43,2	31,7	41,3	35,3	31,4	24,6	48,9	52,5	30,0	29,5
(8) Strikes (lost working days in 1000) 1976	534	42		5011	3284	25378	3253	14	26	20	37860
1977	24	897		3666	10143	16566	1518	236	87	5	35822
1978	4281	1002		2220	9405	10177	1357	8	37	5	39000
(9) Balance of payments (1979) in Mio SDR	-4920	-2640	n.d.	+1188	-2952	+3955	n.d.	-1817	-2027	+1884	n.d.

Sources: Finanzbericht 1982. Bundesministerium der Finanzen, Bonn 1981, pp. 264ff.
ILO: Year Book of Labour Statistics. Geneva 1979, pp. 634ff.
Bundesministerium der Finanzen: Unsere internationalen Währungsbeziehungen. Bonn, Sept. 1977, p. 13
Statistisches Jahrbuch für die Bundesrepublik Deutschland. Stuttgart, 1981, p. 724f.

has made many misstatements. Even defense expenditures, which are borne by the central government in all countries, can be made to appear high if the comparison is made with centralized states where the total budget includes items like education that do not appear in the budget of federal governments. The same is true of the apparently favorable level of expenditures in the Federal Republic for health and welfare. This item can be compared internationally only with the greatest caution in view of the large differences in the ways social security systems are organized. But even if such differences are carefully taken into account, the Federal Republic is still in the lead. Since 1977, however, its expenditures in these fields have fallen as a percentage of the GNP.

Some of the accomplishments of postwar Germany cannot be attributed in any major way to the political system. The advantages for an economy that as a result of its wartime destruction was compelled to undertake a total renewal are tied only indirectly to the political actions of the Adenauer era. The thorough loss of any illusion by this medium-sized state of being a great power gave the Federal Republic a further advantage over Great Britain and France, which had to direct a part of their effort and resources in the postwar period to a failing attempt to play a worldwide role as major powers. The existence of a reserve of industrial workers made up of expellees who were especially highly motivated to prevent the decline of society by individual exertion gave West Germany an incomparable advantage in its new start. Even discriminatory actions, such as the undervaluation of the German mark, became a temporary advantage in the export market.

There is nevertheless little cause for the self-satisfaction with the prosperity of the "German model" that was at times reflected in election campaign rhetoric. During the lengthy period of economic upturn, many a needed adaptation of structural policy was not made. The closed season for competition through specialization in international economic activity is gone. The Federal Republic is beginning to feel the results of increasing competition on the one hand and of growing protectionism on the part of its highly industrialized trading partners on the other. Because of the disproportionate importance of the industrial sector in the economy of the Federal Republic, crises of industrial stagnation tend to affect growth and employment levels more severely than in other countries. Meanwhile, the pressure of other industrial nations on the Federal Republic has also increased. There have been appeals to the dual responsibility of the Federal Republic for economic growth in the West and an improved balance of payments for Germany's trading partners. As late as 1978, the United States and the Organisation for Economic Co-operation and Development (OECD) recommended an increase in the debt, which they considered to be supportive of economic growth.

Other countries increasingly suspect the Federal Republic of strengthening its power as the dominant economy. This suspicion, which has arisen out of differences of opinion on economic policy between German and non-German politicians, has created burdens for those responsible for the policies of the Federal Republic. That government has been placed under increasing pressure to act on the ideas of the majority of industrialized countries without being able to translate its own strong position into the use of power that could influence the common course of action of these countries.

In spite of a number of crisis indicators, the political institutions, basking in the predominantly "fair weather" influence of the postwar period, have so far escaped the need to test their successes. The system gained its legitimacy largely through its economic accomplishments. The assurance of legal protection and the achievements in the field of social welfare overcame, within the democratic rules of the Basic Law, the traditional reluctance of many Germans to participate in politics and especially to tolerate conflict.

These accomplishments in economic productivity may be contrasted with problems in legitimacy, which appear only in times of crisis. The overreaction to symptoms of economic crisis through the political distortions of extremism or terrorism showed, however, that the West German governmental system is subject to special burdens that may endanger the basis of its legitimacy:

- Overcoming the National Socialist period has, as in Italy and Japan, underlined the break in continuity as it affects authority and legitimacy. Because a political elite was not sufficiently reestablished, young people with rigidly moral ideas about politics have repeatedly felt a loss of confidence in the political leadership.
- The tremendous accomplishments of reconstruction by the postwar generation had their emotional price: Young people frequently were given money and employment opportunities instead of human contact and political models with the result that anomic processes were particularly noticeable in the country of the "economic miracle" after the period of the grand coalition (1966–1969).
- The "gift" of so-called socialism on the tips of the bayonets of the Soviet occupying power in the eastern part of the country, which was deprived of constructing its own system through free elections, has widened the gap between national identity and the search for a modern and humane governmental system. In 1945 this gap had appeared to be bridgeable for the very first time. Instead of a

national mentality and normal national awareness, West Germany developed a cartel of "antisocialist" defense ideologies. In hardly any Western democracy has pluralism been so severely limited by the concept of "militant democracy."

- The cartel of the major parties, which appeared as the result of a process of consolidation in the party system, guarantees the stability of the government, which was one of the highest goals of the fathers of the constitution when they distributed governmental powers. The price paid for this, however, was a drastic reduction in the possibility of political organization by fringe groups who feel themselves estranged from the system.
- Germans continue to shy away from conflicts and to be skeptical of any form of direct democracy and of participation in plebiscites. The legitimation of the system was the result of economic success; it lacked nearly all emotional identification. This lack of emotional identification is not totally disadvantageous. It is noteworthy that at the first signs of an economic crisis—more pronounced than in other countries of Western Europe—confidence in the ability of the state and of the political elite to resolve problems remained strong. The lack of emotional identification is undoubtedly disadvantageous in the relationship of the state with those of its citizens who are partially or totally estranged from it. But among the majority, the predominantly cognitive attitude toward the system has the advantage that fewer expectations can be disappointed and that the acceptance of political realities—as well as real or perceived declines in the status of its citizens—can be achieved with less emotional upheaval.
- The political processes in the Federal Republic lack latitude for their actions, a fact that is dangerous in relation to dissent and fundamental opposition. Politics is understood only in narrow parliamentary terms. The possibility of participation through plebiscites is absent. The high degree of bureaucratization of large societal organizations and the impenetrable party system restrict initiatives at the fringes of the political process. Citizen initiatives and "green" (environmentalist) or "multicolored" party lists attempt to compensate for these limitations. A country that is socially homogenized is poor in political and social outlets for political protests. Because the "rump" state of West Germany is ethnically homogeneous, not even the activation of ethnic minorities can be used as a rallying point for fundamental opposition. Movements toward regional unity among West European democracies have not found an appropriate counterpart in the Federal Republic because of the structure of German federalism. Paradoxically, the

continued existence of large ghettos and regions of poor, underprivileged citizens in the United States has taken on a diverting
and absorbing function for protest that is missing in Germany.
Wherever a social commitment is initiated to protest the many
remaining social grievances and disparities, it is met by a highly
formalized labor and welfare policy and by social welfare dispensed
by the bureaucratic apparatus, leaving very little latitude for social
empathy. It is no coincidence that sociologists, educators, and social
workers are well represented in frustrated anti-intellectual groups.

- Problems are also created by the tendency in the Federal Republic
to bring about an increasingly streamlined society by legally regulating group interactions. In only a few states is the legal regulation
of all types of social relationships as advanced as it is in Germany.
Even in the relationship between management and labor, potential
protests find but few causes for the nostalgia of the class struggle.
The mobilization of trade unions in this area develops very little
power of absorption compared to the unorganized potential of
protest. When there are confrontations with anomic movements,
such as extremism and terrorism, the government tends to legally
regulate normal social interactions in order to deal with the exceptional cases.

Readings

Baker, K. L., Dalton, R. J., and Hildebrandt, K., eds. *Germany Transformed: Political Culture and the New Politics.* Cambridge: Harvard University Press, 1981.

Balfour, Michael. *West Germany.* London: Benn, 1968.

Dahrendorf, Ralf. *Society and Democracy in Germany.* Garden City, New York: Doubleday, 1967.

Edinger, Lewis J. *Politics in West Germany.* Boston: Little, Brown, 1977.

Goldman, Guido, *The German Political System.* New York: Random House, 1974.

Sontheimer, Kurt. *The Government and Politics of West Germany.* London: Hutchinson, 1972.

Tilford, R. D. and Preece, R.J.C. *Federal Germany: Political and Social Order.* London: Wolff, 1969.

Chancellors of the Federal Republic of Germany

Konrad Adenauer (1949–1963)

Ludwig Erhard (1963–1966)

Kurt Georg Kiesinger (1966–1969)

Willy Brandt (1969–1974)   Helmut Schmidt (1974–1982)

Helmut Kohl (1982–   )

Presidents of the Federal Republic of Germany

Theodor Heuss (1949–1959)

Heinrich Lübke (1959–1969)

Gustav Heinemann (1969–1974)

Walter Scheel (1974–1979)   Karl Carstens (1979–1984)

Richard von Weizsäcker (1984–   )

KARL HARDACH

6

The Economy of the Federal Republic of Germany: Structure, Performance, and World Position

About a year before the foundation of the Federal Republic of Germany in the summer of 1949, three major economic policy decisions were made that greatly influenced the future economic structure and development of the new state: reform of the currency, admission to the Marshall Plan, and the establishment of a free enterprise system. The United States, as the most powerful of the Western Allies, attempted, like the Soviet Union, to demonstrate to the defeated Germans the excellence of its political order through the superiority of its economic system. The U.S. military governor was obligated to work for the ultimate establishment of the free market doctrine in Germany despite widespread demands for nationalization among the German public and the pro-nationalization policy of the British Labour government. While the Social Democratic party (SPD) from the very beginning advocated national-ization of a considerable part of the means of production and demo-cratically controlled governmental guidance of the economy, the main conservative and future majority party, the Christian Democratic Union (CDU), eventually came out strongly for the competitive profit system. The principles of the neoliberalist school of economics were to serve in phraseology and substance as the main ideological basis for the economic policy concept of a "social market economy," the officially pursued economic policy after the currency reform.

The neoliberalist creed, rooted in economic and political consider-ations, emphasized the need for a well-functioning competitive system as the means of preventing the concentration of public and private power. Dictatorship, state planning and economic controls, and private monopolies created by industrial cartelization could be forestalled by the establishment and proper safeguarding of a free market economy. Besides providing the best insurance against the loss of political freedom, the market economy also represented, to the neoliberalist, a superior device of economic organization leading to a more efficient allocation of resources. This capitalist wonderland was to be reached by maintaining a certain monetary stability (without which all attempts to achieve a competitive order would be in vain) and by adopting various government measures to ensure market competition and economic stability, since an unregulated free market economy of the laissez-faire type had historically led to monopolistic practices and cyclical fluctuations. To ensure competition the government was to restrict cartels and monopolies; countercyclical measures, preferably as automatic as possible to avoid arbitrary intervention, were to maintain economic stability. Social cohesion would be fostered by mitigating major income inequalities, should they appear in spite of competition, through a progressive income tax mild enough not to thwart incentives.

In spite of the fundamental insistence of neoliberalism on polarizing the economic and political systems, with an alleged choice between individual freedom and independence based on comprehensive competition and widely diffused ownership on the one hand and a collectivist system of state ownership and totalitarian planning on the other, a mixed system developed. A combination of the market principle as practiced before 1914 and elements of governmental guidance of the economy as practiced during the wars and the interwar years was precisely what characterized the German economy after the currency reform.

The state of competition in the German economy had been somewhat improved by the Allied deconcentration measures in the coal, steel, and chemical industries, in banking, and in a few other fields. Because the breakup of companies had frequently neither considered established and technologically or organizationally sound integration nor significantly redistributed ownership of the newly created smaller firms, strong incentives for reintegration remained. Throughout the 1950s, 1960s, and 1970s, concentration continued, benefiting the very large enterprises. Many of these large companies, frequently enjoying an international reputation, not only dominated swarms of smaller suppliers and subcontractors, undermining their economic maneuverability and competitive behavior, but also tended to contribute to the restraint of competition among the industrial giants through the establishment of joint subsidiaries.

Stern neoliberalists had to view such an expansion of big business over the years with very mixed feelings, but the political support they were able to command turned out to be quite insufficient to stop economic concentration. The voters were intelligent enough not to demand a simple return to petit bourgeois economic relations. The need to keep abreast of international developments, especially the creation of larger economic areas like the Common Market, necessitated a certain coordination and cooperation on the domestic level. At a time of rapid and capital-intensive technological progress, the trend toward larger production units in factories and greater concentration of capital assets in enterprises could not be halted in a single country. Thus considerations of political principle or business ideology could not be heeded, and no economic Luddism occurred.

But there were other blemishes, at least in the eyes of neoliberalists. Although a general prohibition of cartels denied them the aid of the courts, mild cartel-like arrangements continued to exist in some industries. Furthermore, entire sectors, like agriculture, housing, transportation, banking, and insurance, were exempted from this prohibition, and in these cases the state itself generally supervised the functioning of cartel-like agreements. Public ownership and the entrepreneurial function of the state were continued in areas in which such activity had been traditional. Nationwide transportation (railroads, inland waterways, airlines) and most local transportation systems, telegraph, telephone and postal communications, and radio and television networks, as well as the overwhelming proportion of the utilities, were owned and operated by public authorities at various levels. Government ownership also extended to manufacturing, although this was not the consequence of any conscious nationalization policy. In the 1950s the state held a share of more than one-fifth in the national production of coal, coke, crude oil, pig iron, and steel; around half in automobile construction (Volkswagen) and iron ore, lead, and zinc production; and more than two-thirds in aluminum smelting. In addition, it had substantial interests in other industries like shipbuilding, housing, and chemicals.

Almost all these properties had been inherited from previous governments, and by the late 1970s the federal government alone held interests in several thousand enterprises, despite some previous privatization to encourage the idea of share-ownership in a system of "people's capitalism." The state did not, however, totally divest itself of ownership in these companies but maintained its influence on management and generally retained at least a theoretical option of using its industrial holdings to exert some countervailing power in oligopolistic markets. The state-owned companies were run in a businesslike manner as private enterprises, competing for capital, labor, and customers in the marketplace and paying the penalty of poor performance through the replacement of management.

Besides functioning as an entrepreneur, the state played a much larger role in the economy as an administrator. Federal, state, and local governments constituted the three-tiered hierarchy of the German administrative system. Since many economic and social problems in a small country (actually as large as Oregon) tend to become national affairs calling for a nationwide solution, there has been a trend over the years toward a certain centralization of legislative and administrative powers. The eleven German states do not have the power that state governments in the United States have, but the basic units of local government have been responsible for a much wider range of activities than their U.S. counterparts. These have included the operation of such local enterprises as public utilities, buses, streetcars, slaughterhouses, savings banks, hospitals, museums, theaters, and orchestras. To fulfill its administrative obligations, each level in the three-tiered governmental hierarchy was assigned specific public revenues. In the 1970s their share (including social security contributions) in the gross domestic product amounted to some 45 percent in Germany as against some 30 percent in the United States, a clear indication of the much greater importance in Germany of the public sector.

As Germany honors the right of free association, the representation of private interests, aside from such elected bodies as parties, parliaments, and governments, has been the domain of various semipublic or private organizations that have at times considerably influenced the shaping of economic policy. Such a role has been played by the chambers (of industry and commerce, of handicrafts, of agriculture) representing the regional concerns of their members and by a multitude of economic associations (of farmers, industrialists, bankers, retailers, and others), all of them with hundreds of subgroups and regional federations. Usually these pressure groups have encompassed a great many competing units whose conflicting interests had to be integrated. Since formal procedures for collective decision making were frequently lacking from the outset, such organizations have been repeatedly criticized for their low degree of internal democracy, as well as for the lack of clarity in their relations with the political parties and their influence on official economic policy.

The trade unions and employers' organizations—the "social partners," as the Germans call them—have acted as independent parties in the collective bargaining process, the results of which constitute important macroeconomic data for other economic policymakers. Considerable modifications in the organizational structure of the unions and their depoliticization on principle represented the most conspicuous change in Germany's postwar labor market. Because it was realized that previous

fragmentation into some 200 unions representing different denomina-
tional, political, and craft interests had weakened the unions' cause, a
unified, nondenominational, nonpolitical body, the German Trade Union
Federation (DGB), with its sixteen constituent industrial unions, was
established in 1949. These industry-based unions, which represented all
the workers in a particular industrial sector (e.g., the metal-producing
and -using industries) or related trade groups (e.g., construction and
building materials), abolished the multiplicity and diffusion of the past
and ended, or at least internalized, demarcation and comparability
disputes. The new unions, built up from scratch, showed themselves
incomparably better suited to the modern age than those inherited from
the nineteenth century in some other European countries. They facilitated
a national wage policy and long-term economic budgeting by management,
expedited mediation, and reduced strikes and lockouts, as well as
strengthened the bargaining position of the unions.

Unions and employers not only agreed in jealously safeguarding their
independence and autonomy against any public intervention but also
reached common ground with the DGB's eventual acceptance of the
"social market economy." Inspired by Marxist thinking, the DGB had
initially demanded the transfer to public ownership of such key sectors
as the iron, basic chemical, and energy-producing industries; mining;
the main transportation systems; and all credit institutions. The repeated
rejection of nationalization and comprehensive economic planning by
the majority of voters in the federal elections of the 1950s led the Social
Democrats (in 1959) and unionists (in 1963) to modify their aims
regarding the economic order and to accept the social market economy.
Both now maintained that the market mechanism should be given
priority, assisted, if necessary, by economic planning. That some sort
of macroeconomic planning was indeed advisable was learned by the
conservative parties and their supporters in the business community
during the shocking recession of 1966–1967, which led to a CDU-SPD
"grand coalition" government and general support for the creation of
additional economic policy instruments. The Law for Promoting Economic Stability and Growth of 1967 introduced modern medium-term
economic management through the adoption of a comprehensive set of
new and partly unique economic policy tools. Their skillful use was
henceforth to guarantee the attainment of the four economic policy
objectives set down in the law: price stability, full employment, external
equilibrium, and adequate growth.

Unionists and Social Democrats on the one hand and employers and
the conservative parties on the other could henceforth differ about the
desirable extent of governmental guidance of the economy without
questioning the necessity for such macroeconomic planning. Labor's

request for participation in microeconomic decision making, however, remained a heavily contested issue. On this question of "industrial democracy" the unions demanded and over the years achieved some participation in the day-to-day conduct of business, i.e., "codetermination" in the actual management. The German economy is now characterized by such limiting of entrepreneurial independence; the existence of a bilateral monopoly in the labor market and of a system of relations, contractual and otherwise, among powerful semieconomic and semipolitical organizations; the increasing concentration in industry and banking; the persistence of mild cartel-like arrangements; lasting controls over entire sectors of the economy; the considerable entrepreneurial activity of the state; and the further extension and refinement of its regulatory and redistributive operations. All this, surely, would have not only astonished but probably distressed the ideological founding fathers of this economic system. The question remains whether the term "market economy" provides an adequate description of German reality. But whatever the social market economy has lacked in doctrinal purity—from the neoliberalist point of view—it has made up in actual performance.

The period of nearly half a decade following the currency reform of mid-1948 has quite often been referred to abroad as the years of the German "economic miracle," as the defeated country rejuvenated itself, phoenixlike, in a relatively short time, rising from rubble and ashes to provide a standard of living at, or even above, the prewar level. In the four years until mid-1952, the German gross national product (GNP) rose nominally by more than 80 percent or by 67 percent in real terms. Nevertheless, in terms of the per capita product, Germany was still about 12 percent behind France and 3 percent behind Great Britain in 1952. The economy of Germany was suffering much more than those of other West European countries, owing, apart from a belated start, to various burdens (among them partition, dismantling, forced exports, production prohibitions, and refugees) placed upon the war-devastated country. The causes of the quick recovery immediately following the currency reform are to be found in an adequate supply of capital, labor, entrepreneurship, and markets and in realistic official policies.

To be more specific, the economic rebuilding of Germany necessitated investable funds from either foreign or domestic sources. Although up to October 1954 Germany received foreign aid totaling about $4.4 billion from the Western Allies, these allocations were not really considerable in quantitative terms and, even during the main aid year of 1948–1949, amounted to less than 5 percent of the German GNP. The quantitative importance of foreign aid as a source of investable funds becomes even less impressive when consideration is given to the various burdens the

Allies imposed upon Germany; their aggregate value at the time exceeded the aid received quite considerably, since between 1946 and 1949 an estimated 11 to 15 percent of the Western zones' national product was spent on occupation costs and reparation deliveries. With few exceptions, however, the burdens placed upon Germany taxed only its domestic resources and did not seriously undermine its balance-of-payments position, which was greatly strengthened by the Marshall Plan. This, indeed, was the main contribution of Allied, particularly U.S., aid: to provide Germany with the foreign exchange to acquire vital foodstuffs, raw materials, and other imports. In this qualified sense foreign aid indeed deserves to be ranked beside the currency reform and decontrol as the third main cause of Germany's quick reconstruction.

The Germans themselves kept their belts tightened in order to reach gross investment levels of 20–24 percent of GNP between 1949 and 1953–1954, and none of the major European countries reached the German investment ratio at the time. Relatively few funds were allocated through budgets as part of a centrally guided investment program, and self-financing provided more than 80 percent of all investable funds during the first year after the currency reform and at least one-half during the early 1950s. Given the general capital shortage in the economy and the preference for the market mechanism, a strong emphasis on entrepreneurial self-financing seemed to be the most feasible method of capital accumulation in the face of an illiquid securities market, tight and expensive bank credits, and slim corporate equities. The policy actually pursued (of favoring corporate saving) not only allowed for some governmental channeling of funds into desired directions by means of tax concessions but also provided the basis for future external financing through the building up of equities, apart from creating strong incentives for the individual businessman. That this altogether decentralized form of national capital formation quickly led to a large increase in national product resulted partly from the fact that the substantial existing stock of plant and equipment, although frequently inoperable due to partial damage, dismantling, and wear and tear, permitted the quick com- mencement of operations once a relatively small amount of capital had been strategically applied. On the other hand, the fast growth of com- modity production reflected the policy of German management of investing particularly in fields characterized by a low capital-output ratio and quick returns.

That foreign observers habitually praise German managers represents a platitude that is probably as valid as the cliché of the Germans' extraordinary industriousness. The long list of Prussian virtues that foreign authors like to recite usually includes as typically German characteristics a love for order, a talent for effective organization, a strong inclination to save and invest, a pronounced spirit of inventiveness and enterprise, and above all, a willingness—bordering on a craving—for work. If Spartan standards were advisable for the Germans if they intended to rebuild their economy, such attitudes were a must for the millions of returning soldiers, those who had been bombed out, and all others whose means of livelihood had disappeared. The refugees and expellees particularly had to start from scratch in a new environment. Since in 1950 every fifth person in Germany had recently taken up residence there, this inflow of more than 9 million people presented a major problem at the time as well as a considerable opportunity for the future.

Initially, the refugees and expellees constituted a formidable hindrance to reconstruction, placing an additional burden on such already over-strained facilities as housing, hospitals, schools, and transport. Increasingly, however, as the general recovery progressed, these millions turned out to be an asset instead of a liability for the German economy. The refugees not only had a somewhat larger share of people of working age than the indigenous population; they also lacked local ties and were thus willing to move to where there was employment. Since many of the weak and unfit had succumbed to the rigors of expulsion and the hardships of the westward trek, the survivors represented the more sturdy and alert, who were eager to improve their lot and confront well-established and at times complacent indigenous members of the economic community with new ideas and methods. Such competition was not confined to entrepreneurial circles but was also prevalent among workers, and the availability of refugee labor tended to act as a depressant upon wages. By 1960 the economic, social, and political integration into the Federal Republic of the expelled persons had basically been achieved, and for the first time their unemployment rate remained below the national average. Thereafter millions of foreign workers, mostly from Mediterranean countries, accepted gainful employment in Germany, thereby improving their own standard of living and providing substantial benefits to the German economy as well.

The German workers' restrained wage demands and their steady and industrious efforts were their invaluable contribution to the country's reconstruction. Like the laborers in neighboring countries, they were prepared to work long and hard; but there is little statistical evidence that they did anything exceptional, and the "hard work" thesis of the rapid German recovery has generally been rejected as an unsatisfactory explanation. Labor's restrained wage policy—whether due to a states-manlike sense of responsibility among union leaders or a proper un-derstanding among the rank and file of the harsh realities—contributed greatly to Germany's recovery. Moderate wages permitted the buildup of plant and equipment, ensured the stability of the new currency, and enabled Germany to return to the world market through competitive exports.

For an international trading country like Germany, access to foreign markets, whether as buyer or seller, was of particular importance. The restoration of international economic relations, however, took longer after 1945 than after World War I, because World War II had been preceded by the worldwide economic disintegration of the 1930s. Participation in various new institutions that brought liberalization of trade and multilateralization of payments opened for Germany the doors of nations producing foodstuffs and raw materials. Foreign food supplies were particularly vital, given the loss of Germany's breadbasket in the east and the population increase of about 25 percent due to refugees and expellees. As with food, Germany also had been a long-time importer of raw materials, such as textile fibers, nonferrous metals, natural rubber, and crude oil.

To a considerable extent it was the Korean crisis that enabled Germany to pay for these imports through a surprisingly quick comeback in the world market. For once, the country was not involved in a military dispute; existing industrial capacities and scarce raw materials were not needed for armament programs and were thus free for highly profitable export production in the face of increased international demand and reduced foreign competition. In this situation Germany was favored by its traditional industrial structure, which emphasized capital-goods industries. Germany's ability to supply machinery, industrial equipment, vehicles, and certain electrical and chemical products accounted to a considerable extent for its remarkable reentry into the world market. It could offer these commodities at attractive prices due to its comparatively conservative domestic economic policy, the general undervaluation of its currency, and a variety of export-promotion schemes of the federal government, which also maintained realistic policies in general.

Events in the political sphere played a role of overwhelming importance in Germany's recovery. The relatively rapid breakup of the anti-Hitler coalition into rival ideological camps once the war had ended enabled the Germans in the East and in the West to turn from hated enemies into appreciated allies. Without the East-West split, there can be no doubt, the occupation policies of the Big Four would have been harsher (or less benevolent) and would have lasted longer and weighed harder upon the Germans. In this sense, the latter turned out to be the main, although not the only beneficiaries of the Cold War, which has come to be regarded as the single most decisive factor in Germany's recovery. In party-political terms, the German voters in the Federal Republic contributed to internal stability through their lasting renunciation of extremism of both the right and the left, and their solid support of democratic parties, either of the bourgeois-conservative or the social democratic, laborite variety. The conservative cabinets under Adenauer (up to October 1963) and Erhard (until November 1966) were able to restore confidence in the state apparatus and to revive a somewhat paternalistic spirit of government. The restoration of political order and stability with the active cooperation of a loyal social democratic opposition was no small task in a country where the public had been thoroughly disillusioned by the sequence within little more than a quarter century of constitutional monarchy, democratic parliamentarism, and strong-man dictatorship. Yet such stabilization was essential to bring about entrepreneurial activity, labor peace, and the confidence of foreign businessmen. "Order" for a conservative government meant, of course, the pursuit of an economic policy that was solidly probusiness.

Among all its economic policy objectives the conservative government regarded the pursuit of price stability and a satisfactory balance of payments as virtually obligatory, and its tight monetary and fiscal management implied a rejection of full-employment policies. The German neoliberalists maintained instead that such desirable goals as full employment or economic growth would result in the long run from the steadfast pursuit of internal and external monetary stability. At least as far as Germany during the 1950s and most of the 1960s is concerned it is difficult to contradict them. More mixed, however, was the neoliberalist success with regard to redistribution and social welfare which the advocates of the social market economy also accepted as economic policy objectives in their own right. The policy adopted in 1948 of giving men of action the opportunity to work for themselves in the hope that their success would also improve living conditions in general had certainly proved successful and yielded an ample supply of goods and services for private and public consumption. Nevertheless, it has been frequently asked whether the social market economy really deserves the epithet "social" (meaning "just"), given the quite pronounced inequality in wealth, the small and slow progress toward a more equal distribution of income, the rather limited diffusion of economic power, and—last but not least—the uncontrolled influence on official economic policymaking of vociferous and well-financed pressure groups and cliques. It would appear that social advancement has been lagging behind economic progress.

German economic progress in the roughly three decades after the currency reform was characterized by a tendency for growth rates to decline. In the early 1950s the annual average rate of growth amounted to almost 9 percent; the corresponding figure for the late 1970s was merely 2 percent. To put it differently: In each of the six five-year periods between 1950 and 1980 the rate of growth was 1–1.5 percent lower than in the preceding one.

This declining economic trend is in keeping with theoretical concepts of growth that suggest that in an economy characterized by an imbalance in production factors (a relatively small capital stock and a large labor supply), the correspondingly high productivity of capital will encourage extensive investment, which, in turn, will result in a steep rise of the gross national product. The broad-gauged expansion of the capital stock, however, will in time lead to a reduction in the productivity of capital and a concomitant reduction of future rates of investment, leading to a slower economic expansion. Eventually the capital stock will reach a level at which its further growth (and that of the national product) is determined by the increase of technological knowledge and of the population. Such reasoning can indeed explain the initially steep and subsequently flattened increase of the German GNP. In the late 1940s capital was relatively scarce while labor was abundant, encouraging high investment and resulting in fast economic growth. Over the years the capital stock widened while the labor force grew at a much slower rate due to the reduced influx of refugees and the declining natural population growth. Modern methods came to be used more and more, thereby closing the technological gap so that henceforth new investment would represent merely the normal increase in technological knowledge.

Superimposed on this tendency for growth to decline were fluctuations of such regularity that four complete business cycles can be detected up to the enactment of the Law for Promoting Economic Stability and Growth: 1950–1954, 1955–1958, 1959–1963, and 1964–1967. Each cycle contained an upturn phase lasting about two years, started by a more or less sudden upsurge of demand, leading to overutilization of productive capacities, rapidly rising prices and profits, and after some time, steep wage increases. As the initial flood of demand leveled off, sellers' markets increasingly gave way to buyers' markets; utilization of capacity and employment declined, and for two to three years the German economy would pass through a phase of sluggish growth, to be followed by a new demand-induced cyclical upswing.

Changes in demand were the main cause of these rhythmic fluctuations, which in each case (1950, 1955, 1959, 1964) started in the exporting industries. The pull that foreign demand exerted on the German economy did not necessarily come unexpectedly but was to a considerable extent induced. The preceding recession had not only brought a certain pressure to bear on German prices and shortened the delivery time for German products—both attractive developments for foreign customers—but German producers tended in the face of unsatisfactory domestic demand to intensify their export activities. Through multiplier processes the generally increased demand soon affected the consumer goods industries, which in their turn placed orders for additional plant and equipment. High profits, resulting from lower costs due to better utilization of capacities and the general excess of demand, provided the necessary funds for investment projects. Credits, which for a time remained at relatively low interest rates, stemming from the previous slowdown phase, also facilitated entrepreneurial expansion.

A new phase of sluggish growth began in each cycle (1952, 1957, 1962, 1965) as the consequence of decreasing demand for capital goods. In each case the initial clustering of orders for plant and equipment, their technical indivisibility, and the lengthy gestation period probably broke the investment boom. Businessmen in all likelihood abstained for a time from further capital-widening projects and curbed their demand for producer goods until they had better information on the fate of their recently enlarged capacities. Better empirical evidence is available on the restrictive monetary policy pursued by the central bank to curb inflationary tendencies once each boom got under way. The reduction of funds available from outside sources and declining possibilities for self-financing investments, due to a host of wage increases (typical for the later part of each expansion phase), resulted in shrinking demand for capital goods, particularly in 1952, 1956, and 1965–1966.

Although in all these years public authorities failed to pursue a well-thought-out countercyclical budget policy to diminish the boom by raising taxes and postponing government expenditures, there was a stabilizing effect nevertheless in 1955, 1959, and especially 1965–1966, as a result of the domestic price increases that drove down exports and boosted imports. The ensuing deflationary process in each cycle not only broke the investment boom and concomitant inflationary tendencies, thus leading to equilibrium, but usually overshot the mark by turning into a recession. In the face of declining demand, entrepreneurs tended to adopt a policy of "wait and see" by limiting further expansion of their activities. Thus, in due time their pessimistic expectations materialized. Too sharp a contraction was averted by the rather stable level of private consumption, but this stabilizing effect was insufficient to usher in an upturn. Nor did the increased demand for capital goods, due to new investment projects in response to lower interest rates, manage to do so.

In all cases it was an increased foreign demand that lifted the German economy into the recovery phase of a new cycle, since up to the mid-1960s no major fiscal policy measures were taken to stimulate the economy. This reflected partly the fact that, in the face of high growth rates of 8–10 percent during the speed-up phase, their leveling-off at 5–7 percent during the following slowdown phase was regarded as a welcome damper on excessive economic activity and a return to internal and external stability. However, when in the mid-1960s the recovery phase brought an average growth rate of merely 6 percent and contraction began to mean virtual stagnation (or even absolute decline, as in 1967, when German GNP fell by 0.2 percent), a deliberately expansionist fiscal policy had to be adopted to prevent the recession from becoming a depression.

To put federal fiscal policy on a sounder footing, the Law for Promoting Stability and Growth in the Economy was passed in June 1967. Referred to as the "Magna Charta" of modern medium-term management of the economy, the law provided the federal government with a number of new tools, some of them unique in international practice. Previously the federal government, the eleven state governments, and the approximately 25,000 municipalities had made up their budgets independently of each other. This system virtually precluded fiscal plans spanning several years as well as a combined and coherent fiscal policy. By contrast, the new law brought about a certain centralization of fiscal powers and the first steps toward planning for growth. Instead of the annual and uncoordinated budgets of the past, five-year finance plans and medium-term public investment programs became mandatory at all levels. Moreover, the federal government was required to submit an annual report outlining its economic and fiscal policy objectives for the next year within the framework of an overall five-year projection. In addition, various new instruments of economic policy were created or assumed more concrete form. This enlarged armory of cyclical and growth-policy weapons would bring about—so it was hoped and exuberantly stated—a real annual growth of 4 percent, an annual inflation rate of not more than 1 percent, an unemployment rate not surpassing 0.8 percent, and a foreign trade surplus of 1 percent of GNP. These aims were called "the magic square," suggesting that only a government endowed with magic powers could hope to succeed in bringing all four goals to fruition simultaneously and in their entirety.

In actual fact, German economic policy has been trying in vain to achieve this ever since 1967. In no single year following the passage of the Stability Law has it been possible to bring about an equilibrium in the economy as a whole, i.e., a situation in which the actual economic results managed to reach the fourfold goal. This was the case even though the targets were lowered to less ambitious levels (e.g., acceptable rates of unemployment and of inflation of 3 percent each). The four business cycles of the 1950s and 1960s were followed by three more, 1968–1971, 1972–1975, and 1976 to the present (1981). There is considerable justification for saying that the 1970s witnessed growing economic instability in Germany, which was enhanced by the worldwide economic crisis beginning in mid-1974. German economic growth has been either too fast or too slow, jumping between such extremes as 7.9 percent (1969) and minus 1.8 percent (1975). Fluctuations of the inflation rate in terms of the GNP price deflator ranged from 1.8 percent (1968) to 7.7 percent (1972), and the unemployment ratio varied from 0.7 percent (1970) to 4.7 percent (1975).

In the light of the original objectives of the Stability Law, these figures do not bespeak much success. However, gauged within the international context of a worldwide economic downswing, German progress toward greater stability looks much better. In terms of growth, full employment, and price stability as well as foreign transactions, Germany actually did well in the period 1970–1979 compared with other countries. In the Economic Olympics of the Big Six, the Federal Republic of Germany earned one gold, two silver, and one bronze medals. As it is debatable which of the four stabilization aims is the most important—a trade unionist will choose full employment, a saver price stability, and so forth—it is not possible to award a specific medal for overall performance.

A more detailed breakdown of this performance shows that in the 1970s the average annual growth rate of 3.1 percent of the gross domestic product reflected a good middle position for Germany. Japan (6.1 percent) and France (4.1 percent) grew faster; Italy (3.0 percent), the United States (2.9 percent), and Great Britain (2.4 percent) were slightly behind. Germany did even better during that decade with regard to employment. The German average of 2.5 percent unemployment was in excess of Japan's 1.7 percent but was lower than Great Britain's 3.7 percent or France's 3.8 percent and much better than the United States's 6 percent and Italy's 6.4 percent. In maintaining price stability Germany was the leader of the pack. Its average rate of inflation (5.2 percent) even outdid the solid Swiss, let alone the Americans (7.1 percent), French (9.2 percent), Japanese (9.3 percent), Italians (12.8 percent), and British (13.3 percent). Germany, along with Japan, also achieved an average annual surplus of almost $4 billion in its current account balance of foreign transactions during the 1970s. Italy broke even, while France, Great Britain, and the United States all registered an annual deficit of roughly $1 billion. A look at the whole decade, however, fails to convey the entire story since 1974—a period during which the economy of the Federal Republic has had to face the most adverse winds in its recent history.

Between 1973 and 1980, the nations of the Organization of Petroleum Exporting Countries (OPEC) raised the price of a barrel of crude oil from about $3 to more than $30. This enormous increase in the price of energy was and still is a tough test for all industrial countries. They have not dealt equally well with the resulting burden. Again, the Germans did fairly well, as between 1974 and 1980 they increased their real GNP by 19 percent per capita. This was only 1 percent less than the Japanese and 1 percent more than the French. The Americans and British limped behind, achieving only 9 percent and 6 percent respectively. Although other imported goods did not increase so drastically in price, Germany had to export more than previously and thus was forced to work more for the same amount of imports. The jargon-prone economists call this a considerable deterioration of Germany's terms of trade (1973 = 107, 1976 = 100, 1980 = 91). The layperson will derive more understanding of the situation from an example: In 1973 it was necessary to trade twelve cars—one of Germany's most important export articles—for a certain quantity of crude oil, whereas seven years later almost four times that many cars had to be given in exchange.

Since 1978, when the surplus in the balance of trade represented the second best result ever in the Federal Republic, the foreign trade situation has rapidly deteriorated. In 1979 and 1980 this surplus was less than half that of the previous year, which was insufficient to make up for the traditional deficit in the balance of services and the balance of transfer payments. In the balance-of-service transactions the rising expenditures of German tourists abroad made themselves felt, in the balance of transfer payments, Germany's contributions to Common Market finances figured prominently, as did the paychecks sent home by some 2 million foreign workers. The balance of current transactions which combines these three balances, consequently wound up with a deficit of DM 10 billion (1979) and DM 28 billion (1980) for the first time after about a decade and a half of surpluses. This development occurred in tandem with the reduction of German currency reserves from a record value of more than DM 100 billion in 1978 to just under DM 80 billion in 1980 and also with the depreciation of the deutsche mark vis-à-vis the dollar from 58 cents (January 1980) to 40 cents (August 1981).

Germans thus had to face the question whether this reversal signified the end of an era in which Germany had steadily strengthened its position in world trade: Was there any evidence that it was losing its competitiveness in export trade? The Federal Republic had to fall back upon previously earned foreign assets by having recourse to the currency reserves and to accept foreign indebtedness in the amount of the deficit in the current balance of its international transactions; also, the national debt increased rapidly from 1975 onward. All of these actions suggested the possibility that the Germans had attempted to live beyond their means. It is known from economic history that foreign indebtedness is no cause for alarm if these funds are used for investment (as in the case of the United States in the nineteenth century), but it can become a very serious matter if they are spent on excessive domestic consumption (as in Britain in several decades of the twentieth century). For the Germans then, there were no grounds for panic, but watchfulness seemed indicated.

With its per capita GNP of $13,390 in 1980, Germany held one of the top positions on the economic ladder of the West, behind only the Swiss and the Scandinavians. Its lead over the five main industrial nations was in some cases quite considerable, amounting to 10 percent or slightly more vis-à-vis France and the United States, more than 30 percent as against Great Britain and Japan, and almost 50 percent relative to Italy. It is well known that a comparison of national welfare on the basis of GNP figures can be misleading with regard to comparative levels of individual welfare. Many elements that have substantial bearing on individual well-being fail to be revealed in GNP totals. This is true, first and foremost, of the distribution of income. Among the major industrial countries in 1980, Germany paid by far the highest hourly wages in industrial employment, leading the United States by 2 percent, Great Britain, Japan, and France by 30 to 40 percent, and Italy by almost 60 percent. In respect of the employers' social insurance contributions, as required by law, and sundry fringe benefits, the Federal Republic was on top again; its subsidiary costs connected with the employment of workers were about twice as high as in the United States and more than three times as much as in Great Britain and Japan.

Yet in spite of this relatively favorable situation for the German wage-earner, the disparity between rich and poor in Germany remained quite significant. At the same time, it was less pronounced than in some other industrial countries, e.g., the United States. Among its Common Market partners, Germany alone had shown a slow drift toward greater equality in distribution of income over the years. The distribution of property in Germany was characterized by an even higher degree of inequality than was income. In the late 1970s German private property (i.e., the net market value of real estate and of productive and monetary assets) was estimated at DM 3 trillion. Out of a total of 21.6 million households almost one-fifth was indebted or had no or very little property (up to DM 5,000); almost two-fifths had some minor assets (between DM 5,000 and DM 35,000); another two-fifths had a more or less solid financial cushion (DM 35,000 to DM 500,000); and 3 percent of all households were really wealthy, owning more than DM 500,000 or a total of at least one-fifth of all property.

GNP and growth rates do not indicate how and under what conditions these economic results have been reached. Without a doubt, it is important to know to what extent the national product has been created in collaboration with or dependence on foreign countries. A country with a small external share (as in the United States with 8 percent and Japan with 13 percent in 1980) had far greater potential to control its own economic destiny than those countries with a high foreign trade dependence (France, 18 percent; Italy, 20 percent; Great Britain, 22 percent; and Germany, 23 percent). Almost one-quarter of all German jobs stemmed from export activities, a fact that made Germany dependent on the smooth functioning of world trade like no other major industrial country in the West. As the world's second largest exporter, Germany sold goods valued at $193 billion in 1980. It was outdone by the Americans by about 15 percent but was about 33 percent ahead of the Japanese and some 40 percent in front of the French and British. Germany's share in world trade of about 10 percent reflected partly its rather modest endowment of treasures of the soil and its strong dependence on imported primary energy, which accounted for about two-thirds of domestic consumption. It is not surprising that Germany consistently warns against the dangers of budding protectionism and attempts to diversify its foreign economic activities by type and region.

German exports in 1980 consisted overwhelmingly (84 percent) of finished goods, 9 percent of semifinished goods, and only 2 percent and 5 percent respectively of raw materials and foodstuffs. In chemical products and plastics, bicycles and automobiles (cars, trucks, buses), metalwares and mechanical engineering products, printing products and textiles, Germany was the world's most important exporter; in synthetic fibers, rubber and asbestos goods, fine ceramics, precision instruments and optical goods, iron and steel, coal, nonferrous metals, leather goods, and dairy products, it took second place; and in the exports of the electrical engineering, glass, and aircraft industries, third place.

It would be wrong to assume that Germany, as a highly industrialized country, imported primarily raw materials and foodstuffs and transformed them into finished articles for export. Actually, German imports in 1980 were made up of finished goods (51 percent), semifinished goods (18 percent), and only 18 percent of raw materials and 13 percent of foodstuffs. Approximately one-fifth of domestic supplies of cars, machines, wood and paper, rubber and asbestos, electrical goods, and chemical and mineral oil products and about one-third of all clothing, leather goods, shoes, and precision and optical instruments came from foreign countries. The high proportion of finished and semifinished articles among exports and imports reflected the fact that the industrialized countries trade primarily among themselves and were therefore in a position to make full use of the advantages of the international division of labor. Thus in 1980, 62 percent of German imports came from the industrialized European countries and 11 percent from industrialized overseas countries. This left only a meager 5 percent for imports from communist countries and 21 percent from the developing countries. Roughly speaking, about 10 percent of German imports came from each of such Common Market countries (in declining order of importance) as the Netherlands, France, Italy, Belgium/Luxembourg, and Great Britain; the U.S. share was 8 percent; and only about 2 to 3 percent each came from Japan, the Soviet Union, and East Germany.

The regional structure of German imports was rather similar to that of its exports since, in spite of multilaterality in the international exchange of goods and services, a certain tendency for a bilateral squaring of trade balances exists. Thus in 1980, 69 percent of German exports went to the industrialized European countries, with again roughly 10 percent each to France, the Netherlands, Italy, Belgium/Luxembourg, and Great Britain. The United States took 6 percent, and only about 2 percent each went to the Soviet Union, East Germany, and Japan. In 1980 the share of trade with Soviet-bloc countries amounted to 1 percent for the United States, around 2 percent for Japan and Great Britain, roughly 4 percent for France and Italy, and about 6 percent for Germany. Germany's role as the most important trader with the East was due to geographic proximity and traditional economic ties with East Germany, which accounted for about one-quarter of this trade. Warnings against an all-too-intensive exchange of goods with communist countries have hardly been justified as yet. However, it cannot be denied that such economic relations are susceptible to political hazards.

It is also important to know how much labor goes into a national product. In 1980 the average annual working time—measured on the basis of the metal industry, which frequently spearheads the reduction of this figure—was longest in Japan with 2,094 hours per worker, i.e., 310 hours longer than among the allegedly super-industrious Germans. Even in the land of the proverbial *dolce far niente* working hours were on average 10 percent longer than in Germany; as also in France, where, according to a German saying, one can live just like God, who had a life of ease after the Revolution forced him out of office. The relatively short working hours in Germany were not a consequence of long strikes or absenteeism due to industrial accidents. Indeed, in the 1970s Germany had a particularly good record on average annual loss of working hours caused by strikes. Only slightly more than 50 working days per 1,000 employees were lost, whereas in Japan the number was three times greater, in France four times, in Great Britain and the United States roughly ten times, and in Italy as much as thirty times. As just under 43 percent of the roughly 22 million German employees (23 percent of white-collar workers, 55 percent of blue-collar workers) were members of a trade union at the beginning of the 1970s, one cannot hold a low degree of unionization (as exists in the United States, where only one-fifth of the total labor force are union members) responsible for these limited labor disputes.

Moreover, the level of safety at work has improved greatly in the last two decades in Germany; it came off rather well in a worldwide comparison but held only a middle position among European countries. In Germany in the mid-1970s as many as 175 of 100,000 inhabitants lost their lives through industrial accidents; the corresponding figures were 193 in Italy, 289 in the United States, and 379 in Japan, but only 99 in France and 125 in Great Britain. Safety on the job is one of many factors that influence job satisfaction, e.g., wage level and wage differentials, working conditions such as noise and dirt at the place of work, regulations concerning leisure time and holidays, and opportunities offered for further training and promotion. In the mid-1970s, only 1 percent of German employees considered themselves "dissatisfied" with their occupational activity, whereas 55 percent were "satisfied" and as many as 44 percent were, in fact, "very satisfied." These figures compared favorably with those in both Great Britain and the United States—3–5 percent, 46–48 percent and 49 percent respectively. In the two Mediterranean countries and in Japan the level of satisfaction was much lower, only 25–33 percent of the employees describing themselves as "very satisfied."

It is above all the way the GNP is spent that has an important bearing upon individual welfare. Thus the state's share in the national product along with its inherited functions are of great importance. But such tangible things as one's dwelling, summer vacation, and the possession of consumer durables (a car, refrigerator, washing machine, telephone, television set, and the like) directly determine the perceptions of individuals concerning their well-being. Because of space limitations and because the indicative value of the many socioeconomic indicators regarding individual welfare is often unclear, only housing, tourism, and health in the late 1970s will be analyzed here.

A comparison of the six major Western industrial nations shows that more than two-thirds of the German population lived in apartments as against one-quarter in houses, quite the opposite of the situation in the United States. The German pattern is, however, typical of the continental style of living, in contrast to Great Britain and Japan, where detached housing is even more widespread than in the United States. Only a comparatively small number—one-third—of Germans were the owners of the premises they occupied; the remaining two-thirds paid rent. In other countries the ratio was fairly evenly balanced; only in the United States did one find a ratio of two owners to one tenant. Germans held a much higher position with regard to the size of their living quarters, just above the halfway mark, alongside the Italians and Japanese. One-third each of all Germans lived in premises with, respectively, up to three rooms, four rooms, or five or more rooms. Thus they were much better off than the French but still their situation was a far cry from the large number of rooms available to the Anglo-Saxons, who regard one's home as one's castle.

The quality of housing is affected to a great extent by the availability of electricity, running water, and central heating. Their presence depends on the age of the buildings. Older buildings may have some attractive features, but they usually have fewer physical amenities. It is rare to find houses without a toilet, bath, or shower in Anglo-Saxon countries or in Germany, where wartime damage decimated older houses. This is not so in the two Mediterranean countries and in Japan. Partly in consequence of this—by modern standards—unsatisfactory hygienic situation, one-third of all Italians and more than half of all Japanese are either rather or very dissatisfied with their dwellings; only slightly more than one-fifth of all Americans, British, and French voiced such complaints. The Germans, otherwise quite demanding people, expressed the greatest satisfaction with their living quarters. Obviously satisfaction with one's nest is a very personal thing.

Although quite satisfied at home, the Germans, as in the old tribal days, continue to be noted for their wanderlust. As Germans usually have thirty-five days of paid vacation and legal holidays annually, they were generally—in some cases considerably—better off than the other Europeans at the beginning of the 1970s. The French and Italians were entitled to thirty-two days, the British to merely twenty-five. About two-thirds of all German holidaymakers spent their vacations abroad; exactly the opposite is true in the United States. In accordance with this, Germans spent a great deal on foreign travel—$21 billion in 1980— or as much as the Americans, British, and Japanese combined. Apart from being able to enjoy ample leisure time and a high standard of living, Germans were in a position to visit the Alps and the Mediter-ranean, frequently in their own cars, due to their central location in Europe. Thus, almost two-thirds of the aforementioned sum went (in declining order of magnitude) to Italy, Austria, Switzerland, France, and Spain. Just over 5 percent went to the United States, making this the seventh most popular foreign destination of the German population. Moreover, one-quarter of all Germans, by far the largest group, expressed the desire to visit the United States.

Germany did not offer a particularly impressive health picture by 1980, although the quantitative data were somewhat mixed. An infant mortality rate of 17 per thousand of those born alive was shockingly high compared to those in Japan and France, with only 10 and 12 deaths but in line with the sad situation elsewhere (Great Britain and the United States, 16, and Italy, 21 deaths). The general life expectancy for men and women in Germany of 68 and 74 years respectively was up to 2 years below that in other European countries but quite close to the U.S. figures.

It is difficult to establish causal relationships between these figures and the general level of welfare, housing conditions, or health facilities. German medical care in particular was quite satisfactory in statistical terms. There were almost 20 doctors for every 10,000 inhabitants, whereas in France, Great Britain, and the United States there were only 15 to 16. With respect to the proportion of nurses to every 10,000 inhabitants the ranking was reversed, however, with the figure for Germany being only 37 as against 50 to 65 in the three countries just mentioned. But Germany was on top again with the number of hospital beds—85 inhabitants per bed; the corresponding figure in the other countries was around 100 or much higher.

It is, however, hardly possible to draw conclusions as to the actual state of health of the population in these countries as demonstrated, for instance, by the number of psychiatrists. In Germany there are about 20,000 persons to one psychiatrist; in the United States there are only 9,000. Does a low ratio indicate a better provision of psychiatric help for the individual, or does it show a more pronounced need for psychiatric services? The author, who spent more than a decade of his adult life in each country, would find it difficult to state whether the quality of life is superior in Germany or in the United States. Both countries, as highly industrialized economies and pluralistic societies, guarantee the pursuit of individual happiness to an extent unheard of historically. But contrary to what dictionaries say, "to be happy" and "glücklich sein" do not describe the same emotional frame of mind.

Readings

Arndt, Hans-Joachim. *West Germany, Politics of Non-Planning.* Syracuse, N.Y.: Syracuse University Press, 1966.

Hallet, Graham. *The Social Economy of West Germany.* New York: St. Martin's Press, 1973.

Hardach, Karl. *The Political Economy of Germany in the Twentieth Century.* Berkeley: University of California Press, 1980.

Stolper, Gustav, Häuser, Karl, and Borchardt, Knut. *The German Economy, 1870 to the Present.* New York: Harcourt, Brace and World, 1967.

HANS-ADOLF JACOBSEN

7

The Role of the Federal Republic of Germany in the World, 1949–1982

Maneuverability of Action and Its Determinants

An understanding of the role of the Federal Republic of Germany in Europe and the world requires comprehension of the steadily expanding geographic, political, economic, and cultural flexibility of action the country has acquired over the last thirty years as well as knowledge of the major determinants of its foreign policy decisions, including their possibilities and limitations. This requires clarification of the national interest and an understanding of the starting point in each region; the given international situation; treaty arrangements, dependencies, and involvements; the importance of weapons systems; the domestic social consensus; the many ideological factors; and the ability to give each of these factors its appropriate weight. The foreign policy of the Federal Republic of Germany has always to a large degree been the result of international politics. It has adjusted to them as it has tried to influence the international political system. The available alternatives arose from these factors and their relationship to domestic determinants.

During the years 1949–1955 the initial prerequisites for independent action in foreign policy were created. The victorious powers, however, retained certain special rights (responsibility for Germany and Berlin as a whole and, until 1968, the right to invoke emergency powers), but the reassumption of sovereignty and the return to the family of nations on May 5, 1955, was the culmination of a struggle for equality by the new German republic. It had been achieved by way of the Occupation

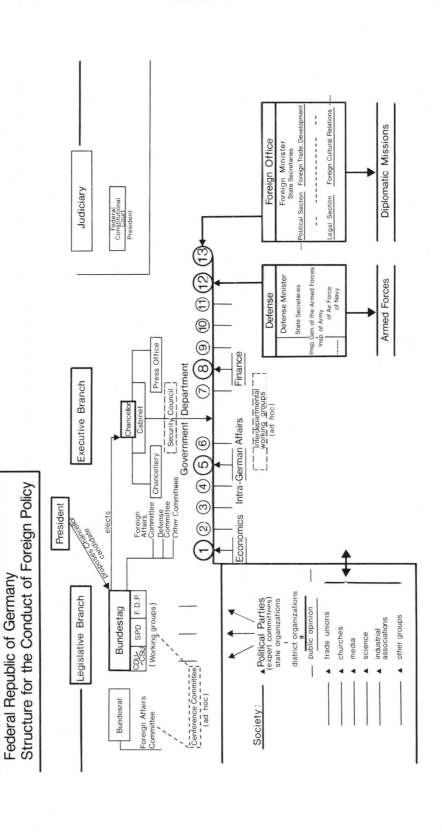

Federal Republic of Germany
Structure for the Conduct of Foreign Policy

Legislative Branch

President

Executive Branch

Judiciary

Bundesrat

Foreign Affairs
Committee

Bundestag

CDU-
CSU   SPD   F.D.P.

(Working groups)

Conference Committee
(ad hoc)

proposes candidate

Chancellor

elects

Foreign
Affairs
Committee

Defense
Committee

Other Committees

Chancellor

Chancellery

Cabinet

Press Office

Security Council

Government Department

Economics   Intra-German Affairs   Finance

Interdepartmental
working groups
(ad hoc)

① ② ③ ④ ⑤ ⑥ ⑦ ⑧ ⑨ ⑩ ⑪ ⑫ ⑬

Defense

Defense Minister
State Secretaries
Insp. Gen. of the Armed Forces
Insp. of Army   of Air Force
                 of Navy

Armed Forces

Foreign Office

Foreign Minister
State Secretaries

Political Section   Foreign Trade   Development

Legal Section   Foreign Cultural Relations

Diplomatic Missions

Federal
Constitutional
Court
President

Society:

Political Parties
(expert committees)
state organizations
|
district organizations
||
public opinion

trade unions
churches
media
science
industrial
associations
other groups

Statute, the Petersberg Agreement, the Treaties of Paris, and the so-called Contractual Agreements between the new Federal Republic and the three Western occupying powers. The Petersberg Agreement enabled the Federal Republic of Germany to resume consular relations with foreign countries. The Office for Foreign Relations in the Federal Chancellery, which had been created in 1950, undertook the administrative preparations for this step. The first Consulates General were established in London, New York, and Paris. The revised Occupation Statute of 1951 expanded the rights to conduct foreign relations. It also, at least partially, restored the right to deal in foreign currencies, and the Federal Republic accepted prewar Germany's foreign debts.

On March 15, 1951, Chancellor Konrad Adenauer added to his functions the newly created post of foreign minister and on that day created the new Foreign Office. Between then and 1955, diplomatic relations were established with numerous West European, African, Asian, and Latin American countries as well as Canada, the United States, Australia, and New Zealand. In 1952 diplomatic relations were established with Yugoslavia and in the second half of 1955 with the Soviet Union. In this manner, a German presence was established in forty-one nations of the world. In the following fifteen years Germany was able to gain access to additional countries of Africa, Latin America, and Asia and, of particular importance, in 1965 established diplomatic relations with Israel. This latter step, however, provided the Arab states with cause to break their diplomatic relations with the Federal Republic. In 1967 diplomatic relations were established with Romania, and in 1968 they were reestablished with Yugoslavia, with which the Federal Republic had broken in 1957 as a consequence of the application of the so-called Hallstein Doctrine (see p. 146).

The third phase, which provided the Federal Republic with considerably more freedom of action in foreign relations, was achieved in the 1970s. As a consequence of the new policies toward the remainder of Germany and the countries of Eastern Europe initiated under the coalition led by Willy Brandt and Walter Scheel, the Federal Republic not only became a member of the United Nations (in 1973, simultaneously with the German Democratic Republic) but was able to establish relations with the remaining communist states, including in 1972 the People's Republic of China. Seven of the Arab states also reestablished normal diplomatic relationships with Bonn. It was only in the beginning of the 1980s, therefore, that the Federal Republic was represented on a worldwide scale (in 161 states) so that it could apply its power globally, primarily through its alliances. Meanwhile it had also become a member of numerous international organizations.

Federal Republic of Germany:
Establishment of Diplomatic Relations (1949-1982)

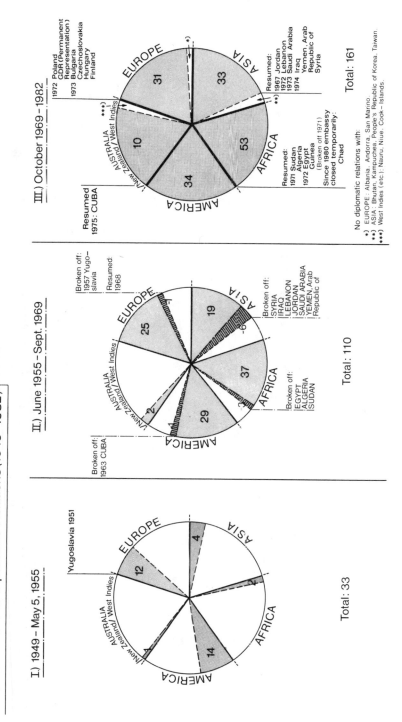

I.) 1949 – May 5, 1955

Yugoslavia 1951

EUROPE 12
ASIA 4
AFRICA 2
AMERICA 14
AUSTRALIA (New Zealand / West Indies) 1

Total: 33

II.) June 1955 – Sept. 1969

Broken off: 1957 Yugoslavia
Resumed: 1968

EUROPE 25
ASIA 19
AFRICA 37
AMERICA
AUSTRALIA (New Zealand / West Indies) 2

Broken off:
SYRIA
IRAQ
LEBANON
JORDAN
SAUDI ARABIA
YEMEN, Arab Republic of

Broken off:
EGYPT
ALGERIA
SUDAN

Broken off:
1963 CUBA

Total: 110

III.) October 1969 – 1982

1972 Poland
GDR (Permanent Representation)
Bulgaria
1973 Czechoslovakia
Hungary
Finland

EUROPE 31
ASIA 33
AFRICA 53
AMERICA 34
AUSTRALIA (New Zealand / West Indies) 10

Resumed:
*) 1967 Jordan
1972 Lebanon
1973 Saudi Arabia
1974 Iraq
Yemen, Arab Republic of
Syria

Resumed:
**) 1971 Sudan
Algeria
1972 Egypt
Guinea
(Broken off 1971)
Since 1980 embassy closed temporarily:
Chad

Resumed 1975: CUBA

Total: 161

No diplomatic relations with:

*) EUROPE: Albania, Andorra, San Marino
**) ASIA: Bhutan, Kampuchea, People's Republic of Korea, Taiwan.
***) West Indies (etc.): Nauru, Niue, Cook – Islands.

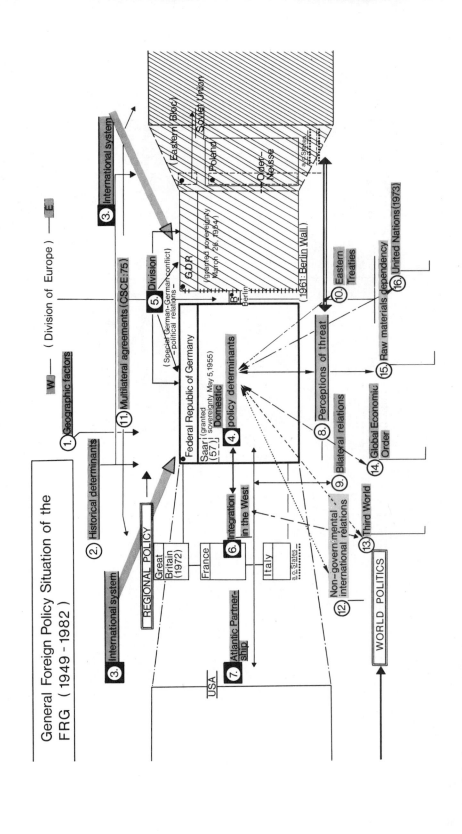

General Foreign Policy Situation of the FRG (1949 - 1982)

Beginning in 1949, the foreign policies of the Federal Republic of Germany were determined by a series of political frames of reference, which must be seen as interdependent with each other. In addition to its geographic position in the center of Europe, which persistently influences the thoughts and actions of German leaders, the primary historic determinant was and is the division of Europe, exemplified by the strongly fortified boundary of 1,381 km (829 mi) between the two German states, and Germany's immediate proximity to the area of communist control. Even very recently, Bonn government representatives justified their attitudes and statements about Poland, which were subjected to considerable criticism, by pointing out that the past German-Polish relationship had been marked by conflict and that it was not permissible to cause further suffering to the Polish people. But relations with France, the Netherlands, Israel, and the Soviet Union, to mention the most important examples, were burdened from the start by special historical mortgages, reminiscences, and the consequences of recent history. Many foreign statesmen, functionaries, and journalists frequently measured the actions and inactions of German leaders by comparing them with the policies of their predecessors.

Even under Adenauer a primary goal was to restore confidence in German policy, in its trustworthiness and its ties to the Western value system, and thereby to pave the way for Germany to reenter the community of free nations. A measure of this effort can be obtained by an examination of the restitution for the injustice done by Germans in the name of the Third Reich to other nations and to those persecuted for racial, religious, philosophical, or political reasons. The timely fulfillment of the debt agreement signed in London in 1952 between the Federal Republic, the three Western powers, and thirty other states (but not the Eastern bloc countries) strengthened the international position of the Federal Republic and its credit position. In the agreement, the Federal Republic accepted the prewar foreign debts of the Reich and Prussia as well as all private debts and trade indebtedness incurred during the years 1933–1945 (about DM 13.5 billion).

The same goal of restoring confidence in German policy pertained to the 1952 agreement between Adenauer and the prime minister of Israel, Moshe Sharett, in which the Federal Republic undertook to pay to the state of Israel DM 3 billion during the next twelve to fourteen years and to the Jewish Claims Conference, which represented Jewish refugees living outside Israel, the sum of DM 450 million. These promises were fulfilled by March 1966.

Moral appeals to Germans to view decisions of the Federal Republic against the background of National Socialist policies and to accept them for this reason were not infrequent. Social Democratic Representative

Carlo Schmid stated in this context: "National dignity also includes an acceptance of one's own history." This is particularly true of the relationship of the Federal Republic of Germany to those nations of the West that suffered during the war under the authority of the National Socialist regime. Today they are its treaty allies, but the relationship cannot escape past experience, in spite of the remarkable change in mutual attitudes. Changes in the course of foreign policy or single events in domestic policy that might be connected to past German attitudes or behavior, as well as numerous days of remembrance, repeatedly inspired open criticism centered on comparisons with the practices of the Nazi regime. On the whole, however, the honest efforts at restitution and reconciliation, the policy of integration, and common interests and values have made an important contribution to the reduction of such feelings of resentment.

In Eastern Europe, however, the barriers to any attempted normalization were much greater. This had become clear during the opening of diplomatic relations with the USSR in 1955. Foremost was the fact that these nations, especially Poland and the USSR, had been subjected to particularly great suffering by the Nazi regime and had been forced to make the greatest sacrifices. Additionally, any attempted reconciliation confronted the differences in political systems. The antagonism between East and West created its own severe limitations. Added to this was the German goal of eventual reunification, which was seen by the Eastern countries as revanchist and was therefore rejected. A breakthrough was not possible until the 1970s. It was symbolized in 1970 by the genuflection of Chancellor Willy Brandt in front of the Warsaw ghetto memorial and the resonance this act released in Eastern Europe.

It is nevertheless true that regardless of the subject—peace or war, legislation, restitution, or balance of payments—Germany's eastern neighbors have always connected these and other problems to the policies of the Third Reich. Although their own propagandistic and ideological goals, directly tied to exaggerated threats, may have played a role in shaping their attitudes, the historical residue of the Nazi regime remained a heavy burden.

German politicians, whenever an international political problem reached crisis proportions, joined in expressing the belief that no war should ever again originate on German soil. This axiom, along with many others, proves clearly the close connection between German history and German policies. This factor remains disquieting yet therapeutic for German leaders, who must always prove their perceptiveness, their responsibility, and their moderation. At the moment, past ideas of the German nation-state, whose realization in the nineteenth and twentieth centuries caused more conflict than peace, are again being subjected to sensitive review, but not very seriously. For it is clear that a strong, united Germany in the center of Europe, encompassing a population of 80 million Germans and the world's second largest industrial potential, would, under current circumstances, continue to be a nightmare for most politicians of both East and West.

Domestic Determinants of Foreign Policy

There can be no doubt that domestic policy considerations were co-determinants in the formulation of foreign policy, particularly in the relationship between means and goals. Inasmuch as the Federal Republic's integration into the West meant a decision in favor of the Western economic and value system, the Basic Law (constitution) became the basis for a comprehensive system of rules for the new, liberal-democratic state. With it came the ties to the tradition of Western constitutionalism.

The constitution is the source, limit, and guidepost for all of the state's power. The authority to conduct foreign relations, including the authority to conclude treaties and to integrate the country into larger groupings, is fundamentally a constitutional power. Foreign policy activities, like all other expressions and actions of the state, are therefore subject to the requirements, limits, and prohibitions contained in the constitution. However, in the Federal Republic of Germany, as elsewhere, the tensions between constitutional theory and reality played a major role, particularly because the self-image and world view of the power elite, the leadership style of the chancellor, specific interests, party-political or bureaucratic views, traditional or new integration ideology—in short, personal and structural variables—were all factors in the foreign policy decision-making process.

After their historical experiences and under the pressures of the occupation powers, the "fathers" of the constitution (1949) set down certain goals and guidelines (directives and prohibitions) for German foreign policy. First among these is the demand for German unity "under conditions of free self-determination." This statement was intended to express the view that the German state had not disappeared. Coupled with the specific renunciation of the use of force—underlined again in Article 26 (unconstitutionality of a war of aggression) and spelled out in the preamble for an active policy of peace—was the idea of a united Europe. The authors of the Basic Law avoided, however, deciding which of these objectives—reunification or European unity—was to have precedence.

Both government and parliament are participants in the execution of foreign policy; the executive branch takes precedence. Article 32 of the constitution regulates the division of powers between the federal government and the *Länder*. It provides that foreign relations are primarily the prerogative of the Federal Government in cooperation with the president of the Republic, who officially represents Germany in relation to other countries. The general rules of international law are an integral part of the law of the Federal Republic.

The special role of the federal chancellor set forth in Article 65 remains of key importance. The chancellor determines policy guidelines and has responsibility for them. Only within their own departments do department heads (federal ministers) direct their departments independently. Their actions may not, however, conflict with the guidelines issued by the chancellor (see p. 129).

The supreme seat of power, which may make legally valid independent decisions, is the Bundestag (parliament), which is directly elected by the people. Through statements by the government, reports on the state of the nation, discussions of foreign policy or the world situation, and question hours and resolutions, this body debates the basic issues facing state and nation—often in emotional and controversial discussions—and, when required, ratifies treaties and passes laws (e.g., laws establishing the military sovereignty of the Federal Republic of Germany). Ratification and implementing legislation were required, for example, in the case of the Schuman Plan, the Paris Treaties of 1955, and the treaties with the Soviet Union, Poland, and the German Democratic Republic (GDR). The Bundesrat (upper chamber) has a considerable voice in this process as the representative of the *Länder*, as does the Federal Constitutional Court. The latter has the responsibility for binding determination of constitutionality without regard to the value or appropriateness of the legislative act under review. Among other actions, its decision of 1973 concerning the basic agreement between the two German states provided a detailed framework for the future policy of the government concerning Germany as a whole.

The formulators of German foreign policy continue to see foreign governments as their most important partners or opponents but also relate to the representatives of international organizations and nongovernmental decision makers. This process is marked by the constant interaction of domestic and foreign policy, by a comprehensive system of communications, by the interrelationships of international economic and security communities, and by the structural interweaving of the various organizations concerned with foreign policy. Added to this are the interrelationships among numerous functional and technical interactions, the attention that must be given to the basis of domestic power (coalitions), and the development of foreign trade. In other words, German foreign policy, like that of many other states, is subject to numerous influences in its formative and decisive stages on the national as well as multinational level. These influences are hardly comparable to those of past eras either in quantity or in quality. Furthermore, it is not possible to measure the new power elite against old standards, for, in spite of some individual continuity at the beginning, the new elite's education, training, values, and realistic evaluation of the international system differ sharply from those of its predecessors.

Early on, the representatives of the Federal Republic of Germany articulated basic national interests and tied them to the constitution. These interests underwent some mutations in priorities and in their terminology. Among the foreign policy guidelines that are still valid are especially those embodying such inviolable principles as peace and freedom, restitution to victims of Nazi persecution, reunification of Germany, renunciation of force, security of life style, self-determination, and the realization of human rights. The policy of integration with the West must also be counted among these basic principles, for every federal government since 1949 has left no doubt that this principle is and will remain fundamental to West German foreign policy, particularly as its realization demonstrates new forms of political coexistence and cooperation by Germans in Europe and in the world. The neutralization of the Federal Republic of Germany—as was the case with Austria—was at no time an option of German foreign policy.

A comparison of the priorities of the foreign policy goals of the governments of Adenauer, Brandt, Schmidt, and Kohl indicates a shift in the rank order. At the beginning, the reestablishment of sovereignty and European unity, military security, the Atlantic alliance, rearmament, economic reconstruction, and reunification had priority. From 1969 to 1974, the priorities shifted to the initiation of a policy of détente and reconciliation with the East, coupled with a simultaneous strengthening of the Western alliance, a regulated coexistence with the GDR, and an intensification of multilateral cooperation in Europe. In the second half of the 1970s, increasing importance was attached to the North-South relationship and to international coordination in dealing with worldwide economic problems. At the beginning of the eighties (1982–1983), there was increased emphasis on strengthening the Western alliance, coupled with a posture reflecting undiminished awareness of the desire for the unity of Germany. Efforts to reach an accommodation with the neighbors to the east continued. These shifts are also indicative of the ability of German politicians to accept the new challenges of the international system and to deal with them appropriately.

The Concept of a Threat

As a consequence of the East-West conflict, the leadership in the two power blocs, including that of the Federal Republic of Germany, accepted the existence of a threat that, after 1945, persistently influenced their thoughts and actions. It is difficult to say whether the widely shared fear that Western Europe was threatened in its existence by Soviet communism was objectively justified. A positive reply would have to be given if it could be established that the Soviet Union intended to achieve its goals of dominance in the Western part of the European continent by military means. On the basis of their subjective evaluation of the situation, the states that joined together to form the North Atlantic Treaty Organization (NATO) took political, economic, and military defensive measures—with the voluntary acceptance of a dependence on the United States as leader of the alliance—in order to be prepared to counter any possible threat by the Soviet Union and its allies. In this they possibly failed to recognize sufficiently that their own decisions (e.g., the declared policy of "roll back") would be interpreted by the other side as endangering its "socialist" interests and the security of the Soviet Union. This was true also for the other side—with a different denominator.

An important consequence of this development was a shift of security policy to the strategy of deterrence and to crisis management. Both East and West were determined to shape their policies so as to maintain internal stability and develop a military potential incorporating technological progress, simultaneously strengthening the self-confidence of the population through the ideology of integration. As a result, any possible aggressor would resist the attainment of his goals by force because the risk of defeat would be greater than the possibility of victory.

The threat syndrome experienced in the Federal Republic was composed of a number of different factors. First, there were the remnants of anti-Bolshevik propaganda slogans of the Nazi period ("offensive anticommunism"); second, there were the personal encounters of Germans, including former prisoners of war, with communism during the war and the postwar periods of flight and expulsion. The start of the Cold War and the evaluation of Soviet policy as expansionist by both the Western powers and exiled German politicians strengthened their determination to retain their existing life style. The Soviet-communist way of exercising power in Eastern Europe, especially in the Soviet occupation zone/GDR and in East Berlin, which had led to a rapidly rising level of refugees (see p. 211), left no doubt about the alternative social policy of Stalinism. The policy of Konrad Adenauer and his followers was based from the start on a widespread concern about the dangers of Soviet communism. The numerous events in Poland (1946), Czechoslovakia (1948), Korea (1950), Hungary (1956), and the GDR (1953); pressures on Berlin in the 1940s and 1950s; the military invasion of Czechoslovakia by the Warsaw Pact countries in 1968 and of Afghanistan by the USSR in 1979; and the Polish crisis of 1981–1982 continually vindicated that policy. Added to this was Moscow's consistent propagation of the victory of communism as the standard for the world, its substantial increase in military armament, and its efforts to expand its influence in the Third World by supporting revolutionary movements.

Today, however, views of the USSR's medium-term goals are no longer uniform. On the basis of historical experience, these goals seem to combine a desire for "super-security" with the need to compensate for unmistakable domestic weaknesses and the failing attraction of communism as an ideology, and with a policy of extensive expansionism in the interest of world revolution. In evaluating the threat felt in the West, it must not be overlooked that the threat ("the cartel of fear") was maximized so that certain domestic measures (e.g., German rearmament from 1950 to 1955) could be given a firmer basis and so that the unified will of the nation could be strengthened. In the Federal Republic of Germany, undifferentiated anticommunism had notable effects as an ideology in strengthening integration with the West, in creating an immunity against communism, and in bringing about an acceptance of Western values.

Only in the course of the policy of détente in the 1960s and 1970s were the representatives of East and West able to conclude that their own security against possible threats had to include the security of the opponent. This new insight provided both opportunities and difficulties for a cooperative arms policy. The new appraisal of Soviet policy was undoubtedly also the result of domestic changes in the Soviet system and in other communist states.

Without doubt, many important national and multinational decisions made in the Federal Republic of Germany since 1949—most of them in concert with its allies—were made or declared to be defensive measures against or reactions to the policy of Soviet communism. In the 1970s, there was no doubt that new, difficult elements arose, posing a danger to its security. The oil price crisis of 1973 made clear that the Federal Republic of Germany—like other modern states with a large dependency on exports—could be as threatened by economic factors as by the arms race and its risks. The stability of a free market economy and the ability of the European Community to function are dependent more than ever on oil supply from the Arab states, which at the end of the 1970s supplied 60 percent of the Community's petroleum imports. So, too, is the economic health of the Federal Republic of Germany dependent on the efficiency of the world economy, as foreign trade constitutes a high percentage of its gross national product (see Chapter 6).

European Unification

Today, the existence of the Federal Republic without its numerous cooperative ties within Europe is hardly conceivable. These ties are without doubt the most important consequence of the two world wars. Only mutual understanding and joint action made it possible to end the deadly cycle of war and peace, victors and vanquished. In the development of the European unification process a decisive role was played by the desire of the European nations to find the best way to protect themselves against possible future conflicts, the dangers of which were made vivid by the Cold War.

The earliest forms of cooperation were agreed upon with a view to the necessary reconstruction of a Europe destroyed by war and the need to ensure common legal values of a state of law and common standards. The European Economic Council (known since 1948 as the Organization for European Economic Cooperation) served as an instrument for the elimination of import barriers and the creation of monetary convertibility; it was a decisive precondition for U.S. reconstruction assistance (Marshall Plan). The Council of Europe became the political forum of the West European states and an agent for the development of legal relationships (e.g., mutual recognition of degrees, diplomas, and courses of study) and for the observation of standards of human rights (the European Convention on Human Rights of 1950 and the European Court of Human Rights, whose decisions are recognized by all members as binding). The essential practical measures, especially the Marshall Plan, benefited the three Western occupation zones and thereby the Federal Republic of Germany after its establishment.

Soon the question arose whether the Federal Republic could participate in these European international organizations and in what manner. It appeared to be in the interest of other West European states, notably France, to be able to incorporate and make use of West Germany's industrial and economic potential, which, in spite of wartime destruction and the payment of considerable reparations immediately after capitulation, remained strong and was in the process of reconstruction. It was also clear in Western capitals that harsh conditions similar to those imposed by the Treaty of Versailles of 1919, which had created a potential for political and economic unrest in the former German Reich (and which had become one of the causes for the outbreak of World War II), should be avoided. Most were aware that the political division of Europe and of Germany in itself constituted a new and different danger.

France, and especially its foreign minister, Robert Schuman, and his adviser, Jean Monnet, deserves credit in the first instance for squaring the circle, namely, for finding a formula placing controls on the defeated enemy and simultaneously gaining German participation in the common effort of reconstruction and collective security. Just how serious and without reservation this intention was is attested to by the unquestioned historical fact that, after decades of "archenmity" between Germany and France, a process of reconciliation was initiated not only between the two governments (in the Franco-German Treaty of January 1963) but also between the German and the French people themselves—a process unique in the history of international relations. Today this relationship is one of the essential cornerstones of Western foreign policy.

Schuman and Monnet proceeded from the assumption that West German economic and industrial potential, in spite of its destruction and a large amount of dismantling due to reparations, had to be viewed as a threatening factor. They believed that it could be effectively controlled only if the corresponding potential of France and possibly of other European states could be subjected to the same controls.

This was the basic formula of the European Coal and Steel Community, established in 1951. In the process of European integration that now began, the Federal Republic of Germany was guided by the idea that it would regain its sovereignty by relinquishing certain sovereign rights and could thereby overcome the political and international isolation of the postwar period. In turn, the victorious Western powers were prepared to remove step by step the economic limitations previously imposed on Germany and to relinquish reparations. The Coal and Steel Community was composed of six countries: Germany, France, Italy, Belgium, the Netherlands, and Luxembourg. All of these states gave up their sovereignty in the area of coal and steel and transferred it to an international authority endowed with its own executive (the High Authority), which was responsible to a control organ (the Council of Ministers). A common assembly made up of representatives of national parliaments was accorded an advisory role. An autonomous body in international law had thereby been created, even though it was limited to a small area of the total economy. (One shortcoming, which burdened the process of integration for nearly two decades, was Great Britain's inability to join the community. It welcomed the creation of the Coal and Steel Community but it still believed that it had to play an autonomous role in international relations.) Since that time, European integration has been the foundation of the economic, trade, monetary, and even foreign policy of the Federal Republic of Germany.

The next step—which failed—was the attempt to find a similar solution for defense: the European Defense Community (EDC). Both the Coal and Steel Community (CSC) and the EDC were to be placed under one political umbrella—the European Political Community. The treaty, developed to its smallest detail and already signed, failed because in 1954 it could not obtain French ratification. Public opinion in that country was not prepared for so far-reaching a relinquishment of sovereignty and for such a joint exercise of new political sovereign rights with the Germans. The British position may again have played a role.

London welcomed the EDC but did not want to join it. The opportunity to form a European federation as a responsible member of the world community was now lost.

Instead, the Federal Republic of Germany was shortly afterwards accepted as a member of the Western defense alliance, NATO. To avoid possible political repercussions among West European members of the alliance, an additional political-military organization—the West European Union—consisting of the six members of the Coal and Steel Community and Great Britain was created, although it had no practical importance. This, too, showed that the process of rebuilding confidence between the former victors and vanquished was proceeding apace.

Completely aside from the defensive alliance, the members of the CSC were now faced with the question of how the process of integration could be extended to the entire economy. The answer came in the signing of the 1957 Treaty of Rome, which created the European Economic Community (EEC) and, in light of the expected use of atomic power, the European Atomic Community (EAC). The foreign ministers of the member countries elected the state secretary of the German foreign office, Professor Walter Hallstein, as the first EEC president. The EEC structure is similar to that of the CSC, with an executive branch (the Commission), a Council of Ministers, and an advisory parliament. A few years later the three existing communities—CSC, EEC, and EAC— were combined into one European Community (EC). The treaties had modified relationships among the six European member states. Although they remained sovereign internationally, they had subordinated their sovereignty to supranational principles in the economic area.

The underlying principle of the Community is the total freedom of movement of persons, goods, services, and capital. Only one area was dealt with by the EEC treaty in detail: the common agricultural market. A strongly interventionist policy protecting Europe's farmers was established. France especially, which then as now had a large rural population, was interested in such a policy. The industrial and geographic advantage (the so-called Rhine track) of the Federal Republic of Germany was in this way redressed for the more farm produce–oriented treaty partners. The Community developed one major weakness; the economic boom that lasted for nearly fifteen years, into the mid-1960s, enabled it to implement freedom of movement in the labor sector, but other measures envisaged in the treaty providing for regional economic steering were neglected. A result of this one-sided development are the different levels of industrialization in the member states and the high percentage of migrant workers who moved to the industrial centers.

It is nevertheless noteworthy that the format for West European integration has remained solid despite the absence of a political community and occasional political crises. These crises have included the departure of France from the NATO military organization, an occasional French veto of the decisions of the Council of Ministers, and different evaluations of the relationship to the Soviet Union and the GDR, as well as a lack of monetary cooperation (the present common currency system—the European Monetary System [EMS]—is not supported by all members and consists essentially of a joint floating of the European currencies in relation to the dollar). None of the Community's members can now conceive of existing without it, no matter how many difficulties the future may hold.

The European Economic Community is a creation of law—an international treaty—rather than a creation of force. The sources and structure of its lawful activities show that the Community "has in fact achieved a fusion of individual national economic policies and national economic law," which are executed not so much by national bodies as by those of the Community itself. There can be no doubt that it continues to have great functional limitations. The road to European union with a common foreign policy, a safeguarding of the security of its members, common economic relationships, and synchronized cooperation in other fields can probably be achieved only by way of a pragmatic, evolutionary policy at different speeds for different members. It could be hastened by "tangible solidarity," a permanent dynamism, and the recognition that the individual states on their own are too weak to master the international challenges of the present and near future.

A special problem is the expansion of the Community. The advantage of including Great Britain and other states (at the present time the EC consists of the six founding nations plus Great Britain, Denmark, Ireland, and Greece) is offset by the disadvantage that the more countries belong, the more difficult it is to arrive at a common policy. This is the reason for the Community's current inability to reform its agricultural policy, to arrive at a common fisheries policy, to initiate regional and social policies, to stabilize the currency system, and above all, to decide on the entry of Spain and Portugal as additional members.

Under these circumstances, it is not surprising that all attempts to "communitize" foreign policy have so far failed. The first direct elections to the European Parliament were held in 1979, but the parliament commands only marginal authority. On the other hand, there have developed methods of informal cooperation among the member states, including a regular summit meeting of the heads of state or government, as well as the Organization of European Political Cooperation, created in 1970. These steps have led to a permanent communications network of the participating foreign ministers, which demonstrated its usefulness during the Conference on Security and Cooperation in Europe (CSCE)

TABLE 1

Some Comparative Figures: The Federal Republic of Germany--
the European Community-- the United States of America

	FRG	EC	USA
Territory (in 1000 sq. km.)	249	1,529	9,363
Population	61,300,000	260,400,000	220,100,000
Population per sq. km.	247	170	24
Annual Production			
Wheat (in 1000 tons)	13,000	93,000	433,000
Milk (in 1000 tons)	24,000	108,000	56,000
Anthracite (in 1000 tons)	86,000	232,000	707,000
Refined Fuels (in 1000 tons)	34,000	206,000	463,000
Steel Ingots (in 1000 tons)	46,000	140,000	126,500
Electricity (in billions of kilowatt hours)	372	1,200	2,250
Automobiles (in 1000)	4,000	10,000	8,500
Imports (in billion $)	127	480	174
Exports (in billion $)	314	1,051	333
Gold and Foreign Exchange Reserves (in billion $)	35	166	15
GNP (in billion $)	600	2,000	2,300
GNP per population ($)	10,000	7,700	10,700

Source: German Federal Statistical Yearbook, 1979.

negotiations and in such delicate questions as the crisis in the Near East and the relationship to Poland and the Soviet Union.

All efforts to provide the Community with a uniform currency have, however, resulted in failure. There could be a solid basis for such a step in the common budget of $25 billion, which equals about 1 percent of the total value-added tax of all the member states. Failure in this area represents a considerable hurdle because, when viewed in light of the worldwide economic crisis and the rise in energy costs, the results of the delays of earlier years have become increasingly clear. Regional distortions in Italy and Great Britain, which cannot be financially overcome at this time, are a burden on the Community and tend to lead to increasing imbalance between the rising costs of the common agricultural policy and the lack of resources for an efficient regional and social policy. This problem is of particular concern during a period of increased unemployment—the Community average has already risen above 12 percent. The reform of the agricultural and financial policies of the Community has, therefore, for years been the main area of contention among the members, especially between the Federal Republic of Germany, which has become a net contributor to the Community's budget, and Great Britain, which can no longer meet its payment obligations (see p. 121).

Policies Toward Other Parts of Germany and Toward Eastern Europe

It has been claimed, probably rightly, that German foreign policy until the mid-1960s was devoted above all to reunification, resulting in many years of limited flexibility. Since 1949, government and parliament have consistently concentrated their efforts on finding ways and means to overcome the division of Germany, and thereby of Europe, which they considered unnatural and dangerous. They believed that such a solution would further the interests of the nation and of peace. Debates on the subject, which were in part emotional and controversial, were carried on in bilateral and multilateral conferences and discussions, accompanied by all kinds of activities for and against specific suggestions and alternatives (including those of the opposition Social Democrats). Such suggestions were discussed, criticized, rejected, changed, and newly conceptualized without, however, coming any closer to the desired goals. On the contrary; the solidification of the positions in East and West on the German question (unification, eastern boundaries, security of Berlin) became more and more apparent, as did the West German principle of placing "freedom before unity."

In those years of the Cold War it is probable that no real opportunity was missed to reestablish the unity of Germany; indeed, it would hardly have been possible to achieve it under the terms inherent in the ideas of Western democracy, given the *fait accompli* established by the victorious powers between 1945 and 1949. Furthermore the division of Europe and the consequent balance of power established during the course of the East-West conflict became an essential basis for European security, implying mutual respect of the interests of the two power blocs and of the respective leadership roles of Moscow and Washington.

The various German federal governments did, however, for a long period (and in concert with their Western allies) support hopes for a revision of the political realities resulting from World War II even though they maintained one basic principle: the renunciation of force. There was, therefore, no policy of revenge comparable to that of previous eras. Germany's dedication to a policy of peace (which the expellees, too, had stressed in their charter of 1950) was not solely the result of political impotence but also of the insight gained from experience that war could no longer be viewed as the extension of policy by other means; it was rather a declaration of policy bankruptcy, conjuring up its own decline. Free elections as an expression of the right of self-determination were the method favored by all the parties in the Federal Republic of Germany. A model for such a peaceful method of resolving conflicts and simultaneously securing the national interest was the inclusion of the Saar in the Federal Republic of Germany on January 1, 1957, following a free referendum by the voters.

While the reconstruction of and reentry into the world economy by the Federal Republic of Germany took place with the assistance of its social market economy (a free market economy modified by measures of social justice), integration with the West and reunification in peace and freedom remained the declared main themes of Adenauer's foreign policy. This also meant the maintenance of the demand for the sole right to represent Germany abroad and a resolution in a peace treaty of the territorial question in the east (the Oder-Neisse Line boundary). The most important diplomatic instrument for this purpose was the so-called Hallstein Doctrine, that is, the basic decision of 1955 that the recognition of the GDR by third countries would be regarded as an "unfriendly act" and would cause an appropriate response (including a break in diplomatic relations, as happened for the first time in 1957 in the case of Yugoslavia). Everything was designed not to sanction the de facto division of Germany. German cultural policy and development assistance were included among the resources available to the Hallstein Doctrine.

In the Adenauer era, the so-called third pillar of German foreign policy, that is, foreign cultural policy, served primarily to present German civilization, the great traditions of the German intellect and humane spirit, as well as to expand Germany's cultural presence abroad. It was simultaneously used as an instrument of all-German policy, in this case to support the nonrecognition of the GDR, and as part of the anti-communist strategy. Beginning in 1969, the new federal government expanded its definition of culture in an effort to show to other peoples, in addition to the "permanent achievements of the past," an image of the intellectual debate and stimulating tension that had become daily reality in this transition period. Cultural policy was no longer limited to the export of culture; it was also an opportunity for and a method of strengthening cultural interaction by states and societies. It now became important to develop models for such interaction in order to avoid isolation and national arrogance.

The Hallstein Doctrine was intended to have an effect on the neutral states and on developing countries with neutralist tendencies. It was initially successful because these new nations were, as a rule, interested in receiving economic assistance from the Federal Republic of Germany. Such assistance was generally tied to the condition of nonrecognition of the GDR. It was easier to succeed in this policy at a time when the nations of the Third World were to be persuaded by capital investment and the stimulation of business initiatives to adopt a free market economy along Western lines. But in the 1960s a reorientation took place in which the reduction of social differences between North and South became a priority, in which development policy was increasingly seen as the domestic policy of the world. In this atmosphere, the Hallstein Doctrine could no longer be applied because it became a decreasingly useful way to enforce the demand that the Federal Republic of Germany be recognized as the sole representative of Germany or to prevent the consolidation and growing international stature of the GDR.

The relationship of the Federal Republic of Germany to the countries of Eastern Europe has been marked since 1949 by a number of determining factors whose importance underwent some changes in the course of the ensuing three decades. In addition to the burdens of history, the East-West conflict, the division of Germany, and the antagonism between the systems made any balancing of interests very difficult. In light of the threats of force and ideology of Soviet communism, only "unity and solidarity of the free nations of the world," as well as an Atlantic pact could, in Adenauer's view, guarantee the security and freedom of the Western nations. Although the Federal Republic opened diplomatic relations with the Soviet Union in September 1955 in order to participate in a dialogue with the fourth victorious power and to influence its decisions, this same objective was not pursued with regard to other communist countries.

Adenauer, who on the basis of his "Potsdam complex" (i.e., fear of agreement among the four powers without German participation) was afraid that Germany might again find itself between two millstones and might suffer renewed isolation, and who also had visions of an anti-German coalition, soon had to recognize that Moscow would not accept reunification with the promise of either a neutralized GDR or indeed of a neutralized, reunified Germany. For some time he hoped to be able to persuade the Soviet leadership to permit some liberalization in the GDR and gain Soviet acceptance of the status quo for a limited period. But this was not a serious alternative for the Soviet Union, especially as it considered, beginning in the mid-1950s, that the existence of two German states with different social systems had become a reality. Even the policy of strength as an anticommunist strategy could not change this attitude. As a result, Bonn's relations with Eastern Europe, particularly as seen against the backdrop of the special conflict between West and East Germany, became more than ambivalent.

At the same time German-Polish relations, quite apart from the burden of their history, were afflicted with the question of the disputed border (Oder-Neisse Line). The West German leadership maintained, on the basis of its interpretation of the Potsdam Agreement, that Poland did not yet have final possession of the former German territories and that the Oder-Neisse Line had not been recognized as a de jure boundary in international law. The Polish government, however, never left any doubt as to its fundamental position. As far as it was concerned, the border question had been solved forever in 1945. When in 1955 Warsaw expressed interest in opening diplomatic relations with the Federal Republic of Germany without preconditions, this overture was rejected by Bonn under some pressure from expellee organizations. Because of Poland's recognition of the GDR, FRG relations with Poland would have violated the Hallstein Doctrine.

The real dilemma of German policy under Adenauer was that neither the government nor the Social Democratic opposition could devise a realistic way to pursue simultaneously integration with the West and reunification, or rather a way in which one would not exclude the other. Perhaps Adenauer, supported in a major way by his American friends, thought then that the unity of Germany might be enforced. If this was the case it proved to be a major illusion and a fundamental misreading of Soviet-communist interests. The "policy of strength" had failed, certainly when the Wall was constructed in 1961 and barbed wire and mine fields marked the zonal boundary—an unmistakable symbol of the division of Germany.

New impulses for the all-German and Eastern European policy came from several sources: from the decision of the Bundestag of June 14, 1961, to improve the relations of the Federal Republic of Germany with the countries of Eastern Europe without jeopardizing the vital interests of the nation; from the appointment of Gerhard Schroeder to the post of foreign minister in November 1961; and from the July 1963 speech of Egon Bahr, one of the closest collaborators of the then mayor of Berlin, Willy Brandt, in which he recommended "change through rapprochement." Schroeder introduced the so-called policy of movement in 1962 in which he stated it to be the task of the Federal Republic of Germany to build bridges to the East without, however, giving up its claim to exclusive representation. The most visible success of this policy was the establishment of trade missions, first in September 1963 in Warsaw, then in 1964 in Romania and Hungary, and finally in Bulgaria.

This new orientation was tied on the one hand to the changes in the international system and the need of the Federal Government to keep in step with them and on the other hand to domestic changes in the Soviet Union that gave rise to a changed evaluation of Soviet communism. A decisive addition to these factors was the change in awareness among the people of the Federal Republic of Germany. Monolithic antipathies began to soften. The basic questions of all-German policy and European security were discussed and led to controversies outside the government and parliament. It was a time of appeals and petitions that slowly caused some rethinking and fostered the recognition that those who seriously desire peace must be willing to make some sacrifices for it. Even among the members of the expellee organizations, who for years had suffered from blindness to reality and had hardly progressed beyond an isolated projection of themselves as the bearers of East German culture, there were many individual expressions of willingness to relinquish the right to return to the old homestead—and old pictures grew paler.

Further noteworthy steps were taken by the grand coalition in the mid-1960s. The Kiesinger-Brandt government (1966–1969) sought direct contact with the states of Eastern Europe. A signal of this desire was the establishment of diplomatic relations with Romania in 1967 and their resumption with Yugoslavia in 1968. In both cases the German politicians avoided confrontation with the Hallstein Doctrine by developing the theory of "birth defects." According to this theory, in the 1950s the East European states, because of their dependence on Moscow, had had no choice but to recognize the GDR; thus they could not be treated like those countries that did have a choice in the matter.

Contrary to the policy of the Erhard government (October 1963–November 1966), which was still marked by a strategy of isolating the GDR, Kiesinger and Brandt tried to include the GDR in their détente efforts. Thus, Chancellor Kiesinger in his government statement of December 12, 1966, renewed the offer previously contained in his "peace note" of March 1966 to exchange mutual declarations of renunciation of force with the communist states. He avoided the previous practice of not taking official cognizance of the GDR as a state and of speaking of its incorporation into the Federal Republic of Germany. He sought to arrive at a regulated coexistence of the two German states, without, however, recognizing the other German state under international law. But he left no doubt that the borders of a reunified Germany could be settled only in a freely negotiated agreement with an all-German government, which itself would create the conditions for a permanent and peaceful relationship with its neighbors.

But these and similar statements continued to demonstrate the inability of the German leadership to adapt the foreign policy of the Federal Republic of Germany to the changed political conditions in Europe. The internal contradiction continued to be evident. On the one hand the federal government was to document its readiness to accept the European status quo; on the other hand it sought to exclude from the status quo such controversial subjects as the claim to recognition of the Federal Republic as the sole representative of Germany, the Oder-Neisse boundary, the a priori invalidity of the Munich Agreement with respect to Germany's relationship to Czechoslovakia, and of course, the nuclear option.

Nevertheless, the grand coalition government had taken the initiative in the post-Adenauer era and created the foundation for a new all-German policy and a new policy toward the East. The change in government to the new Social Democratic–Liberal coalition in 1969 (the Brandt-Scheel government) proved to be the turning point in the policy toward Eastern Europe. The new government's bilateral, and later multilateral, policy proceeded from the newly accepted assumption that the division of Germany would continue for the foreseeable future. This did not mean, however, that it relinquished the long-term goal of the right of self-determination by all Germans. The immediate goal, however, had to be a way to hold the nation together by arriving at a modus vivendi with the GDR and a strategy of mutually interdependent concessions that would improve personal contacts and thereby make the division more bearable.

Although Bonn now took into consideration the political reality of the existence of a second German state, it continued to reject recognition of the GDR under international law because of its own constitutional limitations. A special relationship had to continue to exist; the GDR could not be a foreign country. The security of West Berlin was indissolubly tied to that special relationship. This portion of the former capital of the Reich, a thorn in the side of the GDR and repeatedly at the center of international crises in the late 1940s and 1950s, was to confirm its close ties to the Federal Republic of Germany and to be represented abroad by it. The umbrella agreement signed by the Four Powers on September 3, 1971, regulated the most troublesome questions, even though the interpretation of the agreement has in practice led to tensions on both sides and to mutual recriminations. The transit agreement was to improve travel to and from Berlin, and the basic agreement of December 21, 1972, between the two German states finally established a basis for good neighborly relations on the basis of equality of status.

In its "letter on German unity" addressed to the USSR and GDR, the federal government again expressed its view that the agreement was not in conflict with the political goal of the Federal Republic of Germany "to work for conditions of peace in Europe in which the German people could regain their unity in free self-determination."

The new government was able to continue at the point where new policy considerations toward Eastern Europe had abruptly stopped because of the invasion of Czechoslovakia by the Warsaw Pact forces in August 1968. The government statement of 1969 was clear: The policy of détente was to be continued and previous policies were to be altered with regard to German-German relations, with regard to the Soviet Union, and with regard to Poland and Czechoslovakia. After the signature of the atomic test ban treaty, negotiations were to be initiated with Moscow about a mutual renunciation of force. Bonn hoped thereby to achieve not only a significant improvement in the climate of bilateral relations but also a renunciation of the right of the Soviet Union to intervene in Germany, which is anchored in the UN Charter. Additionally, Bonn expected an official declaration by Moscow, which it considered important both politically and psychologically, that the Federal Republic of Germany was not engaged in "a policy of revisionism and revenge." With regard to Poland, the Federal Republic was prepared to conclude a bilateral border agreement, as had been suggested by the first secretary of the Polish Communist party, Wladyslaw Gomulka, in the spring of 1969, without prejudice to a final settlement in a peace treaty. It was expected that Warsaw would in return recognize the principle of the unity of the German nation.

The first breakthrough of this new policy came with the signing of the treaty with the Soviet Union on August 12, 1970. At its core was the renunciation of force and the recognition of the inviolability of existing borders. With this policy, the basis for the normalization of bilateral relations had been established. But in no way did it imply that Germany would act as an intermediary between East and West. For the representatives of the Bonn government left no doubt about their solid ties to the Western alliance as a precondition of any expanded German role in Eastern Europe, just as they left no doubt about the right of self-determination of the German people. The policy of balance of interests that was given expression in this treaty was also pursued with respect to Poland. The treaty signed in Warsaw on December 7, 1970, was a turning point in German-Polish relations. It constituted the first instance of a voluntary, mutual, and internationally recognized boundary settlement in the history of these two nations. In this agreement, the Federal Republic of Germany recognized Poland's western boundary as legally binding even as its final acceptance under international law was made subject to a peace treaty. This agreement has correctly been termed the closing line of a history of suffering and sacrifice in which nothing was surrendered that Germany had not forfeited long ago, but which did not take the place of a formal peace treaty and did not abrogate the rights and responsibilities of the Four Powers for Germany and Berlin as a whole.

The Social Democratic–Liberal coalition saw these two agreements as important contributions to the policy of peace of the 1970s, as a catalyst for the improvement of German-German relations, and as a real possibility for the expansion of the Federal Republic's area of foreign policy activity. In succeeding agreements, which in addition to questions related to Berlin and the GDR also resolved the differences with Czechoslovakia about the Munich Agreement of 1938, the preconditions were created for the assumption of diplomatic relations with the remaining communist states (see p. 214). After the mid-1970s, the role of the Federal Republic in Eastern Europe also underwent some changes. Bonn increasingly became an indispensable discussion partner, highly regarded because of its importance in Europe. By its expressed desire for a policy of détente, it began to modify the image of Germans even in this part of the continent.

At the end of ten years, the process of reconciliation with the nations of Eastern Europe initiated by this policy was, on balance, far from fulfilling all earlier hopes and expectations. On the one hand this was the result of the continued existence of antipathy, the ties to antagonistic blocs, and the difficulties of regulating political and economic questions; on the other hand it was the result of the global situation. The crises in world politics increasingly influenced the East-West relationship. In spite of this, there has been a multiplication of multilateral relationships, a lessening of certain tensions, and a gradual reduction of mutual prejudices.

The compromise agreements achieved between Chancellor Schmidt and Polish party chief Edward Gierek in the summer of 1975, after long, eventful, and arduous negotiations, covered questions of credit, pensions, and resettlement as well as material restitution to the People's Republic of Poland. They demonstrated the determination of the two governments to continue the process of normalization while safeguarding their own rights and interests. The conditions then negotiated (repayment of a credit of DM 1 billion) and the resettlement of an additional 120,000 German nationals were fulfilled by the early 1980s, despite mutual accusations and recriminations. Thus, Warsaw constantly criticized the German government for failing in its domestic legislation to abide by the letter and spirit of the agreement of 1970. Additionally, certain politicians and functionaries of the Federal Republic continue to support the controversial "right to the homeland" policy by which they refer to former German territories in the East.

There is no controversy about the right to ties with the old homeland, even if it is understandably somewhat transfigured among many older people. There is also no controversy about the formal legal situation, based on the constitution, that only an all-German government can make the final decision concerning this chapter of German history. But the power of the de facto situation long ago created realities that in the interest of peace and reconciliation have to be emotionally accepted even by those who were once directly affected by the process. There is, for one, the undeniable fact that these men and women were long ago firmly integrated into West German society and have made their new home here; their children are hardly capable of dealing with the old terms and ideas. There is, for another, the fact that the former German eastern territories have since 1945 been settled by Poles (mostly people resettled from eastern Poland) and that these Poles have also had children. As early as 1960, these new settlers accounted for 47.5 percent of the Polish inhabitants of these areas. Today's figures speak for themselves. Particularly after the resettlement of many former Germans from what is now Poland to the Federal Republic of Germany (in the 1970s alone these amounted to nearly 200,000) there remains only a very small minority of people of German ancestry in Poland for whom the right to apply for resettlement must continue to exist.

Third, and most important: All German governments, and the organizations of expellees, have renounced force as a method of executing policies. In establishing the priorities of ensuring peace the following principle must be accepted: the right of former refugees, expellees, and resettled persons to a home in the Federal Republic of Germany, that is, in a free state established under law. In the former German eastern territories this right belongs to those Poles who have settled there or were born there—there are already two generations of them.

In all these years an unmistakable change took place in the Germans' view of themselves. It was propelled by economic prosperity, progress in West European integration, and efforts at worldwide détente. Opinion polls, public discussions, and media reports make clear that for the majority of the citizens of the Federal Republic the basic values of their governmental and societal structure, anchored in the constitution, have assumed a much higher value than that of belonging to a unified German nation. There are many indications that a uniform awareness of nationhood has been replaced in both German states by increased individual identity. The evidence of this process has also become clear through a weakened interest in reunification, which has declined steadily since the 1960s. Early in the 1980s, 60 percent of those polled believed that the

Germans in the two states no longer constituted a single nation. In other words, the erosion of a national consciousness appears to have moved more quickly than the numerous statements of politicians and organization representatives would lead one to believe. On one essential point, however, there is a consensus: The call for the maintenance of unity will have validity as long as there is alive a political will testifying to the feeling of the inseparability of the Germans.

Military Power

The role of Germany in the nineteenth and twentieth centuries has, understandably, been tied to that of its armed forces or to what in certain specific instances became known as German militarism and imperialism. It was, after all, the armies of Prussia and Germany that by their armed might forced the unification of the Reich, that spread fear and terror on the battlefields of Europe and Africa, at sea and in the air, but whose efficiency also caused unconcealed admiration. With their help the German leadership twice sought to achieve for Germany a position as a world power.

In 1939 the German armed forces were among the most effective and strongest in the world. On the basis of their tradition, training, management, and the principle of "unquestioned obedience" to Hitler, they had developed into an active force assisting the National Socialist leaders in the fulfillment of their goals; the latter had viewed war as a legitimate means of executing their policies and had wanted to dominate the European continent. This goal must be viewed as one of the decisive causes of the permanent unrest in the world today.

Following the unconditional surrender of the German armed forces and the destruction of Germany's military potential, numerous war crimes trials revealed the guilt and misfortune of the German military, even though the extent of its involvement, its participation in murderous acts in the occupied territories, and the opposition of individual groups of officers was uncovered only in later years in the course of international research. A heavy burden of history remained, constantly giving renewed impetus to an unmistakable renunciation of the program and methods of National Socialism and to a drive for an acceptance of the changed attitude of the German soldier, in the center of whose role now stood the *duty to maintain the peace.*

The summary convictions of German soldiers at the end of the war were, of course, not convincing. But they were a particularly heavy burden on those in the armed forces who had themselves suffered for a number of years, had borne privations, and had considered their assignment to the front as a "moral obligation." After 1945 these people found themselves defamed in an all-inclusive way as "militarists" or "tools of the National Socialists," condemned, and initially economically disadvantaged. In the course of the East-West conflict, the Western powers, in their search for security—initially out of concern about a possible resurrection of Germany as a major military power but gradually more and more out of fear of Soviet expansionism—urged the Germans also to contribute to the defense of the free world. It then became clear that because of the experiences of the immediate past, of the division of Germany and of the bipolar world, the population of the Federal Republic was deeply divided over the existential question of a military contribution. From 1950 to 1955 a slow change of attitudes took place as a result of the achievements of the economic recovery, the successful policy of integration with the West, and the increased assumption that a threat existed.

At the beginning of the public debate on this issue, an attitude of rejection was dominant; there was, in any case, a desire for disassociation from anything military. Gradually requirements of security policy became tolerated and acknowledged because there appeared to be no realistic alternative. Although the number of West Germans who favored partial acceptance of a military contribution increased, the overall attitude remained ambivalent. The proportion of undecided hovered around 20 percent. The lack of support for any rearmament was not, as Adenauer would have it in an oversimplified way, due to the opposition of the Communists, Social Democrats, and many of the media, but because it represented a widespread basic attitude on the part of the Germans and a real crisis of conscience.

The decision to rearm the Federal Republic of Germany was doubtless a consequence of the Cold War. As it developed, the majority of the population began to identify with this policy and with Adenauer's achievements. The election returns of 1957 were conclusive proof: The CDU/CSU was for the first time able to obtain more than 50 percent of the seats in the Bundestag. Later Adenauer correctly pointed to this success and its steadfastness as a basis for confidence in Germany. In fairness it must be added that this process was traceable to the "cartel of fear" of communism that had been created.

After the failure of the plan to create a European Defense Community, the Federal Republic was quickly accepted on May 9, 1955, as the fifteenth member of NATO, which had been founded in 1949. The essential basis for the reconstruction of a new German military force is contained in the defense legislation passed by the second Bundestag, by which the armed forces were structurally tied into the constitutional system of the democratic state.

The primary objectives of the policy, to provide parliamentary controls over the selection process for the higher-ranking members of the officer corps in the interest of democracy, were ensured through this legislation without appreciably reducing the efficiency of the military force. With the proclamation of the law on July 21, 1957, the principle of universal military service for males between the ages of 18 and 45 was established. Initially this service was for twelve months, beginning in 1961 for eighteen months, and since 1972 for fifteen months. The constitution (Article 4, Clause 3) also ensured the right of conscientious objection to protect those who refuse military service involving the use of weapons. The new armed force was called the Bundeswehr (federal defense force) as a clear expression of the fact that it was a creation of the Federal Republic of Germany and dedicated only to defense.

Since the 1950s, the Bundeswehr has had a clearly defined task: to ensure the inviolability of the territory and the Federal Republic of Germany's freedom to develop therein. In periods of relative political calm, its assignment is to preserve peace in Europe as a part of the multinational security community by possessing an effective potential to enforce sanctions; in periods of political tension, its task is to contribute to crisis control and, in case of enemy aggression, to display its determination to assert itself as a military defense force. In the latter case, the only aim can be to restore the status quo ante. The soldiers of the Bundeswehr are aware of the paradox of a military existence that requires preparation for conflict without desiring its realization. Additionally, the Bundeswehr can, should the government so decide, be used domestically if the police and federal border patrol forces are unable to quell conditions approaching civil war.

The organizational structure of the Bundeswehr was completed in several steps. In 1956, army, navy, and air force totaled barely 56,000; in 1965 they had reached a total of 440,000. Ten years after the start of rearmament, the Bundeswehr had essentially achieved the strengths established for it. At that time seven armored infantry divisions, three armored divisions, one mountain division, one paratroop division, fourteen air force squadrons, six air defense rocket battalions, and fourteen floating or flying naval squadrons had been placed under NATO command. At the start of the 1980s the strength of the Bundeswehr was just short of 500,000, including 45,000 officers. Of this force, 45 percent had been selected under universal military service. The force commanded nearly 5,000 tanks, 450 fighter aircraft, and 60 rocket air defense units. In case of war, an additional 700,000 soldiers can be mobilized within three days. So far, more than 2 million reservists have been trained. The Bundeswehr also employs approximately 180,000 civilians.

TABLE 2

The Most Important Sources of Weapons for Third World Countries
(1971-1980)

Country	Total	Approx. Percentage
USA	$26,191 (Mill)	38%
USSR	$22,443 (Mill)	32.5%
France	$ 7,513 (Mill)	11%
UK	$ 4,639 (Mill)	7%
Italy	$ 2,258 (Mill)	3%
Fed. Rep. of Germany	$ 1,093 (Mill)	1.5%
China (PR)	$ 830 (Mill)	1%
Netherlands	$ 669 (Mill)	1%
Other Third World Countries	$ 1,961 (Mill)	3%

Source: International Peace Research Institute, Stockholm, 1981.

The strength of the Bundeswehr is in its conventional strike force. It does not possess any nuclear weapons because the Federal Republic declined the production of atomic weaponry. The leadership of the armed forces has, however, since the mid-1960s participated in NATO's nuclear planning group so that specific German interests would be safeguarded. The percentage of defense expenditures rose as part of the total budget of the Federal Republic from 12.2 percent (DM 6.3 billion) in 1956 to 33.3 percent (DM 19 billion) in 1963 but fell in the second half of the 1960s to below 30 percent. With a 1982 federal budget of DM 240 billion, the defense budget has been set at DM 43.8 billion, i.e., at 18.2 percent. This amounts to about 3.3 percent of GNP. The Federal Republic of Germany, therefore, provides the second highest amount of defense expenditures in the alliance, surpassed only by the United States. The continuing rate of increase in real terms during the period 1970 to 1981 rose from 2.6 percent to 3.4 percent annually. Added to this should be defense assistance to Turkey, Greece, and Portugal since 1964 of more than DM 3 billion. The Federal Republic of Germany has always set strict limitations on the export of arms. These have amounted to less than 0.4 percent of total exports. The largest share of these exports went to NATO countries and only 0.14 percent to the Third World, primarily in the form of ships. In thirty countries—mostly in Africa—the Federal Republic of Germany provides training assistance in such fields as medicine, transportation, and tele- communications without tying any political demands to it, which has contributed materially to the value attached to this assistance by the receiving countries.

Concurrent with the establishment of the Bundeswehr as an orga- nization and structure, a struggle took place within the armed forces over the creation of an internal leadership that could ensure a democratic basis. This was established as part of the total military leadership responsibility with the goal of educating soldiers as "citizens in uniform." As such, the soldiers of the Bundeswehr were to differ from those of previous German military forces by their active commitment to peace, freedom, and democracy. Central to this concept of internal guidance were a series of demands, among them a command system related to contemporary democratic norms, the maintenance of the soldier's political status as a citizen of the republic, and his education to thoughtful sharing of responsibility. This educational process was designed to create a better understanding not only of the role of the soldier's immediate military station within state, society, and environment but also of the value of the defense of the Federal Republic of Germany itself. Special measures of care and welfare for the soldier were to ease his later transition into civilian life.

Of course these measures could provide only a general framework for military behavior. In practice the achievement of these new goals met numerous difficulties, particularly because certain former military traditions appeared to conflict with them. No matter how the internal leadership of the Bundeswehr and its efficiency is evaluated, it can hardly be doubted that in principle the new role has been accepted. Supervisory personnel of all grades, of whom few today are former members of the Wehrmacht (the armed forces of Germany between 1935 and 1945), in general unconditionally identify with democratic norms. This does not preclude the fact that some of them find it difficult to muster understanding for the growing criticism voiced by different social groups of the purpose of defense, of the Bundeswehr, and of NATO.

In contrast to its predecessors, the Bundeswehr is not an instrument of power in the classic meaning of that term in previous eras. Its task is purely defensive. From the beginning it has made its contribution to the joint defense of peace in Europe, but it has also shown in several nonmilitary assignments (e.g., in Agadir in 1960 and during the natural catastrophe in Italy in 1980–1981, when 1,700 men were brought into action) to what extent change has taken place in the self-awareness of the German soldier.

There can be no doubt that the significance of the most important conventional military force in Western Europe has increased, particularly because it is supported by a sizable economic potential and by modern technology. This is also clear from various quantitative data and the assumption of greater defense burdens and greater responsibilities in NATO councils (in the early 1980s more than 700 German officers were assigned to NATO staff positions) as well as by the furnishing of an increased share of actual NATO forces in Central Europe (not counting the special role of France). At the beginning of the 1980s, the Federal Republic of Germany furnished 50 percent of the ground forces, 50 percent of the ground-based air defense forces, 30 percent of the fighter aircraft, 70 percent of the naval forces in the Baltic, and 100 percent of the naval air forces in that sea.

The military power of the Federal Republic of Germany is part of the NATO alliance. The basis and guarantee of its security was and is the tie to the Western security alliance. Only as a member of this group has it been able to extend its influence regionally as well as on a worldwide basis. In light of the East-West demarcation line in Central Europe, the Federal Republic has probably become the most important European pillar of U.S. policy and one of the most decisive factors in the balance of conventional forces between the two power blocs. Unforeseeable consequences would, therefore, result should Germany leave the alliance, and confidence in its trustworthiness, its reliability as an ally, and its accountability would be seriously reduced to its own detriment.

Germany's higher dependency on exports, highly developed level of industry in a small area, above-average population density, and long, open border with the states of the Warsaw Pact (which subjects a maximum area of the country to possible destruction) have caused German military leaders to direct their planning toward a strategy of a believable deterrent (making an attack an incalculably high risk) and of a so-called forward defense. At the same time, they have decisively rejected any deployment of the German armed forces outside the NATO area and in return have sought an improved division of assignments among the pact partners.

An examination of the current role of the German military force requires a look at the morale, condition of training, and motivation of the soldiers as well as the attitude of the West German population toward the Bundeswehr and its task. Despite official statements about the high degree of preparedness of the Bundeswehr, preparedness is in fact very difficult to assess. The Bundeswehr is a mirror image of German society. Polls have established that more than 70 percent of the citizens consider the Bundeswehr important or very important, but this support is much lower among young people, especially those with higher education. The number of conscientious objectors—which rose from 2,500 in 1958 to nearly 70,000 in 1977 and was 58,000 in 1981— and the behavior and frequent appeals of heterogeneous peace movements and other societal groups show that there has also been a lessening in the dedication to self-defense, especially among those subject to military service. The purpose, possibility, and limitation of defense are often subjects of controversy, particularly in view of the weapons of mass destruction and their possible effects. This is also related to the contradictions in policy, that is, the generally acknowledged inability of the world's leaders, in spite of frequent public statements in favor of peace and the necessity for arms control and disarmament, to succeed in lowering the level of the gigantic arms race any more than in meeting the costs for new generations of weapons. In other words, the military force of the Federal Republic of Germany is being challenged at the beginning of the 1980s by new powers and forces, both domestic and foreign.

European Security and Détente

The changes in the international order in the 1960s and 1970s, which served as the new determinants of West German foreign policy, were characterized in Europe primarily by the effort to move beyond the period of permanent confrontation and to initiate a process of partial cooperation. Its goal was to control the tensions between East and West, to restrain existing rivalries, and to delineate areas of common interest. In light of the consequences of a conceivable thermonuclear war and the increasingly difficult situation facing the world economy, highest priority was given to a policy of ensuring peace, coupled with the demand for the renunciation of force in international relations. At least in this question vital to humanity, namely that of its continued existence, all the powers were united, even if they left no doubt that not all conflicts or ideological confrontations would thereby be removed. The antagonism between the systems and blocs was a political reality; its continued existence had to be fundamental to any stability that might be created.

After World War II there were, in addition to the traditional means of diplomacy, collective security, and defense, various efforts to increase security through arms control and disarmament. In these efforts, all possible variants, from a general, total disarmament to unilateral steps and to step-by-step reciprocal processes, were discussed at numerous international conferences without any significant success. But the evaluations of a number of suggestions for disengagement, of each country's military strength including that of potential enemies, of mechanisms for control and sanctions, and of the cost effectiveness of weaponry were all too far apart to permit agreement. A new method to ensure peace was without doubt the policy of Western integration. This was the process of unifying numerous social systems, thereby bringing about the organization of one comprehensive unit through which specific political activities, expectations, and loyalties of the national components could be shifted to a new center whose institutions would take precedence over those of the nation-states. To accomplish this, an expanded communications network going beyond national borders was required, as were strengthened trade relations and continual exchange and cooperation in the fields of culture, technology, and science.

Even though this effort was achieved only gradually and only in specific areas, with differing results and at differing levels of integration— most importantly, so far, in the multilateral security pact (NATO) and in the economy (EC)—this type of voluntary formation of a community, with all its frictions and specific disagreements, must be recognized as a significant element of future security policy. West European integration, made possible in large part by constitutional similarities and homogeneity of values, as well as support from the transatlantic partnership with the United States, has, for instance, led to the peaceful resolution of conflicts between its members, the joint control of major sources of power, and the intertwining of multinational decision processes. At the same time, mutual consultation and information processes were improved, contributing to the reduction of traditional prejudices and lack of confidence.

In this process of integration, numerous difficulties and dangers were, of course, recognized; for instance, the likelihood of the community's experiencing more crises, an insufficient control mechanism, and unsatisfactory democratic participation in the decision-making process. The desired unity and joint effort could, on the other hand, cause increased perceptions of a threat by nations outside the community. Nevertheless, this policy of a regionally limited integration of interests has brought about a higher measure of stability and security than many efforts of diplomacy, strategy, and arms control in the first half of the twentieth century. Chancellor Adenauer was, it is true, always quite skeptical about the numerous suggestions for arms control. These were acceptable to him only if they did not interfere with the ties to the West, implied no discrimination against the Federal Republic of Germany, did not question the stationing of U.S. troops in Western Europe, and did not have as their goal the acceptance of the status quo.

For him and his party, the division of Germany (or, as it was called later, the special German-German conflict) was the main cause of tension in Europe. They therefore believed that negotiations about arms control and disarmament as elements of European security policy could be meaningful only if visible progress had been achieved in the matter of reunification. There was, therefore, from the beginning an interaction between the problem of German unification and European security. When the Western powers, beginning in the mid-1950s, could no longer avoid an informal but growing cooperation with the states of Eastern Europe and sought mutual respect for their respective spheres of interest and influence, the Adenauer government not only had to modify its concept for Germany but had to establish new priorities. For a number of years it tried to solve both problems simultaneously in the framework of East-West détente until it was recognized in the early 1960s that only success in the area of European security could provide favorable conditions for a long-term solution of the German question.

In any case, the agreements reached in the 1960s, which were persistently supported by the Federal Republic of Germany, initiated a process of accords in the arms race, even if France and China preferred their own road to security. The most important of these agreements are the installation of the "hot line" between Washington and Moscow (1963); the Nuclear Test Ban Treaty (1963), the Nuclear Nonproliferation Treaty, which was signed by the federal government on January 18, 1969; and SALT I (1972) and SALT II (1979), designed to establish nuclear parity between the two superpowers. The SALT agreements were to reduce the danger of the independent, dynamic character of modern weapons and thereby the instability of the international order. Measured against the difficult task of ensuring European security, these were very modest steps on the road to a real structure of peace. They were particularly far removed from an agreement offering to the Germans, as a divided nation, some hope to achieve a solution to the German question on the basis of the right of self-determination. The essential factor, however, is that states began more and more to recognize that they had common interests going beyond the contrasts that divided them and to include these in their dialogues and in their actions.

Most of the bilateral and multilateral efforts to create the conditions for a European security conference must be seen against this background. The initiative for it originated with the Soviet Union and other communist states. But their original goals, among them to achieve the separation of the United States from Europe and to slow the process of European unification, could not be harmonized with the policies of the Western alliance. As a result, the Western reaction was negative for a number of years. The attitude of the Federal Republic to these suggestions changed after the Warsaw Pact countries issued the 1966 Declaration of Bucharest (strengthening peace and security in Europe), particularly as Bonn did not want to act as a brake on the efforts at détente. It did not reject the suggested negotiations in principle, but it stated three conditions: the careful preparation of the conference, the centerpiece of which would be the goal of a peaceful European order; the full participation of the United States; and the exclusion of the GDR. Beyond these points Bonn stated its full agreement with the 1967 report of the Belgian foreign minister, Pierre Harmel, in which the future tasks of the Western alliance were set forth in concrete terms. It recommended that in the future, in addition to the required defensive capacity and a functioning deterrent, a second method of achieving security would be finding ways and means to further détente. This indicated the desire to achieve progress in the area of arms control and disarmament to create a stable balance between East and West at the lowest possible level of armament. In a statement emanating from the June 1968 NATO meeting at Reykjavik, in the drafting of which Willy Brandt played a considerable role, the NATO countries challenged those of the East to negotiate simultaneously about mutual and balanced force reductions (MBFR). These negotiations have been taking place in Vienna since 1973 without any notable results.

The invasion of Czechoslovakia by the Warsaw Pact states in August 1968 initially prevented any dialogue about these suggestions for European security. The statement issued by the March 1969 Budapest Conference of the Political Committee of the Communist States was directed to all European countries and had a less tendentious tone. It made clear that the Eastern bloc was willing to accept something less than its maximum demands, a change probably stimulated by the need for increased economic cooperation. As a result, an increasingly intensive process was initiated tied to progress in improved East-West relations, whose quantity and quality was, for the West, guided initially by NATO but beginning in 1973 by the Organization of European Political Cooperation.

Meanwhile the new federal government under Brandt and Scheel also saw a possible Conference on Security and Cooperation in Europe (CSCE) more positively. In the years 1970–1972 it made use of this new evaluation in determining its policy toward the East and toward the remainder of Germany. Like most of its allies, it assumed that a series of bilateral agreements would pave the way for the multilateral preparation of such a conference. Progress in the negotiations with the Soviet Union and with Poland, especially about Berlin, were seen as test cases (see p. 150). The German attitude on CSCE had been governed since 1969 by the following principles: renunciation of force, peaceful resolution of conflicts, peacefully agreed boundary changes, exclusion of the German question from the treaty, a specific tie to the MBFR negotiations, freedom of movement, and practical results. Although the

TABLE 3

Defense Expenditures

	in billions of $		in $ per individual		percent of GNP	
	1975	1980	1975	1980	1975	1979
The Super Powers						
USA	88,983	147,700	417	644	5.9	5.2
USSR	124,000	*	490	*		11-13
China (PR)	*	56,941	*	56		7
Warsaw Pact Countries						
Bulgaria	457	1,140	52	128	2.7	2.1
Czechoslovakia	1,706	3,520	116	229	3.8	2.8
German Democratic Republic	2,550	4,790	148	285	5.5	6.3
Hungary	506	1,080	48	101	2.4	2.1
Poland	2,011	4,670	59	131	3.1	2.4
Rumania	707	1,470	33	66	1.7	1.4
NATO Countries						
Belgium	1,971	3,735	200	378	3.0	3.3
United Kingdom	11,118	24,448	198	437	4.9	4.9
Canada	2,965	4,240	130	177	2.2	1.7
Denmark	939	1,404	185	274	2.2	2.0
France	13,984	20,220	264	374	3.9	3.9
Fed. Rep. of Germany	16,142	15,120	259	410	3.7	3.3
Greece	1,435	1,770	159	236	6.9	*
Italy	4,700	6,580	84		2.6	2.4
Luxembourg	22	42	65	134	1.1	1.0
Netherlands	2,978	5,239	218	374	3.6	3.4
Norway	929	1,570	232	383	3.1	3.1
Portugal	1,088	699	124	71	6.0	4.0
Turkey	2,200	*	55		9.0	*

* - Figure not available.

disentanglement of the power structure could not be the stated goal, the federal government saw the intensification of human contacts and the improvement in the exchange of information between East and West as a key way to lend substance to a policy of détente, to include human beings in a responsible manner and to permit them to benefit from it.

After a preparatory conference and a major conference during the period from 1972 to 1975, the final act of the CSCE was signed at Helsinki on August 1, 1975, by thirty-five states of Europe, the United States, and Canada. It is true that CSCE neither changed the political map of Europe nor made new international law, but it was a declaration of intent created by an unprecedented consensus, at the center of which was a code of conduct for international relations. This code has since left its mark on a number of international policies. Especially in times of crisis, strict adherence to this code was demanded as a measure of appropriate behavior. In this, the negotiating partners proceeded from the acceptance of the reality of different social systems and from mutual concessions in foreign policy. This new characteristic of détente, with its renunciation of the use of force or the threat of force, with economic cooperation, and with cooperation in humanitarian matters, was a move away from the balance of terror to a more stable balance of interests.

In the Federal Republic of Germany the government saw this process primarily as a means to an end; that is, as a transition strategy in moving from the era of the Cold War to a peaceful European order. It probably also saw it as an appropriate substitute for a policy of reunification.

A policy of détente in which both sides were aware of German concerns was seen as the best guarantee for an improvement of relations between the two German states and thereby the maintenance of a sense of cohesion among Germans. In this, the decisive criteria were seen as respect for the territorial status quo, a balance of forces, a guarantee of security, and a resolution of conflicts by nonmilitary means, as well as a reduction in the frequency of crises and a peaceful adjustment of interests at the lowest possible level.

But in the Federal Republic there were divided opinions as to the value and dangers of the CSCE. Leading representatives of the opposition (CDU/CSU) above all criticized the "illusions" of the government. In their opinion, a "realistic" policy of détente had to contain, in addition to a balance of military forces, provisions ensuring the "indivisibility" of détente, a mutual dependence on performance and counterperformance, a realization of human rights, and a national right of self-determination. But this dissent in judging the value of the policy of détente was not exclusively a German problem. Among the allies, it was primarily the United States that doubted such a policy would bring real advantages

TABLE 4

Security Expenditures in the Federal Republic of Germany
(in billions of DM and as percentages of the total budget)

	1970	1972	1974	1976	1977	1978	1979	1980	1981	1982
Total Budget	91	111	136	163	172	190	203	215	231	240
Defense Budget	19.2	24.5	28.9	31.9	32.9	34.9	36.9	38.8	42.0	43.8
Percent	21.0	22.0	21.0	19.5	19.1	18.4	18.0	18.1	18.2	18.2
Personnel Costs	7.4	10.5	12.2	13.8	14.5	15.0	16.0	17.0	17.9	17.8
Capital Costs	8.3	9.6	12.0	12.6	2.9	14.0	15.2	15.7	17.9	19.2
Procurement	3.8	3.9	5.6	6.4	6.3	7.5	8.0	8.7	10.4	11.0
Maintenance	1.7	2.6	3.1	3.0	3.2	3.3	3.5	3.6	3.8	4.0
Construction	0.9	1.0	1.2	1.9	1.4	1.6	1.6	1.6	1.8	2.3
R & D	1.0	1.2	1.3	1.4	1.5	1.6	1.7	1.6	1.4	1.5

to the West. In its view, Moscow had used it to expand its influence in the Third World (Angola, Ethiopia, etc.) and to strive for a position of superiority in the arms race. There can be no doubt that the global extension of the East-West conflict in the 1970s, the invasion of Afghanistan by Soviet forces in 1979–1980, and the situation in Poland in the early 1980s renewed the tensions between the two world powers and severely endangered the policy of détente, providing the Western alliance with a difficult test of its cohesiveness. The crisis in the policy of détente became additionally acute through the appearance of conflicts within Western societies and through economic difficulties due to worldwide dependencies and interdependencies. Opinions differed as to the appropriate use of resources, that is, in which way and with what measures the West should respond to Soviet action and which of these would in fact motivate Moscow to moderation and to arms control negotiations with some expectation of success. Simultaneously, regional and national areas of self-interest became clearer.

The Federal Republic of Germany is fully aware of this difficult international situation. Its decision-making elite know that the continuation of the course of détente, which they desire and consider necessary, can have a chance of success only if the Federal Republic coordinates its decisions within the alliance and also makes its views fully known within that grouping in order to avoid rash unilateral decisions and to obtain agreement on realistic joint approaches. At the same time, it must prove itself capable of engaging in a dialogue with its partners in the East.

The NATO twin decision of December 12, 1979, to station cruise and Pershing missiles in Europe in 1983 and simultaneously to negotiate a reduction in missile strength with the Soviets, which has become controversial in both East and West, must be viewed in this light. Arms control negotiations had started in 1969, concentrating initially on intercontinental strategy and climaxing in the signing of SALT II in the summer of 1979. They were then extended to the area of conventional weapons (the Vienna negotiations), and at the second CSCE Follow-Up Conference in Madrid proposals were submitted by the West for a European disarmament conference and for further confidence-building measures. Geographically these were to extend to all of Europe, i.e., including the European part of the Soviet Union. Until then, medium-range nuclear weaponry (sometimes known as the gray zone of negotiating policy) had been excluded from the discussions. The Soviet Union had meanwhile started to replace its SS-4 and SS-3 missiles with SS-20's. As various Western statesmen repeatedly pointed out, this potentially superior intermediate-range weapon could be used by the Soviet Union as a means of exerting pressure. This regional threat was to be countered by a NATO decision. The suggestion for negotiations on medium-range missiles was to be tied to the deployment of 108 Pershing II missiles and 464 land-based cruise missiles (of these 96 P IIs were to be deployed in the Federal Republic of Germany beginning late in 1983) should the arms control negotiations not lead to a satisfactory result. The United States declared itself ready to relinquish the deployment of the missiles should the Soviet Union dismantle its SS-20 missiles and take older weapons systems out of service (the so-called zero option).

In part because of the pressure of domestic elements (the peace movements), Chancellor Schmidt advised Washington that he strongly supported bilateral negotiations between the superpowers, which were finally initiated in Geneva on November 30, 1981. The Federal Republic and its allies expect concrete and verifiable results; only these can prevent conflicts and ease the resolution of crises, improve the instruments for the maintenance of peace, and lower the balance of armaments to the lowest possible level.

Bilateral Relations and Development Assistance

The foreign policy of the Federal Republic of Germany is, as has been repeatedly emphasized, dependent to a high degree on the Western alliance and its requirements. It has also been shaped by numerous bilateral relations, differing regionally in quantity and quality. Their nature has been prescribed by the German national interest and by the general principles of conduct set forth in the constitution, adapted in every case to the specific environment and to such other specific factors as level of development, intensity of the relationship, goals to be achieved, and the availability of resources.

Whereas relations with Western neighbors were developed by the process of integration through a multiplicity of interrelationships (which did not eliminate tensions, mutual criticism, and differing reactions to world political events), relations with the Third World have been based on traditional considerations, on those of the German-German relationship, on economic concerns, or on the application of the German or United Nations principles of development assistance. During the 1960s and 1970s it became clear that the policies of the Federal Republic of Germany needed increasingly to adapt themselves to a strategy of interdependence. This required that new structures of partnership be sought, that bodies of regional cooperation be supported, and that the creation of special spheres of influence be resisted. This could be done only on a basis of equality and self-determination permitting the maintenance of individual political, cultural, economic, and social structures in the newly created nations. For a country so dependent on exports as the Federal Republic, foreign policy also needed to create stability. The latter was essentially dependent on the voluntary acceptance by all countries of an orderly method for the conduct of relations and an agreement on dependable rules of cooperation. The fundamental changes in the world's political and economic situation presented the Federal Republic with increasing additional challenges that could apparently be mastered only in the framework of the trilateral community: Europe, the United States, and Japan.

The relationship of the Federal Republic to Japan has since 1952 developed into a closer partnership than ever before despite geographic distance and economic competition. Both countries now pursued many of the same interests and goals and were faced with similar challenges. Their common fate in 1945, the loss of territories, domestic political changes in the direction of democratization, the amazing reconstruction, and the high level of economic and technological achievements, combined with a defense against Soviet communism, created the basis for a new beginning that differed basically from the previous models of thought and behavior—the so-called traditional German-Japanese friendship. In economic and cultural foreign policy it was possible to tie into certain older traditions. In contrast to previous periods, however, the leading personalities in both countries favored a policy of harmonization of interests, of a balanced growth of the world economy, and of the use of available instruments for the peaceful settlement of world conflicts. At the same time they decisively rejected all efforts at the establishment of a hegemony. Japan is the most important Asian trading partner of the Federal Republic even though imports and exports (up to 2 percent of the total) remained small, as they had before 1939, and continued a similar structure of exchange of goods and high direct investments. Of special importance are the frequent consultations and resulting cooperation with Japan in international matters and in raw material and energy questions.

Relations with the People's Republic of China (PRC) developed quite differently. Although Peking declared an end to hostilities with Germany in 1955, the normalization of bilateral contacts was a long way off. Contrasts in ideology and power politics, the close U.S.-German alliance, and the support of Taiwan by the Federal Republic initially prevented any rapprochement. Only the sensational world political changes of the 1960s, particularly the increasing tensions between the Soviet Union and the PRC, created the necessary conditions for the agreement of October 1972 establishing diplomatic relations and providing for an exchange of ambassadors. This development was made easier by Bonn's decision to opt for the PRC on the question of relations with Taiwan and by agreement on specific problems of development policy (e.g., the policies of mutual advantage and of dialogue). Since that time, noticeable progress has been made in cooperation between the two states, especially in science, technology, and academic interaction. These are supported by a lively exchange of official and private delegations, which contribute to improved mutual understanding.

The Federal Republic of Germany today imports approximately 45 percent of its copper ore, 53 percent of its iron ore, 18 percent of its manganese, 42 percent of its cobalt, 65 percent of its vanadium, and 21 percent of its chromium from developing countries. At the end of the 1970s, it imported 16 percent of its petroleum needs from Saudi Arabia, 16 percent from Libya, 15.8 percent from Nigeria, 9.3 percent from Algeria, and 8.8 percent from Iran. These selected data make clear to what a large extent the Federal Republic is interested in the political stability of these countries. In addition, nearly 1 million jobs in Germany can be safeguarded only through peaceful, stable development in the Third World, for 23 percent of all German exports and 30 percent of all exports of capital goods go to these countries. Similarly, 30 percent of all German foreign investments are located there.

These, too, are explanations for the vital interest of the Federal Republic in ensuring raw material and energy supplies and the international means for their transportation. Peace and security today are not dependent solely on the maintenance of stability in Europe.

The increasing domestic unrest and external conflicts in Africa, Asia, and Latin America undoubtedly constitute a growing threat to world peace. The Federal Republic therefore must, in coordination with others, assist in furthering stability in these countries, to alleviate hunger and poverty and to provide a model of real partnership in a pluralistic world. It must furthermore make increased efforts to participate in improving economic, financial, and technical cooperation with these areas. This is independent of the domestic political structure of the countries with which it cooperates; Bonn does not wish to impose its own system or values on others. Rather, central to its policies are two goals: to strengthen the independence and self-reliance of these states and as far as possible to permit this policy to function without involving these countries in East-West tensions. Additionally, it desires to overcome the remnants of colonialism and racial discrimination by negotiated solutions and promotion of respect for indispensable human rights.

Although the Federal Republic has nearly doubled its development assistance since 1977, it still remains far from the stated goal of making available 0.7 percent of its GNP as public development assistance. In the first twenty years (1950–1970) it spent nearly DM 57 billion in bilateral and multilateral development assistance, of which 49 percent was from public funds and 51 percent from private sources. The largest sum—DM 17.1 billion—was spent in Asia.

Africa has in recent years assumed a special role in German development policy. More than two-fifths of all assistance goes to this continent, amounting to DM 21 billion by the end of 1980. There is a cooperative development assistance program with nearly every African state. The Federal Republic is Africa's second largest trading partner; imports in 1980 were more than DM 80 billion, exports more than DM 19 billion.

An especially difficult and controversial chapter of German foreign policy concerns relationships with the countries of the Middle East. From the beginning these have been burdened by three factors. First, the moral obligations to Israel resulting from the National Socialist policy of the destruction of European Jewry affected the German-Arab relationship. Second, the claim to sole representation of Germany, which was designed by the Federal Republic to deny recognition to the GDR, was not in conformity with the interests of the Arab states. Finally, there are the additional dangers to the military and economic security of Europe resulting from the continuing Israeli-Arab conflict and its international implications, including the rivalry between the United States and the Soviet Union.

The first crisis in the relationship with the Arab countries arose in the mid-1960s when it became known that the Federal Republic was furnishing weapons to Israel. President Nasser of Egypt threatened to recognize the GDR if these deliveries did not cease. Although the federal cabinet thereupon decided in February 1965 to stop all exports of weapons to areas of tension, the establishment of diplomatic relations with Israel in May 1965 caused a number of Arab states to break relations with Bonn. The dislike of the Arabs for the Federal Republic was strengthened by the fact that German sympathies during the 1967 Six-Day War were clearly with Israel.

It was only in the late 1960s and early 1970s that a change took place in the Middle East policies of the Federal Republic of Germany. This was made easier by a modus vivendi between the two German states and the decision to reject further use of the Hallstein Doctrine. The change in policy began with the recognition that peace and security in Europe were also dependent on stability in the Middle East. The Federal Republic therefore sought harmonious relations with all Arab states, but not at the expense of Israel. It supported UN Security Council Resolution 242 of 1967, which contains the essential elements of a just peace settlement. It demands, *inter alia,* the withdrawal of Israeli forces from occupied territories and the recognition of Israel's right to exist and the territorial integrity of all the states of the Middle East, as well as a just solution to the refugee problem. Since 1970, the joint policy of the European Community has provided an additional policy framework for the Federal Republic, permitting it to support specific principles, which it had not dared to do publicly before.

The Middle East policy of the EC has as its goal the achievement of a permanent, comprehensive, and just settlement of the Arab-Israeli conflict. The heads of state and government and the foreign ministers of the EC countries have expressed this view in numerous statements from 1971 to 1979. In the future, the Palestinian people's legitimate right to a homeland is to be brought into harmony with the right of Israel to exist. This new Middle East policy not only led to a resumption of diplomatic relations between the Federal Republic and all the Arab states, but it is also considered to have made an important contribution to the political stability of the area and the security of energy supplies from the region.

The Western Alliance as a Factor in the Maintenance of Peace

Just as the year 1969, when the Social Democratic–Liberal coalition under Willy Brandt and Walter Scheel formed a new government, marked a significant turning point in the history of the Federal Republic of Germany, so the end of 1982 and the beginning of 1983 must also be seen as an incisive moment in postwar German democracy. On October 1, 1982, for the first time, a constructive vote of no confidence was used by the CDU/CSU and FDP in the Bundestag to topple one federal chancellor (Helmut Schmidt) and to elect another (Helmut Kohl). Increasing tensions between the partners of the previous coalition (SPD and FDP) had significantly contributed to the collapse of the governing coalition and caused the FDP leadership to change its allegiance. This surprising "change of power," noted worldwide, was sanctioned by the German voters a few months later in early Bundestag elections held on March 6, 1983.

One area of major emphasis in the new government's program was domestic and economic policy, especially the reduction of growing unemployment, which will be looked upon as a test of its abilities. Another area was foreign policy, in which substantial continuity was emphasized but in which hints of new emphases were unmistakable, especially in methodology and in the application of resources. Moreover, Chancellor Kohl and Foreign Minister Genscher have left no doubt that the firm alliance of free nations and membership in the European Community will continue to be the basis of their foreign policy. By this they mean honest partnerships founded on jointly held views of freedom, the rule of law, and the precedence to be accorded to human rights and human dignity. They postulated as an irrevocable goal the establishment of a just, peaceful order for all of Europe; in their view, this was the only way to guarantee peaceful change and the exercise of the right of self-determination by the entire German people and thereby to achieve the unity of Germany. Tied to this policy was strict adherence to and full application of the 1971 Four-Power Agreement on Berlin, which also meant strengthening the ties of Berlin to the Federal Republic and the assumption of the city's representation abroad by the government of that republic.

Statements by members of the government contained hints of the shift of emphasis, which could be seen, *inter alia,* in the differing evaluations by the government and the SPD of the threat posed by the Soviet Union and in their differing attitudes toward the division of Germany. On the one hand, it is clear that the new CDU/CSU–FDP coalition government is not oblivious to the changing political frame of reference and to real power relationships and, moreover, firmly holds to a policy of adherence to treaties. On the other hand, without regard to its determination to continue or even improve upon the previously initiated policy of a *modus vivendi* with the German Democratic Republic, the new government does not regard the agreements concerning Germany as a whole to be final settlements. It sees them rather as a temporary condition, which in the long run it hopes to be able to change peacefully to bring about German reunification. It is supported in its view by the legal position on this subject contained in the Basic Law and by the May 1972 joint declaration of all the parties represented in the Bundestag.

The new leadership elite in Bonn sees the role of the Federal Republic of Germany as both demanding and binding: cosmopolitan, ready to reach understandings, working in solidarity with its friends, reliable, true to its agreements and credible, ready for greater cooperation and an adjustment of interests with the member states of the Warsaw Pact, and concerned about greater equity for the Third World. A large portion of the underlying concepts of future policy is understandably devoted to questions of security policy. In the view of the government, military resources will be required to secure the peace until a comprehensive and verifiable disarmament agreement can be achieved. Under the present circumstances, however, the concept of deterrence and a defense based on a balance of power is indispensable. The result is the government's decision to strictly adhere to both aspects of the NATO dual-track decision. Beyond these considerations, however, Chancellor Kohl emphasized once more during his talks in Moscow in July 1983 the so-called dictum of German policy that war may never again be started from German soil. The renunciation of the use of force or the threat of force, therefore, remains at the core of the German policy for the maintenance of peace. In the future, the new "coalition of the center" intends to work intensively to bring about peace with freedom and a concomitant continual reduction of armaments.

This goal of peace, which was the centerpiece of Chancellor Kohl's "Program of Renewal," must, however, be seen not merely as a condition in which weapons are silent but rather as a permanent obligation to use international law and social as well as ecological measures to ensure the continued existence of humanity and to bring about more humane conditions of existence. How such a "positive peace" can be brought about, and even what it would encompass, are and will remain controversial questions. There are no panaceas available, particularly if regional differences and those between the Western democracies and the communist systems are taken into account; relations between the latter two groups continue to be marked by undisguised antagonism. The new government, for its part, has clearly outlined its ideas on this subject and has determined that democratic values, complemented by a striving for an intellectual renewal of the German people, will be the guidelines for its actions and aspirations.

The more the people of the world become aware of current domestic and foreign crises and of their own fears, the more they resent traditional security policies that have so far been developed primarily by experts and bureaucrats and that have accepted the dilemma posed by nuclear deterrence through the threat of suicide. More recently, the debate on security, marked in part by emotionalism and frequently by inconsistency, has stimulated new thought and has caused many politicians to rethink their positions. The raising of this existential question undoubtedly has positive value. Unfortunately, it tends increasingly to lead to the consideration of one's own opinion as solely acceptable, to the disqualification of opposing views as "unrealistic," and to the defamation as warmongering of alliance decisions in favor of military measures to secure the peace. The basic doctrine of the German armed forces—that the forces are fundamentally defensive in nature—is thereby ignored. The heterogeneous peace movements in particular, which surely are not solely a German phenomenon, tend to challenge the democratically established leadership of the Federal Republic of Germany through powerful demonstrations and a variety of other activities. These groups must basically be classified as opposed to nuclear weapons, opposed to their deployment in Germany, and in favor of disarmament (often with differing conceptions); they would be hard put to formulate a uniform positive goal for the creation of a peaceful order in Europe. It is, of course, essential that all possible strategies for peaceful change, for the reduction of the levels of armaments, and for increased security must be taken seriously and must be critically discussed. But they must always be analyzed and evaluated within the basic framework of German policy. To this the following must be added: Alternative policies, no matter how desirable they might appear to be and no matter how morally justified, require, in a democracy, that they can command a majority. They also need a consensus in the alliance. Any negation of these factors would indicate a dangerous lack of a sense of reality. Clarity of arguments and motives cannot be a substitute for the politics of the possible.

This, too, is part of the new role of the Federal Republic of Germany: the recognition that Germans do not live on an island on which they can make their decisions solely on the basis of their own national interest but rather in a world of mutual interdependence. This recognition is first and foremost related to the security of the Federal Republic of Germany, ensured through the existence and effectiveness of NATO. In this area, the new coalition of the center, along with all other German democrats, will be facing a further testing of its policies. Only the future will show whether all of them together will, even in the face of adverse economic conditions and growing societal conflicts, be able not only to cope with a commitment to democracy, maintain a dialogue with those whose opinions differ, and deal with nonviolent protests, but also to retain an unshakable right to their own continued existence.

A Major Medium-Sized Power with Worldwide Responsibilities

The Federal Republic of Germany today considers itself to be part of the surrounding world; it does not act in isolation. As the 1980s begin, the Western community's security and value system remain the fundamental orientation of German foreign policy. This does not exclude factual criticisms of omissions, unilateral measures, or specific actions of its allies or the possibility of differing judgments about political events, the effectiveness of the use of resources, or Soviet policies. Such attitudes have little in common with anti-Americanism. Now as before, the overwhelming majority of the German people support friendship with the United States and the maintenance of NATO. The federal government holds the view that flexibility in its foreign policy and the weight it carries are dependent on the strength of the alliance and on the role it plays in that alliance.

The Federal Republic has accepted its new role as a major medium-sized power. Recently it has been persistently urged to assume greater responsibility in world politics. It can do this only if it appears neither as an "honest broker" nor as a "mediator" between the conflicting powers and does not consider itself a neutral power. The Federal Republic has unmistakably taken sides. Perhaps it can assume the role of "honest interpreter" on behalf of the Western world and perhaps that of a brakeman in order to reduce the danger of collision between the two superpowers. In any case it will have to use all of its strength to make its power count, regionally, worldwide, and in the UN—in consultation with its partners—for a peaceful resolution of conflicts, for a readiness for dialogue and cooperation, for political compromises, for a real balancing of interests, and for the realization of human rights. It must constantly seek to make its voice heard in these questions of human existence.

It is an irony of history that Germans have twice in this century attempted to fight for a role among the world powers in order to have a voice in determining the fate of this earth. Twice they failed. After 1945, the Federal Republic of Germany was prepared to accept the role of a medium-sized power, but it has been constantly burdened with new obligations. This, too, is a reason why its influence has grown greatly. If it shows self-restraint and reticence in the protection of its interests, if it is able to measure accurately balances and relationships and to contribute to the resolution of the North-South conflict as a part of a policy of worldwide partnership and peace—only then will it be in a position to cope with the demands made on it.

In light of the historical experiences of a strong German Reich predominant in Central Europe, and in the light of the importance currently attached to securing peace and ensuring a balance of power, allowing the resolution of many social and economic problems in Europe and the world, it is now important with respect to the question of German unity to proceed from a clearly defined reality, to avoid empty rhetoric, and to differentiate the possible from wishful thinking. Under current conditions there is no possibility of resolving the division of Germany, even if now and then new hopes, usually tied to pacifist-neutralist tendencies, do arise. The question whether this problem can be solved in the framework of a future common European solution cannot now be answered. Furthermore, no politician in the Federal Republic of Germany is either willing or able to predict concretely what reunification would in fact mean for Germany and the world and what new dangers or advantages might result from it. There remains, therefore, only an intensive look at the original concept of the nation: an improvement of close interpersonal relationships and a strengthening of the feeling of belonging together regardless of the ties to different, antagonistic social systems.

One essential task remains for the Federal Republic: to prove through its policies that history is not a one-way street. Its strength and its determination in the alliance, the realized values of its basic order, its economic stability, and its ability to innovate will determine whether human dignity can be ensured in this portion of Germany and whether a more humane, free society can be established whose example can have a positive effect on the other part of the German nation. By concentrating all its energies on this goal, by seeking and by accepting a regulated interrelationship with the GDR, the Federal Republic could in the future, as a medium-sized country with considerable economic and military power, make a far greater contribution to the establishment of peace in Europe, and thereby in the world, than by a policy of contradictions and ambiguity.

Readings

Calleo, David P. *The German Problem Reconsidered: Germany and the World Order, 1870 to the Present.* Cambridge: Cambridge University Press, 1978.

Hanrieder, Wolfram. *West German Foreign Policy, 1949–1963.* Stanford, Calif.: Stanford University Press, 1967.

Joffe, Josef. "The Foreign Policy of the German Federal Republic." Pp. 117–151 in R. C. Macridis (ed.), *Foreign Policy in World Politics.* Englewood, N.J.: Prentice-Hall, 1976.

Merkl, Peter H. *German Foreign Policies, West and East. On the Threshold of a New European Era.* Santa Barbara, Calif.: ABC-Clio, 1974.

Pfetsch, Frank R. *Die Aussenpolitik der Bundesrepublik 1949–1980.* Munich: Fink, 1981.

ROGER MORGAN

8

The Federal Republic and the United States

Postwar Beginnings

The postwar relationship between the United States and Germany was that between the victor and the vanquished: After the unconditional surrender of the Third Reich in May 1945, no German government existed and the United States, together with its allies, exercised supreme authority over the defeated enemy. Quite naturally, there were many aspects of U.S. policy at this time that reflected the mentality of the war—the punitive provisions of the original Occupation Directive of April 1945 or the influence of the Morgenthau Plan for the "pastoralization" of Germany—but elements of a more conciliatory policy were growing in prominence. One of the most striking features of U.S.-German relations in the early postwar years was the speed with which the two ex-enemy countries adjusted their views of each other, forming by 1949 a firm partnership that, although very unequal, was already marked by a high degree of mutual confidence in the supportive role played by each of the partners.

The first guidelines for the policies to be applied in the U.S. zone of occupation in Germany, the Joint Chiefs of Staff Document JCS 1067 of April 1945, were a harsh and negative set of instructions on how U.S. personnel should treat the German population: "Fraternization" was strictly prohibited, any remaining elements of Nazism were to be ruthlessly eradicated, and the standard of living of the Germans was to be drastically reduced in punishment for the evil deeds of the Third Reich. In practice, this savage code proved unrealistic and unworkable, and it was very quickly modified. U.S. occupation forces provided considerable amounts of foodstuffs to avert famine in Germany, the low levels of industrial production originally authorized were rapidly raised,

177

and a revival of political life in the Western zones of occupation was actively encouraged, instead of being repressed.

In the summer of 1947, when the Cold War led to the Truman Doctrine and the Marshall Plan, these changes in U.S. policy in Germany were codified in a new directive (JCS 1779 of July 1947) that was radically different from the 1945 guidelines. U.S. policy now recognized the need for "the economic contributions of a stable and productive Germany" and promised the Germans "a forum of political organization and a manner of political life which, resting on a substantial basis of economic welfare, will lead to tranquillity within Germany and will contribute to the spirit of peace among nations." This spirit of conciliation was applied by the Americans in such policies as the reform of the West German currency in 1948 and also in the form proposed for the country's new political institutions. These institutions, which originally developed separately within each of the Western zones of occupation, were based not only on free elections and the active encouragement of competition among a wide range of political parties but also on the principle of a strongly decentralized federalism.

Throughout the different phases of Germany's political development, from the first local elections of 1946 to the creation of the Federal Republic three years later, the U.S. authorities strongly defended— especially against the original British proposals—the principle that the new democracy of Germany should grow from the grass roots of a decentralized federal system rather than from a centralized model like some earlier German constitutions. The partnership between the leaders of the new Germany and the Americans responsible for the U.S. policy in Germany, from the military governor, General Lucius Clay, downward, laid the foundations for the close cooperation between Germans and Americans that was reflected in the creation of the Federal Republic in 1949.

The Consolidation of a Partnership, 1949–1955

The Federal Republic was brought into existence in 1949 as a subordinate partner of the Western powers and of the United States in particular. In the years that followed, many world affairs consolidated this relationship. One of the major themes in the history of U.S.-German relations from 1949 to 1955 is the way in which the worsening of the Cold War between the Western and Soviet alliances made the United States increasingly build up the status and independence of its West German partner, whose leader, Konrad Adenauer, was able to count on the support of Washington and to use it to improve the position of his country.

One symbol of the worsening of the Cold War was the continuing East-West deadlock over the future of Germany. After the foreign ministers of the Soviet Union and the Western powers had failed to reach agreement on Germany's future in June 1949, there were no East-West meetings until the Berlin Conference early in 1954, at which a further discussion was held on the future of Germany, again without any progress toward a settlement. It was against this background, and the further failure to agree at the Geneva Summit Conference of 1955, that the United States proceeded with its policy of building up the Federal Republic as a close European ally and welcoming it as an important European member of the Atlantic alliance.

The process of U.S.-German reconciliation was also helped by the dramatic development of the Cold War outside Europe. When North Korean forces invaded South Korea in June 1950, many people in the United States and in Europe feared that there would also be an attack by communist East Germany on noncommunist West Germany, and this fear strengthened the American idea (which had already been expressed at the end of 1949) that West Germany should be rearmed in order to add its military strength to that of the West. The issue of West German rearmament was one on which Adenauer was able to use the international situation, quite legitimately, to demand an improvement in Germany's status. When the United States pressed for a West German contribution to the defense of Europe, and France responded with some reluctance by suggesting the idea of an integrated European Defense Community, Adenauer responded that Germany would indeed join a European army but only on the basis of full equality with the other members. Even though the European Defense Community as originally proposed by France in 1950 was in fact fated to collapse four years later, the net result was that the Federal Republic, when it joined the North Atlantic Treaty Organization (NATO) in May 1955, did so as a close and valued partner of the United States.

One important reason for this was the very close personal understanding between the two groups of leaders who were responsible for the conduct of policy in Washington and in Bonn. Both President Truman and his secretary of state, Dean Acheson, had great confidence in Chancellor Adenauer, and the latter's relations with Eisenhower and John Foster Dulles, after the Republicans took office in January 1953, were even closer. In particular, a relationship of deep trust and understanding developed between Dulles, the secretary of state in the Eisenhower administration, and the German chancellor, who acted as his own minister for foreign affairs. Both Dulles and Adenauer were deeply religious, and they also shared a profound skepticism about the possibilities of any lasting agreement with the Soviet Union: This meant that they had a strong common interest in forging the closest political ties between the United States and the Federal Republic. It also helped this partnership that the infant Federal Republic had a number of features in common with the United States, including a commitment to the economics of private enterprise and a political system based on federalism.

In the first half of the 1950s, the leadership of the United States guided the Federal Republic through a number of stages that transformed the original dependence of the new state into virtually full sovereignty and independence by 1955. As early as November 1949, the United States was a firm supporter of the view that the dismantling of German industry should be stopped and that Germany should be allowed to develop its steel production, shipbuilding industry, and other economic activities. The United States also took the lead in bringing the Federal Republic into membership of the Council of Europe, the International Monetary Fund, the World Bank, and the Organization for European Economic Cooperation.

In 1951, under U.S. leadership, the Federal Republic established a Ministry of Foreign Affairs, and the Allied rights of supervision of German legislation were reduced; in 1952, when intensive discussions were being held on the restoration of German sovereignty the United States again—partly because of the strong U.S. wish to rearm the Federal Republic—took the lead in arguing that Germany's status should be upgraded. In order to ensure that the Federal Republic kept a government friendly to the Western alliance, Dulles also took the unusual step of intervening publicly in the West German election campaign of 1953 in favor of Adenauer and against the Social Democratic party, which was arguing in favor of the neutralization and reunification of Germany.

After the 1953 election, when Adenauer's parliamentary majority was greatly increased, thanks partly to this U.S. support, the argument about German rearmament continued. Both before and after the defeat of the European Defense Community in the form originally proposed by France, there was close cooperation between the governments in Bonn and Washington, and there was no doubt that Germany's entry into NATO in May 1955 was due essentially to this close partnership.

A further reason for the growing identity of views between Washington and Bonn was that neither of the two governments saw any prospect of useful negotiations with the Soviet Union. In Washington, those advisers who argued that a final split between East and West in Europe was not inevitable and that there should be negotiations to try to reunify Germany (for instance, George Kennan) were not taken seriously by those who held power, particularly Acheson and Dulles; in West Germany, similarly, the Social Democratic party led by Kurt Schumacher, with its ideas of neutralizing Germany by East-West agreement, was also kept away from any effective influence by Adenauer and was rejected by the German voters in the elections of 1953 and 1957.

A further element of similarity between the U.S. and German approaches to East-West relations was that both Dulles and Adenauer, at least in theory, were committed to changing the map of Europe to the advantage of the West. Some at least of Adenauer's popularity was due to his promise to try to reunify Germany by a policy of "negotiation from strength," and Dulles—at least up to the time when he took office in 1953—argued in favor of "liberating" Eastern Europe through the "roll-back" of Soviet power. Neither of these policies was in fact put into practice—the risk of war was much too great for that—but the theoretical commitment of both the U.S. and the West German governments to extend Western freedom to the East created a strong bond between them. The U.S. government was particularly strong, among the Western allies of the Federal Republic, in its insistence that the West should give no official recognition to the East German regime and that the reunification of Germany should one day take place through the holding of free elections throughout the country—elections that, so Adenauer and Dulles confidently asserted, would certainly lead to a reunified Germany that would join the Western alliance.

First Strains in the Alliance, 1955–1960

By 1955, a fairly stable pattern of relationships in Central Europe appeared to have been established: The Federal Republic had joined NATO, the German Democratic Republic had joined the Warsaw Pact, and the Soviet Union appeared to have accepted the fact that West Berlin had close ties with the Federal Republic. The optimistic idea of some observers in the West that Germany could be reunified and neutralized by international agreement, like Austria after 1955, had been rejected as unworkable, and the Federal Republic seemed set on a course of close partnership with the Western world and with the United States in particular.

By 1960, even though many of the same statesmen were still in office (Adenauer continued to be chancellor until 1963, Eisenhower remained president until January 1961, and Dulles continued as secretary of state until shortly before his death in 1959), some minor questions had begun to arise about the long-term stability of the U.S.-German partnership. One reason for these questions was the apparent relaxation of East-West hostility, marked by a number of visits by Western leaders to the Soviet Union and vice versa. Even though there were renewed outbreaks of East-West crisis, such as the crushing of the Hungarian uprising late in 1956 and the renewal of Soviet pressure on West Berlin in November 1958, the idea continued to gain ground that the Cold War period of East-West confrontation was gradually giving way to a more relaxed relationship. This opened up the prospect of negotiations with the Soviet Union about a variety of issues, including arms control and the future of Berlin, and when East-West negotiations on such questions came to be considered, there were inevitable differences of perception between Washington and Bonn.

At the same time, there were signs of disagreement between the two governments about the slow progress of West German rearmament (some spokesmen in Washington expressed disappointment that the German defense contribution was not growing more quickly) and also, more important, on the question of the U.S. military presence in Germany. A number of aspects of this problem created difficulties: For instance, it began to appear to some Americans that the United States was paying a disproportionate amount of the cost of stationing conventional forces in Germany, and Germany was pressed to make a bigger financial contribution to offset this cost. Again, there was great alarm in Germany in the summer of 1956 when it was reported that Admiral Radford, chairman of the Joint Chiefs of Staff, was contemplating a plan for the reduction of U.S. ground forces by as much as 800,000 men and that he proposed to substitute for them increased reliance on nuclear weapons. Rumors that the "Radford Plan" would be adopted as official U.S. policy naturally created great alarm in Bonn, and it was some time before German opinion was reassured. Indeed, John Foster Dulles himself had gone some way toward endorsing the reduction of U.S. ground forces as an option to be seriously considered (it was probably a natural line for the Republican administration to take in 1956, an election year), and it was only after strenuous opposition from Adenauer and other German leaders that the plan was finally abandoned.

Renewed friction between Washington and Bonn was caused by the rather ambiguous reaction of John Foster Dulles to the new Soviet pressure on Berlin at the end of 1958. This began with a speech by Khrushchev on November 10, in which he announced that the Soviet Union no longer wished to abide by the Potsdam Agreement but proposed to hand over its responsibilities for Berlin to the German Democratic Republic. A number of Western leaders responded to this ultimatum by saying that the West probably ought to negotiate with the Soviet Union; and even Dulles, in a press conference on November 26, replied to the question whether the United States could accept the control of traffic to West Berlin by the East Germans instead of the Soviets (a suggestion the West had previously flatly rejected) by saying that if the East Germans were recognized as agents of the Soviets, the Soviet suggestion might be considered. This flexibility on the part of Dulles gave Adenauer a very unpleasant shock (and also reinforced his growing alliance with de Gaulle, one of the Western leaders who took a strongly anti-Soviet position at this time), as it signified just the kind of diplomatic upgrading of the East German state that had previously been taboo from a Western point of view.

Among the possible explanations for this apparent weakening by Dulles (he was in fact mortally ill by this time and had only a few more weeks of office left) is that he really was contemplating a serious shift in the policy of the United States, in fact a first step toward de facto recognition of the GDR and thus of the division of Germany. It is reported that Dulles made it quite clear to Adenauer, whom he visited for the last time in February 1959, that the vital interest of the United States in preserving world peace was not to be compromised by rigid adherence to the principle of nonrecognition of the GDR, however important this principle was to West Germany.

In another case, in January 1959, speculation by Dulles at a press conference appeared to the Adenauer government to amount to the abandonment of an agreed Western viewpoint. When asked whether he still believed that free elections throughout Germany were a necessary first step toward the reunification (this had always been the Western view), Dulles replied: "It seems to us to be a natural method. But I would not say that it is the only method by which reunification could be accomplished," and he went on to suggest, among other possibilities, a confederation between the two German states as an alternative first step toward reunification. Even though this sort of remark by Dulles— worded in deliberately speculative terms—aroused less alarm in Germany than his statement of November 26, which had implied official recognition of the GDR, it still helped to contribute to German fears that the determination of the United States to support the previously agreed point of view on the German question was flagging.

It should be emphasized that, despite these alarming remarks by Dulles and other statements by President Eisenhower that also led the Germans to fear that the U.S. position on recognition of the GDR was weakening, the Eisenhower period on the whole closed as it had begun with a very solid partnership between Washington and Bonn. Even though some differences of opinion inevitably arose from the different perspectives of the United States (a world power with a responsibility for conducting East-West relations as a whole) and West Germany (an exposed and not fully armed European state with the unresolved problem of national unity on its mind), these differences were not strong enough to have a serious influence on the very high degree of understanding prevailing between the two nations and the two governments.

"Ich bin ein Berliner," 1961–1963

One of the best-remembered sayings of President John F. Kennedy is his dramatic phrase "Ich bin ein Berliner," which was greeted with rapturous enthusiasm by a massed crowd outside the City Hall of West Berlin in June 1963. In view of this, and of the generally high popularity of Kennedy in Germany, it is ironic to recall that the period of his presidency in fact included a number of quite serious crises in U.S.-German relations.

The starting point for this relatively troubled period was that the Kennedy administration, unlike that of Eisenhower, included a number of officials and advisers who saw the main tasks of U.S. foreign policy essentially in terms of building a better relationship with the Soviet Union. This was the case with the "arms control lobby," who attached the highest priority to negotiating East-West agreements to limit the spread of nuclear weapons, and it was also true of such senior officials as George Kennan (appointed by Kennedy as ambassador to Yugoslavia), who continued to believe that a peaceful settlement of differences between Eastern and Western Europe—including the German problem—should be actively pursued by the United States.

These attitudes, and particularly the readiness to negotiate with the Soviet Union even at the cost of tension with West Germany and other European allies, played a part in creating difficulties between Washington and Bonn as the Berlin crisis that had started in 1958 dragged on and was made worse by the building of the Berlin Wall in August 1961. There were, however, many other issues on which the standpoints of Washington and Bonn tended to diverge during this period.

A further source of trouble was that the foreign and defense policies of the Kennedy administration were not in fact very clearly defined. For the first eighteen months of the Kennedy administration, at least, Washington was the scene of conflict between rival factions, some of which wished to consolidate the Atlantic alliance (particularly after the challenge to its policies and organization by General de Gaulle in 1962–1963), others of which insisted on giving priority to arms control negotiations with the Soviet Union. These differences of perspective on defense policy produced a situation in which a group of officials in Washington were able to launch the project of a multilateral nuclear force (MLF) to be commanded jointly by the United States and some of the European members of NATO. It was argued by this "European" faction in Washington (particularly in the State Department) that West Germany was actively interested in acquiring nuclear weapons—or at least a share in the control of them—and that if the United States did not act to deal with this problem, the Germans would react by following

President de Gaulle in the direction of developing an independent national nuclear strike force. These apprehensions were in fact greatly exaggerated—indeed, the German officials who expressed an interest in the multilateral force that Washington now proposed as an antidote to the temptations of Gaullism probably did so largely because they thought the proposal represented an active desire of the United States. However, the MLF proposal, which occupied much of the attention of the alliance from 1962 to 1964, was based on misperceptions in both Washington and Bonn, and the pursuit and the final killing of this well-meant but ill-conceived project resulted in a good deal of tension between the two allies.

At the same time, there were further signs that the financial burden of stationing U.S. ground forces in Germany was also imposing a strain on the relationship. An agreement reached between Washington and Bonn in November 1961 provided for the Germans to make a substantial contribution toward offsetting this cost by purchasing U.S. military equipment, and the agreement was renewed in 1963. However, there remained a certain amount of strain arising from the common agricultural policy of the European Community, of which Germany was now a member. The commercial relations between the United States and the European Community were dominated in the early 1960s by the so-called chicken war, in which U.S. poultry farmers accused the Community of unfair subsidization of exports of poultry to the United States. This relatively minor issue led to quite acrimonious exchanges between Washington and Germany before a compromise solution was reached through the General Agreement on Tariffs and Trade.

The greatest source of trouble between Washington and Bonn during the Kennedy years was, however, the development of relations between the Western alliance and the Soviet bloc. In his first meeting with Khrushchev in June 1961, and still more after the Cuban missile crisis of autumn 1962, Kennedy showed himself determined to strive for an agreement with the Soviet leadership that would make the world a safer place by improving communication between the capitals of the two superpowers and by banning the proliferation of nuclear weapons. Although the German government in general supported these aims, it found some of the implications most unwelcome; Chancellor Adenauer (who was now an extremely old man) regarded the youthful U.S. president's pursuit of East-West détente as potentially dangerous. In particular, it appeared to Adenauer that Kennedy might go further than Dulles had appeared willing to go in 1958–1959 and actually make an agreement with the Soviet Union that would compromise interests that Germany regarded as vital. For instance, Kennedy's pursuit of an overall East-West arms control dialogue—starting with the Nuclear Test Ban

Treaty signed in Moscow in 1963—appeared likely to involve the acceptance of the German Democratic Republic as a fully equal signatory of this and other East-West agreements; this of course compromised the long-standing West German view that the East German state should not be recognized.

On another sensitive issue, that of Berlin, the Kennedy administration began in 1961 (after the building of the Berlin Wall) to discuss with the Soviet Union a number of specific proposals for improving the situation in and around Berlin, including such dangerous (to the Germans) ideas as the notion that access to West Berlin should be controlled by an international authority of which the GDR should be a member. When Adenauer's government was informed by Washington early in 1962 that ideas along these lines were being discussed between Washington and Moscow, Adenauer's reaction was to leak the draft proposals to the press and then to make a speech in Berlin (May 8, 1962) in which he violently denounced the Kennedy administration for being prepared to betray vital German interests. This incident led to the recall of the West German ambassador in Washington, at the request of the U.S. administration, and to the worst crisis in U.S.-German relations in the entire postwar period.

In the months before Kennedy's assassination in November 1963, much was done both in Washington and in Bonn to smooth over the conflicts of the previous year: For instance, the U.S. administration made it absolutely clear that there was no question that the Test Ban Treaty of 1963 would be extended into a general East-West nonaggression pact, which would have further upgraded the status of the GDR. The lessons of the Kennedy administration, as far as U.S.-German relations were concerned, were summarized in an article in the *New York Times Magazine* of December 15, 1963, by the wise elder statesman, Dean Acheson:

> My thesis is that in making political and military judgments affecting Europe a major—often *the* major—consideration should be their effect on the German people and the German government. It follows from this that the closest liaison and consultation with the German government is an absolute necessity. . . . Unexpected or unexplained action nearly always causes consternation in Bonn. Sensible action after careful consultation, even when there has been some difference of view, rarely does.

A Period of Stable Partnership, 1963–1969

The presidency of Lyndon B. Johnson was a period during which the underlying harmony of interests between Bonn and Washington was reaffirmed after the dramatic episodes of the Kennedy presidency. There were several reasons why the alliance during this period was so harmonious. In the first place, the men in control of policy in both the United States and the Federal Republic had more in common with each other than Kennedy and Adenauer, who had been so sharply opposed in temperament and political philosophy. Second, there were no major threats to Berlin or to European security, comparable to those of 1961, to bring U.S.-German divergences to light; and third, the attention of the United States was increasingly concentrated on the problems of the Vietnam War, so that there were no dramatic European initiatives from Washington that were liable, like the MLF proposal under Kennedy or the "Year of Europe" launched by Kissinger in 1973, to create confusion and division in Germany.

The main problems that arose in U.S.-German relations during the Johnson years were in fact caused by economic difficulties. The cost of the Vietnam War and the continuing problems of the U.S. balance of payments led Washington to press the Federal Republic to take over a larger share of the costs of U.S. forces in Germany. At the same time, however, the Federal Republic itself was running into increasing economic difficulties—it was in fact the economic recession of the mid-1960s that was to remove Chancellor Erhard from office in 1966 and to lead to his replacement by the "grand coalition"—and there were fairly strict limits to what the Germans felt they could afford to pay. Chancellor Erhard's visit to Washington in September 1966, when he agreed under strong U.S. pressure to maintain the existing level of German offset payments, led to the revolt of the Free Democratic members of his cabinet and their resignation from office. Thus started the chain of events leading to the creation of the Christian Democratic Union–Social Democratic party (CDU-SPD) "grand coalition" under Kiesinger and Brandt at the end of the year.

One of the lessons German politicians drew from this episode was that a German chancellor might be at risk if he allowed a U.S. president to drive too hard a bargain with him, as Johnson appeared to have done with Erhard. From now on, for this and other reasons, West German leaders developed a tendency to be more outspoken in public defense of German interests in their dealings with Washington, even though in the last resort all Germans understood that the position of the Federal Republic depended on the support of the United States.

Yet, it should again be stressed that U.S.-German relations during the Johnson administration were on the whole very harmonious. This was particularly true of the attitudes that the governments in Bonn and Washington both took toward the crucial issue of relations with the Soviet bloc. Whereas Bonn and Washington had gotten badly out of line on this issue during the period following the building of the Berlin Wall in 1961, both governments were now agreed that better relations with the East should be pursued, but only in slow and careful stages. The cautious steps taken by the Johnson administration in the process, which the president characterized as "bridge-building" between East and West (the development of economic and commercial exchanges, closer cultural relations, and so forth), were closely in line with the policy of East-West reconciliation through "small steps" pursued both by Erhard and by Kiesinger. The U.S. administration was extremely careful not to antagonize the Federal Republic by taking any hasty steps in the direction of recognizing the GDR (a policy made easier by the fact that the Soviet Union was not actively pressing the issue during this period), and Bonn likewise kept in line with the U.S. approach by developing more flexible views of its own on some of the key aspects of the problem. For instance, it was generally accepted in Bonn by 1969 that the aim of reunifying Germany within the 1937 frontiers was an unrealistic and untenable objective and that the Federal Republic must accept at least a minimal degree of formal relations with the GDR as a state in order to improve the chances of bringing about closer contacts between the German people on both sides of the dividing line.

In the concrete issues that were the subject of East-West negotiations during this period, notably the Nuclear Nonproliferation Treaty, Washington and Bonn thus acted with a high degree of mutual confidence and active cooperation. They also agreed on the general redefinition of the aims of NATO, which were defined in the Harmel Report of 1967 as the pursuit both of defense and of détente.

Brandt's Ostpolitik and Nixon's "Era of Negotiations," 1969–1974

The close understanding that had developed between Bonn and Washington in the course of a partnership lasting more than twenty years was to be put acutely to the test during the period of dramatic changes in international relations that occurred in the early 1970s. It had been relatively easy for the United States and the Federal Republic to keep their overall aims and perspectives in close harmony with one another during the Cold War period of the 1950s, when both Washington and Bonn were convinced that there were no prospects of successful negotiation with the Soviet Union and that the overriding priority for both of them was to build up the military strength of the Western alliance. It was much more difficult for the two partners to keep in step when the confrontation of the Cold War gave way to the much more flexible prospects of East-West détente. In this new situation, there was vastly increased scope for misunderstanding and mistrust between the two capitals. From Washington's point of view, there appeared to be considerable risk that the new Ostpolitik pursued by Chancellor Brandt— a policy of flexibility and negotiations with the Soviet Union and other Eastern countries—might lead to a sellout of some important Western interests; and in Bonn there was a certain fear that the developing dialogue between the two superpowers—in a period President Nixon characterized as the "era of negotiations"—might result in a deal that would damage the interests of Germany, for instance, with regard to the problem of Berlin. It is a remarkable tribute to the strength of the partnership between the United States and the Federal Republic, and to the skill and good sense of the political leaders and diplomatic officials in both capitals, that this highly delicate period of East-West diplomacy was brought to a successful conclusion without major German-U.S. conflicts—even though, to be sure, there were some moments of considerable friction.

By the time Brandt and Nixon left office in 1974—the former resigning from the chancellorship in May as a result of the scandal of the discovery of an East German spy in his entourage, the latter resigning the presidency in August as a result of the Watergate scandal—there had been many important changes in the framework of East-West relations in Europe. President Nixon's visit to Moscow in May 1972, which followed some years of intensive negotiations between the superpowers, saw the formal signature of a group of very precise U.S.-Soviet undertakings concerning nuclear weapons: These undertakings covered limitations on both defensive (antiballistic missile) and offensive nuclear systems, and they were accompanied by a comprehensive U.S.-Soviet declaration on the general principles of détente and coexistence. This attempt at understanding between the two superpowers, particularly in the crucial area of nuclear weapons, was confirmed when Soviet leader Brezhnev visited Washington a year later.

Meanwhile the determination of the Brandt government to create a new relationship with Eastern Europe had been symbolized by the chancellor's visits to Moscow in August 1970 and to Warsaw in December 1970 (on the latter occasion Brandt dramatically expressed the German wish for reconciliation by kneeling in a spirit of penitence on the site of the former Jewish ghetto in Warsaw). The West German treaties with the Soviet Union and with Poland, signed on the occasion of Brandt's two visits, were ratified by the West German parliament after stormy debates that nearly brought about the downfall of the Brandt government in the spring of 1972. These treaties embodied West Germany's acceptance that the German frontier with Poland (the Oder-Neisse Line) would in effect be recognized as the permanent eastern frontier of Germany; the treaties also accepted the principle that the German nation was likely to remain divided into two states for some time.

In addition to these U.S.-Soviet agreements and the direct agreements made between the Federal Republic and the states to the east, a third major East-West agreement was negotiated in 1970–1971 and came into force in June 1972. This was the Quadripartite Agreement on Berlin, signed between the Soviet Union on the one hand and the United States, Britain, and France on the other. This agreement, an essential part of the stabilization of East-West relations that was desired both by Bonn and by Washington, embodied a number of important concessions the Soviet Union made to the Western point of view, especially the right of West Berlin, under Allied responsibility, to enjoy easier access to the outside world and guaranteed links of all kinds (except constitutional ones) with the Federal Republic.

The Berlin agreement was in turn followed by a gradual improvement in relations between the two German states. In the new atmosphere of better communication between East and West, both East and West Germany were prepared to negotiate on such matters as the improvement of transport, trade, telephone and postal communications, and closer relations generally; these negotiations prepared the way for the Basic Treaty they signed in December 1972, by which they agreed to recognize each other as states.

The fact that the close understanding between Bonn and Washington survived all the strains and possible misunderstandings caused by the negotiation of the vast complex of East-West agreements is all the more remarkable in view of the other changes in the world at the same time, many of which had a direct bearing on the U.S.-German relationship. The worsening situation in the Middle East, for instance, which led to the Yom Kippur war in the autumn of 1973, brought to light some major differences in perception between Washington and Bonn. Whereas Washington was determined to come to the aid of Israel in the war and even used U.S. military bases in Germany to send reinforcements to the Israeli army, Bonn had by this time moved a good deal closer to the Arab states, and there was great concern in Bonn that Germany's involuntary association with the pro-Israeli policy of Washington might do serious damage to Germany's relations with the oil-producing Arab states.

Another source of friction between the United States and the Federal Republic during the period was, as often before, economic problems affecting the political relationships of the Western world. The enlargement of the European Community from six states to nine through the incorporation of Britain, Ireland, and Denmark, which took place in January 1973, created a European trading bloc in which certain elements of conflict between the United States and Western Europe (including the Federal Republic) showed signs of becoming more acute. There had already, indeed, been considerable friction between the United States and the West European allies (especially the Federal Republic) as a result of the monetary crisis of the spring of 1971, which led to the program of emergency measures announced by President Nixon on August 15, ending the Bretton Woods monetary system and bringing a degree of protectionism into international trade relations.

One reason the Washington-Bonn partnership was so successful in overcoming these difficulties was that the men occupying the top leadership positions in both capitals, despite their very different political and ideological backgrounds, in fact proved very pragmatic and flexible in their approach to the problems facing them in office. Thus their points of view could be relatively easily reconciled. It had been feared by some observers that the U.S.-German relationship would suffer when a right-wing Republican administration took office in Washington at the same time as the political balance in Germany shifted fairly decisively to the left, Willy Brandt being the first member of the Social Democratic party to be chancellor of Germany since 1930. In the 1950s, indeed, the Social Democratic opposition in Germany, led by Kurt Schumacher, had shown strong resistance to the pro-Western alignment of German foreign policy under Adenauer and had opted for a distinctly neutralist position between East and West. At the same time, the economic policy of the SPD, until the adoption of a new program at the party's conference in Bad Godesberg in 1959, still showed strong traces of the Marxist origins of the party: There was a strong commitment to nationalization of large sectors of the economy and an increase in government regulation of business.

By the time the Brandt administration took office, however, the SPD had decisively shifted its position both on foreign and on economic policy; in foreign affairs, the SPD under Brandt and other leaders (particularly Fritz Erler and Helmut Schmidt) had become a strong supporter of the Federal Republic's membership in NATO and other Western organizations, and in economic policy the Godesberg Program had broken decisively with the strict principles of socialism and made a clear commitment to the principles of a mixed economy. Chancellor Brandt and his main political colleagues—who included Karl Schiller and Herbert Wehner, as well as Schmidt—thus represented an administration that was not as far removed from the political and economic philosophy of the United States as might have been the case; this moderation in the policy of the SPD was further confirmed by the presence in government of Brandt's coalition partner, the Free Democratic party (FDP), led by Walter Scheel, who served under Brandt as vicechancelloi and minister for foreign affairs. The FDP, like the SPD, had indeed shown some tendencies toward a neutralist foreign policy in the 1950s, under their leader of the time, Thomas Dehler, but by the time the Brandt-Scheel government took office the FDP's foreign policy orientation was entirely pro-Western.

In Washington, the situation was in some ways parallel. In terms of the general traditional orientation of the Republican party, it might have been feared that the transition from the Democratic Johnson administration to the Republican administration under Nixon would bring a shift to the right both in economic policy and in regard to East-West relations. There was indeed some friction between Washington and Bonn over economic questions (particularly at the time of the so-called Nixon measures of August 1971 and also when some of the U.S.–European Community trade issues became more difficult a couple of years later), but in terms of its foreign policy orientation the Nixon administration took a line that was essentially compatible with Bonn's, and these questions of foreign policy were in fact the most significant ones for the Washington-Bonn partnership. Nixon's determination to go down in history as the president who transformed the era of confrontation into the era of negotiation was the main factor that produced an underlying harmony between his policy and that of Brandt. Not only President Nixon himself but also many of the leading figures concerned with U.S.-European relations in his administration showed a sensitive appreciation of the problems and objectives of the German government. President Nixon's most influential adviser on foreign policy, Henry Kissinger, was of course German by origin: He had an excellent knowledge of the political situation in Bonn, and he had been disturbed by what he regarded as the insensitive handling of Germany by the Kennedy administration. In the State Department, the important post of assistant secretary for European affairs was now occupied by Martin Hillenbrand, a career diplomat who had acquired an extremely close understanding of Germany in the course of many years' work on German matters both in Washington and as counselor of the U.S. Embassy in Bonn. The Nixon administration's ambassador to Bonn, Kenneth Rush, even though he was new to diplomacy (he was a former law professor, president of the Union Carbide Company, and a friend of Nixon's attorney general, John Mitchell), proved to be an extremely able promoter of U.S.-German cooperation, particularly during the delicate negotiations of 1971 on the Berlin agreement. His very close relations with President Nixon were of great importance in maintaining U.S.-German harmony at this stage.

Among the issues facing the leaders in Bonn and Washington, in addition to the dramatic developments in high diplomacy concerning relations with the East, were the familiar issues of the cost of U.S. troops stationed in Germany. As negotiations began for the renewal of the U.S.-German offset agreement, which was due to expire in June 1971, the U.S. balance-of-payments deficit reached a record level. This gave force to the arguments put forward by Senator Mike Mansfield and other critics of the high cost of the U.S. military presence in Germany. In 1971 the so-called Mansfield Resolution, demanding that Western Europe should either pay a higher percentage of the cost or face reductions in U.S. forces there, was debated by the Senate. The administration succeeded in having the resolution rejected but at the same time found it necessary to take a fairly tough line in negotiating the next two-year agreement (to cover the period 1971–1973) with the Federal Republic. For the first time, the 1971 offset agreement included a considerable contribution by the German authorities toward the modernization of barracks and other U.S. facilities in Germany. This new element in the agreement—which also included the by now traditional German commitment to purchase U.S. military equipment and U.S. Treasury bonds—reflected not only a tough U.S. bargaining position but also the willingness of the Bonn government to pay a somewhat higher price for U.S. support at a time when its Ostpolitik was arousing a certain degree of mistrust and controversy. It was particularly important to the Brandt government to maintain the public support of the U.S. administration at a time when the German opposition was criticizing Bonn's Eastern negotiations on the grounds that they would create a breach in the Atlantic alliance.

The course of Bonn's negotiations with its eastern neighbors from 1969 onward was in fact punctuated by constant rumors that Brandt's approaches to the East were causing concern in Washington. Although these reports, which were promoted by the German opposition for reasons of party politics, were greatly exaggerated, they were not wholly without foundation: There were moments during the rapid development of Brandt's Ostpolitik when some officials in Washington felt that the process of preliminary discussion had not been as full as it might have been. The main U.S. concern was not that the substance of Ostpolitik was taking the Federal Republic in a direction that did not reflect U.S. sentiments about the realities of Germany's position; it was rather that, by making premature concessions that might remain unreciprocated, the new German government might provoke a public reaction in Germany so violent that it would endanger both the policy of East-West détente and the West German regime itself. This applied particularly to Bonn's dealings with Moscow; it was feared in Washington that the German government, in its eagerness to make progress in relations with the Soviet Union, might be tempted into making unwise concessions. Chancellor Brandt, in a public review of German exchanges of views with the U.S. government during the year 1970, indicated revealingly that whereas allied consultation on matters concerning Berlin had been constant, detailed, and effective, the exchanges between Bonn and Washington on the separate question of how to deal with the Soviet Union had been rather less effective. In fact, when the West German–Soviet Treaty was signed in August 1970, the U.S. response was basically one of approval, and the same was true of Brandt's agreement with Poland at the end of the year.

By the spring of 1972, when the whole package of East-West agreements had been ratified and brought into force, the underlying unity of purpose between Washington and Bonn had been confirmed. A major symbolic event of this period was a speech given by Willy Brandt at the Harvard University commencement in June 1972, commemorating the twenty-fifth anniversary of the Marshall Plan. In a comprehensive review of twenty-five years of U.S.-German partnership, Brandt underlined in particular the identity of views between the Federal Republic and the United States on the fundamental principles of democracy and also the shared objectives of the two countries in questions of foreign policy. To give tangible expression to West Germany's deep feelings of gratitude for the Marshall Plan, announced by Secretary of State Marshall at the same university twenty-five years before, Chancellor Brandt announced that the West German government was providing a large sum of money to establish the German Marshall Fund of the United States, a foundation devoted to the support of cooperative endeavors of all kinds between the United States and Western Europe.

During the remaining two years of the Brandt administration (1972–1974), developments in U.S.-German relations were less dramatic. Building on the foundations laid by the diplomatic breakthroughs of the early 1970s, both Washington and Bonn devoted themselves to the pursuit of East-West détente on a multilateral rather than a bilateral basis. This meant essentially that East-West negotiations were conducted within the broader international frameworks of the Conference on Security and Cooperation in Europe, which opened in Helsinki in 1973, and the more technical discussions on Mutual and Balanced Force Reductions, which began in the same year in Vienna. In both these sets of negotiations there was close understanding between the United States and West German negotiators on the objectives to be pursued. In the Vienna talks on troop reductions, to be sure, there was a major issue of principle to be resolved, namely, whether the negotiations should cover military forces from the countries within the area affected by the proposed agreement (i.e., West German troops in particular) or only the forces of the superpowers stationed within the area in question, but this question was resolved by amicable discussions between Washington and Bonn.

Thus, by the time President Nixon and Chancellor Brandt had handed over the reins of the office to President Ford and Chancellor Schmidt, the partnership between their two countries, originally established in the years of the Cold War, appeared to have been fully confirmed and even reinforced by the challenges of the period of détente.

Schmidt Faces Ford, Carter, and Reagan, 1974–1980

There were many elements of change in the relationship between Washington and Bonn between the mid-1970s and the early 1980s, particularly the three changes during that period in the U.S. presidency. On the other hand, there were a number of elements of continuity, not least the fact that Chancellor Schmidt continued to hold office in Bonn without interruption or serious challenge; after taking over from Willy Brandt in May 1974, he was triumphantly reelected to office in 1976 and again in 1980. During this period, while there were frequent changes not only in Washington but also in other NATO capitals (for instance, London from 1974 to 1979 had four prime ministers—Edward Heath, Harold Wilson, James Callaghan, and Margaret Thatcher), Bonn remained a pillar of stability and continuity. It was also noteworthy that Chancellor Schmidt during this period developed a very close working partnership with the other European leader to enjoy a long term of office, namely Valéry Giscard d'Estaing, the president of France from 1974 to 1981. Thus, despite all the variations in the Washington-Bonn relationship during these years, from one point of view they can be considered as a whole: the period of Chancellor Schmidt's leading role in the affairs of the Western alliance.

The rising influence of Germany within NATO and within the European Community—which led to the publication of numerous commentaries under such titles as "Germany Steps Up" (an article by R. G. Livingston in the spring 1976 *Foreign Policy*)—was due not only to the personal position of power enjoyed by the West German chancellor. A further factor was that the West German economy came through the world recession of the mid-1970s in rather better shape than many other Western countries. By the late 1970s the Federal Republic represented one-third of the wealth of the European Economic Community of nine nations (the Federal Republic was twice as rich as the United Kingdom and about 30 percent wealthier than France), and the stability of the German mark stood in clear contrast to the instability of the dollar.

The rising economic power of the Federal Republic, combined with the relative instability of some of its European partners and with the passage of time since the end of the Third Reich, combined to make the new chancellor feel able to speak with rather more independence and authority in world affairs than his predecessors. Chancellor Schmidt was in any case more outspoken than Chancellor Brandt in criticism of both German officials and Germany's foreign partners, and this is one of the reasons why his relations with President Carter were marked by a good deal of friction. The self-evident rise in the international authority and standing of the Federal Republic in fact led some U.S. commentators to suggest that the Federal Republic should be given the formal status of the United States's leading partner in the management of the affairs of the Western world. In the last year of the Ford administration, for instance, this argument was very strongly put by the eminent economist C. Fred Bergsten, who argued in a widely publicized article that the United States should base its European policy squarely on a relationship of "bigemony" with the Federal Republic. In economic terms, there was much to be said for this argument, even though critics of Dr. Bergsten argued that he went too far in asserting that the European Community was so incoherent as a partner for the United States that Washington should look to Bonn and forget about Brussels. In political terms, however, it was not acceptable to any of Washington's European partners, and not even to the Federal Republic, that the overall relationship between the European and U.S. components of the Atlantic alliance should be reduced to a relationship between Washington and Bonn.

Moreover, a number of factors of discord were beginning to develop in the Bonn-Washington relationship, and they became worse once the Ford administration was replaced by the Carter administration in January 1977. One source of the trouble was very obviously the fact that President Carter and Chancellor Schmidt approached political matters from quite different standpoints. From Schmidt's point of view, the incoming Carter administration represented the worst sort of idealistic approach to world problems, of a kind that had tended to be characteristic of the Democratic party. Just as the youthful President Kennedy and some of his more idealistic advisers had alarmed the Adenauer government and disrupted the U.S.-German consensus in the early 1960s, so President Carter's idealism and willingness to experiment in international affairs proved difficult for Bonn to cope with after 1977. President Carter's tendency to approach world problems, both East-West and North-South, in terms of general concepts or slogans of a rather naive kind alarmed the pragmatic and tough-minded Schmidt. It was also no comfort to Bonn that President Carter's main adviser on international affairs, Zbigniew Brzezinski, adopted an approach to world politics that appeared to give relatively low priority to the specific concerns of Germany. Both President

Carter and his adviser, although they expressed good intentions about the management of world problems, appeared to be operating on a level of abstraction that was somewhat removed from the more concrete preoccupations of the government in Bonn.

In addition to these differences in temperament and style, there is no doubt that major substantive differences between Washington and Bonn began to develop during this period on a number of issues. There were at least five such issues, which were to cause serious friction. They were, first, a conflict between the economic policies pursued by the United States and those of the Federal Republic; second, conflicting policies with regard to nuclear energy and particularly the policy pursued by the Federal Republic of transferring advanced nuclear technology to Brazil and other foreign purchasers; third, a number of disputes on issues within the Atlantic alliance, including both the problem of competition between Bonn and Washington for the sale of military hardware to their NATO allies and also a major clash about the deployment of new weapons systems in the European theater; fourth, an acute difference of opinion on how to deal with the Soviet bloc on East-West questions, especially human rights; and fifth, disagreement about how to respond to the demands of the developing countries of the world for a new economic order in North-South relations.

The first issue—that of economic policies—arose when the United States put pressure on the Bonn administration to make a contribution to international economic recovery by reflating the German economy faster than Bonn wished or intended. This was described as making the Federal Republic of Germany the "locomotive" of economic revival in the Western world as a whole. As soon as the Carter administration took office in January 1977, Vice-President Walter Mondale put strong pressure on Chancellor Schmidt to take the lead in economic revival; he argued that the Federal Republic, like Japan, should use its strong economy and its substantial financial reserves to embark on a policy of reflation that would hasten the recovery of the world economy.

As was to be expected, the German response to this demand was negative. The fear of inflation, stimulated by memories of Germany's catastrophic inflations of the 1920s and 1940s, is a dominant feature of German thinking in financial policy, and in 1977 Bonn was not prepared to go beyond the modest increase in spending on economic infrastructure that was already planned for the years ahead. Even though the difference in approach was reduced by discussions between Chancellor Schmidt and President Carter when they met for the first time at the Western economic summit conference held in London in May 1977, an underlying difference of opinion between the two capitals continued to create friction in the relationship.

The second major issue, that of nuclear energy, appeared for a time even more likely to create acute tensions between Washington and Bonn. The Federal Republic's heavy reliance on imported energy, which was dramatically confirmed in the 1973–1974 oil crisis, led to a national policy of actively developing the production of nuclear energy; as a by-product of this, the Federal Republic became one of the world's leading exporters of nuclear technology. In a major agreement signed in June 1975 with Brazil, the Federal Republic undertook to deliver eight nuclear power stations, as well as a complete fuel-reprocessing cycle, including an enrichment plant for uranium. In Washington, the prospect of the transfer of this technology to Brazil—which would provide Brazil with the capacity to manufacture nuclear bombs—aroused deep misgivings, which were all the greater because Brazil had refused to sign the Nuclear Nonproliferation Treaty. Much was at stake for both sides. President Carter and his advisers saw the proposed Brazilian deal as a precedent that would unleash a worldwide wave of nuclear proliferation, whereas for the Federal Republic, the earnings from this deal, and the economies of scale in the production of a longer run of nuclear power stations, would help to meet the high cost of Germany's own nuclear program, and the abandonment of the deal would endanger thousands of jobs. After intensive negotiations between Washington and Bonn a compromise was reached in June 1977, by which the United States lifted its objections to the German sale to Brazil and Bonn in exchange confirmed that Germany would make no further sales abroad of nuclear recycling technology, at least "for the time being." As with the issue of macro-economic policy, however, differing approaches to nuclear policy remained a potential source of conflict.

The third problem, that of U.S.-German competition in the provision of military equipment for NATO, represented the development of a long history of wrangling on this issue. Ever since the U.S. balance of payments began to worsen in the early 1960s, Washington had pressed the Germans to offset the cost of stationing troops in Europe by purchasing U.S. weaponry, as well as by making contributions in other ways. Under the Ford administration, agreement had been reached in principle that the essential components of the new battle tank to be used by the U.S. and West German armies in the 1980s should be standardized. In the early months of the Carter administration, however, Bonn officials accused the Americans of undermining this agreement by publicly arguing that the U.S. tank, the XMI, was superior to the German Leopard II tank, which implied that the proposed standardization of components would have to be reconsidered. This dispute became linked with another over the financing of NATO's new Airborne Warning and Command System (AWACS); the United States wished the European share of the cost of the system to be as high as possible. There was hard bargaining over the link between these two issues, with Washington resisting the purchase of a full share of German tank components and Bonn retaliating by resisting the idea of contributing to the cost of AWACS.

In another issue concerning the military equipment for NATO's European theater, there was a spectacular clash between Washington and Bonn late in 1977, when the Carter administration decided to press ahead with plans for deploying "neutron bombs" (enhanced radiation nuclear weapons) on German soil. This prospect stimulated vigorous protests by the West German peace movement, but Chancellor Schmidt, in the interests of Bonn's alliance with Washington, lent his support to the proposal. In so doing he incurred considerable enmity on the left wing of his party, and it was therefore highly embarrassing and irritating for him when the Carter administration unexpectedly changed its mind and decided not to proceed with the proposed deployment.

A fourth source of friction between Bonn and Washington in the Carter period was the question of how to deal with the Soviet Union on questions of human rights. President Carter, when he set out the new administration's view on this issue, condemned Soviet violations of human rights in terms that almost amounted to an ultimatum; in fact, the Carter administration made the promotion of human rights one of the central planks of its foreign policy throughout the world. Although Chancellor Schmidt shared the essentials of the U.S. viewpoint, he regarded explicit condemnation of Soviet practice as counterproductive; in particular, he argued that the position of the 17 million Germans in the GDR, and the chances of emigration for German minorities throughout Eastern Europe, could be improved only by patient negotiation and not by public polemics. Semipublic criticism of the U.S. position by Schmidt in the spring of 1977 set the scene for further disagreements between Washington and Bonn in the course of the international conference convened later in the year in Belgrade to review the carrying-out of the Helsinki Agreement on Cooperation and Security in Europe. Human rights continued to be an issue on which the German and U.S. points of view were very different.

Fifth and last, it should be noted that German and U.S. points of view diverged on the issues of North-South economic relations. The Conference on International Economic Cooperation, which met in Paris throughout 1976, waited until early 1977 to see what view the new U.S. administration would take. At this major conference on the relations between developed and developing countries, President Carter in fact took a view distinctly opposed to that taken by the Federal Republic in earlier negotiations: The Carter Administration was sympathetic to international planning arrangements that would provide large buffer stocks of primary commodities, whereas Bonn held that such stocks would be very expensive and would distort the operation of market forces in setting the prices of raw materials. This difference in perspective, which continued to play some role in U.S.-German economic discussions until the end of the Carter administration (when the Reagan administration in fact took a view nearer to that held in Bonn), was a minor but not a negligible factor in stimulating U.S.-German discord.

Washington and the Kohl Administration

The unexpected collapse of the SPD-FDP coalition in the autumn of 1982, followed by the appointment of the CDU leader Helmut Kohl as chancellor and the triumphant success of his party in the election of March 1983, created a new situation in relations between Bonn and Washington.

The main cause of the sense of relief—even jubilation—expressed in administration circles in Washington when the CDU thus returned to office after thirteen years in opposition was the fact that this change made the security and political situation in Europe look much safer from the U.S. point of view. As usual, Washington's relations with Bonn were influenced by its perspective as a superpower: The U.S.–West German relationship was dependent to some extent on the U.S.-Soviet one. As the East-West military balance had deteriorated, from a Western point of view, during the late 1970s, the West German administration under Helmut Schmidt had at first taken a strongly pro-U.S. position: Chancellor Schmidt himself was primarily responsible for the "two-track decision" taken by NATO at the end of 1979, which committed the alliance to the stationing of Pershing II and cruise missiles in Western Europe if East-West talks did not succeed in reducing the Soviet SS-20 arsenal. By 1982, however, under the influence of the antinuclear movement in West Germany and elsewhere, Helmut Schmidt's party—particularly when he was replaced as leader by Hans Jochen Vogel after the coalition with the FDP collapsed—moved to a position more critical of the U.S. commitment to deploy these new weapons in Europe. During the federal election campaign of February–March 1983, the CDU took a line very much nearer to that of Washington than that of the SPD, and this was the main reason why the victory of Kohl was greeted so warmly in Washington. The new administration of Chancellor Kohl, which included several men who were well known and well liked by the Reagan administration (including the new minister of defense, Manfred Wörner), laid special stress in its early declarations on the need to maintain close relations with Washington during the difficult period of East-West negotiations that lay ahead.

The East-West situation, however, was not the only reason why the Reagan administration felt such sympathy with the new men in office in Bonn. In the field of economic and monetary affairs, the Kohl administration promised to undertake a policy of credit restraint and curbs on public spending that brought it more in line with the Reagan approach to economic policy than the previous Schmidt administration had been.

By the summer of 1983, therefore, with right-of-center administrations in office both in Washington and in Bonn, there appeared to be at least a good prospect of continuing close agreement between the two allies both on international and domestic matters. It was, however, clear that this agreement would not be problem free. On the question of economic dealings with the Soviet bloc, for instance, Chancellor Kohl and his ministers (who included both Vice-Chancellor Genscher and Economics Minister Lambsdorff, who had served in the same post under Schmidt) made it clear that Germany had a continuing interest in maintaining economic links with the East. Lambsdorff, for instance, insisted on the right of the Federal Republic to follow through on its gas pipeline deal with the Soviet government, and when Chancellor Kohl visited Moscow in early July, he again emphasized the particular interest of the Federal Republic in maintaining good relations with the Eastern bloc. One of the fundamental sources of recurrent irritation in the U.S.–West German relationship—the tendency of Bonn and Washington to look with different perspectives on relations with the East—thus remained.

Conclusion: Toward a Partnership of Equals?

By 1980, when President Reagan was elected, there were other issues on which distinct differences between German and U.S. perspectives could be detected. On the central issue of East-West relations, for instance, a deep U.S. skepticism about the viability of détente (strongly reflected in the incoming administration) stood in sharp contrast to the insistence of the German government and large sections of German opinion that the fruits of East-West détente for Germany had been very considerable and that they should not be put at risk. Already, under the Carter administration, Germany had hesitated to accept the need to bring a new generation of nuclear weapons into the European theater of NATO; this hesitation was reflected in the so-called two-track decision taken by NATO at the end of 1979, according to which new weapons would be introduced into Western Europe only if negotiations with the Soviet Union failed to achieve a reduction in Soviet missile strength by 1983.

All these different elements of disagreement between Bonn and Washington added up to an impression, by the early 1980s, that the future of the U.S.-German relationship was not at all as secure as in the past. On the other hand, public opinion polls both in Germany and in the United States repeatedly showed that the majority of the citizens of both countries still had considerable faith in the other as an important ally. Looking at the situation more optimistically, it could even be argued that U.S. policy in Germany after the war, the policy of building up the defeated enemy into a mature and self-confident democracy, had met with very considerable success in creating the kind of Federal Republic with which the United States had to deal by 1980: a democratic state self-confident enough to be able to speak in clear and straightforward terms to its U.S. partner in a relationship between adults. This relationship could indeed be described as one between two partners possessing full equality of rights, even though their economic and material strength continued to be unequal.

Readings

Gatzke, Hans. *Germany and the United States: "A Special Relationship."* Cambridge, Mass.: Harvard University Press, 1980.

Hillenbrand, Martin. "The United States and West Germany." Pp. 73–92 in Wolfram F. Hanrieder (ed.). *West German Foreign Policy: 1949–1979.* Boulder, Colo.: Westview Press, 1980.

Morgan, Roger. *The United States and West Germany, 1945–1973.* London and New York: Oxford University Press, 1974.

Morgan, Roger. *West Germany's Foreign Policy Agenda.* Beverly Hills and London: Sage Publications, 1978.

Smyser, W. R. *German-American Relations.* Beverly Hills and London: Sage Publications, 1980.

RÜDIGER THOMAS

9

The Other German System: A Look at the German Democratic Republic

Introduction

With the founding of two German states in 1949, postwar Germany became the focal point of a dual conflict: the confrontation between two power blocs and between two competing political-economic systems. In the global East-West conflict, the division of Germany became an outstanding example of the former. At the same time, developments within the two German states made them into the most vivid locale for the comparison of the advantages and disadvantages of the alternative political systems of East and West.

The political steps that finally led to the end of a single German state were initiated as early as the first few months after the start of the military occupation of Germany. By the end of 1946 at the latest, despite continuing assurances to the contrary, the division could no longer be averted. The formation of communist regimes in Eastern Europe strengthened Western fears of Soviet expansionist policy, and the sociopolitical ideas put forward by the East German Communists were felt to be a threat to free democratic principles. Both of these trends led to a skepticism that, as early as October 1945, motivated Konrad Adenauer to state somewhat epigrammatically: "Half of Germany whole is preferable to the whole of Germany half." The dominance of security interests turned rhetorical demands for reunification into an incalculable risk. The division of the country was the tribute paid to the force of power politics, which served as the basis for the decision in the fall of 1944 to split Germany into occupation zones. For a long time an attempt was made in the Federal Republic to avoid intellectual acceptance of the political effects of the division of Germany by declaring the split provisional. The German Democratic Republic was, as Ernst Richert put it, a "state that must not be," and as a result, failed to be the subject of any differentiated perception and scientific analysis until well into the 1960s. Anyone wanting to understand present-day Germany will have to take into account the fact of its unwanted but unavoidable dual existence. Only in the overall context of the totality of postwar German history will it be possible to consider anew in what ways the "unity of the German nation" now exists.

History of the German Democratic Republic

Three separate periods can be distinguished in the historical development of the German Democratic Republic (GDR). The *formational phase,* ending with the founding of the GDR on October 7, 1949, is referred to as an "antifascist democratic revolution." The Sozialistische Einheitspartei Deutschlands (Socialist Unity Party of Germany—SED) defines the period from 1949 to 1961 as a stage in the "socialist revolution" in which the "foundations of socialism" were created. These terms are used to describe a comprehensive structural change that was intended to alter radically the political system, the economy, and society. This revolution from above, carried out by the SED and supported by the Soviet occupying power, was accompanied by a concentrated use of repressive power and represented a highly controversial long-term process of transformation. This revolutionary phase ended on August 13, 1961, when the GDR sealed itself off from the West by the construction of the Berlin Wall. The period since 1961 can be described as a phase of postrevolutionary consolidation characterized by the expansion of the socialist system and the "shaping of the developed socialist society."

The Formational Phase. The basic outlines of the strategy used by the German Communists had been worked out under the direction of Wilhelm Pieck and Walter Ulbricht during their wartime exile in Moscow. Immediately after the end of the war the Communist Party of Germany (KPD) promoted the creation of a broad political alliance, in which it assumed that it would have dominant influence on the basis of its close ties with the Soviet occupying power. The alliance of all newly formed political groupings was intended to prevent any competition among parties likely to result in a minority position for the German Communists. In order to dispel the misgivings of their partners, the Communists assured them that initially they did not intend to establish a socialist society but rather an "antifascist democratic order." All political forces were to join together at the moment of defeat ("*Stunde Null,*" or "zero hour") to liquidate forever the foundations of National Socialist tyranny and complete the bourgeois revolution in Germany.

The KPD expressly stated in its program of June 1945 that "it would be wrong to impose the Soviet system on Germany" and advocated a "parliamentary democratic republic with all democratic rights and freedoms for the people." Communist policy was directed toward all of Germany and strove to obtain major influence on developments in all of the occupation zones, which it could hope to achieve only by a strategy of alliance.

In July 1945 a "united front of antifascist democratic forces" was constituted in the Soviet occupation zone. It included the newly established middle-class parties, i.e., Liberals and Christian Democrats, in addition to Communists and Social Democrats. The KPD's interest in a "bloc policy" of all political parties was displaced at the end of 1945 by the forced unification of the two working-class parties, the KPD and the SPD. Despite a decisive rejection by the Social Democrats in the Western occupation zones, the KPD succeeded in overcoming the misgivings of the SPD leadership in the Soviet zone. The SED was formed at a party unification conference on April 21 and 22, 1946.

However, the Communists had still not achieved their aim of gaining control over and imposing conformity on all political forces. During the regional elections in the fall of 1946, the Liberals and Christian Democrats together received about the same number of votes as the SED. In light of this unexpectedly strong competition from the nonsocialist parties, which above all advocated their own economic policies, considerable integration problems manifested themselves in the ranks of the SED. Despite a number of programmatic and organizational concessions on the part of the German Communists, the unification of the KPD and the SPD had failed to eliminate the skepticism among many Social Democrats about Communist domination. The SED's unstable condition was made apparent by numerous resignations of former Social Democrats and considerable differences of opinion on political doctrine.

In June 1948 Walter Ulbricht, who later became secretary general of the party, succeeded in forcing through the organizational transformation of the SED to make it a "party of a new type" patterned on the Soviet model. In doing so, he definitively decided the controversy over the political direction of the party in favor of the Communists. After the Soviet Union's break with Yugoslavia, which took place at the same time, the principle previously put forward that each country should take its "individual road to socialism" was permanently discarded. A bitter war was declared on "social democracy," and any attempt to turn the SED into an "opportunistic party of Western character" was vigorously opposed. By liquidating any remaining virulent Social Democratic thinking in the SED, German Communism completed its alignment with Soviet policy, a situation aptly described by Kurt Schumacher's comment: "The Communist Party is inseparably tied to a single and independent power, i.e., to Russia as a national and imperialist state, and to its foreign policy objectives."

Following their unexpected success in the election of 1946, the nonsocialist parties came under growing political pressure, which restricted their ability to advocate alternative positions and led to an ever-increasing relinquishment of their original Liberal and Christian Democratic principles. Some of the leaders of these parties refused to accept the political conformity demanded of them and were forced to move into the Western occupation zones. By the middle of 1948 a political doctrine had been established in the Soviet occupation zone that was based largely on the model of socialism provided by the Soviet occupying power and that carried out the process of social transformation by a revolution from above, i.e., by a progressive reduction of opportunities for democratic involvement.

The economic policy in the Soviet occupation zone resulted in fundamental changes in proprietorship. The land reform introduced in September 1945 led to the elimination of all private landownership exceeding 100 hectares (about 247 acres). As a result, 2.2 million hectares (5.4 million acres) were seized and distributed to approximately 500,000 persons for private farming. A partial nationalization of industry resulted from the uncompensated "expropriation of war criminals and Nazi activists" justified on the basis of a plebiscite held in Saxony in June 1946. The government-administered Volkseigene Betriebe (People's Enterprises—VEB) accounted for about two-fifths of industrial production in 1948, private enterprises for another two-fifths, and "Soviet corporations" (Sowjetische Aktiengesellschaften—SAG), i.e., confiscated companies operated and exploited directly by the Soviet Union for its own economy, for one-fifth. The opposite directions taken by political and economic development in the Western zones and in the Soviet zone were underscored by the introduction of separate currencies in June 1948. This was the factor that triggered the Soviet blockade of Berlin.

Other political focal points in the first postwar years included denazification, which was accompanied by a broad reorganization of the judicial and administrative systems, as well as a "democratic school reform" (introduction of a uniform school system) and the restructuring of higher education, which was to provide increased access to higher education for working-class children. Through the establishment of special preparatory institutes, later known as "workers' and farmers' faculties," the proportion of working-class children in institutions of higher learning had risen to 36 percent by 1949. Through this educational policy the SED sought not only to participate in the realization of equal opportunity ("elimination of bourgeois educational privileges") but also to create a reservoir of politically reliable and professionally qualified managerial people.

Even though the prospects for the success of an all-German policy began decreasing in the summer of 1946 in the wake of the sharpening East-West conflict, the SED continued to project itself as an advocate and champion of German unity. In November 1946 the SED presented a draft constitution for an undivided German Democratic Republic, designed to underline its all-German claims. However, the failure of the June 1947 Munich Conference of all German Minister Presidents (the prime ministers of all the German *Länder*), at which it was not possible even to achieve agreement on an agenda, made it evident that mutual mistrust and profound political differences had created an unbridgeable gap between the eastern and western parts of Germany. Thereafter, the SED attempted to organize all-German activities outside the formal framework of existing political institutions by a propagandistic mobilization of the masses. This concept was the basis for the People's Congress Movement, an attempt made beginning in November 1947 to establish a pseudoparliamentary representation for Germans in a German People's Congress. An effort was made to gain the participation of political groups in the Western zones—unilaterally and with marginal success—in order to gain more public approval for the SED's own objectives.

In June 1948 the People's Council, formed by the Second German People's Congress, declared itself to be the "authorized representative for all of Germany" and began drawing up a constitution. Based on the Weimar constitution, the draft constitution also incorporated the concept of "people's democracy" as advocated by the SED, i.e., the government was to be composed of representatives of all political parties. The transition from a "formal" to a "real" democracy was to be brought about by this unification of all political forces into a common "national front." The Third German People's Congress, elected in May 1949 on the basis of a single "unity" list, established the Second German People's Council, which—after the convening of the German Bundestag on September 7, 1949—named itself the Provisional People's Chamber without any prior parliamentary elections and proclaimed the founding of the GDR on October 7, 1949.

The effect of the simultaneous founding of the two German states was that each blamed the other for the division of Germany. The GDR accused the Federal Republic of "separatism"; the Federal Republic refused legal recognition of the German Democratic Republic and claimed under international law to be acting in the name of all Germans.

The antagonism between the two governments emerged with particular clarity in Berlin, where the occupying powers had established a joint administration of the city at the end of the war. The basic conflict between a liberal-socialist and a communist orientation manifested itself in the former German capital in connection with the founding of the SED in April 1946. The Social Democrats held a primary election in the western sectors of the city at the end of March. An overwhelming majority of party members rejected an organization merger with the KPD, although they approved of cooperative activity with it. Characteristically, the Soviet military administration had prohibited any such documentation of public opinion in the eastern sector of the city. In the Berlin City Assembly election in October 1946 the SED received just under one-fifth (19.8 percent) of the vote while nearly half of the voting populace (48.7 percent) supported the SPD. With this result, the Communists lost most of their influence on overall developments in Berlin; they then concentrated on expanding their control over the eastern sector with the support of the Soviet occupying power. In June 1948 the Soviet representatives left the Kommandantura, the Four-Power command structure for Berlin, and in November a separate city administration (Magistrate) was formed in East Berlin. This was the beginning of the process of integrating East Berlin into the Soviet occupation zone that was to lead in 1949 to the naming of East Berlin as the capital of the GDR and the seat of its government.

The polarization of political objectives in Germany was doubly concentrated at its focal point in Berlin. It was there that the Western occupation powers matched forces with the Soviet Union during the Berlin blockade, and it was there that the basic political contrast between the two Germanys was most immediately evident as the formation of two alternative societal models continued in the 1950s. In 1948 the "social market economy" was introduced in the Western occupation zones and steps were taken to initiate a parliamentary democracy, the principles of which were anchored in the constitution (Basic Law) of the Federal Republic of Germany (FRG). In the Soviet occupation zone a centrally planned economy was established, based on a progressively increasing degree of government ownership of industry. It was combined with a political system that formally defined itself as a multiparty system but in actual fact was dominated by the SED.

The Socialist Revolution Stage. The takeover of political power by the SED and the founding of the GDR by no means marked the end of the revolutionary restructuring of society. On the contrary, the decisive phase now began. The political leaders of the GDR were faced with a double legitimacy deficit: They governed a state without international recognition and without citizens. To compensate for these deficiencies, the GDR made its policy on Germany and the economy the central areas of activity in establishing a Soviet-style socialist system.

In their policy on Germany the GDR and the Soviet Union pursued a double strategy through which they hoped to influence Western positions. As a consequence of its own policy of nonrecognition, the government of the Federal Republic rejected all official contacts between the two German states. It considered the government of the GDR to be nothing more than an executive organ of Soviet interests and thus felt that it would be possible to overcome the division of Germany only by integrating the eastern part of Germany into the West German "core state." The federal government's adoption of this position under Konrad Adenauer, which was intended to weaken the GDR by its systematic isolation, motivated the GDR's political leadership to try to erode this attitude by constantly proposing negotiations. Under Otto Grotewohl the GDR government repeatedly emphasized the urgent need for accelerating the conclusion of a peace treaty and the restoration of German unity through agreements between the two German states. Despite the slogan "Germans at one table," the GDR's German policy failed to find a partner or to evoke a response.

As a result, the Soviet Union developed a German policy initiative of its own aimed primarily at preventing the intended integration of the Federal Republic of Germany into the West on the basis of security considerations. On March 10, 1952, the Soviet Union sent a note to the Western powers containing principles for the draft of a peace treaty aimed at neutralizing Germany. The Western powers agreed with Chancellor Adenauer that the risk of political neutralization was an unacceptable price for a possible realization of German unity. Although the German Social Democrats pointed out that integration into the West and the rearmament that this implied would necessarily make a solution of the German question extremely difficult, negotiations for a European Defense Community were continued while the Soviet initiative bogged down in a multiple exchange of notes that produced no results.

After the failure of the Berlin Conference of Foreign Ministers early in 1954, each side's policy on Germany was increasingly reduced to an effort to justify its own position in the light of irreconcilable views. Western demands for free all-German elections without preconditions while refusing to recognize the GDR as a separate state were faced with Eastern proposals for *a priori* conclusion of a peace treaty, recognition of the GDR as a negotiating partner, and the neutralization of Germany.

The feeling that political unification was hopeless, which was reinforced by the Korean War, resulted in the final emergence of an integration policy through which both German states advanced to membership in the opposing alliances. The line dividing Germany at the same time became the line dividing Europe between the opposing systems of East and West. When the FRG became a member of the North Atlantic Treaty Organization (NATO) in May 1955 after conclusion of the Contractual Agreements, the Soviet Union, for its part, stabilized the GDR's political status by means of the Declaration of Sovereignty of March 25, 1954, and the treaty of September 20, 1955, which formally ended occupation status. The Soviets created the Warsaw Pact on May 14, 1955, with the participation of the GDR as a visible expression of the formation of military blocs in Europe. Paramilitary units had been established in the GDR in 1952 under the name of the Encamped People's Police; the GDR, after joining the Warsaw Pact, established its own military forces, the National People's Army, in 1956.

The integration of the two German states into the respective alliances permanently consolidated the political division of Germany in 1955. Despite the Western policy of nonrecognition, the maintenance of "provisional status" had become an illusion, as the Soviet Union had drawn the GDR into its sphere of power and, as such, guaranteed the existence of its political system. In support of this status, the following statement was made at the Third SED Party Conference in March 1956: "The development of the German Democratic Republic can now no longer be separated from the development of the entire socialist camp."

With the founding of the GDR, Soviet socialism became the established form of government, but it was still not the constituent basis of society. Party and government leaders could achieve political legitimacy, i.e., recognition of the new political system from within, only if they gave proof of economic and social successes that would substantiate the asserted superiority of the Soviet-socialist system.

In doing this, the GDR had to cope with a difficult situation. In the Soviet occupation zone some 45 percent of industrial productive capacity had been destroyed in the war, more than twice as much as in the Western zones, where the destruction rate was 20 percent. There was a major disproportion between a poorly developed basic materials industry (especially metallurgy and building materials) and a high-quality metal-processing industry (machine tools, textile machines, precision mechanics and optics, electrical engineering). The steel industry in the Soviet occupation zone, for instance, had accounted for only 7.3 percent of total German production in 1936, as opposed to 92.7 percent in the Western zones. Except for large soft coal deposits, the GDR is a country extremely poor in raw materials. The lack of anthracite and metal ores made it very difficult for the GDR to build up its own metallurgical industry. The GDR could not, therefore, simply strive to rebuild its prewar industries. Instead, it had to undertake a far-reaching restructuring of its industry, strongly orienting it toward foreign trade as far as this was possible in light of the overall political situation. An acceleration of economic development was further hindered in the first postwar years by the considerable reparations demanded by the Soviet Union, which continued to January 1, 1954.

Although the transfer of industrial ownership to the government begun in 1946 provided the political leadership with direct economic power, it was accompanied by the loss of qualified managerial people for which the party cadre at first could supply no equivalent replacement. In addition, the SED had to reckon with resistance from the traditional social elites who had been deprived of their powers. Understandably, they did not want to come to terms with the new system and thereby inhibited its consolidation. In this difficult situation, the SED pushed ahead with the implementation of its revolutionary policy. After the GDR reattained its prewar level of industrial production in 1950, the 1951–1955 Five-Year Plan was adopted, envisaging an acceleration of economic growth. Following the permanent failure of the all-German neutralization policy, the "building of socialism" was declared to be "the fundamental task in the German Democratic Republic" at the SED's Second Party Conference in July 1952. The conversion of individual farms into "agricultural production cooperatives" was first planned in 1952, initially on a volunteer basis and without much success.

Attempts by the political leadership to increase economic production by means of an administrative measure imposing higher work norms triggered growing dissatisfaction in the population that culminated in the uprising of June 17, 1953. This demonstrative denial of loyalty on the part of the workers in opposition to the arrogance of the "workers' and farmers' state" clearly showed that the rule of the SED could be guaranteed only through the use of Soviet occupation forces.

The SED's position of power, in which it also made political use of the legal system to eliminate its opponents, could not be challenged as long as it existed in the framework of the Soviet-supported system. However, "the aggravation of the class struggle" (as it was termed by Walter Ulbricht) became clearly apparent in another form. The citizens of the GDR had no choice between political alternatives in their own society, but they were able to choose between two German societies. They were able to withdraw from the state's claim to absolute power by moving to the West, by "voting with their feet." The latent basic conflict within GDR society, which the SED had institutionally blocked by eliminating any form of opposition, was shifted to competition between the two German states. An inner-societal class conflict became an inter-societal conflict between two systems. The stability of rule guaranteed by the Soviet Union was itself the cause of social instability. "Fleeing the republic" not only belied the supposed political consensus, it also caused a considerable loss of economic resources. An analysis of this mass exodus pointed to three causes: A large number of the refugees came from those social groups that were immediately affected by revolutionary restructuring; political motives caused many citizens to leave who were disillusioned by the restrictions imposed on freedom; and the visible success of the "economic miracle" in the Federal Republic of Germany provided an increasing number of economic incentives to leave the GDR.

As it considered the higher standard of living in the Federal Republic to be the primary motive for fleeing, the SED at its Fifth Party Congress in 1958 formulated as its "priority economic task" the objective of attaining and surpassing West German per capita consumption of food and essential consumer goods by 1961. At the same time it continued its socialization policy, using governmental actions to decree the collectivization of agriculture in but a few months' time, a process that was completed on April 19, 1960. But the party's ambitious economic aims were rapidly seen to be unattainable, and the attitude grew stronger among party and government leaders that the exodus of qualified workers would have to be stopped by force. After obtaining the approval of the Soviet Union and the other Warsaw Pact countries, the GDR began to seal off its border with the West by beginning construction of the Berlin Wall on August 13, 1961. This determined self-isolation of the GDR demonstrated that the rigorous policy of social revolution had not found the broad approval the SED claimed. The demonstration of power revealed that the SED was unable to gain acceptance of its political message by the people. At the same time, the "shock therapy" represented by the erection of the Wall was the decisive prerequisite for consolidation within the GDR.

Before 1961 about 3 million people had left the GDR for the West, i.e., nearly one-sixth of its population. The abrupt end of this refugee movement became the basis for economic stability and an acceleration of economic growth. Once the possibility of refusing to cooperate with the state's claim to absolute power over the individual had been eliminated, it became mutually necessary for the political leadership and the population to come to terms. The SED continued its monopoly on political power, but this development became the basis of a social compact that has turned the GDR into an achievement-oriented society. In order to provide the GDR population with greater incentives, the political leaders sought to reward economic growth by providing pay increases and improved social benefits. The rise in the material standard of living and the expansion of a Soviet-socialist policy were supplemented by the opportunity to climb the ladder of success in GDR society, primarily by the acquisition of educational qualifications. In this way it was possible to create a partial identity of interests between politics and society that disguised the continuing absence of political legitimacy of the regime and laid the foundations for "cooperative solidarity" in GDR society.

The Postrevolutionary Consolidation Phase. The collectivization of agriculture and the securing of dependable economic development by sealing the country off from the outside were, in the SED's view, the last two decisive elements for the "victory of the socialist means of production." Beginning in 1962, developments in the GDR entered a period of consolidation characterized by considerable economic successes and noteworthy results in educational and social policy, as well as stronger orientation of its overall policy toward the satisfaction of consumer needs.

After completing the process of revolutionary social restructuring, the SED adopted its first party program, summarizing its basic political positions, at the Sixth Party Congress in January 1963. It is based on a broad interpretation of German history since World War I and contains detailed characterizations of postwar developments in both parts of Germany intended to justify the SED's own political actions. Central to the program is the contention that the "Age of Socialism" had begun on German soil. The dominant aspect of the program, however, is economic development and associated with it is a detailed appreciation of science as "the direct source of productive power."

The first consequence of the modernization policy introduced in the wake of the Sixth Party Congress was an economic reform policy initiated in June 1963 as the "new economic system of planning and economic management." It contained a decentralization of economic decisions, oriented the economy more toward profitability, and created material incentives for higher production levels, all intended to overcome the manifest shortcomings of rigid bureaucratic planning, with its strictly quantitative orientation. The scientific orientation of SED policy was further strengthened at the Seventh Party Congress in April 1967, after the economic reform had shown initial positive results. The theory of a "scientific and technical revolution" served as a basis for establishing technocratic socialism, intended to guarantee policy efficiency through specific applications of cybernetics, information theory, electronic data processing, and social forecasting.

Inasmuch as the original GDR constitution of 1949, intended for all of Germany, did not coincide with constitutional reality, even in a formal sense, a new socialist constitution was adopted in a plebiscite on April 6, 1968. The new constitution defined the GDR as a "socialist state of the German nation" (Article 1) and embodied "socialist ownership of the means of production, planning and management of social development in accordance with the most advanced scientific knowledge" (Article 2).

Walter Ulbricht's proclamation at the SED's Seventh Party Congress of the "economic system of socialism" initiated the second stage of economic reform. Further economic upswing was to be attained by means of technological innovations in key sectors of the economy and by concentrating investments on products, processes, and technologies directly related to the party's goals for the structure of the economy. This one-sided policy led to a weakening of economic growth in 1969 accompanied by shortages of consumer goods, which in turn led to a correction of economic policies in December 1970. Erroneous economic policy decisions after 1967 and a rigid posture in the negotiations between the two German states that began at the end of 1969 can be considered the primary reasons for the end of the Ulbricht era, which had determined political developments in East Germany for a quarter of a century.

The Eighth SED Party Congress in June 1971, following Walter Ulbricht's resignation in May and his replacement as first secretary of the SED by Erich Honecker, marked the beginning of the most recent phase in the history of the GDR. In the 1970s the principle of "unity of economic and social policy" moved into the foreground in the process of "shaping a developed socialist society." The core of the "primary economic task" is a "further raising of the material and cultural standard of living," which necessarily presupposed a corresponding rate of economic growth.

The changed international political status brought about by the conclusion of the Treaty on Intra-German Relations (signed on December 21, 1972), which led to worldwide diplomatic recognition of the GDR and to a considerable increase in travel from the Federal Republic, had a greater effect on domestic policy than was the case in the previous period (1961–1970). International recognition of the political existence of the GDR represented an important factor in the political stabilization of the country, but it also generated expectations for domestic changes and for a fundamental change in the relations between the two German states. However, it thereby revealed considerable shortcomings in the legitimacy of the political system in the GDR and confronted the country's political leaders with new problems.

By fundamentally dissociating itself from the principle of the unity of the German nation, the GDR intended to dispel any illusions about a potential sociopolitical rapprochement between the two German states or the possibility of their ideological coexistence. Integration in the "community of socialist countries," in particular the close relationship with the Soviet Union, was given priority over the common historical tradition of the two German states, resulting in the need for a strict separation from the Federal Republic. The far-reaching changes in and amendments to the GDR constitution that became effective on October 7, 1974, were intended primarily to eliminate the references to one German nation (Article 1) and to the prospect of possible German unification (Article 8).

The potential for conflict that had arisen from the GDR's all-German policy could, however, be neutralized only in part by this policy of disillusionment. Freedom of movement and human rights emerged once again as subjects of public discussion following the signing of the Final Act of the Conference on Security and Cooperation in Europe in Helsinki on August 1, 1975. Individual Marxist scientists as well as numerous writers voiced their grievances about conditions in the GDR and demanded realization of a socialist democracy in which freedom of public criticism and political pluralism would be guaranteed. The political leaders of the GDR responded with the repressive use of government power, including the expulsion of some citizens (Wolf Biermann), their social isolation (Robert Havemann), or their arrest (Rudolf Bahro), and condoned the movement of a number of artists to the Federal Republic. As the debate about peace developed in Western Europe, a peace movement was also formed in the GDR by writers and religious groups. It is critical of the arms buildup and military propaganda in the GDR and avoids blaming the West alone for the East-West military confrontation.

The development of public criticism in the GDR is, however, narrowly limited by government controls. Any apparently justified criticism must be refuted by ideological propaganda and by the expansion of socialist welfare policy. Economic success is of particular importance for the stabilization of society. While maintaining price stability since 1971, the GDR has succeeded in attaining a steady annual economic growth of 4–5 percent, resulting in a rise in the standard of living as well as in a number of remarkable improvements in social policy. The drastic rise in raw material prices on the world market over the last few years has considerably increased the burdens on the GDR economy so that economic growth in the future can be maintained only by a far-reaching "intensification of production," i.e., optimum use of all available resources and constant appeals to the citizens of the country to keep up production levels. The key function of the economy in further "shaping a developed socialist society" was clearly stressed in the new party program (1976) and at the Tenth SED Party Congress (April 1981), at which the accelerated development of microelectronics was announced. Taking stock of the political situation, Erich Honecker announced the fundamental objective for the 1980s: "We will stay on our course with high continuity."

Political System

The political system in the GDR is characterized by the following fundamental factors:

Political and Social Leadership by the SED. The SED's claim to leadership is expressly and irreversibly laid down in the constitution of the GDR (Article 1). The SED justifies its central role in the political system by arguing that it has a scientific weltanschauung, namely Marxism-Leninism. As a result it feels able to achieve scientifically based policies. At the same time the SED claims that as "the conscious and organized vanguard of the working class and laboring population" it represents the interests of the majority of the people in the GDR. Although the SED lays down the basic policy lines, the state is defined as the "main instrument of policy." The party, therefore, has the policy-directing function; the state has the executive and administrative function. The decisions of the party (directives) are implemented through measures of the state (laws).

Elimination of the Principle of Competition. From the Marxist-Leninist point of view, the cause of class conflict is removed when the means of production have been socialized. In principle there is, therefore, a basic identity of interests in all of GDR society. The function of politics is no longer to resolve conflicts among competing programs and parties but has been transformed into an "alliance of policies." Various parties and social organizations associated with diverse social classes and groups still exist in the political system of the GDR. However, their aim is not to represent specific interests but to work toward their integration into the system. Politics is defined as "joint action." "The alliance of all of the powers of the people is expressed organizationally through the National Front of the German Democratic Republic" (Article 3 of the constitution). In this framework political opposition is a phenomenon contradictory to the system and is suppressed with the instruments of power available to the state. The freedom to form coalitions guaranteed in the Constitution of the GDR is restricted to organizations that approve the principle of the alliance of policies and that acknowledge the SED's claim to a leadership role.

Overall Social Planning. The GDR economy is based on public ownership of the means of production. The nationalization of industry took place with the formation of the Volkseigene Betriebe, whereas a system of state-controlled production cooperatives was established for agriculture. The socialist restructuring of industrial ownership, from which only small businesses in manual trades and services are exempted, is the basis of the socialist planned economy in the GDR. The principle of management and planning applies not only to the economy, however, but also to all other areas of activity (Article 9). Overall social planning is a consequence of the state's claim to control of all social resources. It is intended to express the rational character of politics. In the process of planning, the state translates the political directives and basic decisions of the party into concrete and controllable measures. The state has the function of guaranteeing, in Erich Honecker's words, "the scientific, precisely balanced and uniform guidance and planning of social development."

Political Mobilization of the Masses. "Socialist democracy" is supposed to establish comprehensive participation by all citizens in the shaping of political, economic, social, and cultural life and is based on the principle "work together, plan together, and govern together!" (Article 21). Membership in political parties and social organizations is, therefore, strongly encouraged. However, political participation is limited to efforts to implement objectives laid down by the party and the state. The media have an important role in creating a uniform political orientation. Their function is to disseminate the political principles formulated by the SED and, in the same manner as educational institutions, to promote the development of a uniform "socialist consciousness."

Socialist Legal System. In contrast to the Western democracies, the GDR takes the view that there is no independent and neutral legal order guaranteeing universal basic and human rights. The legal system is viewed as an instrument of power for use in defending specific class interests. In accordance with the principle of the concentration of powers advocated in the GDR, the "socialist system of law" (Article 19) is seen as part of the unitary power of the state. Judges are subject to the directives and controls of the state and can be removed from office by the legislature. The basic rights guaranteed in the constitution are in fact guaranteed only insofar as they do not question the political system.

Integration in the Community of Socialist Countries. The origin and consolidation of the GDR was decisively influenced by the Soviet Union.

The close relationship to the Soviet Union is stated in the constitution to be "irrevocable" and a guarantee of the GDR's continued existence. At the same time it is emphasized that the GDR is "an inseparable part of the community of socialist states" (Article 8). The SED's irreversible claim to a leadership role establishes a specific structure in the domestic political system; at the same time the GDR's membership in the worldwide Soviet-socialist system under the leadership of the Soviet Union is elevated to an immutable constitutional principle.

To analyze the functioning of this political system, it is necessary to understand the party organization and its decision-making process. The SED has more than 2.1 million members, i.e., one out of six GDR citizens over 18 belongs to the party. It is organized in both industrial and geographic units. Individual party groupings are formed where members work and in their areas of residence. Party leaders are in full control in ministries, administrative authorities, and industrial enterprises. The fundamental organizational principle of the SED is that of democratic centralism, a definition of which is found in the Party Statute. It reads as follows (Item 23):

a) All Party organs, from the lowest to the highest, are elected democratically;

b) the elected Party organs are obliged to report regularly to the organizations that elected them;

c) all decisions made by higher Party organs are binding on subordinate organs, strict Party discipline must be observed and minorities as well as individuals must submit to the decisions of the majority.

Since party officials who have been elected to leadership positions have to be approved by higher bodies in the party hierarchy, the party's central organization clearly has supremacy. The Party Congress is considered the "highest organ of the party" and is convened once every five years to coincide with the periods of economic planning. However, the real decision-making bodies are the Central Committee, the Politburo, and the Central Committee Secretariat. The Central Committee can be viewed as a parliament within the party that decides on basic medium- and long-term policies. At the Tenth Party Congress (1981) a total of 213 people (156 members, 57 candidates with an advisory vote) were elected to the Central Committee, to serve with full-time party and government officials, managers of production units, and high-ranking military officers, as well as representatives of the educational, scientific, and cultural sectors. According to its statute, the Central Committee must meet in plenary session every six months, but it has met on an average of every three months. The Politburo consists of about twenty-

GDR:
Organizational Structure of the SED

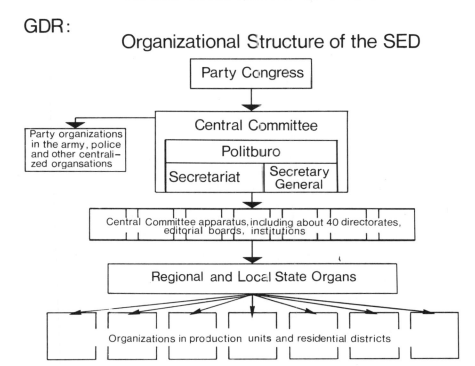

five people from the Central Committee who provide continuous political leadership; it meets weekly. It functions as the party government. The Central Committee Secretariat, on the other hand, must be seen as the party executive responsible for implementing and controlling party decisions in government and in society. It has at its disposal an administrative apparatus of more than 2,000 people assigned to more than forty units in the various government departments.

Research into the actual distribution of power within the party would show with certainty that the Politburo of the SED is the GDR's most important organ of political leadership. The extent to which the Central Committee exercises effective independent functions in decision-making and control is not clear. It would seem to assume real significance in the decision-making process only if differences within the Politburo should reduce that body's ability to act or if serious differences should arise between the party cadre and the party leadership, i.e., in exceptional situations in which the Politburo's ability to perform its functions was reduced. The Central Committee Secretariat cannot be viewed as an independent power factor inasmuch as its key members are usually also members of the Politburo. Instead, it provides through its specialized departments a comprehensive apparatus for the decision-making processes within the Politburo and monitors the implementation of its directives at all party levels.

An analysis of the functions of the various members of the Politburo in the party and state apparatus and an awareness of the existing generation gap between them (including differing historical experiences and differing values based on these experiences) and their differences in professional qualifications gives greater credence to the hypothesis that a pluralism of interests exists within the Politburo. Economic efficiency criteria, objective pragmatism, interest in political stability, appeals to basic ideological positions, and the authority of the party are probably the primary factors. At times it may have seemed possible to differentiate clearly between the two groupings, i.e., a "strategic clique" (the representatives of party bureaucracy) and an "institutionalized counterelite" (the economy-and-technology-oriented wing of the party). However, simply saying that there are differences between dogmatists and technocrats overlooks the fact that the political role of all representatives of the party leadership provides them with an equal interest in securing power and championing efficiency. The differences in behavior are based less on fundamentally divergent views and more on differing assessments of specific problems and tasks. Even though it is hardly possible to make reliable forecasts of political trends on the basis of a limited and nonpublic conflict, it can be said that as a result of the increased presence of scientifically qualified elites within the party hierarchy, the rational element in the political decision-making processes is present to a greater extent than in the past, thereby enhancing the effectiveness of party leadership.

In the GDR the state is defined as the "main instrument of policy" and is clearly distinguished from the political leadership provided by the SED. The People's Chamber is "the supreme body of state power," and its function is to decide on "fundamental questions of government policy" (Article 48 of the constitution). It consists of a total of 500 deputies from seventy-two voting districts. The People's Chamber is elected every five years on the basis of a single list of candidates of the parties and mass organizations contained in the National Front of the GDR (the last election was in 1981). Since the People's Chamber is convened only four to five times per year, it can exercise its constitutionally defined responsibility as the supreme organ of the state (regardless of the actual distribution of power) to only a very limited extent. It has mainly a "rubber stamp" function, a fact also clearly evident from the unanimity of its decisions.

The Council of State acts as a collective head of state. The president of the Council of State is the secretary general of the SED, Erich Honecker, who also heads the National Defense Council. The GDR's

System of State Organs in the GDR

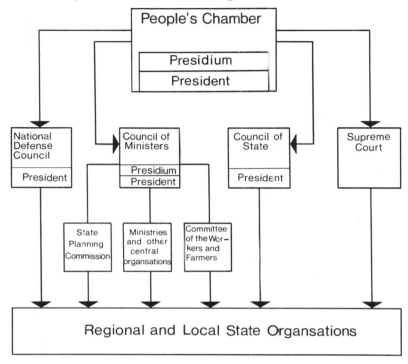

Council of Ministers heads the executive branch of the government and is supported by a large administrative apparatus and by committees of experts. The council was limited largely to economic functions in the political regime of the 1960s, but the present GDR constitution makes it responsible for "the uniform execution of government policy" (Article 76).

The high degree of integration between party and government offices ensures that the government will implement the SED's basic policy decisions. The Party Statute already requires the members of the SED to enforce party directives in the government and economic sectors; party decisions are also directives legally binding on the Council of Ministers and its members as well as on all other members of government. It could thus be assumed that government institutions in general are only executive organs without any real decision-making responsibility of their own. This would, however, overlook the fact that party decisions as a rule are confined to fundamental issues so that a limited decision-making area remains open in the actual implementation of policy; this, too, is of course subject to party control at all levels.

Effects of Socialist Policy

In assessing the history of the GDR over the more than thirty years of its existence, both successes and failures must be registered. The positive side of the balance sheet includes the relative stability of the economy and strong social mobility (in part implementing the goal of equal opportunity), as well as a high degree of social security.

Economic Development. Since the early 1960s, the GDR has had considerable economic success. Even if the problems involved in making international comparisons are taken into account, the GDR ranks about tenth among the industrial nations of the world in terms of economic productivity. Its 1980 national income (i.e., the net national product, consisting of manufacturing, construction, farming, transport and telecommunications, and domestic trade) amounted to just under 174 billion marks. This represents growth by a factor of eight since 1949. If economic development is measured on the basis of per capita output, the GDR is at about the same level as Great Britain. This is about 30 percent less than in the Federal Republic of Germany and about the same amount above the average per capita output in the other countries of the Council for Mutual Economic Assistance (COMECON).

The fact that the GDR is counted among the developed industrial countries is a result of the significance of the contributions of its industrial sector to the net product of its economy. The share of industry in the national income (including construction and manual trades) rose from 49.2 percent in 1950 to 68.8 percent in 1980; the share represented by farming and forestry declined from 30.8 percent to 9.1 percent in the same period. Until 1950 it had been nearly impossible to correct the disproportions in the GDR economy, but in the ensuing period efforts were made in new industrial sectors. Emphasis was placed on the development of export-intensive industries such as machine-building and motor vehicle production, chemicals, electrical technology, and electronic instrument construction, which at present are responsible for about half of total industrial production and regularly register above-average growth rates. The extensive growth in industrial production in the 1950s was based primarily on increasing the number of workers; later development has been due mainly to an increase in productivity. The primary reasons (according to Western estimates) that the GDR's productivity is about a third lower than that of the Federal Republic are less efficient use of time, lower capital productivity, and lower levels of automation.

Developments in the farm sector were marked by intensification and concentration, resulting in a substantial decline in the number of agricultural workers and a considerable increase in the size of individual farms (average size 5,000 hectares, or 13,350 acres). GDR agriculture equaled the prewar production levels in 1957 and achieved considerable growth in the 1960s, more or less equaling that in the Federal Republic. On the other hand, production results in the 1970s were in part unsatisfactory, leading to the planning of some restructuring in the agricultural sector.

The importance of foreign trade to the economic growth of the GDR is comparable to the importance it has for the economy of the Federal Republic. In both German states exports amount to about one-quarter of the gross national product. The differing economic systems of the two states are reflected in foreign trade by differences in organizational structures, forms of activity, and regional focuses. As a result of the GDR's political integration in the Warsaw Pact and its membership in COMECON since 1950, two-thirds of its foreign trade is conducted with the COMECON countries. About 25 percent is with Western industrialized countries and about 6 percent with developing countries. More than one-third of the GDR's total foreign trade is with the Soviet Union, which supplies the GDR primarily with raw materials (oil, gas, coal, cotton, cellulose) and metallurgical products.

In analyzing the structure of the GDR's foreign trade, it becomes evident that capital goods (machines, plant equipment, transport vehicles) dominate exports; the major imports consist of raw materials and semifinished products. There are, however, considerable differences depending on the countries involved. Technological imports, for instance, play an important role in the GDR's trade with the West.

In the 1960s the GDR's balance of foreign trade was nearly always positive (deficits in trade with the West were compensated for by surpluses in other trade relations), but the drastic rise in oil prices in 1973 resulted in a constantly growing balance-of-trade deficit. The cumulative deficit in trade with the Western industrial countries for the period from 1971 to 1979 amounts to about $9.6 billion. Beginning with the new Five-Year Plan (1981–1985), the GDR has made considerable efforts to reduce its foreign trade deficit through a major increase in exports. An export growth of 5 percent was attained in 1981 by increasing the quality of products, lowering energy consumption levels, and introducing efficiency measures.

In the GDR, the government not only has a monopoly on economic planning and decision making but also acts as the central distribution authority. Wages and prices are administratively determined. Prices for basic necessities, public services, rents, health services, social services, education, and culture are highly subsidized; luxury goods such as television sets and automobiles are subject to heavy consumer taxes.

Annual change in national income

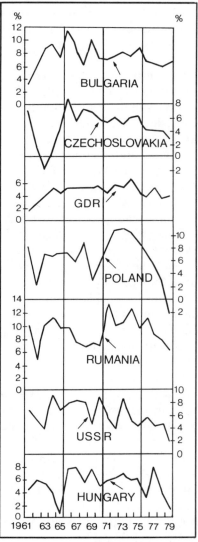

Sources: Statistical yearbooks and plan fulfillment
reports of the Comecon countries, DIW 80

German Institute for Economic Research:
Weekly Report 20/80, p. 220.

The GDR is the only country to show a relatively constant
rate of economic growth.

In 1980 the average monthly net income of a family of four was approximately 1,500 marks. Indirect allocations from the "social funds," referred to in the GDR as the "second paycheck," meant that the government added another 880 marks per month to this income.

The individual standard of living in the GDR is significantly higher than in the other COMECON countries. It is, however, lower—about one-third by Western estimates—than in the Federal Republic. Income is much more evenly distributed in the GDR than in the Federal Republic as a result of the government's redistribution policy. Consumer behavior in the GDR shows a growing tendency to follow West German trends.

Social Mobility in the GDR's Education-Oriented Society. The transformation of the political and economic system initiated in 1945 and interpreted by the SED as a revolutionary restructuring of society has brought about profound social changes in the GDR. A considerable regrouping of social classes took place when the middle class was deprived of the power it had derived from ownership and education and simultaneously reliable worker cadres, promoted by the SED, climbed up the social ladder. The mass migration into the Federal Republic until 1961, involving an above-average number of educated and trained people (university graduates, students, skilled workers) had a negative influence on the population structure. The resulting labor shortage is an essential reason for the high rate of employment among women. About 50 percent of all employed individuals in the GDR are women, as compared with about 37 percent in the Federal Republic. The high level of female employment has been a major factor in social emancipation of women and the enhancement of their social status. Even though it cannot be denied that the double load many women bear by working and having a family leads to numerous individual conflicts, a changed sense of confidence and the presence of a remarkable number of women in middle-management positions in GDR society can be observed. It is important to note, however, that there are almost no women in the GDR's top-level political decision-making bodies.

As a result of the reduced labor potential caused by migration, the GDR is especially in need of producing a highly qualified work force. In 1980 three-fourths of the working population in the GDR were trained and qualified for a vocation. Of the total working population, the proportion of academic and vocational school graduates rose from 6.7 percent in 1962 to 18 percent in 1980. The proportion of skilled workers and master craftsmen rose in the same period from 33.7 percent to 57 percent. Because of the labor shortage, part of this training took place in part-time courses (adult training in correspondence and night school courses). Under these conditions, there can be no doubt that there are considerable pressures for achievement. It must be added, however, that educational qualification, along with the required fundamental political loyalty, is an essential criterion for the acquisition of social status and is a determining factor in the comparatively high level of social mobility. As private ownership of the means of production has been eliminated, except in the case of the manual trades, and success in a society marked by technical progress and automation depends mostly on proof of professional qualification, at least in the middle-aged and younger generations, the observable trend toward an education-related society can be viewed as an important step toward the realization of equality of opportunity.

Intensive support of the orientation toward education is especially marked among young people. Their careers will be determined largely by their successful completion of educational training, requiring a high level of achievement. Access to higher education is also influenced by proof of political activity and, to a lesser degree, by social origin. To fulfill the requirement for political activity, about 75 percent of young people are members of the GDR's only youth organization, the Freie Deutsche Jugend (Free German Youth—FDJ). The proportion of members is higher among secondary school students, university students, and soldiers than among apprentices. The objective of the FDJ is the development of "socialist consciousness," but it also provides leisure-time activities for young people in youth clubs. It is, however, easily observable that Western models and fashions influence the behavior of young people in the GDR. The GDR writer Werner Heiduczek correctly observed that these young people "sometimes lead a schizophrenic existence, one an official life and the other the private life among each other."

Social Security. As the government in the GDR is the predominant employer of the population, it can in fact comply with the right to work guaranteed in Article 24 of the constitution. This right forms the basis of a comprehensive system of social security in which the limited latitude for individual decisions is offset by the assurance of a secure livelihood.

The uniform system of social insurance for the work force, covering more than 85 percent of the population, is managed by the GDR's trade union, the Free German Confederation of Trade Unions (FDGB). The members of production cooperatives, self-employed manual workers, and other self-employed persons are covered by GDR state insurance. Social insurance benefits include free medical treatment at the work place, free medical care in case of sickness, and provision of sick pay, as well as an old-age pension.

The principle of "unity of economic and social policy" advocated in the GDR was stressed again in 1972 by the introduction of comprehensive "social packages." They include, among other things, increases in the level of pensions, the gradual reduction of the work week to forty hours, benefits for shift workers, and especially, considerable relief for working mothers. As of May 1976, maternity leave of twenty-six weeks will be granted. Working mothers will be able to benefit also from the granting of paid leave up to thirteen weeks if their children are sick. In addition, social benefits include scholarships for university students and professional trainees, which are granted to 90 percent of full-time students.

Any overall assessment of social policy in the GDR must evaluate as positive the specific support provided to families with a large number of children and to working women. In addition, the support of training programs, including a considerable easing of qualification requirements in job-related education programs for working adults, must be considered an important part of the success of the GDR's educational policy. However, alongside these respectable achievements of socialist welfare policy, considerable failures must be pointed out that determine the "real existing socialism." They can be grouped under four headings: participation, efficiency, distribution, and orientation.

1. *Participation.* The exaggerated political demands placed on the GDR population by the multiplicity of social obligations (membership in parties and mass organizations, participation in competitive initiatives to fulfill economic plans, and so on) lead to a high degree of formal political participation but in fact promote a depoliticizing of broad sections of the population. Many people concentrate primarily on working toward the realization of individual goals and on their careers. This political apathy is the expression of a profound frustration resulting from the realization that social commitment is limited to actively working for objectives dictated from above, whereas the formulation of individual positions and any expression of social criticism are tabooed as "hostile to the system" and repressed by government measures. As a result, political activity is degraded to the level of the demonstrative assurances of loyalty required as a condition for social advancement. It becomes nothing more than a ritual completed without any inner conviction. "Socialist democracy" is thereby reduced to "democracy by assent." The fiction of consent can, however, never take the place of true acceptance. Political legitimacy is the result of the formation of a political consensus in the entire population and not the product of a proclaimed fictional identity of interests. The guarantee of basic social rights cannot compensate for limitations on individual freedom.

2. *Efficiency.* The centralism of the political and economic order in the GDR led to the establishment of a bureaucratic structure that has

a negative influence on effectiveness and flexibility. No institutionalized mechanisms exist for the resolution of conflicts; thus the capacity of the system to deal with conflicts is relatively small, and the party and state leadership tend to overreact whenever disturbances and conflicts appear.

The pursuit of efficiency in political and economic decisions is impaired by the limited information flow resulting from the canalization of public opinion by the government's media policy. The formation of a greater number of advisory bodies, giving the political system a "consultative authoritarian" character, is only partly able to remedy this defect.

The administrative steering of the economy hinders individual initiative and willingness to accept risk at the middle-echelon leadership levels and in production management. It favors a "system of organized irresponsibility." The far-reaching elimination of competition is detrimental to economic profitability and to the willingness to engage in technological innovation.

3. *Distribution.* The shortage of material goods and services in the GDR causes problems in distribution, which, however, cannot be openly expressed and remedied. The GDR's trade union, the Free German Confederation of Trade Unions, sees itself not as an independent representative of workers' interests but rather as a "conveyor belt" (in Lenin's words) in the implementation of political objectives. The distribution of the national income and other social resources is carried out bureaucratically and, as a result, the process is removed from popular influence and control.

Problems of distribution also arise in the field of education. Because of its shortage of skilled personnel, the GDR has since the beginning of the 1970s based access to higher education on projected future needs. This limitation on the availability of attractive educational opportunities frustrates individual career aspirations and raises the issue of the right of access to education. A suspicion of special privileges for the ruling elite is nurtured by the existence of educational privileges, indicative of the formation of a "new class," as Milovan Djilas termed it. Social mobility in GDR society is reduced by a growing trend toward self-reproduction by the official elite.

4. *Orientation.* The swing toward technocratic socialism in the postrevolutionary consolidation phase, begun in the 1960s, means that the party and state leadership owes the loyalty of the masses primarily to those economic and social policy successes that can be subsumed under the paradigm of "industrial society" and that can be characterized by "efficiency," "achievement," and "affluence." The political dilemma of "real socialism" lies in a progressive erosion of its ideological credibility, a phenomenon that could be described as the secularization

of Marxism-Leninism. Acceptance of the system is the result almost exclusively of its competence as a welfare state, not of the internalizing of specific socialist ideas. Social models and specific needs of GDR citizens are largely identical with the predominant values and behavioral norms in the Federal Republic. The GDR has become a success as an industrial society but has remained unidentifiable as a socialist society.

This development calls in question the Marxist hypothesis that social existence determines individual consciousness. On the contrary it can be seen that differences in social structures by no means correspond to differences in awareness. This paradox in historical experience will also have to be borne in mind when the "German question" is given renewed consideration.

Two German States, One German Nation?

Social policies and all-German policies have been curiously intertwined in German postwar history. Both sides formulated binding claims for the model of society they developed, although with differences in form and reasoning, and both sides declared that the acceptance of their political concept was a precondition for the restoration of German unity under one political system, which they proclaimed as their objective until the end of the 1960s. The Federal Republic of Germany used legal instruments to engage in the battle between the two German systems, i.e., by refusing to recognize the GDR as an independent country and by claiming the right to sole representation of Germany internationally; the German Democratic Republic based its claim as a model for all of Germany on ideological arguments. The SED declared that in the materialist view of history the GDR was "an entire epoch ahead" of the Federal Republic because it had definitively overcome capitalism.

The hopelessness of the situation resulted from the dependence of German reunification on the capitulation to the demands of one side or the other. This hapless situation resulted in an immobility in the intra-German relationship, particularly after the Berlin Wall was built in 1961, leading to a drastic reduction in meetings between the people in the two Germanys and to the danger of a growing alienation between them.

The new intra-German policy initiated at the beginning of the 1970s sought a normalization of the relationship through contractual relations between the two German states. It was motivated primarily by the desire to preserve the unity of the nation through intensified personal contacts. On March 19, 1970, the first meeting between the two German heads of government, Willy Brandt and Willi Stoph, took place in

Erfurt, on GDR soil. At that meeting Chancellor Brandt reviewed postwar developments and attempted to define the German situation:

> Despite all the reconstruction on both sides, German policy after 1945 was primarily a function of the powers that defeated and occupied Germany. The power confrontation between the East and the West has since then dominated the German situation and divided Europe. We are in no position to act as though this division had not taken place. However, we can make an effort to mitigate the effects of this division and actively contribute to a development aimed at filling the trenches that separate us, in Europe and in Germany. In this I assume the continuing and living reality of a German nation. . . . The conflicts we have with each other are different from those between two foreign nations. They are related to our national unity.

After a long period of a policy of strict nonrecognition, the recognition of the political existence of the GDR by the Federal Republic was the subject of vehement controversy between the governing coalition (SPD and FDP) and the Christian Democratic opposition. However, it was a necessary condition for the negotiation of a gradual facilitation of human contacts between the two Germanys. Together with the Berlin Four-Power Agreement (September 1971), the Treaty on Intra-German Relations signed in December 1972 was intended to develop "normal good-neighborly relations" between the two German states (Article 1). Since then it has been possible to expand considerably the volume of travel from the Federal Republic and West Berlin into the GDR. In many other areas the hopes for far-reaching progress in the relations between the two German states have not been fulfilled. This again confirms an observation once made by a former president of the Federal Republic, Gustav Heinemann, who said that Germany is a "difficult fatherland."

Now, almost forty years after the end of World War II, the question arises as to whether the provisional establishment of two German states has become final and irreversible. A look at the political structures and the economic systems alone makes evident fundamental differences that appear unbridgeable, even on a long-term basis. Still, it can be said that the two German states expressly recognize the necessity of "antagonistic cooperation." As Erich Honecker and Helmut Schmidt jointly stated in December 1981, a realistic policy must "assume that different socio-political systems exist in the two States and that they belong to different alliances." However, both sides confirmed a special responsibility based on their common history, "that war must never again originate on German soil." Located in the center of Europe and on the dividing

Territory and population

Federal Republic[1] by states
GDR by districts

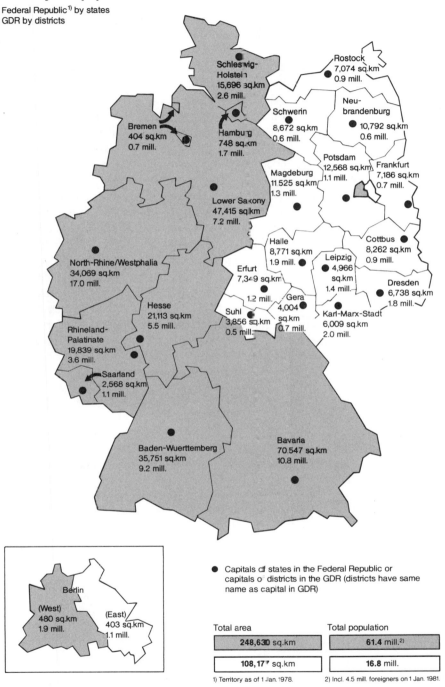

Schleswig-Holstein
15,696 sq.km
2.6 mill.

Rostock
7,074 sq.km
0.9 mill.

Schwerin
8,672 sq.km
0.6 mill.

Neu-brandenburg
10,792 sq.km
0.6 mill.

Bremen
404 sq.km
0.7 mill.

Hamburg
748 sq.km
1.7 mill.

Potsdam
12,568 sq.km
1.1 mill.

Frankfurt
7,186 sq.km
0.7 mill.

Magdeburg
11,525 sq.km
1.3 mill.

Lower Saxony
47,415 sq.km
7.2 mill.

North-Rhine/Westphalia
34,069 sq.km
17.0 mill.

Halle
8,771 sq.km
1.9 mill.

Leipzig
4,966 sq.km
1.4 mill.

Cottbus
8,262 sq.km
0.9 mill.

Erfurt
7,349 sq.km
1.2 mill.

Gera
4,004 sq.km
0.7 mill.

Dresden
6,738 sq.km
1.8 mill.

Hesse
21,113 sq.km
5.5 mill.

Suhl
3,856 sq.km
0.5 mill.

Karl-Marx-Stadt
6,009 sq.km
2.0 mill.

Rhineland-Palatinate
19,839 sq.km
3.6 mill.

Saarland
2,568 sq.km
1.1 mill.

Baden-Wuerttemberg
35,751 sq.km
9.2 mill.

Bavaria
70,547 sq.km
10.8 mill.

Berlin
(West)
480 sq.km
1.9 mill.

(East)
403 sq.km
1.1 mill.

● Capitals of states in the Federal Republic or capitals of districts in the GDR (districts have same name as capital in GDR)

Total area	Total population
248,630 sq.km	61.4 mill.[2]
108,177 sq.km	16.8 mill.

1) Territory as of 1 Jan. 1978.

2) Incl. 4.5 mill. foreigners on 1 Jan. 1981.

line between the two major systems in the world, the two German states cannot undertake independent political action unless they want to embrace a neutralism that is as dangerous as it is illusory. However, as Schmidt pointed out, they can "work actively within their respective alliances to reduce tensions, avoid confrontations, and settle potential conflicts by means of reasonable compromises."

German history did not begin as the history of a divided country in 1945. A unified German state was only an ideal and a political claim over long periods of time and not an existing political reality. This historical experience makes it clear that political unity is not a necessary condition for national identity. As long as communication is maintained between the two German societies, Germans will continue to have a special relationship to one another. In an awareness of their historical identity, both German states should see each other and themselves as positive reciprocal challenges, as a "dialectical unit." Only if the existing antagonism between the two systems is perceived not as an immutable contradiction but rather as the basis for productive competition leading to a better society, only then will it be possible for "national unity" to retain a constructive meaning. In this perspective the answer to the "German question" lies in the development of a society that provides comprehensive realization of freedom and social justice and makes an effective contribution to peace. This interest unifies the Germans; it is the program for "Germany's double future" in our world.

Readings

Legters, Lyman H. (ed.). *The German Democratic Republic, A Developed Socialist Society*. Boulder, Colo.: Westview Press, 1978.
Ludz, Peter C. *Die DDR zwischen Ost und West. Politische Analysen 1961 bis 1976*. Munich: Beck Verlag, 1977.
McCauley, Martin. *Marxism-Leninism in the German Democratic Republic. The Socialist Unity Party (SED)*. New York: Barnes & Noble Books, 1979.
Sontheimer, Kurt, and Bleek, Wilhelm. *Die DDR-Politik, Gesellschaft, Wirtschaft*. Hamburg: Hoffmann und Campe, 1979.
Steele, Jonathan. *Socialism with a German Face; The State That Came in from the Cold*. London: Cape, 1977.
Thomas, Rüdiger. *Modell DDR. Die kalkulierte Emanzipation*. Munich: Carl Hanser Verlag, 1981.

Part 2

— □ —

Literature and the Arts

FRANCIS M. SHARP

—————— **10** ——————

Literature in German, 1871–1933

Naturalism in Imperial Germany

Literary history cannot be understood as a mere chronicle of individual writers, works, and movements taken out of the broader historical context. During the period under discussion here, the two historical-political events that shaped all aspects of cultural life in Europe were the founding of the Second German Empire in 1871 and World War I, from 1914 to 1918. With the unification of the German states and the impetus it gave to industrial expansion in the last quarter of the century, Germany entered a phase of nationalistic fervor and economic prosperity it had never experienced before. The "belated nation" finally came of age, becoming Europe's greatest industrial power after 1900, second only to the United States on a world scale.

In the years following the founding of the empire, Germany strove self-consciously to create cultural works commensurate with its newfound political and economic muscle. Monumental was the aesthetic order of the day and most of the literary works, as well as the sculpture and architecture, in this style have fallen happily into obscurity. The Bismarck towers that still dot the German landscape, and grandiose monuments like the Niederwalddenkmal (Lower Forest Monument) near Bingen on the Rhine, still stand as reminders of this period in German history. Richard Wagner's *Gesamtkunstwerk* (total art work) is one of the few cultural artifacts that satisfied the aesthetic and nationalistic demands of the German bourgeoisie of the time and that has sustained a lively, if controversial, existence to the present day. The tetralogy *The Ring of the Nibelung* (*Der Ring des Nibelungen*) was performed in its entirety for the first time in August 1876 over a period of five days before enthusiastic audiences. These performances inaugurated the theater in

Bayreuth that had been constructed specially for Wagner's works and were the first of the annual festivals devoted to his music.

The flood of patriotic literature after 1870 testified to the exuberance of the new nation and celebrated its claim to cultural as well as military superiority. Friedrich Nietzsche (1844-1900) was one of the first to recognize the hollowness of this national pride. He proclaimed the military and political triumphs of the empire to be a defeat for the German spirit, which had become infected by complacency, materialism, and shallow optimism. Nietzsche's cultural pessimism, heard by only a few at the time, became increasingly influential toward the end of the century. For the intellectual life of the twentieth century, there has been no voice more powerful, no influence more widely felt, than Nietzsche's. To Gottfried Benn, he was the earthquake of his generation and the greatest genius of the German language since Martin Luther.

Young writers too began to feel at odds with the temper of their times as their attention was directed to the ugly social realities behind the euphoric mask of fashionable literature. Hidden underneath this mask was the suffering of broad strata of society that was the unwelcome but inevitable by-product of industrialization and unchecked capitalist growth. This suffering was concentrated particularly in the large cities where the growing pains of the rapidly developing industrial state were most acute. It was there that groups of writers in the 1880s gathered to discuss the possibilities of a new literature that would be faithful to the realities of their age. Berlin, the new capital of the empire, and Munich, long a magnet for artists, intellectuals, and bohemians, became the centers for a young generation of writers whose catchwords were, above all else, realism, naturalism, and modernity. A programmatic statement from Durch (Through), a Berlin literary club, called for "nature's truth" in the work of art and a turn from antiquity to modernity in the search for artistic ideals.

For the writers associated with Durch and similar groups, such as the one founded around the periodical *Die Gesellschaft* (Society) in Munich, the decade from 1880-1890 was mainly a time of theorizing about a German naturalistic literature that could compare favorably with the French, Russian, and Scandinavian literatures of the age. Ultimately German literature failed, however, to produce an internationally acclaimed writer of the stature of Zola, Dostoyevsky, or Ibsen. Arno Holz (1863-1929), known to his contemporaries as a poet without poetry, formulated a radical German version of Zola's famous formula for naturalism: "L'oeuvre d'art est un coin de la nature, vu à travers un tempérament." It was Holz's ambition to outdo his foreign models, to be more consistent, more modern. The element of the artist's "tempérament," the factor of subjectivity, should be eliminated to the greatest possible extent. "Art has the tendency to return to nature," Holz proclaimed. His mathematical formulation "Art $=$ Nature $-x$," reflects the tremendous influence natural science had on German naturalism. The scientist, in his apparently detached relationship to nature, was admired and emulated by artists and writers. In 1887 Wilhelm Bölsche published a work in which he attempted to establish the "scientific" foundations and purposes of literature. Wilhelm Scherer, a leading literary historian, proclaimed natural science the pervasive ruling force of his age, the power behind Germany's rapid technological progress no less than the basis of literary investigation.

With a declared defiance of contemporary literary and political life, a group of young writers—Holz among them—published in 1884 an anthology of their poetry entitled *Modern Poets of Character* (*Moderne Dichtercharaktere*). Thematically, the poems touched upon new ground: social injustice, prostitution, machines, and the city were favorite themes. Formally, however, they lacked any claim to innovation. Real formal innovation did not appear in literary works until the end of the decade. Holz formulated the key concepts of "consistent naturalism" and the *Sekundenstil* (style reflecting each second) only at the beginning of the 1890s in his work *Art: Its Essence and Laws* (*Die Kunst; Ihr Wesen und ihre Gesetze*). Together with Johannes Schlaf, he had published in 1889 the literary counterpart of his theory, the three narrative sketches entitled *Papa Hamlet*. The sketches, consisting mainly of dramatic dialogues, are an attempt to reproduce exactly the sights and sounds of short scenes from the lives of their characters. The intent was to copy a slice of life onto the written page. The gestures, grunts, groans, and dialect of the figures are reflected from one moment to the next (*Sekundenstil*) as if the writers were mere recorders. Ironically, Holz and Schlaf published this model of ultrarealism as a translation of a fictitious Norwegian writer, Bjarne P. Holmsen, in order to lend it the literary prestige of the more progressive Scandinavian literatures. Holz collaborated a second and final time with Schlaf using the techniques of naturalism in the drama *Familie Selicke,* a work set on a Christmas Eve in the household of a poverty-stricken family. A dying child, a drunken father, and a daughter willing to sacrifice her future for the family form a melodramatic picture of human life caught up in the unbending laws of milieu and circumstance. The novelist Theodor Fontane wrote enthusiastically about the play, which was first staged by the Freie Bühne (Free Stage) in 1890.

The Freie Bühne, an association modeled after the Parisian Théâtre Libre, had been founded the previous year in Berlin in order to provide a stage for naturalistic dramas. Public stagings of many of these had been banned by the censor, and they were performed for the first time before the private audiences of the Freie Bühne. Ibsen's *Ghosts* was the first play put on by the association. Shortly thereafter, on October 20, 1889, in the Lessing Theater, Gerhart Hauptmann's (1862–1946) first drama, *Before Dawn* (*Vor Sonnenaufgang*), was staged, a work soon recognized as a turning point. It marked the arrival on a German stage of a German play written with an eye to the naturalistic guidelines laid down by Holz and Schlaf, but more important, a play written by a talented dramatist. Although contemporary reaction was far from unanimous, Fontane accorded the work the ultimate praise as the "fulfillment of Ibsen." The honors and accolades of his countrymen as well as the world at large had, however, just begun to fill Hauptmann's long and productive life. Much like Goethe before him and Thomas Mann after him, he came to be accepted as a representative figure of his age.

The themes of *Before Dawn* are typically naturalistic ones: alcoholism, moral degeneracy, and heredity. A young, idealistic socialist arrives in a mining village to investigate the economic conditions of the population. While there, he falls in love with Helene, the daughter of the family with which he lives, and he becomes engaged to her. After he discovers the environment of alcoholism and immorality in which she has grown up, however, he abandons her to the milieu from which he believes she can never escape. And, indeed, her final suicide seems her only way out. Detailed stage directions, the banishment of monologue, and the lack of a hero all contribute to the play's realism. At one performance a member of the audience unwittingly lent support to this realism. Helene's unmarried sister in the play is expecting a child and when she begins labor offstage, a midwife is loudly called for. At that moment, a doctor in the audience responded by tossing a pair of delivery forceps onto the stage, a gesture reportedly made out of disgust rather than support. The controversy that surrounded the play soon reached beyond the world of the theater even into the political circles of the Prussian parliament. There an irate deputy referred to it as an "intellectual brothel."

Hauptmann's novella *Flagman Thiel* (*Bahnwärter Thiel*), originally published in 1887 in *Die Gesellschaft*, is still widely read as a masterpiece of the genre. It was, however, his dramas *Before Dawn, The Reconciliation* (*Das Friedensfest*, 1891), and *The Weavers* (*Die Weber*, 1892) that established him as the leading German naturalist. And it is mainly for these and a small number of his other early dramatic works that he is remembered today, although later in his career he published several novels and even some lyric poetry. Hauptmann was at his strongest in the creation of memorable stage characters. The talent for dramatic characterization, together with his social consciousness—*not* socialistic, as he insisted—accounted for a large part of his early success. Sustaining his sympathies for the poor and oppressed, which today seem at times to border on the sentimental, was an idealistic faith in scientific progress rather than political conviction.

The revolt of the oppressed lies at the center of *The Weavers,* a historical drama about the uprisings of the Silesian weavers in 1844. Hauptmann wrote a version of the play in the Silesian dialect of his forebears—his grandfather had been a weaver—and dedicated it to his father. *The Weavers* lacked the timeliness of Heine's famous poem about the same revolt, yet it unleashed a storm of controversy and gained its author European notoriety. Hauptmann's sympathy for the situation of the weavers a half century before, hardly a topical issue in the 1890s, was evidently interpreted as subversive. A public performance was initially forbidden by the police censor, and *The Weavers* was first seen on the stage of the Freie Bühne. The ban was eventually lifted, however, and the Deutsches Theater (German Theater) in Berlin performed it publicly in 1894. The kaiser, evidently in agreement with the censor's initial opinion, promptly canceled the royal box.

The decade after *The Weavers* was the most productive period of Hauptmann's life, when his eclectic intellectual tastes led him simultaneously in quite divergent directions of study. Dreams, fairy tales, myths, and legends of his native land as well as those of antiquity, the Middle Ages, and the Reformation all found expression in his dramatic and epic works. *The Assumption of Hannele (Hanneles Himmelfahrt,* 1893), published only a year after *The Weavers,* depicts the dreams and visions of a dying child. In *The Sunken Bell (Die versunkene Glocke,* 1896), Hauptmann appears to have turned completely to a neoromantic style, yet in the same year he published *Florian Geyer,* a drama like *The Weavers* in which the masses, not the individual, are central and that realistically depicts the historical tragedy of the Peasants' Rebellion in sixteenth-century Germany. Among the other lasting achievements of his early career is that rarity in the history of German drama, a successful comedy (*The Beaver Coat; Der Biberpelz,* 1893). Other attempts in this genre either failed or ended in the hybrid form of tragicomedy—*The Rats (Die Ratten,* 1910), a "Berlin tragicomedy," is the primary example. The two tragedies *Drayman Henschel (Fuhrmann Henschel,* 1898) and *Rose Bernd* (1905) pay homage once more to a naturalistic view of the milieu, but naturalism as a literary movement had reached its highest point with Hauptmann's *The Weavers.* None of its other exponents, with the possible exception of Hermann Sudermann and Max Halbe, are of more than historical interest today.

The social novelist Theodor Fontane (1819–1898) belongs at least on the periphery of naturalism not merely for his support of the young playwrights in his reviews, but for certain aspects of his own works as well. Although he was sixty when his first novel appeared, he made a significant contribution to the history of the genre during the remaining years of his life with his *The Adulteress* (*L'Adultera,* 1882), *Trials and Tribulations* (*Irrungen, Wirrungen,* 1888), *Frau Jenny Treibel* (1892), *Effi Briest* (1895), and *Stechlin* (*Der Stechlin,* 1897). Fontane returns again and again to his native Berlin and its surroundings for his settings, often alluding to actual restaurants and cafés as the backdrop for the lives of his characters. These characters inhabit a social stratum far removed from the world of the lower classes in naturalist drama, yet even in these upper bourgeois and aristocratic circles, human action and behavior are determined. Lives are played out according to the strict regulation of social codes and conventions, many of which are historical relics of a Prussian feudal society that disappeared completely only after World War II.

Typical of Fontane and in many ways his masterpiece is *Effi Briest,* the story of a marital mismatch that leads to a tragic end. Effi is married at seventeen to her mother's former lover, a man many years her senior. Treated like a child and often left alone, she inevitably becomes bored with her provincial life and falls into a short-lived adulterous affair. Many years afterward, when the affair comes to light, unwritten social codes demand that certain actions be taken. Without real conviction or emotion, Effi's husband kills her former lover in a duel and sends her home to her parents, where a short time later she dies. At the end of the novel, her father rejects the mother's suggestion that her guilt be examined more closely, an attitude typical of Fontane, who withholds moral judgment by letting his fictional figures act out their lives according to the implacable conventions of their society. However great their differences, the younger generation of naturalists returned Fontane's admiration by comparing him with their idols, Zola and the Russian novelist Turgenev.

Art Versus Life at the Turn of the Century

Even while naturalism was celebrating its successes in Germany, its dominance was being challenged by other literary currents imported from abroad. Stefan George (1868–1933), a young poet from the Rhineland, visited Paris in 1889, where together with the circle of poets around Mallarmé he explored the aesthetic and artistic credo of French symbolism in Mallarmé's own work and that of Baudelaire, Rimbaud, and Verlaine. In the 1890s George became the most accomplished German virtuoso of aestheticism, a literary style and philosophy opposed in every respect to naturalism. Poetry, he maintained, should rise above the "unrefined clamor" of the day, reject involvement with life, and constitute in language a realm of pure beauty. George expressed his aloofness from the common and ordinary even at the most basic level. His sparsely punctuated poems are filled with foreign and archaic words. Nouns begin with small letters and a specially developed script lends a visually ornamental effect. The highest aspiration of art in this vein is to gild or transcend life, not to mirror it or right its injustices. Social concerns or faith in science have no place in it. Exotic, formal gardens, their sands strewn with semiprecious gems, are the counterparts in George's poetry to the sordid urban landscapes of naturalist drama. The title figure of one of his first collections (*Algabal,* 1892) exemplifies in the extreme the ideal of the insulated life devoted to aesthetic pleasures. Ethical considerations are entirely foreign to this tyrant, whose slave forfeits his life when he inadvertently interrupts his master's daily ritual. The work was dedicated to the memory of Ludwig II of Bavaria, and Algabal's model in history was the third-century Roman emperor, Heliogabalus.

By 1892, George had reached a crisis in his life and poetry. It seemed as if the isolation he had striven for could bear no further intensification. In launching his journal *Blätter für die Kunst* (Pages for Art), he created an outlet and sounding board for his poetic energies, although it circulated among only a few friends in Germany and initially had a greater impact on foreign admirers of the new German direction in France, Belgium, the Netherlands, and the Scandinavian countries. In the mid-1890s a circle of followers began to gather around the charismatic George, providing him with the resonance he had sought. Some of these poets, artists, and intellectuals later gained a reputation in their own fields, but in most cases only after they had broken with George. Friedrich Gundolf, the poet and scholar, was an exception. During the long years of his loyalty to George, he wrote several successful works of literary history, including volumes on Shakespeare and Goethe, and disseminated George's ideas to a wide audience. Certainly the most bizarre chapter in the circle's history began with George's "discovery" of the schoolboy Max Kronberger on the streets of Munich. Celebrated in George's volume of poetry *The Seventh Ring* (*Der siebente Ring,* 1907) as a divine incarnation, Maximin became for a time the focal point of the circle. The boundaries between poetry and liturgy, between poet and priest, were obscured.

Bizarre as this deification and poetic worship of a schoolboy may have been, it represented the antidemocratic bent and the increasingly cultish direction in which the circle and George's own poetry (*The Star of the Covenant; Der Stern des Bundes,* 1914; and *The New Empire; Das neue Reich,* 1928) were moving. Some of this later poetry was ambiguous enough to be misread by the Nazis as a herald of the new political Reich they proclaimed in early 1933. Following George's death in Switzerland in December 1933, a few months after his emigration, the official arm of the new regime for literature had planned a ceremony in his honor. These plans were canceled, however, allegedly by Goebbels himself, who had received from George before his death a letter rejecting National Socialism. The prospective prophet had turned out to be but another "undesirable." One of George's favorites among his late disciples, Count Claus von Stauffenberg, later turned this intellectual rejection into a heroic though vain deed when in July 1944 he led the assassination attempt on Hitler's life.

George had led the way for literary aestheticism in Germany of the 1890s; the Viennese writer and critic Hermann Bahr (1863–1934) played a similar role in Austria. Less a poet than a promoter, Bahr had, like George, also come under the spell of the French during the years 1889–1890. In the next few decades he earned the reputation as the bellwether of literary trends in German literature. Much later in his life, Bahr made the justifiable claim to have participated in almost every "intellectual fashion" of his day before it had become fashionable. A rival critic once called him the "man of the day after tomorrow." Even before naturalism had reached its peak in Hauptmann's drama *The Weavers,* Bahr had predicted its demise in *The Overcoming of Naturalism* (*Die Überwindung des Naturalismus,* 1891). His novel *The Good School* (*Die gute Schule,* 1890), whose subtitle announced its main concern with "states of the soul," foreshadowed the intense pursuit of spiritual and mental subtleties in the literature of the following years.

A number of terms were used at the time and have been used since to characterize literary styles and practices during the last decade of the century. Hermann Bahr popularized the term "modernity" but offered no prescriptive replacement for naturalism. He, in fact, criticized the naturalists' mania for programmatic literature and recommended certain young Austrian writers whose only common aim was to be "modern" at all costs. Among those Austrians Bahr mentioned were Arthur Schnitzler and Loris, a pseudonym for Hugo von Hofmannsthal, who at the time he began writing was still a schoolboy. Modernity had earlier been a catchword for the naturalists and signified that they no longer considered antiquity as the ideal of art. To be modern meant to intensify literary realism by focusing on contemporary social themes taboo in bourgeois literature, such as sexuality and the misery of the poor. For Bahr, however, modernity meant a "romantic-aristocratic flight" from naturalism as the focus of art shifted from the realm of the social to the psychological. The highest goal of art was, moreover, no longer a quasiscientific truth about nature, but beauty.

In an early essay on the Italian Gabriele d'Annunzio, Hofmannsthal remarked on two qualities of life that to him were characteristically modern: "the analysis of life and the flight from life." The flight, which both Bahr and Hofmannsthal mention, has the same ultimate goal and refuge: the ivory tower of aestheticism. In its numerous variations, the juxtaposition of art and life is perhaps the most frequently encountered theme of recent German literature. Its modern roots lie in the intellectual revolt against the materialism of Bismarckian and Wilhelminian Germany, a revolt most eloquently formulated by Nietzsche. In the 1890s, when Nietzsche's works were coming into wide circulation, there were, however, discernible differences in the attitudes of major writers toward aestheticism. It was an article of faith for Stefan George, whose poetic figures stroll through artificial landscapes, dwell in subterranean realms, and cultivate strange flowers that exist only in the imagination. Barriers to life exist everywhere in George's poetry as well as in his biography. Thomas Mann's ambivalence toward the juxtaposition of art and life is a source of irony not only in his early prose, but even in his last published work, *Confessions of Felix Krull, Confidence Man* (*Die Bekenntnisse des Hochstaplers Felix Krull*, 1954). The characters of Hofmannsthal's early lyrical dramas, on the other hand, revel in the beautiful life devoted to art and the spirit but come to tragic ends because of their neglect of its moral and ethical aspects. It is already evident in these works that Hofmannsthal could never have followed George into the purer realms of *l'art pour l'art*.

Further along in his essay on d'Annunzio, Hofmannsthal elaborates on the analytical aspect of modern life with a metaphor describing the anatomical dissection of the psyche (*Seelenleben*), a strikingly appropriate metaphor for a contemporary of Freud's. With this metaphor, Hofmannsthal also strikes close to the heart of what was to become known as literary impressionism. A term borrowed from painting, impressionism implies in contrast to naturalism both an interiorization of the writer's vision and an affirmative recognition of the role of subjectivity in the creative process. In one sense, Hofmannsthal, Schnitzler, and the early Rilke redirected the naturalists' keen power of observation of the phenomenal world toward the inner life of their characters. For these characters, however, the phenomenal world was of secondary importance to their own dreams, moods, and sensations. At the university in Vienna, the widely known physicist and psychologist Ernst Mach lectured to his students—Hofmannsthal among them—that sense impressions were the *only* reality. Not far away, but for the moment without an audience, Sigmund Freud laboriously gathered evidence for his new science of the psyche that would soon make radical claims about the significance of man's inner life. His seminal work on dream interpretation appeared in 1900. In his later years Freud himself was to draw a parallel between his work and that of Arthur Schnitzler. He recognized in Schnitzler a "double" who had attained through the medium of literature insights into the human psyche that paralleled his own.

One characteristic that binds together numerous writers of various styles over the entire span of the years between 1871 and 1933 is an antibourgeois sentiment. The naturalists perceived the middle class as complacently smug and unfeeling toward the lower classes; the next generation commonly saw it as a class of narrow-minded philistines with little aesthetic sense. Rilke and George reacted with elitist and aristocratic pretensions designed to put themselves and their art beyond the reach of the dull-witted masses. For the ironical Thomas Mann, the burgher is recognizably philistine in his tastes and life style, yet at the same time he represents the healthy principle of life as opposed to the decadent artistic types. Mann's first novel, *Buddenbrooks* (1901), tells the story of four generations of a north German merchant family whose vitality is gradually drained in direct proportion to an increase in artistic sensitivities. Hanno, the youngest Buddenbrooks heir, is frail, is addicted to music, and dies an early death. The widespread antibourgeois sentiment received heady intellectual sustenance from Nietzsche's attacks on the culture of the middle class and his call for a reevaluation of all values. In the 1890s one wag made the suggestion that government revenues might be greatly enhanced by placing a tax on Nietzsche's ideas, which seemed to be everywhere.

In Austria, particularly Vienna, the situation was somewhat different. The antagonisms between burgher and artist seemed less pronounced; at least they were further below the surface in a society in which the arts were integrated into the lives of large numbers of the population. The Viennese filled the nightly performances of Austrian composers and dramatists and celebrated the stage performers like folk heroes. Among Austrian artists the antibourgeois sentiment often took the form of a bohemian life style that flouted public conventions of dress and morality; experimentation with drugs, mental lability, and even suicide were the extreme forms of this defiance. One of the more harmless of the Viennese bohemians was Peter Altenberg (1859–1919), a habitué of numerous coffeehouses in which artistic and literary discussions flourished. Supported by his brother and several other patrons, Altenberg lived a life devoted to the present, recording many of these ephemeral moments in short, impressionistic sketches. He himself denied these vignettes a claim to literary merit, preferring to call them simply "extracts of life." Had it not been for the Viennese coffeehouse society of artists, writers, and intellectuals, Altenberg's talents might have gone undiscovered. It was at the Café Central that he came to the attention of Arthur Schnitzler, who, along with the journalist Karl Kraus, arranged the introduction to his eventual publisher.

Poetic Language, Its Crisis and Its Masters

Karl Kraus (1874–1936) later became one of the most independent and polemical spirits in Vienna, but around 1890 he frequented the Café Griensteidl, where Hermann Bahr presided over literary discussions. By 1897, when the Griensteidl was closed, Kraus wrote scornfully of Bahr in his first essays *The Demolished Literature* (*Die demolierte Literatur*). Two years later, Kraus conceived and initiated a satirical journal, *Die Fackel* (The Torch, 1899–1936) to which in its early years Heinrich Mann, Frank Wedekind, and August Strindberg, among many others, contributed. From 1911 on, Kraus wrote everything that appeared in the biweekly journal, a mixture of poetry, aphorisms, and critical essays. A moralist, he attacked with well-aimed and well-turned phrases what he saw as the shams, pomposities, and hypocrisies of Austrian culture. On satire, he wrote that if it could be understood by the censor, it deserved to be censored. And even disciples of psychoanalysis can admire the wit if not the message of his famous barb that psychoanalysis was itself the sickness for which it claimed to be the cure. Kraus was not only a master at using language; he also saw a writer's use of it as the primary indicator of character. Language, in fact, became the unifying focus of his writings, and he often began essays with excerpts from other journals and newspapers that he subjected to close scrutiny. A foe of modern journalistic writing, he carried on a ceaseless feud with the establishment press in Vienna. The significance Kraus accorded to language is indicative of a central intellectual and artistic concern that began to surface in *fin-de-siècle* Vienna and that is still very much alive today.

In the multinational, multilingual Hapsburg Empire, it was perhaps inevitable that language itself should become a crucial issue in intellectual discourse. To the philosopher Fritz Mauthner (1849–1923), who grew up in Bohemia with three native tongues—German, Czech, and Hebrew—language was the main topic of philosophical inquiry. And it was the Viennese Ludwig Wittgenstein (1889–1951) who in his *Tractatus Logico-philosophicus* (1922) drew the boundaries of language in the famous few words: "What can be said at all can be said clearly, and what we cannot talk about we must pass over in silence." During the decades on each side of the turn of the century, poets too became acutely conscious of the raw material of their craft, language itself. The crisis of faith in the adequacy of language for human communication has not been surmounted; it has become a permanent fixture in the

German intellectual tradition. Martin Luther's crisis of faith and Immanuel Kant's crisis of knowledge have been pointed to as precursors of the crisis of language that marks the twentieth century.

Hugo von Hofmannsthal's (1874–1929) fictional "Letter of Lord Chandos" ("Chandos Brief," 1902) embodies better than any other contemporary source the loss of naive trust in language to mirror a changed experience of reality. The imaginary Lord Chandos writes to his friend Francis Bacon to explain his renunciation of literary activity and to describe his inability to use language even in an everyday sense in making the customary abstractions and judgments about reality. Words seem to dissolve in his mouth like "mouldy fungi" as language loses its function as an intersubjective mediator of experience. It is obvious from Hofmannsthal's highly articulate description of Chandos's quandary that his own situation at the time cannot be equated with that of his fictional letter writer. Hofmannsthal did not renounce literary expression, although his writing did find new direction at this point. After the subjective lyricism and aestheticism of his early career, he turned to dramatic expression, hoping to find the way to broader cultural and social significance.

Hofmannsthal began to write and publish his poems and essays under the pseudonym Loris even before he had completed his secondary education. When he was first introduced into Bahr's circle at the Griensteidl there was considerable amazement that the poet behind the pseudonym was a mere boy, not a diplomat or man of the world. Yet he was already conversant with much of world literature by the time he was eighteen years old and eventually learned to write five and read eight foreign languages. Hofmannsthal's literary sophistication was immediately evident with the publication of *Yesterday* (*Gestern,* 1891), the first of seven lyrical dramolets he wrote during the 1890s. Situated in Italy during the late Renaissance, this "dramatic study in one act in verse" mirrors the life of the upper classes grown decadent through the pursuit of pleasure. The following year, in *The Death of Titian* (*Der Tod des Tizian,* 1892), the eighteen-year-old Hofmannsthal depicts the pupils of the dying Italian painter as they sing the praises of their master. This paean to aestheticism appeared in the first issue of Stefan George's journal *Blätter für die Kunst.*

George had immediately recognized in Hofmannsthal a kindred spirit when he had visited Vienna in 1891. His hopes to share with Hofmannsthal a kind of artistic dictatorship over literary taste were soon shattered, however, when Hofmannsthal refused to be drawn into a relationship of dependency on the imperious George. Moreover, as the next and best known of Hofmannsthal's lyrical dramolets illustrates, his attitude toward the aesthetic life had become more openly critical.

Claudio, the foolish hero of *Death and the Fool* (*Der Tor und der Tod*, 1893), stands at the end of a life that has been devoted to books and art while void of meaningful human relationships. In order to indulge his private world, he has remained without commitment to family and friends. With the arrival of the allegorical figure of Death on stage, Claudio is for the first time made aware of the life that he has missed. Death parades the wronged spirits of his mother, a lover, and a friend before his contrite eyes, but it is too late for him to mend his ways. His only consolation is that he has at least been awakened from the dream of his life at the moment of his death.

In their unstrained formal elegance and expressive imagery, Hofmannsthal's lyric poems must be ranked among the finest in the German language. It is a poetry enriched in meaning by the subtle gestures and movements of its poetic figures. The gait of the woman in "The Two" ("Die Beiden"), for example, the light touch of the rider on the reins of his horse, and their trembling hands in the final strophe are indispensable elements of the poem's effect:

She bore the goblet in her hand—
her chin and mouth firm as its band—
her stride so weightless and so still
that not a drop would ever spill.

So weightless and so firm his hand:
he rode a young horse for his pleasure
and, looking like incarnate leisure,
compelled it; trembling it must stand.

But when he should take from her hand
the goblet that she lifted up,
the two were quivering so much
that each hand missed the other's touch,
and heavy grew the weightless cup
till dark wine rolled upon the sand.

The miscarriage of the lovers' symbolic meeting suggests the lack of permanence and stability in human relationships. Uncertainty and ambiguity, Hofmannsthal once wrote, marked his epoch as they had never done in previous generations. His poetry as well as his lyrical dramolets exhibit an acute awareness of the change that time brings about. In "Stanzas in Terza Rima on Transitoriness" ("Terzinen. Über die Vergänglichkeit"), the speaker puzzles over the perceived presence of his lover, who is separated from him in time. Time has alienated him totally from the person he was as a child, and he seems perplexed at the thought of the close bond between him and his long-dead ancestors.

Hofmannsthal was later to interpret the period of his lyrical works in the 1890s as a time of mystical relationship to the universe, which he called "preexistence." He saw it as a "glorious, yet dangerous" condition prior to the real entry into life through personal commitment and social responsibility. After the crisis portrayed in the Chandos letter, Hofmannsthal gave up the lyrical orientation of his youth for the more publicly oriented dramatic mode of the mature writer.

Drama of Greek antiquity, Elizabethan England, and medieval Germany provided models for Hofmannsthal's reorientation. His *Electra* (*Elektra,* 1904) was a free adaptation of Sophocles' tragedy that gained psychological depth from Freud's work on hysteria, but it finally resembled Oscar Wilde's *Salomé* (1893) more closely than its Greek predecessor. In an attempt to renew the genre of tragedy, Hofmannsthal reinterpreted myth in several other dramatic works. He was to attain a wider audience, however, through his collaboration with the composer Richard Strauss. Their joint efforts began with Strauss's musical adaptation of *Electra* in 1909. Two years later, their *The Cavalier of the Rose* (*Der Rosenkavalier*), a comedy of human types set to music, was performed in Dresden for the first time. With Vienna of the eighteenth century as its setting, *The Cavalier of the Rose* is a lively frolic of love and lechery, of reality and appearance, that has delighted audiences around the world. Hofmannsthal focused on his own society in his comedy *The Difficult Man* (*Der Schwierige,* 1921). After returning home to Vienna from the battlefields of World War I, Count Hans Karl Bühl has become withdrawn and he attempts to limit his social contacts to a minimum. He has a deep mistrust of language, believing that he can only bring about confusion when he opens his mouth. The play provides ample illustration of this comic side of the language crisis depicted in the Chandos letter, but Bühl is finally reconciled to his proper place in the social order. *The Difficult Man* attests humorously yet honestly to Hofmannsthal's deep attachment to the Austrian nobility, which had become an anachronism even before World War I.

Hofmannsthal spoke in his later years of a "conservative revolution," but his concern was for the fragmentation of the entire social structure, not just the aristocracy. In the *Salzburg Festival* (*Salzburger Festspiele*) he helped to create in the postwar years a forum in which all classes could focus on tradition and the common cultural heritage. His own contribution to the festivals included *The Play of Everyman* (*Jedermann,* 1911), an adaptation of the *Everyman* drama of fifteenth-century England. Produced in the open air by Max Reinhardt in front of the Salzburg Cathedral, this drama of the "death of the rich man" became a popular success. Several other of Hofmannsthal's works have been performed at the festival. Among those is his last work, *The Tower* (*Der Turm,*

1925), a tragedy set in a place and time resembling a legendary Polish kingdom of the seventeenth century.

It was characteristic of Hofmannsthal to look outside the everyday world familiar to him for backdrops to works that are primarily of symbolic significance. Vienna and Viennese types, on the other hand, are almost always the limits of Arthur Schnitzler's (1862–1931) fictional world, a world in which psychological and social aspects are dominant. He consistently works with a certain cast of characters in both his drama and his prose; the naive working girl, the woman of the world, the philanderer, and the cheated husband are the stars of the cast. They are even partially recognizable in that play exceptional for Schnitzler, a play set not in contemporary Vienna but in prerevolutionary Paris hours before the storming of the Bastille. A play within a play, *Green Cockatoo* (*Der grüne Kakadu*, 1899), presents a troupe of actors working in an inn acting out the hostilities of the lower classes on the inn's noble patrons. The jaded customers enjoy the abuse as much as the actors until the reality of the incipient revolution in the streets outside invades the theatrics within. Although not typical in its setting, *Green Cockatoo*, through Schnitzler's wit and masterful interweaving of reality and appearance, is one of his liveliest works.

Schnitzler began his writing career—he was a practicing physician as well—with a cycle of one-act plays that depict encounters in the love life of the title character (*The Affairs of Anatol; Anatol*, 1893). A prologue in verse by Hofmannsthal sets an impressionistic mood for what he calls the "comedy of our souls." In each of the plays on stage, Anatol himself plays at life, embellishing the emotions of the present moment while retaining complete inner freedom for the next moment. Although he has no compunctions about his infidelities and spends the night before his wedding with another lover, Schnitzler portrays him sympathetically as a likable if amoral roué. The short dramatic sketch was well suited to Schnitzler's ability to evoke atmosphere and mood. *La ronde* (*Reigen*, 1896–1897), the most openly erotic cycle of one-act plays, is actually a series of ten dialogues and sexual encounters between five men and five women from various social strata. In each scene, one person remains behind from the preceding one as one configuration of social and psychological factors after the other is explored. Originally banned by the censor, *La ronde* still caused a scandal when first performed in 1920. *Light-o'-Love* (*Liebelei*, 1895), on the other hand, had its premiere performance in Vienna's prestigious Burgtheater and was Schnitzler's first stage success. Similar in mood and theme to *Anatol*, it ends in tragedy, however, when the unsuspecting Christine learns that her lover has been killed in a duel over a married woman.

Schnitzler wrote a great many other dramatic works, a large majority of them exploring the psychology of sexuality. Less prominent but of personal as well as sociological interest are his depictions of the role of the Jew in Austrian society in the play *Professor Bernhardi* (1912) and the novel *The Road to the Open* (*Der Weg ins Freie*, 1908). The latter work is atypical in its length; Schnitzler preferred the short form in prose as he did in drama. And in prose, too, the relation between the sexes was the favorite theme. *Dying* (*Sterben*, 1892) illustrates the basic selfishness of love: A woman who has promised to accompany her lover into death finally chooses life over the romantic *Liebestod*. Freud was only one commentator among many who have noted the similarities to psychoanalysis in Schnitzler's fiction. The term "study" has been suggested as a genre designation for his short prose, and parallels with Freud's case histories have been drawn for *Rhapsody* (*Traumnovelle*, 1926), *Beatrice* (*Frau Beate und ihr Sohn*, 1913), and *Fräulein Else* (1924). In the latter work and some years before in *None But the Brave* (*Leutnant Gustl*, 1901), Schnitzler made early use of interior monologue to expose his characters' inner lives, a narrative device related to Freud's technique of free association. The interior monologue has since been adapted by twentieth-century novelists, most ingeniously by James Joyce, as a literary tool for exploiting the psychology of the unconscious.

The honor of being called the "German Joyce," however, fell not to Schnitzler but rather later in the century to his countryman Robert Musil (1880–1942), who had been an avid reader of the Irish novelist since the late 1920s. Such praise abounded in the press reviews when Musil's mammoth novel *The Man Without Qualities* (*Der Mann ohne Eigenschaften*), a work whose single volumes had appeared in 1930, 1933, and 1943, was newly published in a complete edition in 1952. The thirty-year-old Ulrich, the central figure of the novel, is a talented, highly educated man who, despite connections to the best circles of Viennese society, has been unable to accomplish anything concrete in life. And without accomplishment, his identity remains in a kind of amoebic state; he is Musil's image of a man "who had more to hope for from the unpredictable than the certain." Set in Vienna just before World War I, the novel centers on the preparations for the eightieth-birthday celebration of the Hapsburg monarch in 1918. As honorary secretary of the committee making the preparations, Ulrich comes into contact with a great many people, some of whom Musil copied from prominent personalities of the day. Musil, who worked his entire adult life on the novel, was himself a man of many possibilities. Technology and engineering had originally lured him away from the military, and he was later to study seriously psychology, philosophy, and logic.

Among his other literary works, his first novel, *Young Törless* (*Die Verwirrungen des Zöglings Törless,* 1906), stands out for its realistic, unsentimental depiction of adolescent sexuality and brutality against the backdrop of a military academy. Törless, the intellectually precocious hero, becomes involved with two of his more sinister classmates, Reiting and Beineberg, in the physical and psychological persecution of a third classmate. His brief homosexual encounter does not seem to bother Törless; it is rather the disparity between the intimacy of the physical relationship and the contempt he feels toward the victim, whom in the end he finally helps. Sexuality is, in fact, subordinate in the novel to the theme of power and how it is appropriated and misused by the two main culprits, of whom Musil said in the 1930s: "Reiting, Beineberg: today's dictators in embryo."

Hermann Broch (1886–1951), a Viennese-born novelist and essayist, exhibited a versatility equal to that of Musil when in 1927 he gave up a career in textile manufacturing in order to take up studies of mathematics, philosophy, and psychology. His first novel, a trilogy entitled *The Sleepwalkers* (*Die Schlafwandler,* 1931–1932), traces the decay of social and ethical values during the years from 1888 to 1918. Like so many other intellectuals and writers, the Jewish Broch was forced to emigrate after the Nazi takeover of Austria and wrote the works of his maturity abroad. Under arrest by the Nazis, Broch was particularly fortunate to have had a number of influential friends, James Joyce among them, who came to his aid.

Rainer Maria Rilke:
A Classic of Modern German Poetry

In 1900, the year of Nietzsche's death and of the appearance of Freud's *Interpretation of Dreams* (*Traumdeutung*), Richard Dehmel (1863–1920) was considered Germany's greatest living poet. Dehmel's name and reputation have faded over the years, and many today have permanently awarded his briefly worn laurel to the Prague-born Rainer Maria Rilke (1875–1926). Hardly established as a poet in 1900, Rilke spent from May to August of that year in Russia, a second trip to the land he would call a spiritual homeland. Accompanied by Lou Andreas-Salomé, an intimate friend at various times of both Nietzsche and Freud, Rilke was received by Tolstoy, but his most lasting impressions were of the Russian peasants. Their religious piety and resignation to a life of poverty found poetic reflection in his *Book of Hours* (*Stundenbuch,* 1905). Through the persona of a Russian monk, Rilke develops themes and perspectives that return over and over again in his work. The most prominent of these are the highly unorthodox, un-Christian views of

God, religion, and death as well as a somewhat feudalistic social viewpoint. A pantheistic conviction of the suffusion of all being with divine presence coexists in the poems with the view of an evolving god dependent on man for his continuing creation. Religious grounds also underlie Rilke's admiration of the peasants' submissiveness and courage in the face of their hard lot. Poverty is the necessary condition in the lifelong preparation for the personal, nonalienated experience of death, what Rilke called the "great death."

Although the *Book of Hours* was inspired by concrete experience, the poems are highly subjective reflections of that experience. Rilke's development as a poet traces a movement away from a direct expression of inwardness to an expression mediated through images. Shortly after his return from Russia, he began his apprenticeship with visual artists that would lead in this direction. At Worpswede near Bremen, where in 1901 he married the sculptress Clara Westhoff, he lived and worked in the artists' colony of painters and sculptors. The pictorial poems in the volume *Book of Images* (*Das Buch der Bilder*, 1902) mark the first stage in Rilke's new direction. In 1902 he embarked upon the more significant second stage when he left his wife and Worpswede for Paris in order to write a commissioned monograph on Clara's former mentor, Auguste Rodin. The results of his studies and personal relationship with the sculptor—he lived with Rodin as an unofficial secretary during one period—were the two volumes of *New Poems* (*Neue Gedichte, Der neuen Gedichte anderer Teil*, 1907, 1908), a high point in any history of German lyric poetry. It was the craftsmanship and discipline in Rodin's artistry that Rilke sensed was lacking as a counterbalance to his own poetic inspiration. From Rodin he learned, as he later wrote, how to work "like a painter or sculptor *before nature*" and how to turn the objects of the external world into poetic images that contained the modulations of his interior life. Rilke strove to make both body and soul visible on the surface of his images, as Rodin was capable of suggesting inner movement by the distribution of light on the surface of his sculpture. The source of these images was the daily life of Paris, especially the human types, animals, and objects of the Jardin des Plantes that passed in front of the poet's newly opened eyes. Separate poems to a torso of Apollo open each of the volumes of the *New Poems*, one ending with the famous imperative of the work of art to its viewers: "You must change your life." Probably the best-known single poem, "The Panther" ("Der Panther"), was also the first of what came to be called Rilke's "*Dinggedichte*" (object poems):

His sight from ever gazing through the bars
has grown so blunt that it sees nothing more.

It seems to him that thousands of bars are
before him, and behind them nothing merely.

The easy motion of his supple stride,
which turns about the very smallest circle,
is like a dance of strength about a center
in which a mighty will stands stupefied.

Only sometimes when the pupil's film
soundlessly opens . . . then one image fills
and glides through the quiet tension of the limbs
into the heart and ceases and is still.

The object, or central image, is the animal nervously pacing back and forth behind the bars of his cage, his benumbed gaze betraying the paralysis of an inner center of strength.

Rilke's greatest talent was for lyrical poetry, but at least one of his prose works, written in the form of a poet's notebooks, belongs to world literature. Begun in 1904 and completed in 1908–1909, *The Notebooks of Malte Laurids Brigge* (*Die Aufzeichnungen des Malte Laurids Brigge*) recount the inner life of a young, hypersensitive Danish aristocrat living alone and alienated in Paris. His notebooks are the unordered account of his memories and impressions, all written under the threat to his existence from the spectacle of urban degeneration, poverty, and impersonal death. Malte is both autobiographical and imaginary, a representation that channeled the destructive effects of Rilke's own fears and anxieties from life into fiction. Toward the end of the work, Malte develops Rilke's recurrent notion of a "love without possession." The great lovers of history, all of whom in his opinion were women, are cited as evidence that the act of loving ennobles, but to be the object of another's love constricts and destroys. The novel ends with a reinterpretation of the parable of the prodigal son as "the legend of him who did not want to be loved."

Rilke viewed the separation from his wife and his own restless movement from place to place in much the same terms: as a flight from the intrusion of human attachment upon the loneliness that he considered essential to his poetry. Between 1910 and the beginning of World War I in 1914, he traveled ceaselessly, finding a temporary respite in the castle of Duino, near Trieste, from October 1911 to May 1912. Here he was able to nurture in isolation the poetic energies that lay latent in him and here he wrote the first of the ten *Duino Elegies* (*Duineser Elegien*) as though dictated to him by the voice of inspiration. Rilke's muse faltered, however; the tumultuous years of the war were followed by the unstable postwar years, and the elegies were not completed until 1922. In the hierarchy of existence in this famous, yet puzzling, cycle of poems, the figure of the angel towers over all other images, embodying Rilke's conception of an absolute existence. Man is but a frail shadow in comparison to these self-sufficient beings who do not know the human distinction between subject and world. Only in the greatest works of art and in the selfless, unpossessive love of a woman does mortal existence approximate that of the angels. Shortly after the long gestation period of the elegies was over, Rilke produced in less than thirteen days all fifty-five of the sonnets constituting his *Sonnets to Orpheus* (*Sonette an Orpheus,* 1923). Art again is accorded the top rung in the scale of human values. The song of praise is the highest task of the poet, whose mythic embodiment is Orpheus. Rilke, who himself has often been elevated to mythical rank by his commentators, lived out the last years of his life in a Swiss chateau sheltered from everyday social and political realities, a life lived to the end in the service of art.

The Diversity of German Expressionism

Even while under Rodin's influence, working like a sculptor "before nature," Rilke's strategy had little in common with the mimetic intentions of the naturalists. The objects of the *Dinggedichte* are merely the means by which the poet gave contour to the shapeless subjectivism of his earlier poems, not an end in themselves. Naturalism, as the utmost fidelity to nature, is commonly seen as the last stage in the intensification of realism in the nineteenth century. The twentieth century adds yet another chapter in the history of the term "modern" in its relation to art and literature: the chapter of the nonobjective, nonmimetic work of art. Addressing the earth at the end of the ninth elegy, Rilke asks rhetorically: "What, if not transformation, is your insistent commission?" Not fidelity, but transformation is the mission the modern artist in the twentieth century receives from nature. Nature herself is relegated to a position subservient to the vehicle of this transformation, the human faculty of *Geist,* or spirit. In the first decade of the century, it was painting that led the movement away from mimesis toward abstractionism. The program of Die Brücke (the Bridge), an association of artists founded in Dresden in 1905, emphasized existential expressiveness and the independence of colors from their objects in nature. A few years later another group of progressive artists formed Der Blaue Reiter (the Blue Rider) in Munich, a group that counted Wassily Kandinsky and Franz Marc among its membership.

In 1912 Kandinsky published his influential work *Concerning the Spiritual in Art* (*Über das Geistige in der Kunst*), declaring the emancipation of art from nature and the allegiance of the artist to the law of inner necessity. Spirit replaces matter as the ultimate reality in the aesthetics of twentieth-century modernism. In his pioneering study, *The Writer in Extremis*, Walter Sokel interprets this shift of priorities as the belatedly drawn consequences of the Kantian alienation of mind and world. If, as Kant asserted, we are limited in our knowledge of the world by *a priori* categories of mind, then the attempt to "copy" this world in a mimetic work of art becomes a questionable undertaking. Rilke shared this skepticism and the belief in the primacy of the spirit with a great number of very diverse artists and writers, none perhaps so radically different from him in other ways than those associated with the phenomenon in German cultural history known as expressionism.

Under the term "literary expressionism" is usually understood the generation of writers born between 1880 and 1890, that is, the generation that came to artistic and intellectual maturity at the time when World War I was creating havoc. During the years 1910 to 1925, their lives and art were indelibly marked by the prewar sense of impending catastrophe, the incredible destruction of the war itself, and finally, the postwar sense of deep disappointment and spiritual impotence. No one school, leading personality, literary style, or set of artistic principles bound them together, although many found common outlets for their writing in journals like *Der Sturm* (The Storm, 1910–1932) and *Die Aktion* (Action, 1911–1932). The diversity of styles and convictions among expressionist writers becomes apparent in the editorial policies of these two leading journals. To Herwarth Walden, founder and editor of *Der Sturm*, contemporary artistic quality was of primary importance. Radical innovators of nonobjective art such as Wassily Kandinsky, Oskar Kokoschka, and August Stramm, the minor postal official who developed the theory and practice of "word-art," found a powerful patron in Walden. This declared antitraditionalist and defender of the new art was also responsible for the importation of Italian futurism—he published Marinetti's manifestos and distributed promotional leaflets on the streets of Berlin—as well as for exhibiting the works of the young expressionist painters in his private salon. Franz Pfemfert's *Die Aktion*, on the other hand, sought to strike out in new directions in poetry as well as represent politically the "idea of the great German Left." A widespread politicization of literature in the sense of antiwar sentiment, pacifism, and later, revolution, could begin in earnest, however, only at the outbreak of the war. The poets who early found their way into print on the pages of *Die Aktion*—Jakob van Hoddis, Georg Heym, Gottfried Benn, and Ernst Stadler, for example—were not political in this sense. Their poetry embraced rather than rejected the atmosphere of apocalypse that hung over Europe during the last years before the war.

It was just this atmosphere in van Hoddis's famous poem "World's End " ("Weltende," 1911) that caused such a stir among his contemporaries in Berlin:

The bourgeois's hat flies off his pointed head,
The air re-echoes with a cry.
Roofers plunge and hit the ground,
And at the coast—one reads—seas are rising.

The storm is here, the savage seas hop
On land and crash thick dams.
Most people have a cold.
Trains fall off bridges.

If, as the poem describes it, the end of the bourgeois world is near, the beginning of a better world cannot be far away. According to Johannes R. Becher, the poem became a rallying point of antibourgeois sentiment among the young expressionists, solidifying them in their defiance of the older generation. Stylistically, these lightly ironic eight lines reflect typical features of much prewar expressionist poetry. Each line seems to exist in its own right with no connection between the highly visual images. Linked neither in space nor in time, they appear simultaneously and perhaps reflect, as has been suggested, the simultaneity of diverse perceptions of the big-city poet.

Many of these poets, van Hoddis among them, gathered regularly in Berlin's Neopathetisches Cabaret, where the newest verse was read and discussed. Georg Heym (1887–1912) soon overshadowed them all both as a poet and personality. According to accounts of contemporaries, the short-lived Heym, who died prematurely in an ice-skating accident, had a robust and magnetic personality that seemed to belie the grotesque, sinister imagery of his poems. Borrowing his symbolic use of color from van Gogh—his diaries reveal a strong desire to paint—Heym conjured up the modern nightmares of technology and the city in graphic scenes populated by mythological figures. War he knew only in his imagination, and in his poetry as well as his diaries, he eagerly anticipated it as a release from a general feeling of malaise and constriction. As for the millions of others who greeted the actual outbreak of hostilities with jubilation in the summer of 1914, war seemed to promise a vitalization of an existence grown stale in the soulless materialism of Wilhelminian Germany. Heym's poetry shares with that of Gottfried Benn a strong element of provocation and cynicism toward the outwardly placid, secure world of the philistine as well as the intact cosmos of traditional poetry. Heym attacks romanticized symbols of this security in "The War" ("Der Krieg"), for example, in which the personified figure of war crushes the moon in its "black hand." The reassuringly familiar images and symbols from an earlier poetic tradition are consciously thrown out of focus on Heym's feverish landscapes.

Of the innovators among the early expressionist poets, only Gottfried Benn (1886–1956) lived out a normal span of years, surviving both wars and emerging late in his life as the major spokesman for German lyric poetry after 1945. His earliest works are marked by the startling incorporation of the experience and vocabulary of his "other" life as a physician. The nine poems in his first collection *Morgue and Other Poems* (*Morgue*, 1912) left the bourgeois press aghast with their frank glimpses into the dissecting room and the cancer ward, an effect envied and emulated by many of his expressionist contemporaries. The baroque display of physical decay and disease was, however, meant not merely to shock, but also to expose the frailty and arrogance of man's claim to the highest rung on the evolutionary ladder. Benn's verse soon found eager acceptance on the pages of several expressionist journals.

A second collection of poems dedicated to the eccentric and talented poetess Else Lasker-Schüler (*Sons: New Poems; Söhne. Neue Gedichte*, 1913) was followed by still another volume in 1917 (*Flesh: Collected Lyric; Fleisch. Gesammelte Lyrik*) and a series of novellas revolving around the central figure of Dr. Rönne. In a discontinuous narrative style that breaks sharply with the classical form of the German novella, Benn mirrors the disintegration of Rönne's personality and the loss of normal ego boundaries. To others this process of depersonalization appears as madness. To Rönne, it is a welcome escape from the sufferings of consciousness into dreamlike and visionary states. The Rönne-novellas illustrate a central facet of Benn's thought, a disgust with highly developed forms of conscious life and an atavistic desire to reverse the process of evolutionary development. Man is not the crown of creation, he tells the reader in an often-quoted poem, but a swine burdened with a brain. A prime specimen of the intellectual poet, Benn yet extols in verse the decerebration of life and yearns for a return to a primitive, vegetative state of existence far down the scale of evolution; the poem "Songs" ("Gesänge") begins:

O, that we were our primitive ancestors.
A lump of slime in a tepid bog.
Life and death, impregnation and parturition,
Would issue forth from our mute fluids.

A speck of algae or a sand dune,
Formed by the wind and heavy at its base.
Even a dragonfly's head, a gull's wing
Would go too far and suffer too much.

Benn spent the years of the Weimar Republic in Berlin, mainly attending to his practice in skin and venereal diseases and writing articles on diverse medical topics for professional journals. He continued his literary activities, however, and new collections of his poetry and prose appeared in 1927 and 1928. His election to membership in the prestigious Prussian Academy of the Arts in 1932 attests to his growing literary stature at the time. For many this stature was permanently besmirched when he supported the ascension to power of the National Socialists. The politically naive Benn greeted the Nazis as the new biological type of the future and saw their theories of race and breeding as reflections of his own thinking, which, to be sure, showed strongly racist and fascist tendencies. Reality rapidly overran theory, however, and the disillusioned Benn soon opted for what he haughtily called the "aristocratic form of emigration" into military service.

The Alsatian Ernst Stadler (1883–1914) was one of the first to recognize the poet's voice behind the shocking imagery of Benn's earliest verse. In his own development, Stadler was as vehement as Heym in rejecting the impressionistic, aesthetic mode of poetry that had directly preceded them. Heym labeled George a "weak cadaver" and cast aspersions on Rilke's masculinity; Stadler rejected Hofmannsthal's early influence on him as "poisonous." In 1914 Stadler published his later poems under the collective title *Breaking Out* (*Der Ausbruch*), a title that suggests the inherent energy and dynamism of their eruptive imagery. In one well-known poem, the reader finds himself in an express train that seems to wrest itself free of its attachment to the earth as it hurtles onto a bridge over the Rhine. Empirical reality remains perceivable in the rest of the poem's long, rhythmic lines but serves primarily as a springboard for the ecstatic visions of death and rebirth at the poem's end. Stadler fell during the first months of the war in France.

At about the same time, on the eastern front the war indirectly claimed another poet, the Austrian Georg Trakl (1887–1914), who in spite of his limited lyrical production has earned a world-wide literary reputation. Trakl took his own life with an overdose of drugs while he was in a field hospital undergoing psychiatric observation. A macabre scene of the war's carnage some days before had precipitated the suicide. Yet the war finds a subdued, even serene poetic expression in his "Grodek," one of his last and finest poems that transfigures the experience of the battlefield:

In the evening the autumn woods resound
With deadly weapons, the golden plains
And blue lakes; the sun rolls
More gloomily over them; the night embraces

Dying warriors, the wild lament
Of their shattered mouths.
Yet quietly in the pasture's hollow,
Red clouds, the spent blood gathers—
There a wrathful god lives, lunar coolness;
All roads empty into black decay.
Under golden branches of the night and stars
The sister's shade sways through the silent grove,
To greet the spirits of the heroes, the bleeding heads;
And softly the dark flutes of autumn resound in the reed.
O prouder grief! You bronze altars,
A powerful pain nourishes today the hot flame of the spirit,
The unborn grandsons.

Trakl's poems mingle recognizable scraps of Baudelaire's and Rimbaud's poetic vocabulary with hallucinatory, surrealistic visions that originated in the shifting structures of his own psyche. Drugs played an early and crucial role in this instability, as did an abiding sense of guilt toward his sister. Trakl's first collection of poetry appeared in 1913 in "Der Jüngste Tag" ("Judgment Day"), a series of inexpensive volumes published by Kurt Wolff that introduced several expressionist writers to a broader reading public. Stadler's work appeared in the series, as did that of Benn, Walter Hasenclever, Albert Ehrenstein, Franz Werfel, and Franz Kafka. Trakl, who rarely left Salzburg, Innsbruck, and Vienna, had little direct contact, however, with any of the expressionist writers or with the communal existence of expressionism. The real focal point of the intellectual and artistic activities that made expressionists identifiable as a group was Germany, particularly Berlin. Oskar Kokoschka, the Austrian painter and dramatist, was able to arrange improvised stagings in Vienna for his two shockingly avant-garde one-act plays in 1907 and 1908, but it was Herwarth Walden who in the first year of *Der Sturm* published one of them, *The Hope of Women* (*Mörder, Hoffnung der Frauen*), along with Kokoschka's illustrations. Kokoschka was one of the few major artistic talents with whom Trakl had contact in Vienna. Of much greater personal importance were his ties to the periodical *Der Brenner* (The Brenner Pass), its publisher Ludwig von Ficker, and its circle of contributors.

Trakl's imagery is more daringly modern, further removed from mimetic art than the imagery of either Stadler or Heym who, moreover, often clung to quite traditional formal structures. Enigmatic figures, sometimes with names, but always with unstable identities, walk across the poetic landscapes. Abrupt changes of tense and perspective often catch the reader unawares, jolting expectations and conjuring up the effect of shifts in the level of consciousness. Disembodied colors and autonomous metaphors enrich a poetic language of autumnal colors and melancholy. Like Kafka's enigmatic prose, Trakl's poetry simultaneously fascinates and frustrates the casual reader.

The language of expressionist poetry covers a broad spectrum of styles, ranging from the verbosity of the tendentious lyric written by Johannes R. Becher to the culmination of abstract poetry, parallel to Kandinsky's painting, in the verse of August Stramm. Several anthologies published in the declining years of the movement demonstrate this range. The best known of these was *Mankind's Dawning* (*Menschheitsdämmerung,* 1919), edited by Kurt Pinthus, who claimed that the quality of the expressionist poem was to be measured by its intensity. Such intensity ages rapidly, however, and can easily deteriorate into rhetorical excess. The explosive garrulousness of Becher (1891–1958), who later became minister of culture in the German Democratic Republic, is a prime example of a poetic language in which political motivation is paramount. Franz Werfel's (1890–1945) passionate call for the brotherhood of man, on the other hand, has lost the intensity of its historical moment. Werfel, the single best-represented poet in *Mankind's Dawning,* appealed directly to the reader for the solidarity of mankind, an anticipation of a central message of expressionist drama. Compared to Trakl's detachment, his lean vocabulary and reluctance to "waste" words, Werfel's poetry today seems oversaturated with words and pathos. The effect of Trakl's work is highly dependent on the visual image and metaphor, whereas Werfel's ethical convictions demand a more discursive language.

August Stramm (1874–1915) pared language even more severely than Trakl. The building blocks of his poems were words—words freed from all syntactical restraints, neologisms, nouns used as verbs, and verbs used as adjectives. Stramm's radical concentration of language into its smallest semantic unit was intended to return a kind of primordial meaning to the liberated word. Although here as elsewhere expressionist practice was often less convincing than theory, the dissolution of language was carried yet one step further by the poets of dada in their "sound poems."

The date and place of birth of dadaism can be fixed with a precision uncommon in literary history. In February 1916 Hugo Ball (1886–1927) opened the doors of the Cabaret Voltaire in Zurich, welcoming a mixture of artistic and political anarchists to join in an intentionally absurd show of defiance of what they judged to be an absurd world. Artists, intellectuals, and pacifists of all nationalities had found their way to neutral Switzerland, where they could escape both the war and its censorship. Ball, Hans Arp, and Richard Huelsenbeck, along with the Romanians Tristan Tzara and Marcel Janco, were the founding fathers of the group that declared its motto to be: "Dada means nothing." The word itself, a children's word in French for hobbyhorse, they had found in a French-German dictionary. The dadaists rejected totally the political aspects of expressionism and asserted their own antipolitical stance. Special forms of entertainment at the Cabaret Voltaire were the production of "noise-music," with all varieties of instruments and simultaneous poetry in which sentences, sounds, and words from different texts and in different languages were simultaneously declaimed. Not all of the forms of art practiced by the dadaists were so ephemeral. The construction of collages has become accepted artistic expression, and "sound poems" such as "Caravan" ("Karawane") by Hugo Ball are forerunners of concrete poetry. The effects of the sounds and rhythms of the artificial language are unmistakable:

jolifanto bambla o falli bambla
großgiga m'pfa habla horem . . .

It is ironic that at this extreme of abstract expression these "effects" are mimetic in nature. The sounds and rhythms of "Caravan" plainly imitate the real phenomenon.

By 1916, when it had become obvious that the war was no panacea for the existential stasis plaguing so many artists and intellectuals, a more politicized form of expressionism was well under way. Voices critical of the war had gathered in Zurich by 1915 around René Schickele and his journal *Die weissen Blätter* (The White Pages), in which articles appeared on the "political" poet. Kurt Hiller published the first of his cautiously critical *Ziel* (Aim) yearbooks in 1916, including a reprint of Heinrich Mann's essay "Spirit and Action" ("Geist und Tat"), written in 1910. In this essay, Mann compares the relationship between the intellectual and the masses in Germany and France. In France they have functioned well together; in Germany, spirit (*Geist*) has soared high over the heads of those who could translate it into action (*Tat*). Mann calls on the intellectuals to bring their lofty thoughts to earth, to become "agitators" and lead the masses against the social and political forces that oppress them both. René Schickele, Kurt Hiller, and Heinrich Mann are typical of the activist branch of this antimaterialistic generation. The political weapons they appropriated for themselves were neither guns nor Marxism, but pacifism and socialist utopianism. Spirit was the key element of their artistic as well as their political arsenal. They were later to be denounced as aesthetically degenerate by Hitler and politically ineffectual by the Marxist critic Georg Lukács.

The sociopolitical idealism of expressionism found its most congenial literary vehicle in the drama, a genre naturally compatible with the pathos of this idealism. The central moral axiom of man's capacity to realize an inner regeneration, to discover a more compassionate inner self under the distorting layers of identity imposed by society, was inherently dramatic. That "man is good" is the forthright message and title of one of Leonhard Frank's short stories. With a seemingly unlimited faith in man's spiritual power, the dramatists of expressionism broke the grip of the scientific determinism that had immobilized the image of man in naturalist drama.

The age-old conflict between the generations was particularly well suited as a literary vehicle for the social criticism of expressionist dramatists. In Frank Wedekind's *Spring's Awakening* (*Frühlingser-wachen,* 1891), a predecessor of expressionist drama proper, the parents of a teenage girl fail to enlighten her on sexual matters and she dies during an attempted abortion. For Wedekind (1864–1918), the schools are as remiss as the parents in carrying out the function of educating youth. The pressures of the German *Gymnasium* coupled with those from home drive one youth to suicide. Wedekind's biting satire of the tyrannical pedagogue reflects the Nietzschean disdain for the German educational establishment, which placed the accumulation of historical knowledge above creativity and life itself. Heinrich Mann's novel *Small-Town Tyrant* (*Professor Unrat oder Das Ende eines Tyrannen,* 1905), a work that later won great popularity as a film (*The Blue Angel; Der blaue Engel,* 1928), is perhaps the best known of a number of contemporary literary works with a similar theme. The one youthful figure in *Spring's Awakening* who escapes the stunting influence of the older generation is the carefree, sexually open Ilse, a prefiguration of the elemental female Lulu in Wedekind's *Earth-Spirit* (*Erdgeist,* 1895) and *Pandora's Box* (*Die Büchse der Pandora,* 1904). Lulu is the personification of untrammeled sexuality set loose upon an uncomprehending world that finally destroys her.

With the dramatic examples of Wedekind and August Strindberg, openly sexual themes find their way onto the expressionist stage. Kokoschka's *The Hope of Women* depicts the battle of Man and Woman in a strangely mythical world beyond sociological and psychological dimensions. In Carl Sternheim's comedy *The Underpants* (*Die Hose,* 1911), Frau Luise Maske accidentally exposes her panties to public view, a sight that brings two new tenants into the Maske household. But the would-be Casanovas, one a melancholy barber, the other an intellectual and poet, fail in their endeavors at seduction. Just as it appears that the latter will be successful, he rushes from the room to eternalize his feelings in a poem. The real hero is the worldly-wise philistine, Herr Maske, who himself seduces a neighbor during the course of the play and will use the new source of income from his renters to finance a family. As much as the expressionists loved to despise and satirize the narrow-minded burgher, they yet had to admire him for his sexual prowess and animal vitality.

In *Parricide* (*Vatermord,* 1920) Arnolt Bronnen crassly exploits the confluence of sexual and generational conflict at its lowest oedipal coordinates. It centers on incestuous passions and the parricide committed by the son, who does, however, finally reject his mother's sexual advances. The son in Reinhard Johannes Sorge's play *The Beggar* (*Der Bettler,* 1912) also kills his father, but out of pity rather than passion. Typically expressionist, the characters are not individuals but nameless types, as is also the case in Walter Hasenclever's play *The Son* (*Der Sohn,* 1914). The Father/Son conflict here is seen as the modern version of the elemental clash between the privileged and the oppressed. Twenty years old and kept under virtual house arrest by his Father, the Son finally revolts under the Nietzschean banner of Life against the suppression of urges that define him as a human being. His passionate appeals to the "human" core underneath his Father's social mask are rebuffed. He is finally driven to violent insurrection, but as he raises his gun, the Father dies of a heart attack, conveniently absolving the Son of a crippling guilt that would block the vaguely defined path to self-realization upon which he enters in the last scene.

What in Hasenclever's play remained unrealized and tentative became the focal point around which the many dramatic works of Georg Kaiser (1878–1945) constantly revolved. Kaiser, a major link in literary history between Frank Wedekind and Bertolt Brecht, repeatedly attempted to realize on stage the image of the "new man." This he most eloquently accomplished in his *The Citizens of Calais* (*Die Bürger von Calais,* 1914), a dramatic reproduction of the siege of Calais in 1347, in which one man's selfless action—his suicide—sets an example for the noble actions of others. *From Morn to Midnight* (*Von morgens bis mitternachts,* 1916) depicts the futile and frantic attempts of a bank cashier to break out of the narrowness of his life with stolen money, attempts that are predestined to failure. Kaiser makes no attempt to enlist the spectators' sympathy for his characters; they are, as he insisted, embodiments of ideas, not flesh-and-blood beings. Writing a drama is not creating characters, but "thinking a thought to its end," Kaiser once wrote, and the task of the audience is to reconstruct this intellectual process. Instead of an organic structure with mounting and falling tension, Kaiser's dramas present a series of loosely connected scenes or "stations." He stripped the stage as well as his language of words around the essence of the dramatic idea. The sparse, "telegraphic" style of his characters'

264 Francis M. Sharp

speech contrasts sharply with the wordy *Sekundenstil* of the naturalist drama.

Kaiser's trilogy, *The Coral* (*Die Koralle*, 1917), *Gas I* (*Gas I*, 1918), and *Gas II* (*Gas II*, 1920), epitomizes the hopes as well as the disillusionment of what has been called ethical expressionism. The dramas trace three generations of a family, from the attempts of a capitalist billionaire to insulate himself with his fortune from the abrasions of poverty to the billionaire's grandson, who in a final act of nihilism hurls poisonous gas among his fellow workers. In the middle piece of the trilogy, the son has rejected his father's mania for accumulating wealth and has introduced a socialist system of management into the family gasworks. Industrialization itself, in its dehumanization of the workers, has replaced capitalism as the evil force at large. After an explosion they refuse to heed the calls of the son to turn their backs on technology and find simple human fulfillment in a pastoral setting. The play ends on a note of hope, however, as the billionaire's daughter promises to bear the "new man." A war rages in the background of the third play as this representative of the next generation attempts to realize his mother's hopes. But he too, is frustrated by the uncomprehending mass of workers, who steadfastly refuse to share his utopian dreams. The play ends on an utterly pessimistic note, reflecting not only Kaiser's but the general disappointment with the course of political events in the aftermath of the war.

Kaiser was himself a pacifist who, like many others, was bitterly disappointed that some kind of human renewal had not resulted from the chaos of the war. Unlike his contemporary Ernst Toller (1893–1939), however, he remained a passive spectator of postwar events. Toller took an active part in the revolutionary stirrings of the time, once passing out excerpts of his drama *Transfiguration* (*Die Verwandlung*, 1919) among striking workers in Munich. More serious in the eyes of officials was the part he played in establishing a short-lived Soviet republic in postwar Munich. Both efforts earned him jail sentences, in the latter case for five years. It was here that he completed *Transfiguration* and wrote three of his best-known plays, *Masses and Man* (*Masse Mensch*, 1920), *The Machine Wreckers* (*Die Maschinenstürmer*, 1922), and *Hinkemann* (1923). His plays reflect both the initial idealism of Kaiser as well as the ensuing pessimism. Again on the existential level, the central figure of *Transfiguration* experiences a conversion of his war enthusiasm into a belief in brotherly love. The main figure of *Masses and Man*, on the other hand, is a woman whose visions of radical change are denounced as strongly by the establishment as they are by the revolutionaries who reject her pacifism and nonviolence.

German Novelists of World Literature:
Thomas Mann, Hermann Hesse, and Franz Kafka

The energies, idealism, and pathos of expressionism gradually played themselves out in the years after the war and were memories by 1925. A much more subdued generation of writers and intellectuals dominated the cultural scene of Weimar Germany in the 1920s. A *Neue Sachlichkeit* (New Objectivity) had set in among those harshly schooled in the limitations of the power of the word in political matters. There was a widespread belief that the ecstatic outcry of expressionists for the "New Man" had actually been politically counterproductive, draining energies from the pragmatic work of social change. But before we look more closely at the cultural and literary canvas of the 1920s, we must pick up the threads of some individual literary careers, particularly those of three writers of fiction who more than any other modern German literary figures have found a secure place in world literature.

The three are Thomas Mann (1875–1955), Hermann Hesse (1877–1962), and Franz Kafka (1883–1924). As with Rilke, their stature rests on individual achievement that is unduly limited by any single label of literary history. In the German-speaking world, Hesse's reputation has clearly lagged behind that of either Mann or Kafka, yet his popularity abroad has at times been something of a cultural phenomenon. More than any other writer of any nationality, Hesse became, for example, the spiritual authority for millions of young Americans who participated in or who were affected by the American counterculture in the 1960s and 1970s. Kafka easily transcends the expressionist label sometimes attached to his work, although he shared the expressionist preference for nonmimetic art, the expression of subjective reality over the imitation of nature. The climate of expressionism was, in general, not favorable to the more leisurely and expansive pace of narrative fiction. Few works of expressionist prose have survived. Georg Heym, Gottfried Benn, Kasimir Edschmid, Klabund, Heinrich Mann, Leonhard Frank, Carl Einstein, and Alfred Döblin all wrote narrative fiction during the expressionist years, but none of it approaches Kafka's work in stature.

The origins of Thomas Mann's prose lie mainly in foreign models, the great French, Russian, and Scandinavian novelists of the nineteenth century. The principal German source upon which he could draw were the realistic novels of the Berliner Theodor Fontane, with their focus on social problems and conflicts. The first of Mann's works was published in the naturalist journal *Die Gesellschaft* and won the praise of Richard Dehmel. It was, however, his long two-volume novel *Buddenbrooks* (1901), subtitled "The Decline of a Family," that established him as a major writer. Mann was later to wonder whether this would perhaps be his one work that would withstand the test of time. The characteristic dualism that marks his works until the end of his life was already worked out in this novel. Here, the decline in the fitness for life of the Buddenbrooks, a family of patrician grain merchants in Lübeck, is matched by a parallel rise in artistic sensibility. The patriarch of the first of four generations is a robust, uncomplicated man whose zest for life and business laid the foundations for the material fortunes of the clan. Hanno, the last of the male heirs, presents the starkest of contrasts. He is sickly from birth, is oversensitive, and dies at an early age from a typhus infection. The family's decline is gradual, however, reaching a critical point in Hanno's father Thomas, who can no longer sustain the necessary energy and enthusiasm for the competition of the business world. A sign of his loss of *élan vital* is his infatuation with Schopenhauer, for whom the extinction of the will is the only way to inner tranquillity. The growing Buddenbrooks family's fascination with music, particularly that of Wagner, is a further omen of the family's gradual demise.

The opposition between burgher and artist, life and spirit, is a fundamental element of Mann's fictional world. Unlike his brother Heinrich and many other antibourgeois writers, Thomas remained uncommitted to either pole of his dualism, preferring a position between them from which he had an ironical view of both. Like the hero of his novella *Tonio Kröger* (1903), Mann despised the philistine world of the middle class, yet by birth he felt a deep attachment to it. Mann projected the split of his own life into Tonio, a split between the northern German world of his father and the suspect inheritance of his mother— southern, artistic, bohemian. Neither inheritance is fully embraced or rejected. Tonio finds that for him to be productive artistically, he must maintain contact, albeit muted and indirect, with the "blond, blue-eyed" Inges and Hanses of the world; i.e., the mindless but healthy specimens of life.

In the two decades after 1890, Mann wrote a series of short works, all revolving around the confrontation of the artistically sensitive hero with the world of the burgher. With an acute sense for psychological nuance, Mann details the triumphs and suffering of these heroes while avoiding the sentimental by satirizing their narcissism. Detlev Spinell, the pompous aesthete in "Tristan," is put to flight by the "joyous screams" of his rival's healthy offspring. Mann's irony and satire do not shy away from the cruel and grotesque. The deformed Herr Friede- mann in another of these short pieces undergoes a scurrilously harsh rejection by a beautiful woman when after long years of abstinence, he relaxes the rigid control of his emotional life.

In Mann's masterwork of this series, *Death in Venice* (*Der Tod in Venedig,* 1911), a highly respected and aging artist whose entire life had been devoted to the rigorous discipline of his art falls prey to the physical beauty of a young Polish boy. Gustav von Aschenbach, the very model of the artist working at the edge of exhaustion, succumbs at a weak moment to the temptation to flee from his customary self-discipline in the north and to escape to the south and Venice, the city of Nietzsche, Wagner, and the romantic poet Platen. It is a sojourn filled with omens of his death. Several chance encounters with pitiable figures along the way foreshadow the depths of Aschenbach's own fall. Venice, whose existence at the edge of the sea is precarious at best, is further threatened by the plague. Life itself seems to take its revenge on Aschenbach, who for so long had been able to shut it out. It drags him through the degradation and humiliation of homoerotic passions and finally releases him into death.

At the time of the publication of *Death in Venice* Thomas Mann was not that much older than most expressionist writers. Yet the vast difference in artistic temperaments is immediately apparent in the measured pace, polished language, and mythological allusions of his novella. Politically as well as artistically, Mann's attitudes contrasted sharply with those of his antibourgeois contemporaries. In the patriotic enthusiasm with which he greeted the outbreak of the war, however, he was far from alone. His essay "Frederick the Great and the Grand Coalition" ("Friedrich und die grosse Koalition," 1915) underscored his allegiance to the Prussian spirit and his support of the war. It drew a biting retort from his brother Heinrich, whose own essay proposed Emile Zola as an ideal more worthy of emulation. Thomas was clearly meant in his brother's essay as the intellectual with a sense of misguided nationalism. After this exchange the brothers were estranged until 1922.

In 1918, however, Thomas published a long rationalization of his nonpolitical views in *Observations of an Unpolitical Man* (*Betrachtungen eines Unpolitischen*). Underlying his thoughts is the fundamental dualism between "civilization" and "culture," the first being endemic to France and England, the second to Germany. Politics, rational thought, and materialistic values characterize the first; metaphysics, irrationality, and spiritual values are characteristic of the latter. The governing body of a culture is conservative and authoritarian, functioning as a shield against politics. Democracies flourish in civilizations; culture is the natural home of the artist. Mann was for years thereafter associated with the antidemocratic stance he assumed in this work, but this is an injustice to the democrat of later years. At some of the darkest points in the history of the Weimar Republic, he was to take a courageous stance in its defense. In this republic that was notoriously lacking in republicans, Thomas Mann was a shining exception.

Despite its length and its numerous digressions into essays on arcane areas of knowledge, Mann's *The Magic Mountain* (*Der Zauberberg,* 1924) sold extremely well and has since won a solid place in world literature. The novel owes its success to a large degree to its very ambitious intent, that is, to symbolically depict European civilization on the eve of World War I, with its multiplicity of conflicting ideological and intellectual tensions. Mann went about this task by reducing the scale of the setting to a tuberculosis sanitorium in Davos, Switzerland, where the "sick" from both East and West are gathered in a volatile mixture. In the middle of these tensions stands Hans Castorp, a young North German burgher from the flatlands who comes for a short visit with his cousin and remains seven years. During this time, Castorp is buffeted between the shaping forces that reside on the mountain, leaving at the end of his stay for the battlefields of Europe. Many of these forces are the very same ones over which he and his brother Heinrich had openly feuded some years before. Castorp's fate is left open, but his education—Mann called the novel a parody of the German subgenre *Bildungsroman* (novel of education)—culminates with the resolution to deny death the "mastery over his thoughts." Thus his departure from the mountain at the end of the novel signifies a reentry into life, even though the specter of war looms large in the flatlands. The path Mann himself took in 1933 led him in precisely the opposite direction as his fictional hero. Already in Switzerland on a lecture tour with his Jewish wife when Hitler came to power, he received an initially puzzling phone call from his children advising him of the "unfavorable weather" in Germany. This bad weather prevented him from setting foot onto German soil until 1949.

Mann was honored in 1929 by the world literary community with the Nobel Prize, an honor accorded to Hermann Hesse seventeen years later. For all the thematic similarities in their works, Hesse lacked that sense of irony that allows readers to smile along with Mann at the figures in his novels. The artist's calling was from the beginning an entirely serious matter for Hesse. His own literary mission had become clear to him at the age of twelve while reading a Hölderlin poem. Like Hölderlin, Hesse came from a strongly religious background and began his studies as a student of theology. Yet in the age of Nietzsche, metaphysical assurance was even harder to find than in Hölderlin's time, some hundred years before. Hesse's personal search took him to India in 1911 and later to a study of Indian and Chinese thought. The literary reflection of these experiences found expression in *Siddhartha* (*Siddharta,* 1922), the story of a Brahman youth who finds enlightenment.

Hesse's success as a writer had begun some years earlier, however, with his *Peter Camenzind* (1904), a lyrical novel of a young man's development as he travels through the world. A romanticized nature is the hero's main source of instruction, and when he returns to his village at the novel's end to become an innkeeper, he also has the beginnings of a nature poem stowed away in a drawer. *The Prodigy* (*Unterm Rad,* 1906), Hesse's autobiographical school tragedy, also belongs to his prewar literary output. Numerous stories published in literary magazines of the time are filled with enthusiasm for nature and a romantic *wanderlust.* The generally placid waters of his fiction begin to show the disturbance of Hesse's marital problems (*Rosshalde,* 1914), but the artists, wanderers, and solitary figures at the focus of his narratives remain relatively unproblematic until the outbreak of the war.

The pacifist Hesse reacted immediately in September 1914 with an article in a Zurich newspaper condemning the hostilities and the widespread nationalistic fervor, a view that earned him heavy criticism in the press. He was, however, as he told his friend Romain Rolland, unpolitical and believed not in a united Europe but in a united humanity. Personal crises during the war years led him to psychoanalysis, and from 1916 to 1917 he underwent a series of sessions with a disciple of C. G. Jung. The works of the immediate postwar period (*Fairy Tales; Märchen,* 1919; *Klingsor's Last Summer; Klingsors letzter Sommer,* 1920; *Demian,* 1919) give ample evidence of this self-analytical preoccupation, and Harry Haller in *Steppenwolf* (1927) is the archetype of modern man at odds with himself, a man split between his conflicting natures. In the "magic theater," Haller finds that the dualistic division between saint and profligate is a simplification of the vast number of selves, the almost infinite possibilities for transformation, that each human being possesses. From this modern setting of *Steppenwolf,* Hesse moves backward in time to the Middle Ages to find the backdrop to his next major novel, *Narcissus and Goldmund* (*Narziss und Goldmund,* 1930). The juxtaposition of spirit and flesh in the two title figures was already thoroughly familiar to the readers of this very prolific writer.

His writings include not only a great deal of narrative fiction in books and journals, but also essays, book reviews, and a large number of lyric poems. It was, however, Hesse's *Siddhartha* and *Steppenwolf* that had such tremendous impact on the Beats and "hippies" in an American youth culture frustrated by the Eisenhower years and rendered outwardly impotent in their social and political protests during the 1960s and 1970s. The interior journeys in Hesse's novels, heavily dependent on Eastern mysticism and Western psychoanalysis, seemed like existential guidebooks for youth already under the spell of Jack Kerouac's *On the Road* (1957) and, later, Timothy Leary's pronouncements on drugs. Leary's essay on Hesse ("Hermann Hesse: Poet of the Interior Journey") marks a high point in his American reception, according

Steppenwolf the ultimate recognition by the counterculture as a psychedelic journey.

Hesse's German audience has largely viewed his work with more sobriety and with more of an eye toward literary history. From this vantage point, it represents a continuation of nineteenth-century romanticism and seems at times to be curiously out of place in the twentieth century. By contrast, scarcely another writer is so much a product and representative of this century as Franz Kafka, the German-speaking Jewish writer born in Prague as a citizen of the crumbling Austro-Hungarian Empire. "Kafkaesque," a term that has long since become a commonplace in our literary vocabulary, drew its original meaning from the particular circumstances of Kafka's life.

The implicit sense of estrangement and of seeing reality through a distorting mirror has multiple roots in Kafka's biography. As a Jew who spoke German among a Gentile majority who spoke Czech, Kafka met alienation at every turn in his daily life. At home and in the insurance office where he worked for years, the reality of his existence as a writer clashed painfully with his life as a dutiful son and employee. He found the labyrinthine models for the tortuously twisting paths of his heroes in the bureaucracy of his company and the maze of streets winding through Prague. The characteristic of mind that underlies the strange curvature of Kafka's fictional universe is a pervasive ambivalence directed not only toward his father, but toward his own art as well. It was both his salvation and his curse, as he often complained to his fiancée, who after two broken engagements was finally unable to wrest him away from what he called his "scribblings." His writing was his existence, yet he directed in his will that three unfinished novels be destroyed after his death. Fortunately for world literature, Max Brod knew well his friend's wavering nature and arranged for the posthumous publication of *The Trial* (*Der Prozess,* 1925), *The Castle* (*Das Schloss,* 1926), and *America* (*Amerika,* 1927).

The landscape of Kafka's narratives is that of a dream in which metaphor becomes reality and in which mimesis mixes disconcertingly with grotesque and fantastic elements. His prose, however, in contrast to that of many of his expressionist contemporaries, retains its sober, unadorned quality even in the most outlandish situations. The tension between such situations and the apparently unaffected narrator is an integral part of the effect Kafka's fiction has on the reader. In *The Metamorphosis* (*Die Verwandlung,* 1915), one of his early masterpieces, Gregor Samsa awakens one morning to find that he has been metamorphosed into a giant insect. From this point on, his existence is not *like* that of vermin but has indeed *become* that of vermin. Both Gregor and his family perceive this change with horror, but as a fact to which they must adjust their lives. Gregor's new shape seems to be as real to them as his old one. Kafka's short tale "The Judgment" ("Das Urteil," 1913), written during one night of intense concentration, gradually shifts from its initially realistic plane to that of a grotesque nightmare. Ordered by his father to commit suicide for what seem to the reader to be trifling reasons, the hero Georg Bendemann rushes from his home and throws himself off a bridge, declaring with his last breath his filial piety. In another of his stories, "In the Penal Colony" ("In der Strafkolonie," 1919), culprits are punished by having their sentences inscribed into their bodies by a devilishly ingenious torture machine. The punishment is the literal materialization of a metaphorical idiom in everyday German.

As has been remarked, the courtroom atmosphere of much of Kafka's fiction has less to do with his training in law than with the way he encountered the world. The arbitrary justice meted out by his tyrannical father seems to be a more direct source than his studies of the constant mismatch of crime and punishment. Nowhere in his fiction is this mismatch more central than in *The Trial*. K., the thirty-year-old hero of the novel, wakes up one morning to find himself under arrest by functionaries of a faceless and unreachable authority. The only thing certain about this authority is its infallibility. The very fact that proceedings are under way against him, K. is assured, is a sign of his guilt. During the year in which he struggles in vain to find his way through the maze of the court system and to come in closer contact with his judges, no crime is ever specified. The dreamlike frustration at being unable to approach an existentially powerful source of authority also pervades *The Castle*. The invisible inhabitants of Kafka's castle are perhaps more benign than the judges of *The Trial*, yet they are every bit as obscure and unreachable. K.'s guilt is neither legally, morally, nor psychologically grounded but seems to lie in the very fact of his existence. His persecution and punishment—he dies "like a dog" at the hands of the court's functionaries—were strikingly paralleled in the fate of millions who some years later perished under the arbitrary system of justice of National Socialism.

Kafka was no prophet, but he has touched the wound of metaphysical homelessness in twentieth-century man more deeply than any of his contemporaries or literary heirs. If there is a God, man appears to have no chance of finding him. And what seems even worse, this absent God has left behind a set of entirely arbitrary laws that man is bent on following, even to his self-destruction.

Bertolt Brecht and the New Objectivity in Weimar Germany

Kafka's fiction leaves the reader with a sense of powerlessness in the face of an overwhelming and unknown adversary. The inherently quietistic effect contrasts vividly with the dramatic theory and practice of Bertolt Brecht (1898–1956), who sought to employ literary means for political persuasion. Brecht was convinced that he had found the identity of man's worst enemy in capitalism and that the function of the dramatist was to enlighten his audience, to rouse them from their passive state as spectators in the political arena to partisans on the side of Marxist historical necessity. Brecht's first play (*Baal,* 1918), however, was entirely at one with the agitated style and hectic mood of expressionism. His next work *Drums in the Night* (*Trommeln in der Nacht,* 1922), the prize-winning drama of the disillusioned soldier returning from the front, established Brecht's success as a playwright. But it was only gradually during the 1920s and 1930s that he developed and refined his theory of "epic theater," a theory he opposed to the traditional Aristotelian theater.

When Brecht moved to Berlin in 1924, he came to the liveliest cultural center in Europe at a time when theater was already in a state of ferment in the hands of such great stage directors as Max Reinhardt, Leopold Jessner, and Erwin Piscator. The employment of new technical means, including film, in the political theater of Piscator, greatly influenced Brecht. Brecht accused the traditional theater of enticing its audience into a world of illusion in which man's suffering appears eternal and unchangeable. His epic theater works to break this illusion and reach the spectators' capacity for rational contemplation of the plight of the dramatic figures on stage. These figures should be perceived as products of historical circumstances rather than representative of a timeless human condition. The underlying premise of Brecht's theory is that because this circumstance has been made by man, it can be changed by him.

Brecht used several stylistic means to help break the illusion of traditional theater and alienate the audience from an identification with the action on stage. Special lighting effects, the deliberate neglect of the three unities of classical drama, and the avoidance of a traditional curve of rising and falling tension all contribute to the spectators' alienation. Actors are instructed to play their roles as if they were commenting on them rather than identifying with them. At times they directly address the audience as the mouthpiece of the playwright himself. Most prominent among these *Verfremdungseffekte* (alienation effects) are the songs Brecht placed at strategic places in the plot in order to prevent the audience from being caught up in dramatic tension.

Whether as alienation effects or as pure entertainment, the songs of Kurt Weill played a large role in the enormous success of Brecht's *Threepenny Opera* (*Dreigroschenoper*) when it was first performed in Berlin's Theater am Schiffbauerdamm in 1928. The cosmopolitan cultural public of Berlin proved to be as receptive to Weill's jazz-inspired songs as it was to the new music of Arnold Schönberg, Paul Hindemith, and Alban Berg. High culture flourished in the concert halls only short steps away from a milieu of worldly pleasures in which Mac the Knife would have felt right at home. Brecht and Weill's collaboration on *The Rise and Fall of the City of Mahagonny* (*Aufstieg und Fall der Stadt Mahagonny,* 1929) followed shortly after the success of *The Threepenny Opera*, but no comparable reception greeted their efforts. From this point in his career until his emigration in 1933, Brecht's drift to the doctrinaire left mirrored one direction of political polarization in Weimar Germany as a whole. And with this radicalization came an increasing tendentiousness in his plays that he was not to overcome until after several years of living in exile.

In Brecht's appeal to rationality over emotion and in his attempt to theoretically ground the function of literature in the political process, he is a representative figure of the *Neue Sachlichkeit* in the 1920s. The term itself, however, is far less common and even more loosely defined than expressionism. When it was first used in 1925 by Gustav Hartlaub, it was little more than a convenient description of a general mood of sober and sometimes cynical reflection on the ephemeral utopias of the years of war and revolution. The image of the writer as prophet and leader yields to that of the writer as teacher working rationally toward the end of political enlightenment. Upton Sinclair's literary exploration of contemporary social and economic conditions was the foreign model held up for emulation by German writers. Documentation and eyewitness accounts of events found their way into the literature of the period. Political journalism rose to the level of art in the essays of Carl von Ossietzky and Kurt Tucholsky.

Although the Weimar Republic took its name from the residence of the mature Goethe and the home of German classicism, its nerve center remained Berlin, where Wilhelminian Germany had focused its ostentatious display of wealth and might, where the naturalists had revealed the underside of this display, and where Fontane had set his novels examining the habits and mores of its upper classes. In the latter part of the nineteenth century Mark Twain had labeled this city on the Spree the "German Chicago." Gottfried Benn, who spent the 1920s in Berlin, described the city as "flourishing, half Chicago and half Paris, corrupt and fascinating." The poverty and misery that had accompanied the city's rapid growth a half century earlier had been made even worse by the war and its aftermath of strikes, riots, unemployment, and inflation. But the night life was perhaps the most exuberant in all of Europe, running the gamut from theater to film and political cabaret, from opera to burlesque. While bloody political battles between left and right were fought on the streets, the arts flowered in the galleries and museums and the sciences flourished in the academies. The artists and craftsmen of the Bauhaus were drawn to Berlin's stimulating atmosphere as visitors until in 1932 the city provided the world-famous school for design and architecture a last, short refuge. Albert Einstein was a professor at the University of Berlin during the 1920s and a member of the Prussian Academy of Sciences.

Almost without exception, reminiscences of life in the city at the time describe it as free and exhilarating, frenetic and charged with excitement. "The tensions and conflicts of German intellectual life are more perceptible there than in Vienna," Robert Musil remarked about his own move to Berlin little more than a year before Hitler drastically transformed the city's image. With the advantage of hindsight, many have seen the cultural ferment in the Berlin of the Weimar Republic as a kind of dance of death that preceded the extermination of intellectual freedom and curiosity in the Third Reich. Many of the fruits of this ferment in the arts, sciences, and social sciences were rescued, however, in the more tolerant climes of exile.

Among the better-known literary figures of the 1920s and early 1930s were Hans Carossa, Erich Kästner, Hans Fallada, Anna Seghers, Carl Zuckmayer, and Alfred Döblin. Erich Maria Remarque's highly successful *All Quiet on the Western Front* (*Im Westen nichts Neues,* 1929) ranks among the finest antiwar novels ever written in its unsparing, detailed depiction of trench warfare in World War I. Alfred Döblin's *Alexanderplatz, Berlin: The Story of Franz Biberkopf* (*Berlin Alexanderplatz,* 1929), reflecting the general literary preference for contemporary reality, captures the panorama of urban experiences of a released convict who struggles to master his new freedom. Berlin at the turn of the century is the backdrop for Zuckmayer's tragicomedy *The Captain of Köpenick* (*Der Hauptmann von Köpenick,* 1931), a masterful satire based on an actual incident that pokes fun at the German respect for uniforms and authority. Like Biberkopf, the unemployed cobbler Wilhelm Voigt also has a prison record to contend with. Unable to obtain work because he has no identification papers and unable to get these papers because he has no work, Voigt takes the situation into his own hands. Donning a captain's uniform, he uses this symbol of authority to commandeer a group of soldiers, arrest the mayor, and raid the town hall in search of the papers he needs to legitimize his existence. Although the system finally defeats this act of individual bravado and Voigt later learns that he has searched in the wrong place, even the kaiser is said to have found the incident amusing. *The Captain of Köpenick* provided Germany with one of the last laughs it would enjoy at its national idiosyncrasies before the deadly serious literature of *Blut und Boden* (blood and soil) became the official literary norm of the Third Reich.

Readings

Closs, August, ed. *Twentieth-Century German Literature.* New York: Barnes & Noble, 1969.

Daemmrich, Horst S., and Diether H. Haenicke, eds. *The Challenge of German Literature.* Detroit: Wayne State University Press, 1971.

Furness, Raymond. *The Twentieth Century, 1890–1945.* New York: Barnes & Noble, 1978.

Gay, Peter. *Weimar Culture: The Outsider as Insider.* New York: Harper & Row, 1968.

Gray, Ronald. *The German Tradition in Literature, 1871–1945.* Cambridge: Cambridge University Press, 1965.

Hatfield, Henry. *Thomas Mann.* New York: New Directions, 1961.

Mileck, Joseph. *Hermann Hesse: Life and Art.* Berkeley and Los Angeles: University of California Press, 1978.

Pascal, Roy. *From Naturalism to Expressionism: German Literature and Society 1880–1918.* New York: Basic Books, 1973.

Politzer, Heinz. *Franz Kafka: Parable and Paradox.* Ithaca, N.Y.: Cornell University Press, 1966.

Sharp, Francis Michael. *The Poet's Madness: A Reading of Georg Trakl.* Ithaca, N.Y.: Cornell University Press, 1981.

Sokel, Walter H. *The Writer in Extremis: Expressionism in Twentieth-Century German Literature.* Stanford, Calif: Stanford University Press, 1959.

SANDER L. GILMAN

—————— **11** ——————

Literature in German, 1933–1945

Prologue

When it all began, it seemed it would pass quickly. When the Reichstag burned at the end of February 1933, it was obvious that it would not. At the beginning of 1933, Thomas Mann (1875–1955), Germany's first and only winner in the interwar period of the Nobel Prize for literature, was touring France and the Low Countries lecturing on the "sufferings and greatness of Richard Wagner." Ernst Toller (1893–1939), the author who had headed the Bavarian Soviet during its short-lived existence in 1918, was also out of Germany. The Bavarian folk-writer Oskar Maria Graf (1899–1967) was on a lecture tour as well when the Reichstag burned. None returned to Germany.

Heinrich Mann (1871–1950), Thomas Mann's brother and the chairman of the Section for Literature of the Prussian Academy, quietly packed a suitcase, took his umbrella, and left for France on February 21. Six days later, when the Reichstag burned, the floodgates opened and the leading German intellectuals fled. On February 28 the playwright-poet Bertolt Brecht (1898–1956) left Berlin for Prague; the novelists Johannes R. Becher (1891–1958), Alfred Döblin (1878–1957), and Bruno Frank (1887–1945), and the poet Karl Wolfskehl (1869–1948), and the communist publicist Willi Münzenberg (1889–1940) fled the same day. On March 1, 1933, Alfred Polgar (1873–1955), the drama critic, and Berthold Viertel (1885–1953), the novelist, left; on March 2, the poet Max Herrmann-Neisse (1886–1941); on March 3, the dramatist Friedrich Wolf (1880–1953); on March 4, the writers Alfred Wolfenstein (1883–1945) and Gabriele Tergit (b. ca. 1900); on March 5, the editor and essayist Theodor Lessing (1872–1933); on March 8, the publisher and writer Harry Graf Kessler (1868–1937); on March 10, Leonhard Frank (1882–1961), the novelist, and Leopold Schwarzschild (1891–1950), the liberal editor; on March 12, Alfred Kantorowicz (1899–1979), the publicist, and Thomas Mann's daughter, Erika (1905–1969), herself an established actress; on March 13, Thomas Mann's son Klaus (1906–1949), the novelist; on March 14, the novelist Arnold Zweig (1887–1968). The list of those who fled continued until the rupture of German intellectual life had drained the "spirit of Weimar" from the "New Germany."

The new exiles were, however, the lucky ones. The novelist Anna Seghers (1900–1983), the newspaperman Egon Erwin Kisch (1885–1948), the writers Manès Sperber (b. 1905) and Karl August Wittfogel (b. 1896), all spent time in jail, and writers such as the Marxists Willi Bredel (1901–1964) and Ludwig Renn (1889–1979) spent between one and two years in prison. Even less lucky were those writers who were seen to be direct opponents of the new regime. The writers and publicists Erich Baron, Erich Mühsam (1878–1934), and Klaus Neukrantz (1895–1941) all died in the Nazi prisons or newly created concentration camps. The editor and essayist Carl von Ossietzky (1888–1938), arrested and tortured by the Gestapo, the new German political police, was awarded the 1936 Nobel Prize for peace while still in the camp at Papenburg-Esterwegen. Ossietzky was released from the camp but remained under house arrest in a sanatorium in Berlin until he died of the results of his imprisonment in 1938.

It was not merely writers who fled, nor was it the writers alone who were imprisoned and tortured. Liberal intellectuals, and later conservative opponents of the "Thousand Year Reich," as well as Jews, all felt the hatred of the regime. But writers held a special place in the fanaticism of the Nazis. In the struggle for public opinion during the Weimar Republic writers, editors, and publishers of the center and left were felt to be the enemy of the right. The various political tendencies all had their publishing houses, news services, newspapers, as well as authors who wholeheartedly supported one party or another. On the right the press czar was Alfred Hugenberg (1865–1951), who, among other things, owned the major German film studio; on the left was Willi Münzenberg, editor of the *Workers' Illustrated News* and head of the Marxist news service. The ideological struggle between right and left was carried out in the media, and the media became identified with this struggle.

Adolf Hitler, in his programmatic statement of Nazi goals *Mein Kampf* (*My Struggle,* 1925/1926), commented over and over again on the power of the press and the writer in society. Hitler attacked the "so-called 'freedom of the press,'" arguing that the state "must make sure of this instrument of public education" (p. 242). But the press and the writer were not simply the enemies of the "new order." They were the tool of the Jews: "The state authorities either cloak themselves in silence or, what usually happens, in order to put an end to the Jewish press campaign, they persecute the unjustly attacked, which in the eyes of such an official ass, passes as the preservation of state authority and the safeguarding of law and order" (p. 324). Hitler's charge of a Jewish conspiracy against their enemies has, of course, a very specific focus. Hitler, in the preface to his work, sees the rationale for writing it as the need "to destroy the foul legends about my person dished up in the Jewish press" (p. vii). The press accounts of Hitler's abortive coup attempt in 1923 had been for the most part comic. Hitler struck out against the press as the tool of his "hidden enemy," the Jews. The power of this association between the Jew as the enemy and the press (and writers) as his ally in attacking the Germans illustrates the conflation of images the Nazis used to present the image of the writer. His importance was all out of proportion to his role, as he was manipulated by a greater and hidden power. Here the vilification of the opposition becomes a metaphysical condemnation as agents of demonic forces of all who oppose Hitler.

The political implications of the Nazis' image of the writer as the mouthpiece of the Jews can be seen in the first list of Germans whose citizenship was revoked. On August 23, 1933, this list appeared; on it stood Willi Münzenberg, Leopold Schwarzschild, Heinrich Mann, Ernst Toller, Kurt Tucholsky (1890–1935), and the novelist Lion Feuchtwanger (1884–1958). Indeed, in all the lists of those who had their German citizenship revoked (which continued until 1939, with over 8,000 individuals listed), the proportion of writers was extraordinarily high. In addition, the Nazis' creation of the Reich Cultural Organization in September 1933 marked the establishment of a new definition of the writer within German society: the supporter, rather than the opponent, of established order.

The elimination of most writers of international status from Germany did not create an intellectual vacuum. For within the structure of the literary world of the Weimar Republic there had been a large number of writers who were either advocates of the right or whose ideological position permitted them to function under the new literary codes. Rooted in the intellectual conservatism of the late nineteenth century, these writers defined themselves as the "conservative revolution" against the cosmopolitanism and experimentalism of the Weimar Republic. Writers such as Wilhelm Pleyer (1901–1974), with his novels of German-speaking peasants in Czechoslovakia, Hans Grimm (1875–1959), with his evocations of the lost German colonies in Africa, and Ernst Jünger (b. 1895), with his bittersweet novels of the glories of World War I, all contributed to the intellectual opposition to a literature that was seen as sterile, proletarian, city-based, and Jewish. All of these writers, as well as many other conservative thinkers, saw in the purification of German intellectual life their chance to create a new German literature. But one must also stress that this desire to be liberated from that which they viewed as the "disease of internationalism" and to see "literature as the intellectual locus of the nation" (so ran Hugo von Hofmannsthal's programmatic essay of 1927) had been the wish of many conservative writers following World War I. Writers such as Hofmannsthal (1874–1929), had he lived, would have been excluded from this "new community" on racial grounds. Other conservative writers who had wished for a "third Reich," such as Stefan George (1868–1933), made a conscious decision in 1933 not to collaborate with the reality of the Third Reich as created by the Nazis.

Perhaps the best pragmatic example of the tensions of the first year after the Nazis' assumption of power can be found in their restructuring of the Section for Literature in the Prussian Academy. During the Weimar Republic its chairman had been the liberal writer Heinrich Mann, who saw as its prime goal the restructuring of the function of literature in the republican state. To this end the Section for Literature sponsored a new history textbook for the schools of the Weimar Republic. Even before the Ministry for Propaganda was formed under the direction of the Ph.D. in German literature and failed novelist Joseph Goebbels, the conservative president of the Prussian Academy, Max von Schilling, had demanded from all the members of the Academy oaths of loyalty to the new regime. Thomas Mann, Alfred Döblin, and Ricarda Huch (1864–1947) resigned immediately in protest. Ten more writers of international reputation, including Franz Werfel (1890–1945), Jakob Wassermann (1873–1934), and the pacifist René Schickele (1883–1940), were excluded after the Enabling Act of May 23, 1933, placed the Academy under the overall direction of Goebbels. But the other members of the section, including Gerhart Hauptmann (1862–1946), signed. Eventually replacing Heinrich Mann as chairman was Hanns Johst, the author of *Schlageter* (1933), a play dedicated to Adolf Hitler and commemorating the execution of a German nationalist during the French occupation of the Ruhr in 1923. But even within the newly reorganized section on literature, the identification of conservative writers with the new regime was not total. Among the new members proposed by Goebbels for the section on literature was Ernst Jünger, whose glorifications of war had placed him at the forefront of conservative literature during the 1920s. Jünger informed the president of the Prussian Academy that he refused election because of his sense of the role of the writer as individual rather than as part of any collective voice.

Exile in Europe

The writers who found themselves in exile in France, Austria, the Netherlands, and Czechoslovakia, despite their heterogeneous political and aesthetic views, focused on their opposition to the Third Reich. Most thought of their exile as short-term and were convinced that the sound intelligence of the German people coupled with their own propagandistic opposition would soon topple the government and restore the Republic. Bertolt Brecht, sitting in exile in Denmark, admonished his readers in his poem "On the Designation Emigrant" ("Über die Bezeichnung Emigranten") that one should stay "close to the borders / waiting for the day of return." The focus on the inner political workings of the Nazi state as well as the sense of a temporary exile permitted many writers to absolve themselves of responsibility for any active opposition to the state. Only a few writers, such as Jan Petersen (1906–1969), drifted into the political underground in Germany, remaining to actively organize whatever opposition forces remained. In 1935 he appeared at the First International Writers' Congress in Paris and reported on life in Nazi Germany, wearing a black mask to disguise himself; he quickly became one of the cultural heroes of the literary opposition to the Nazis as the "Man With the Black Mask."

The opposition to the Nazis for the most part took literary form. Through the newly created publishing houses, such as Willi Münzenberg's Edition du Carrefour, or new lines in established houses, such as the liberal Querido Press in Amsterdam, a broad spectrum of works by exiled writers began to appear in German for distribution illegally in Nazi Germany and to the growing exile community in Europe. What is striking about this literature is that it paralleled the development of the new literature of Nazi Germany in its selection of literary genres, modes of presentation, and tone. Actually, this should not be so surprising, as both the fascist and antifascist traditions continued propagandistic models for the function of literature in society that had been well established in the Weimar Republic.

Three major thematic or genre traditions can be observed in both the official literature within Germany and the writings of the exiled opponents of the regime. First was the use of volumes of popularized documents as a means of commenting on contemporary events. The most widely read of these early works of documentary montage was the 1933 *Brown Book on the Reichstag Fire and Hitler Terrorism* (*Braunbuch über Reichstagsbrand und Hitlerterror*), compiled by Willi Münzenberg's exile publishing house as a means of countering the anticommunist propaganda associated with the trial of those accused of having started the Reichstag fire. The quasi-official Nazi publishing houses, such as the Franz Eher Press in Munich, brought out similar compilations of documents on the Jewish press.

But even more striking is the second parallel, the search for historical models of contemporary events as a means of examining the rise of the Nazis. What would seem on the surface a flight from exactly the type of pseudo-objectivity implied by the documentary reveals itself to be merely the fictionalization of documentary evidence. The most successful work of this genre that appeared during the period immediately following the Nazi seizure of power was Lion Feuchtwanger's *The Family Oppenheim* (*Die Geschwister Oppenheim*, 1933), a study of a Jewish middle-class family in the period immediately before the Nazi takeover. The attempt to examine a Jewish family as paradigmatic for the blindness of the German middle class proved to be controversial, even among the German writers who supported Feuchtwanger's views. For indeed the abrupt rise of Nazi power also meant the establishment of anti-Semitism as an official policy of the state, and many writers "discovered" the Jewish identity only when they were labeled as "Jewish." On the side of the fascist writers, the interest in the period immediately before 1933 continued as a justification for the new regime. On April 13, 1933, Richard Euringer's (1891–1953) *German Passion 1933* (*Deutsche Passion, 1933;* 1933) was broadcast throughout Germany as a literary sign of the transition. Euringer's radio-play is a pseudometaphysical recreation of the post–World War I era in mock-classical style. It serves much the same function as such novels as *The Family Oppenheim*, to situate the present political situation within the continuum of political history, at least as perceived in 1933.

The conservative tradition that became established as the primary mode of literary expression within Germany and the liberal tradition of those writers who found themselves in opposition to the new regime in 1933 also shared one final common tradition, that is, the tone of their literary works. The polarity of political discourse in the 1920s had so destroyed the possibility of writing outside polemic that the harsh, condemnatory tone of personal vituperation was heard on both sides of the literary discourse. Coming from the supporters of the "New Order," with their training in the anti-Semitic tradition of Dietrich Eckardt (1868–1923) and Julius Streicher (1885–1946), this does not come as a surprise. But that the tone of many early antifascist works reflected not an understanding of the implications of such rhetoric but its incorporation makes many of these early works quite problematic. Klaus Mann's 1936 novel *Mephisto*, based on the career of the actor-director Gustaf Gründgens (1899–1963), exhibits not only Mann's personal animus against Gründgens as an individual and a type (the opportunistic supporter of whatever regime is in power) but also many of the racist attitudes of prefascist Germany. Mann's portrayal of the hero's black mistress especially echoes distinctly fascist racism. The tone of Mann's diatribe is found in many works of the first few years, especially once the illusion vanished that the Nazi terror would be swept away in the course of a normal change in government.

The End of the First Phase

The initial phase of reaction by writers both within and without Germany following the Nazi assumption of power ended by the end of 1936. By then it had become evident that the Nazis had no intention of sharing power even with their conservative political allies and that they were certainly not going to vanish from the scene. With the laws concerning the nature of German citizenship promulgated in 1935 it also became evident that both Jews and politically unwelcome writers were not going to be able to function, even marginally, within the Nazi state. Immediately after the Nazi seizure of power major writers such as Thomas Mann and René Schickele, although themselves in exile, continued to publish within Germany, but this became more and more difficult with the solidification of power within the state. Writers in exile began to consider the establishment of a unified front to oppose the Nazi state.

In December 1935 a group of German intellectuals spanning the spectrum from orthodox communists, such as Johannes R. Becher, to independents, such as Lion Feuchtwanger, published the first appeal to the Germans that came from all political tendencies. On June 9, 1936, the planning committee for a unified political opposition was constituted under the direction of Heinrich Mann. The intellectual organs of the exile community had begun to reveal a common opposition to the Nazis. No longer was it the communists or the socialists or, indeed, the exiled conservative opposition alone; all of these groups began to consider themselves as elements in a common struggle against international fascism.

The debates within the exile community on the nature of fascism revealed how superficially the German exiles understood the nature of the historical process that had led to the rise of Hitler. Their discussion, like the polemics written in 1933, attempted to pinpoint specific historical errors, and they saw these errors in the mirror of literature. The most evident and naive attempt to place the blame for the rise of the Nazi mentality is seen in the so-called expressionism debate that raged among Marxist exiles in the Moscow-based periodical *Das Wort* (The Word) during 1937 and 1938. The primary participants in this debate were the playwright Bertolt Brecht and the Hungarian Marxist theorist Georg Lukács (1885–1971). The debate began with the publication of an essay by Klaus Mann on the poet Gottfried Benn (1886–1956), whose personal views on racism made him acceptable to the Nazis during the period of their coalescence of power. Klaus Mann saw in Benn's flirtation with the Nazis the result of the expressionists' vitalism and stress on the irrational. Alfred Kurella (1895–1975) stated the case even more baldly in a subsequent issue of *Das Wort*: "We can see today who the intellectual children of expressionism are and where its spirit led—to fascism."

The view that the expressionists, such as Benn, Arnolt Bronnen (1895–1959), and Hanns Johst, were in some manner preprogrammed for their later movement to fascism and that Marxist writers, such as Johannes R. Becher, Bertolt Brecht, and Friedrich Wolf, moved to the left in spite of their roots in expressionism became the touchstone of the debate. It became the duty of the exile writers, according to Kurella, to abandon the experimentalism and self-absorption of expressionism. This meant, of course, the move to realism. As the debate in the late 1920s concerning the role of realism (or the "new realism") in social change had been a natural reaction to the experimentalism of the expressionists, it was no surprise that the answer to the pathology of expressionism, with its natural progression to fascism, was realism.

Lukács had already, in 1934, stressed the flight from reality of the expressionists and seen in realism the only possible tool for combating the fascist mentality. In June 1938 Lukács published an essay on realism in *Das Wort* in which he stated that "political unity, nearness to the true nature of the people and true realism" are the three central tenets of oppositional literature. This naive attempt to see in modes of narrative the truth or falsity of political values, to trace the roots of fascism to styles of staging or experiments in form—in general to give literature or culture the determining role in political history—was understood even by Lukács's contemporaries as a superficial means of establishing the official Soviet version of "socialist realism" as the true creed of the progressive. Bertolt Brecht, in a series of unpublished essays of the period, and the philosopher Ernst Bloch (1885–1977), both questioned this assumption. The static, formalistic criteria of the expressionism debate were revealed by Brecht and Bloch to be little more than the imposition on literature of yet another external set of determinants. Literature had become a surrogate for political life. Since the writers in exile could affect neither the political world of Nazi Germany nor that of their exile, they fled into that world in which they had complete control, the world of letters. The impotence of the German intellectual in exile can be measured by the importance given the expressionism debate.

The belief that literary traditions determined political direction was in no way limited to the exiles. As early as 1933 Paul Kluckhohn

(1886–1957), one of the most respected academic critics in Germany, published his programmatic essay on "the conservative revolution in contemporary letters." This was paralleled by a series of conservative literary histories that saw the sole salvation of Germany as an intellectual and cultural entity, not in the pluralism of the Weimar Republic, but in a monolithic, homogeneous literature "of the people [*Volk*]." This conservatism was often, but not always, linked to a negative image by which the "people," the source of all virtue and truth in letters, was defined. And this negative image was that of the Jew, who became the embodiment of "cosmopolitanism," of "asphalt literature," of "internationalism," of "degenerate literary experimentalism."

Drawing on the mix of populist (*völkisch*) and racist literary criticism present in the works of critics such as Adolf Bartels (1862–1945), who spent most of his career as a critic determining the racial and therefore (at least in his mind) the intellectual pedigree of German writers, racist literary theory became paramount in Germany. What is most fascinating is that it drew on conservative tendencies in literary scholarship that, as seen from their roots in the 1920s, did not seem inherently racist. Parallel to Bartels was the Austrian critic Josef Nadler (1884–1963), who wrote a "literary history of German lands and tribes" in which he attempted to determine the particular nature of, for example, Austrian as opposed to Prussian literature, just as elsewhere critics were trying to differentiate American from British letters. Nadler's *völkisch* literary history was quickly subsumed under the more general tradition of a quasi-official literary criticism, which again differentiated between positive literature, i.e., the various strains of *völkisch* writing, and Jewish writing (which often was not written by Jews). Just as there developed a German physics to counter the work of Albert Einstein, so too there developed a German criticism. Because of the nativistic bias in literary criticism, which exists even today, "German criticism" sounds more benign than does "German physics." It is not. It led to work such as that by Johannes Alt (b. 1896), which attempts to determine with "scientific" precision the true nature of Jewish letters.

But the movement from *völkisch* to racist literary theory is not as difficult to understand as the movement of existential literary theory from the realm of abstract philosophy to racist literary segregation. Martin Heidegger's (1889–1976) own strong support of the Nazi movement was not merely a personal aberration; rather it grew quite naturally out of his preoccupation with the existential essence of the literary text. His literary disciples, primarily Hermann Pongs (1889–1979), placed existential literary criticism squarely in the service of the new state. Pongs was able to write in a programmatic essay on the "new duties of literary scholarship," published in 1937, that "more populist power and populist spirit can be found in the rough, archetypal prose of Paul Ernst [1866–1933] than from the linguistic suppleness of the lost bourgeoisie of Thomas Mann." Here the very nature of the description carries racist tones. For "linguistic suppleness" is a code phrase for "Jewish falsity of language," for their manipulation of German to their own ends, while "rough" and "archetypal" point toward the *Volk* with their truthful, pure use of language. The racism of such a view of language is clear. Here the goal of literary theory, as in the so-called expressionism debate is the placing of blame, the creation of scapegoats. It also stresses the importance of the written word for the Nazis as a means of presenting their "revolution" as one with legitimate intellectual credentials. Unlike the exiles' debate about the origin of literary fascism, the racist theories of German literary criticism led to the burning of books throughout Germany on the night of May 10, 1933, and as Heine had written a hundred years before, "Where books are burned, people too can be burned."

The War Begins

Between March 11, 1938, and August 23, 1939, political events in Europe radically altered the nature and role of the exiled writer writing in German. On March 11, 1938, Germany annexed Austria. German writers who had found a home in Austria, which shared a common literary language with Germany, as well as those who had settled in Prague, which fell to the Germans in March 1939, fled once again. In September 1939 a nonaggression pact was signed by Stalin and Hitler, which isolated the German intellectuals who had found refuge in the Soviet Union. Indeed, many German exiles who were viewed as dangerous to order in the Soviet Union were summarily turned over to the Nazis and vanished into concentration camps. A similar fate befell Carola Neher (1900–1942), Bertolt Brecht's Polly in the original *Threepenny Opera* (*Dreigroschenoper,* 1928), who was interned in a Soviet labor camp and shot in 1942. By the end of August 1939, war was seen to be inevitable. The Nazi invasion of Poland on September 1, and the subsequent invasion of Western Europe destroyed whatever refuge the German exiles had found in Europe. They fled, if they could, or like Walter Benjamin (1892–1940), the German social theorist, committed suicide as a means of escaping the Nazi advance.

Flight from Europe was also flight from the organs of literary expression that had developed to state the position of the exiles. The publishing houses in France and the Netherlands were closed (although the S. Fischer Press managed to relocate to neutral Sweden), and the journals ceased publication. Much of this suppression was undertaken with the active support of the powers in the now conquered nations of Western Europe. The French govenment under Pétain, which established itself at Vichy, promulgated laws that disenfranchised Jewish exiles and other nonnatives quite independently of any German pressure. Feelings against the exiles were quite negative, at least on the part of the conservative, anti-Semitic leaders of the "new" France.

Flight to the rest of the world was difficult, if not impossible. The sense of despair that engulfed the intellectual exiles, cut off from their potential reading public and robbed of any direct link with their language, can be measured in one of the major works to come out of this period, Anna Seghers's novel *Transit* (*Transit*). Published in 1944, the novel chronicles the reactions of a group of refugees in the summer of 1940 who attempt to flee the German invasion of France and find themselves in the port of Marseille. The struggle for a visa to escape the Nazis becomes the focus of the lives of all the characters. The loss of personal identity, the overriding importance of that small piece of stamped paper, the visa, which determines one's identity as much as one's fate, becomes the central theme of the novel. The fate of the hero, who assumes one identity after another as he acquires different sets of papers, and his eventual decision to abandon his flight to join the French Resistance constitute the idealized answer to the exiles' feeling of having abandoned the fight against the menace of the Nazis. Seghers herself found refuge in Mexico, where this novel was first published in Spanish.

Seghers's fate, and the fate of her novel, can stand as emblematic of some of the problems faced by other writers who fled France, the Soviet Union, the Netherlands, or Denmark following the German invasion. They were forced to abandon a literary infrastructure of journals and presses and established, if illegal, links to daily life in Germany. They were, moreover, forced to abandon their language and attempt to function in a world that spoke English or Spanish and for which German did not exist as a cultural second tongue. Writers fled to the United States, to Great Britain, to Mexico, indeed as far away as to New Zealand. Exile had become real, as it had become exile not only from Germany but from continental Europe.

In Germany itself major changes had come about as the passage of time had given an ever greater sense of legitimacy to the Nazi regime. Without a doubt, the major international event that provided the Nazi leadership with the label of international respectability was the Olympic Games of 1936, held in Berlin. As Nazi official propaganda, the games, and the resulting film made by Leni Riefenstahl (b. 1902), a product of the conservative Hugenberg studios of the 1920s, served to provide the Germans with a model for public entertainment. German sports activities during the 1920s, especially in the Sportspalace in Berlin, had already acquired the image of a public spectacle. Through the influence of Dietrich Eckardt the Nazis began to exploit the idea of public spectacle as a means of achieving the uniform support of the masses. Through the creation of populist public theater, the *Thingspiel*, as well as the creation of pseudopublic events, such as party congresses, the Nazis were able to manipulate large numbers of people. By the use of film, the official agencies of party propaganda were able to extend their reach into every town; and by the use of radio, they were present at every hearth.

The solidification of power in Germany also meant that some of the more tenuous agreements with intellectuals allied with the Nazis were abrogated. Gottfried Benn, whose quirky racism, similar to that of the American poet Ezra Pound, had enabled him to be used by the Nazis, was quickly returned to the rubbish heap of writers viewed as "swinish." Even major figures such as Hans Grimm, the author of the quintessential colonial novel, *People Without Space* (*Volk ohne Raum,* 1926), broke at least partially with the regime. What developed out of the older traditions within Germany was a new, party-oriented literature.

The conservative literary traditions in Germany before 1933 have been generally classified as "blood and earth" literature (*Blut-und-Boden-Literatur*). Writers such as Wilhelm von Polenz (1861–1903), who glorified the peasant and vilified the city-dweller, were succeeded by an entire generation of writers during the 1930s and 1940s who seemed able to generate an endless stream of paeans to the German peasant. Joseph Georg Oberkofler's (1889–1962) novel *The Forest Preserve* (*Der Bannwald,* 1939), with its mythic reconstruction of German social conflicts and the most popular novel of the 1930s, Josefa Berens-Totenohl's (1891–1969) *The Secret Court* (*Der Femhof,* 1934), with its stress on the irrational, are typical. The use of historical fiction and drama, which serve in the works of older writers such as Hans Friedrich Blunck (1888–1961) or Erwin Guido Kolbenheyer (1878–1962) as the historiographic foundation for a new German literary mythology, was paralleled by the exile writers' attempts to present historical analogies to the rise of Nazism. These included the brilliant tetralogy *Joseph and His Brothers* (*Joseph und seine Brüder*), published between 1933 and 1943, on which Thomas Mann worked during the majority of his years in exile, as well as his brother Heinrich Mann's series of novels on the life and times of King Henri IV of France. The idea of the novel as a cryptohistory of the present day was used by writers both within and without Germany. Within Germany such attempts to adapt older literary forms had a pragmatic purpose in the daily life of the German people. They served to change the Germans' sense of history, wiping out the entire period from the Treaty of Versailles to the rise of the Nazis. The role of such novels outside Germany was less evident, and although in retrospect their value as flashes of historical illumination can be seen, contemporary writers were doubtful of their efficacy in documenting the horrors of the Nazi regime. Younger writers, such as Klaus Mann, sought contemporary events, such as those presented in his novel of exile, *The Volcano* (*Der Vulkan,* 1939), rather than historical analogies.

Within Germany the passage of time brought forth a series of younger writers who contributed pure party literature. Poets such as Heinrich Anacker (1901–1940), Hans Baumann (b. 1914), and the head of the Hitler Youth, Baldur von Schirach (1907–1974), contributed volume after volume of salutes to the new state. Schirach is typical of those writers who combined false pathos with propaganda, as in his poem "Hitler":

> You are many thousands behind me
> and you are me and I am you.
>
> I have not lived an idea
> which has not beaten in your heart.
>
> And when I speak words, I know none
> that is not one with your will.
>
> For you are me and I am you,
> and we all believe, Germany, in you.

Such a text, in thousands of variations, can be found in the numerous volumes of hack poetry written by and for party functionaries. Poetry had become the servant of the state, glorifying the leader and identifying itself as the one true voice of the people. One major writer who saw himself in this role was the poet Josef Weinheber (1892–1945), whom many of his contemporaries viewed as the natural heir of Stefan George. George, who had emigrated to Switzerland and died there in 1933, never acknowledged the Nazis' expressions of interest in him. With Weinheber they acquired a major poetic voice who saw the Nazi dictatorship as the creation of a natural order. Weinheber's early lyric, full of the pathos of a world in collapse, gave way to the crudest glorifications of the heroism of the fascist state.

Literature in Opposition

If the passage of years enabled party poetry to flourish within Germany, it also drove some writers who remained within Germany ever further into what became designated after 1945 as their "inner emigration." Mainly conservative writers, they remained in Germany, where their

public existed. Often their writing was intended for a future generation
and was consigned for the present to the recesses of a desk drawer.
Poets such as Oskar Loerke (1884–1941) and Wilhelm Lehmann
(1882–1968) sought poetic refuge in nature poetry but also kept running
commentaries on their hidden intent in diaries and letters. Some of the
conservative writers, such as Ernst Wiechert (1887–1950), wound up
in more or less direct opposition to the state. Wiechert, for example,
was sent to a concentration camp for opposing the arrest of Pastor
Martin Niemöller. While in the camp he was able to have his works,
viewed by the party and state as exemplary presentations of the universal
values that opposed the "asphalt civilization," placed in the camp
library. Younger writers, such as Marie Luise Kaschnitz (1901–1974),
Elisabeth Langgässer (1899–1950), and Eugen Gottlob Winkler
(1912–1936), were able to publish their conservative, but not oppositional,
writings in the few literary journals, such as the *Deutsche Rundschau*
(German Review), that would still accept nonfascist literature.

At least one clearly liberal writer, the satirist Erich Kästner (1899–1974),
whose works were banned by the Nazis, remained in Germany during
the Third Reich. Forbidden to earn his living by writing, he turned
out hack works under a series of pseudonyms. When, however, the
official film company of the Reich wanted to celebrate its twenty-fifth
anniversary with a film of the tales of the fabulous liar Baron von
Münchhausen, they were forced to allow Kästner a "special permit" to
write the film, which appeared in 1942. A few writers used the literary
traditions of the conservative mode of literature for hidden, oppositional
purposes. Reinhold Schneider's (1903–1958) 1938 novel *Las Casas Before
Charles V* (*Las Casas vor Karl V*) centers on the racist persecution of
the Indians by the Spanish conquistadors. The king is moved to action
by the monk's plea, which illustrates to no small degree the chasm
between the reality of racism (and the nature of the leader) in fact and
in the wish-dreams of fiction.

No work of the "inner emigration" was better accepted by the official
state reviewers than Werner Bergengruen's (1892–1964) novel *A Matter
of Conscience* (*Der Grosstyrann und das Gericht*). Bergengruen was a
Baltic German, whose works were widely accepted within Germany as
part of the conservative wave of appreciation for writers who represented
the border Germans (*Auslandsdeutschtum*). These writers were seen as
outposts of German culture abroad, often in exactly those lands, such
as Bohemia and Moravia or the Baltic region, where German hegemony
was to be established by military means. In 1935 Bergengruen published
his novel of the murder of a functionary in a Renaissance city-state
and the involvement in the murder of the ruler. The official party
newspaper, the *Völkischer Beobachter* (Populist Observer), heralded it

as the "Führer-novel of the Renaissance." By 1940 it had sold 182,000 copies. The work, a thinly veiled attack on the totalitarian state, used the device of the historical novel to its full advantage. It showed the inner corruption of the state, the flaws of any leadership that claims an absolute right to rule. The polis had been seen as the highest good. Yet in Bergengruen's novel the murder of the functionary, shown to have been committed by the ruler of the city-state for "reasons of national security," reveals the center of the state to be corrupt. The immediate references in the novel are clear. They are to the Röhm putsch of 1934, which revealed the rotten inner circle of Hitler's "SA" ("Storm Troopers") to the world. The novel lent itself to two possible interpretations. One, which was seen and accepted by the state, was the need for a strong leader who could undertake even murder for the good of the state; the other presented such an action on the part of a Christian leader as unthinkable and self-condemnatory. This inherent ambiguity enabled those who wished to read into the novel a negative critique of contemporary events to do so; for those who saw in it only historical escapism, the contemporary analogies could easily be overlooked.

Parallel structures of ambiguity can be found coded into other novels of the period, such as Ernst Jünger's *On the Marble Cliffs* (*Auf den Marmorklippen*) of 1939. But this ambiguity could also have a negative side. Karl Aloys Schenzinger's (1886–1962) party novel *Hitleryouth Quex* (*Der Hitlerjunge Quex*, 1932), a hagiography commemorating the murder of a fascist youth group member by the Communists, was banned after extensive distribution because the central figure seemed to have some inner doubt about his sacrifice—an ambiguity impossible in a novel about contemporary events in the Third Reich. In the historical novel, such as Jochen Klepper's (1903–1942) 1937 novel of the life of Frederick the Great, *The Father* (*Der Vater*), just such ambiguity was permitted. For Klepper, Prussia became the true German state and Frederick the true ruler, with the implied contrast to the Nazi regime, which itself wished to claim Prussia as its model. Bergengruen survived the war, Klepper did not. He committed suicide with his Jewish wife and their daughter, sensing their eventual fate.

Within Germany there was also a small nucleus of writers who joined the active underground opposition to the regime. Jan Petersen, "the Man with the Black Mask," assumed the leadership of the Organization of Proletarian-Revolutionary Writers in 1933. By 1935 this organization of Marxist opponents of the regime had been infiltrated and destroyed by the Nazis. Such organizations circulated literally millions of broadsides and pamphlets, the latter often disguised as cookbooks or tracts on hygiene. They contained not only straightforward documentation of the realities of Nazism but also literary texts aimed at exposing the horrors of German fascism. In 1936, according to the Gestapo's own figures, 1,643,200 such texts were seized, more than 70 percent stemming from the various communist underground organizations. Poets such as Albrecht Haushofer (1903–1945), whose *Moabit Sonnets* (*Moabiter Sonette*, 1946) were found in his hand after he was executed by the Nazis for his participation in the abortive July 20, 1941, attempt to assassinate Hitler, were published in this manner. Haushofer, whose father's concept of a "space to live" (*Lebensraum*) had been adopted as Nazi ideological jargon, felt himself drawn to the antifascist opposition. Like many other conservative writers, he saw the corruption of the German language as indicative of corruption in the German soul. Their organizations attempted to create alternatives to the existing state, none of which succeeded in altering the ongoing policies of the Nazis. Of the oppositional groups perhaps the most interesting was the Schulze-Boysen/Harnack group, labeled by the Gestapo as the "red band," which consisted of communist as well as conservative writers and thinkers. Beginning in 1941 this group published the illegal periodical *Die innere Front* (The Inner Front). Its members included the writer Adam Kuckhoff (1887–1943) and the novelist Günther Weisenborn (1902–1969). By 1943 the group had been discovered by the Nazis and forty-nine of its members, including Kuckhoff, had been executed.

The inner-German opposition to the Nazis, in terms of both political and literary strategies, was a failure to some extent because of the factionalization of the opposition groups. In the late 1930s the Communists, under the direction of Stalin, abandoned the antifascist struggle, only to assume it again once the Soviet Union had been attacked. The conservative writers either ceased to write or melted into the background, writing the type of nature poetry that was so protean that it could function both under the Nazis and later under the occupying forces and eventually assume the primary direction of German letters once the Federal Republic was created. Few joined the opposition. But this state of affairs was paralleled within other nations in Europe under fascist domination. Neither in the occupied countries nor in the fascist states was a unified intellectual opposition to the Nazis to be found until Nazi domination began to wane. Exceptions to this acquiescence, such as the great Danish poet Kai Munk (1898–1944), who was murdered by the Nazis, prove as difficult to find outside Germany as within its borders.

The Final Solution

On January 20, 1942, members of the Nazi hierarchy met at a villa on Berlin's Wannsee Lake and formalized the Third Reich's plan for the "final solution to the Jewish problem." Jews had been brought into concentration camps in ever-increasing numbers since 1933. Often the Germans were aided in their "removal" by anti-Semites and fascists of the occupied countries. By 1942 the rate of death through "natural" causes—typhus, malnutrition, and so on—was not great enough for the Nazis, and a plan for the systematic destruction of the Jews of Europe, as well as other groups, such as Gypsies, homosexuals, and Jehovah's Witnesses, was begun. Six million Jews died in the concentration camps, such as Buchenwald, and in the death camps, such as Auschwitz. Among them were poets such as Gertrud Kolmar (1894–1943), Arthur Silbergleit (1881–1944), and Gertrud Kantorowicz (1876–1945). Nelly Sachs (1891–1970), the joint recipient of the 1966 Nobel Prize for literature, was rescued from a concentration camp in 1940 only through the intercession of the Swedish government.

Most remarkably, young writers began to express themselves in the camps. Often all that is left of their memories is a fragment of a poem smuggled out from the camps. Such is the case of Friedrich Karl Pick, who is known only from a tiny notebook with the title "A Few Thoughts About Theresienstadt—On 9.1.43," which was found in the papers of a Czechoslovakian refugee going to Israel. In the camps the need for sanity, for a sense of stability, often drove young writers to search for the most stable, conservative forms to express the horrors they were living. The use of strict meter, of classical poetic form, of traditional images, was a means of grasping the sanity of the schoolroom that had existed before the corruption of literature and art by the Nazis. The thirteen-year-old Ruth Klüger (b. 1931), who survived Theresienstadt, wrote the following poem in Auschwitz in 1944:

Daily behind the barracks
I see smoke and fire.
Jew, bend your back,
No one can escape *that*.
Do you not see in the smoke
A distorted face?
Does it not call out, full of mockery and sarcasm:
Five million I now contain!
Auschwitz lies in my hand,
Everything, everything will be consumed.

Daily, behind the barbed wire
The sun rises purple,
But its light seems empty and hollow
When the other flame appears.
For the warm light of life

has had no meaning in Auschwitz.
Look into the red flame:
The only truth is the furnace.
Auschwitz lies in his hand,
Everything, everything will be consumed.

Some have lived full of horror
faced with threatening danger.
Today he looks with equanimity,
offering up his life.
Everyone is depressed by suffering,
No beauty, no joy,
Life, sun are gone,
And the furnace glows.
Auschwitz lies in his hand,
Everything, everything will be consumed.

Don't you hear the moans and the groaning
As from someone who is dying?
And between them bitter mockery,
The furnace's horrid song:
No one has yet outrun me,
No one, no one will I spare.
And those who build me as a grave
I will consume at last.
Auschwitz lies in my hand,
Everything, everything will be consumed.

The totality of destruction, the blackness of a vision obscured by the foul-smelling clouds belching from the crematoria smokestacks, is cast in this remarkable poem in formal, controlled terms. How different from the radical experimentalism of Paul Celan's (1920–1970) "Fugue of Death" ("Todesfuge"), written retrospectively in 1945. Ruth Klüger survived the death camps, which claimed the lives of her father and brother, and emigrated to the United States, where she now teaches literature.

The Final Exile

The literature of the camps survived as fragmentary documents, buried in gardens, hidden in mattresses, smuggled out in the minds and memories of the survivors. The more extensively published and preserved production of the exile writers, who had fled their refuges in 1938, 1939, and 1940 as the Nazi menace advanced, provided a more comprehensive context for their work. Rather than fragmentary texts and snippets of poems, the exile communities in Britain, the United States, Canada,

Australia, and New Zealand provided a new, English-language context
and inspiration for their writings. Some, such as Thomas Mann, who
arrived in the United States in 1939 for an extended exile, had long-
established American contacts, translators, and publishers. His brother
Heinrich was not as lucky. Although the final volume of Heinrich Mann's
life of Henri IV was published to great critical acclaim in 1939, it
proved to be the last volume of Mann's works to appear in English.
The author, accompanied by his wife, the popular author Lion Feuchtwanger, Franz and Alma Werfel, and Golo Mann, Thomas Mann's
author-son who had just escaped a Vichy internment camp, crossed the
Pyrenees on foot in the fall of 1940 in order to reach neutral Portugal
and a ship that would eventually take them to New York. In New York
and later in California, where he settled, Heinrich Mann lived for the
most part on the bounty of his younger brother.

This final period of exile for the German liberal establishment also
coincided with the beginning of the end of the Nazi domination of
Germany and Europe. The exile writers had begun to see their exile
as the material for their literary creations. Their gaze was not fixed on
Germany, their ears were not constantly attuned to the inner-German
situation. They began to sense the need to create a new literature that
reflected their own experience but that used a radically new means of
achieving an expression denied the now corrupt German language. A
series of works evolved out of the productive interaction between the
literature of their new hosts and the problems they still saw as central
to their creative endeavors.

Such work was the major play of Bertolt Brecht's California exile,
The Life of Galileo (*Das Leben des Galilei*), which premiered in the
Zurich playhouse in September 1943. The play and its productions
present an excellent case study of the life and creativity of the exile
writers during the final years of their English-speaking exile. Brecht's
dramatized life of the Renaissance scientist was his first play to treat
distant history. All of his dramatic works to that point either had treated
contemporary events or were set in the immediate past. Part of this
shift was due to the search for historical analogies, as found in the
works of Thomas and Heinrich Mann; but more than that, Brecht's
role in the Hollywood film colony of the 1940s determined his choice
of material as well as his perspective. For Brecht wrote the play with
the British film actor Charles Laughton in mind for the title role.
Laughton had starred in a series of historical films during the 1930s,
the best known of which was *The Private Life of Henry VIII*, and
Brecht wished to capture the strengths of Laughton's characterization
of the "great man" under stress. Laughton in fact collaborated on the

English version of the play between 1944 and its American premiere in 1947.

But even more than Laughton's character, his role as an expatriate British actor paralleled Brecht's sense of distance, which was reflected in the play. For the central motif of Brecht's play is the trials of the exile. Galileo is, at least at the beginning of the drama, a more or less voluntary exile; by the play's close he is the captive of the church (and his family), which monitors his very thoughts. This is not Brecht's mirror of Nazi Germany. His work had come far from his fixation on the inner workings of the Nazi state, as in his *Private Life of the Master Race* (*Furcht und Elend des Dritten Reiches,* 1938). What Brecht incorporated in the sense of isolation was the Marxist exile's impression of life in the wartime United States. With the Federal Bureau of Investigation (FBI) monitoring the daily life of the left-wing exile community, with spies from their own ranks reporting on their every statement, it must have seemed to Brecht that his exile in the United States was quite like Galileo's Italy, full of cabals. This theme was coupled with the issue of the responsibility of the scientist, a prefiguring of the questioning surrounding the beginning of the atomic age and the bombing of Japan in 1945. Galileo is the peripatetic scientist, driven to ask difficult, perhaps unanswerable questions in a world that believes itself to be in the possession of absolute truth. The exile, seeing himself as a marginal man, is in much the same position. Brecht's drama, with its American inspiration, its Swiss premiere, its British collaborator, and its Renaissance setting, is in many ways the true product of the American exile of the German intellectual. Those who were able to integrate the American experience, at least to a limited degree, into their work were able to cope creatively with their new environments. This group included Brecht; Max Reinhardt (1873–1943), the theater director; Kurt Weill (1900–1950), the composer; Peter Lorre (1904–1964), the actor; and Felix Salten (1869–1947), the author of *Bambi* and innumerable film scripts. Other writers and intellectuals were more or less destroyed by their exile, turning inward and romanticizing the Germany that remained in their fantasy.

Brecht's work for the theater, with its complex theoretical framework and its intent to educate as well as entertain, was perhaps the greatest achievement of the Marxist exiles. The conservative wing of the exile community also produced a series of major literary works during the last four years of the Third Reich. Two of the greatest works of twentieth-century fiction drew on the exile experience. Hermann Broch's (1886–1951) *The Death of Virgil* (*Der Tod des Vergil,* 1945) drew on the reconstruction of the thoughts of the dying and exiled Virgil cast in the form of an interior monologue. By far the greatest contribution of Broch's creation was its fusion of classical, psychological, and political themes into a work of truly international status. The other great novel to come out of the exile community at the end of the war was Thomas Mann's *Dr. Faustus*, the story of the German composer Adrian Leverkühn as told by a slightly obtuse friend. The story, published in 1947, reconstructed the inner life of the quintessential German artist, representing that which Germany claimed as its greatest gift to the world—German culture—as it regressed from creativity to irrational primitiveness. Mann used the life of the German philosopher Friedrich Nietzsche as his primary model but incorporated into the figure of the composer many traits and views of recognizable contemporaries. Casting the entire work in the form of a biography written by a pedant, Mann gave the novel his own ironic touch, distancing himself from the German misery through his vantage point as an exile. *Dr. Faustus* and *Galileo* are the two sides of the exile's image of the world. Neither would have been possible without the rich literary and intellectual tradition in which the exiles found themselves while in the last stages of their diaspora.

Cultural life and literary production during the period from 1933 to 1945 was most probably the most fragmented in the tradition of German letters. The scattering of the exile writers and thinkers throughout the civilized world, the regimentation of cultural life within the German state, the mass murder of the concentration and death camps, had no parallel in Western experience. German intellectual life after 1945 was marked with the stigma of the Nazi period. This inheritance has remained the primary focus of German letters in the post-war era.

Readings

The following works are suggested for further reading in this area. Quotations from the works mentioned in the text have been taken from the editions cited here.

The background to the Third Reich is outlined in two major works: Fritz Stern, *The Politics of Cultural Despair* (Berkeley: University of California Press, 1961); and George L. Mosse, *The Crisis of German Ideology* (New York: Grosset & Dunlap, 1964). The cultural history of the Weimar Republic is presented in an overview by Wolf von Eckardt and Sander L. Gilman, *Bertolt Brecht's Berlin: A Scrapbook of the Twenties* (Garden City, N.Y.: Anchor Press, 1975). My discussion of Nazi literary theory is based on Sander L. Gilman, ed., *NS—Literaturtheorie* (Wiesbaden: Akademische Verlagsgesellschaft Athenaion, 1971). The best general overview of the literary history of this period is to be found in Jan Berg et al., *Sozialgeschichte der deutschen Literatur von 1918 bis zur Gegenwart* (Frankfurt: Fischer, 1980). Detailed studies of the major writers of the period are available: Nigel Hamilton, *The Brothers Mann: The Lives of Heinrich and Thomas Mann, 1871–1950 and 1875–1955* (London: Secker and

Warburg, 1978); Michael Morley, *Brecht: A Study* (Totowa, N. J.: Rowman and Littlefield, 1977); Wolfgang Kaempfer, *Ernst Jünger* (Stuttgart: Metzler, 1981). Documentation of the takeover of cultural life is available in Joseph Wulf, ed., *Literatur und Dichtung im Dritten Reich* (Reinbek bei Hamburg: Rowohlt, 1966), as well as in George Mosse, ed., *Nazi Culture: Intellectual, Cultural, and Social Life in the Third Reich* (New York: Grosset & Dunlap, 1966). Quotations from Hitler's *Mein Kampf* are from Ralph Mannheim's 1943 translation (Boston: Houghton Mifflin).

A survey of life in the camps as mirrored in the literature of the death camps is available in Terence Des Pres, *The Survivor: An Anatomy of Life in the Death Camps* (New York: Oxford University Press, 1976). For the historical background to the "final solution" see Lucy Dawidowicz, *The War Against the Jews, 1933–1945* (New York: Holt, Rinehart and Winston, 1975). Literary texts from the camps are available in the anthology edited by Heinz Seydel, *Welch Wort in die Kälte gerufen* (Berlin: Verlag der Nation, 1968). On opposition poetry see Charles W. Hoffman, *Opposition Poetry in Nazi Germany* (Berkeley: University of California Press, 1962); and on exile literature, William K. Pfeiler, *German Literature in Exile* (Lincoln: University of Nebraska Press, 1957), and David Pike, *German Writers in Soviet Exile, 1933–45* (Chapel Hill: University of North Carolina Press, 1982).

EHRHARD BAHR

———— **12** ————

Contemporary Theater and Drama in West Germany

By the end of World War II about 37 percent of all theater buildings within the 1937 borders of Germany had been completely destroyed, and the remainder had suffered severe damage. But by the fall of 1945 theaters were already reopening. The records show 133 active theater companies for the 1947-1948 season in West Germany and West Berlin. Because of the lack of public funds after the currency reform of 1948, the figure dropped below 100 for 1948–1952. After the founding of the Federal Republic of Germany in 1949, there was a brief period of cautious reorientation, but within three years the West German theater had been restored to its original function as a cultural institution dependent on public expenditures. By 1952-1953 the theater in West Germany and West Berlin had experienced an "economic miracle" with the construction of a great number of theater buildings equipped with the latest in modern stagecraft. The number of theater companies rose with every season, reaching a peak of 181 companies in 1974-1975. At the beginning of the 1980s there were approximately 200 full-size theater companies in West Germany and West Berlin, performing for a population of 60 million in an area the size of the state of Oregon.

Most of today's theater companies operate under the triadic system, uniting drama, opera/operetta/music, and ballet under one management, as Arno Paul pointed out in his structural analysis of West German theater. According to Ingo Seidler, the statistics confirm West Germany's claim to "the greatest density of theatre anywhere in the world" (p. 193). The majority of the theaters are repertory companies, generously subsidized by public funds. Private and commercial theaters are in the minority in West Germany and West Berlin, and even they receive some public funding—for example, the touring companies. To the American observer, West German theater "presents the somewhat unusual

combination of intense intellectual/esthetic exploration and large production budgets." As Michael Kirby, editor of the *Drama Review*, has
said,

> It is almost as if the experimentation of Off-Broadway were being presented
> on Broadway. This does not mean that extensive formal theatrical orga-
> nization, elaborate working rules and regulations, and pressures to cater
> to as broad an audience as possible do not ultimately take their toll in
> innovation. As in other systems, experimentation is not completely un-
> hampered. But the wide-spread theatre in West Germany tends to be
> much more intellectual and esthetic than professional theatre [in the United
> States] (p. 2).

The unique situation of West German theater as a state-supported
institution can be explained in terms of the history of German theater
which grew out of the court theaters of the numerous principalities in
early eighteenth-century Germany. These theaters tried to compete with
the court and theater of Louis XIV at Versailles. Eighteenth-century
German particularism (*Kleinstaaterei*) and the patronage of courts
account for the modern theater system in Germany. The court theaters
were transformed into state theaters, a process that took almost two
hundred years. After World War I, there were still some twenty court
theaters left, which were then converted into tax-supported state institutions, joining the group of theaters supported by state governments
(today's *Landesbühnen* or *Staatstheater*) or local municipalities (so-called
Stadttheater). "State" refers here to the federal states, or *Länder*, of
West Germany. There is no centralized federal support of the theater.

West German taxpayers contribute an ever-increasing amount in
subsidies to their theaters. In the past, public funding of German theaters
accounted on the average for less than two-thirds of their budgets; by
the 1980s public support made up more than three-quarters. In absolute
figures, the total support at the beginning of the 1980s amounted to
more than DM 1.5 billion. The recent economic recession has, however,
threatened some budget cuts or even the closing of some theaters in
smaller cities. In addition, political arguments have been raised against
public support of an elitist institution that serves only the educated
middle class. Only 3.5 million—or 5 percent of the total population—
go to the theater, i.e., 95 percent of the population pay indirectly through
their taxes for the entertainment of the remaining 5 percent, who could
well afford higher ticket prices. Actually, the total figure for occupied
seats per year has declined from 20 million during the 1960s to
approximately 17 million in the early 1980s. Efforts to raise the percentage
of working-class attendance or to organize special theater festivals for

trade union members—for example, the annual Ruhr Theater Festival for coal miners, have not been totally successful. The *Volksbühne* movement ("theater for the people"), founded in Berlin in 1890, was also a failure in this regard, as it turned into a middle-class institution during the course of its history. Only the student protest movement of the late 1960s produced some forms of theater in opposition to the cultural establishment, such as children's theater, youth theater, and so-called free groups, comparable to the American guerrilla or street theater.

Although public subsidies guaranteed a large degree of artistic independence to the German theater, contemporary drama has never dominated its repertory. Classical dramatists still provide about 40 percent of the plays performed; "modern" authors, living between 1850 and 1945, represent 25 percent of the repertory. This leaves approximately 35 percent to contemporary playwrights, of whom a mere 15 percent are German-language authors. German theater has always had a strong tradition as a showcase of international drama. This tradition was continued after World War II, when there was a great demand for international drama on the German stage, an almost feverish craving to catch up with the developments in international theater of the previous twenty years. The favorite foreign-language playwrights of the German stage after 1945 were Eugene O'Neill, Arthur Miller, Thornton Wilder, Tennessee Williams, T. S. Eliot, Jean Anouilh, Samuel Beckett, Jean Giraudoux, Eugène Ionesco, Jean-Paul Sartre, and Federico Garcia Lorca. Of the 15 percent of German-language authors among contemporary dramatists approximately two-thirds are either Austrian (Wolfgang Bauer, Thomas Bernhard, Peter Handke), East German (Bertolt Brecht, Volker Braun, Peter Hacks, Heiner Müller), or Swiss (Friedrich Dürrenmatt, Max Frisch). This leaves roughly 5 percent for contemporary West German authors on the stages in West Germany and West Berlin. Of course, the stages in Austria, Switzerland, and to a lesser degree in the German Democratic Republic are also open to West German playwrights. West German theater would, however, be unthinkable without Dürrenmatt and Frisch during the 1950s, Bertolt Brecht during the 1960s, and Bernhard, Hacks, Handke, and Heiner Müller during the 1970s.

For the period 1947–1975, the leading playwright on the West German stage was Shakespeare, followed by Friedrich Schiller, George Bernard Shaw, and Bertolt Brecht. The only West German author among contemporary dramatists was Carl Zuckmayer, in twelfth place; Swiss playwright Friedrich Dürrenmatt occupied fourteenth place, behind Sartre and before Henrik Ibsen. Among the most performed plays for the period 1947–1975, the first six positions were held by classical authors, with Gotthold Ephraim Lessing's *Minna von Barnhelm*, Goethe's *Faust*, Heinrich von Kleist's *The Broken Pitcher* (*Der zerbrochene Krug*), Schiller's *Maria Stuart* and *Intrigue and Love* (*Kabale und Liebe*), and

Shakespeare's *As You Like It* in the lead. The first modern play was Gerhart Hauptmann's *Beaver Fur (Biberpelz)*, in seventh place, while contemporary dramas were in ninth place (Zuckmayer, *The Devil's General; Des Teufels General*), fifteenth (Zuckmayer, *The Captain of Köpenick; Der Hauptmann von Köpenick*), thirtieth (Karl Wittlinger, *Do You Know the Milky Way?; Kennen Sie die Milchstrasse?*), thirty-seventh (Brecht, *Mother Courage and Her Children; Mutter Courage und ihre Kinder*), thirty-eighth (Brecht, *The Threepenny Opera; Die Dreigroschenoper*), and fortieth (Dürrenmatt, *The Physicists; Die Physiker*).

These statistics show that the history of West German theater and of contemporary West German drama do not go hand in hand. Their periods of success and decline do not overlap. Duirng the first successful decade of West German theater, from 1950 to 1960, contemporary West German dramatists were neglected and Bertolt Brecht's experiments with dramatic form and style were ignored, whereas the crisis of West German theater in the late 1960s occurred during a period of great creativity in West German drama. During the 1950s productions of classical authors were preferred, while contemporary drama was represented by T. S. Eliot's *Cocktail Party, Family Reunion,* and *The Confidential Clerk.*

The Gründgens Era: Restoration of Pre-Nazi Repertory and Hauptmann Renaissance (1948–1963)

The most influential example for the West German theater of the 1950s was set by Gustaf Gründgens (1899–1963) as managing director and leading actor of the theaters at Düsseldorf and then Hamburg. Gründgens represented the continuity of the German theater tradition from the early 1930s to the beginning of the 1960s. From 1934 to 1943 he had been managing director of the Prussian State Theaters in Berlin, and his career under the Nazi regime had provided the model for Klaus Mann's novel *Mephisto*, which was the basis for the 1982 Academy Award–winning film of the same title by Istvan Szabo. As before the war, Gründgens cultivated a repertory of classical authors. Under his directorship the program offered exemplary productions of Shakespeare's *Hamlet*, Goethe's *Faust* (which also appeared as film), and Schiller's *Wallenstein* and *Don Carlos*. Gründgens also included a few contemporary plays in his repertory, but they were almost exclusively foreign-language dramas. The first contemporary German play of significance to be performed under his directorship was Bertolt Brecht's *St. Joan of the Stockyards (Die Heilige Johanna der Schlachthöfe)* in 1959; the first West German play of significance was Siegfried Lenz's (b. 1926) *Time of the Guiltless (Die Zeit der Schuldiosen)* in 1961. But these productions were neither innovative nor trendsetting. By 1959 performances of plays by Brecht, who had died in 1956, were already on the rise in West Germany, with 610 performances in 1959-1960; and the action of Lenz's political drama occurs in a symbolic place and time and is couched in imprecise and unanalytical terms.

The first successful decade of West German theater coincided almost exactly with Gründgens's directorship at Düsseldorf and Hamburg from 1948 to 1963. The prevailing tendency of this decade was one of restoration. West Germany's return to economic prosperity was accompanied by a collective repression of its fascist past. This psychosocial phenomenon was explained by Alexander Mitscherlich in his book *The Inability to Mourn* (*Die Unfähigkeit zu trauern*, 1977). After the defeat of fascism, the Germans had denied their support of Hitler. By making Nazi leaders their scapegoats, the majority of Germans regarded themselves as released from responsibility for their past. As a consequence, it was considered unnecessary to examine the recent past and to come to terms with the facts of war crimes, concentration camps, and genocide. West German theater of the 1950s reflected this tendency in its repertory.

There were two notable exceptions that, however, after close examination, only confirm the rule. The first is Carl Zuckmayer's (1896–1977) drama *The Devil's General*, which had more than 2,000 performances in 1948-1949. Although this drama dealt with the immediate Nazi past, it nevertheless supported the ideology of collective repression. The protagonist's involvement as a general of the Luftwaffe with the Nazi war machine was presented in terms of the devil's pact of the Faust legend, so familiar and dear to all Germans. The equation of fascism with diabolical forces was a comforting message to the postwar German audience, because it resorted to mythology rather than analysis—especially a national mythology that had included the automatic salvation of the guilty protagonist since Goethe's version of 1832. Portrayed as a noble figure instead of an opportunist, the general was shown involved in a tragic conflict rather than in complicity with a criminal regime. The vulgar and evil Nazi figures served as facile scapegoats. With his "Faustian" general, Zuckmayer provided West German audiences with a figure of mythological dimensions whose heroism and uniform they could admire and applaud without guilt feelings. That the representative of the resistance movement appeared in a rather dubious light was another factor that contributed to the phenomenal success of this rather conventional play. Against his better intentions, Zuckmayer, who had spent the Nazi period in exile in the United States, found himself contributing to a political ideology he had fought to destroy. In 1963 Zuckmayer withdrew his play. His attempt to effect its comeback on the West German stage in a revised version in 1967 proved to be a failure.

The other important drama of 1947-1948 was Wolfgang Borchert's (1921–1947) *The Man Outside* (*Draussen vor der Tür*), which was first performed as radio drama and then on the stage. The protagonist was a young soldier who returns home from a prisoner-of-war camp and finds all doors closed to him. He is "the man outside." He cannot find any work. His parents are dead, his wife has left him, his former commanding officer denies any responsibility for sending him and twenty other men on a suicide mission. The protagonist's desperate pleas for help remain unanswered in a society that was unable to mourn because it had resorted to the collective repression of its past. Thus the protagonist finally commits suicide. Wolfgang Borchert died one day before his play premiered in Hamburg. Although it was one of the most provocative plays of early postwar German drama, there were only a few productions, so that *The Man Outside* never entered into the statistics of German theater history. Like the last question of its protagonist, Borchert's challenge to the postwar mentality remained unanswered.

West German theater returned to safer ground when it inaugurated the Hauptmann renaissance of 1952-1953. More than two-thirds of all West German stages put on one of eleven plays by Gerhart Hauptmann (1862–1946), whose image corresponded to the prevailing tendency toward restoration. Hauptmann was one of the few contemporary German writers who had not gone into exile in 1933 when the Nazis came to power, but he had played a rather disappointing role under the regime when compared to his promising beginnings as a naturalist dramatist and socialist sympathizer. His ninetieth birthday was a poor excuse for the Hauptmann boom of the next few years. It was rather a collective identification with Hauptmann's past greatness, which had become uncontroversial and was restored for the spiritual and moral vindication of the postwar generation.

The lack of contemporary postwar drama in West Germany during the 1950s was made up by the Swiss playwrights Friedrich Dürrenmatt (b. 1921) and Max Frisch (b. 1911). They were best qualified to fill this vacuum because they had stayed in close contact with German exile drama, which had found its refuge in the Zurich theater. There many of the plays by exiled dramatists, such as Bertolt Brecht, Ferdinand Bruckner, Ödön von Horvath, Friedrich Wolf, and Carl Zuckmayer had been produced during the 1930s and 1940s, and some of the best German actors and directors had found employment after 1933. Whereas Dürrenmatt cultivated the genre of grotesque comedy, Frisch concentrated his dramatic efforts on coming to terms with the origins and crimes of German fascism. Dürrenmatt's tragicomedy *The Visit* (*Der Besuch der alten Dame*), which premiered in Zurich in 1956, dealt with the sell-out of humanitarian values to the promise of prosperity, reminding

West German audiences of the shaky moral basis of their "economic miracle." The plot shows the natives of a small village in Central Europe willing to dispose of one member of their community for a great sum of money. The play must have struck a responsive chord within Western consciousness, because it became a great international success, including a film starring Ingrid Bergman and Anthony Quinn. *The Physicists* (1962), Dürrenmatt's other international success, dealt with the moral responsibility and madness of modern nuclear research and its threat to the future of mankind.

Max Frisch presented in *The Fire-Bugs* (*Biedermann und die Brandstifter*, 1958), "a morality play without a moral," a parable about the origins of fascism, attributing them to the middle class that was willing to tolerate "fire-bugs," or arsonists, in its own house because of cowardice and self-deception. In his play *Andorra*, which premiered in Zurich in 1961, Frisch attempted to expose the dynamics of anti-Semitism in a mythical country, placing the perpetrators in a witness stand on the forestage. In spite of the play's symbolic locale, the routine declarations of the characters that it was not their fault must have reminded West German audiences of the 1960s of their past involvements and present protestations.

It took until 1956-1957 for a dramatization of the Nazi genocide against the Jews to be shown on a great number of West German stages. It was in *The Diary of Anne Frank*, by Frances Goodrich and Albert Hackett, that the West German audience was confronted for the first time on a larger scale in its theaters with the Nazi Holocaust.

The Piscator Era: Political and Documentary Drama (1963–1966)

Although the *Diary* was a success—it was performed by forty-four theaters—the Holocaust remained taboo for another seven years, until Rolf Hochhuth (b. 1931) achieved a breakthrough with his *Deputy* (*Der Stellvertreter*) which was premiered in a West Berlin production in 1963 under the direction of Erwin Piscator (1893–1966), the grand old man of German political theater of the 1920s. As Gründgens was the representative director of West German theater during the 1950s, Piscator earned this distinction for the 1960s by launching socially critical documentary theater in West Berlin.

Like no other drama in the history of German theater, Hochhuth's play stirred up a vehement international debate. At the center of the controversy was his accusation that Pope Pius XII had been a failure as "God's deputy" on earth when he did not intervene publicly against Nazi genocide against the Jews. Hochhuth's drama dealt with the fate of a Jesuit priest who is shocked by the pope's lack of compassion for the victims of the Holocaust. Therefore the priest accompanies a transport of Jews to Auschwitz and their death, thus becoming "God's true deputy" through his martyrdom.

The major flaw of Hochhuth's play was his attempt to come to terms with the past in the form and blank-verse style of Schiller's historical dramas. As critics were quick to point out, in modern history there can no longer be individual heroes when tragedies are carried out on a worldwide scale by anonymous bureaucracies and automated extermination machines. Yet Hochhuth was not easily discouraged, and he continued to write a number of highly controversial and muckraking plays with varying degrees of success. One of his plays, *Soldiers* (*Soldaten*, 1967), dealing with Churchill's decision to undertake strategic bombings of German cities, resulted in a libel suit; another of Hochhuth's writings caused the ouster of the head of government of one of the West German *Länder* in 1978 because of his involvement in the miscarriage of justice during the Nazi period.

Hochhuth's *Deputy* was an indication of the change of mentality in West Germany during the 1960s, signaling the trend toward a theater involved in coming to terms with the past. The most immediate influences originated from the newspaper reports of the Eichmann trial in Jerusalem in 1961 and the Auschwitz trials in Frankfurt in 1964–1965. The attempts to understand the rise of fascism in Germany and to assess the Germans' implication in Nazi crimes were reflected in a number of dramas that examined West German society in its relationship to fascism, past and present, by authors such as Martin Walser (b. 1927) and Tankred Dorst (b. 1925). The most remarkable result of these concerns was documentary drama, the most important development in German theater since the war. For the first time a new influence on world theater had its origin in West Germany, as Michael Patterson has pointed out.

This development, however, was not free from interruptions, irregularities, and obstacles. By 1963-1964 Hochhuth's *Deputy* had lost ground in the statistics to *Mary, Mary,* a superficial comedy by Jean Kerr. Then there was the interfering influence of the Theater of the Absurd, which also came to the fore during the 1950s with the production of new plays by Samuel Beckett, Eugène Ionesco, and Sławomir Mrożek. Absurd drama, however, found only a few imitators among German dramatists, such as Wolfgang Hildesheimer (b. 1916) and Günter Grass (b. 1927) in an early phase. Technically speaking, Hochhuth's *Deputy,* with Schiller's historical drama as its model, was not documentary drama, although it represented a breakthrough for the theater of fact. Neither were Peter Weiss's *Marat/Sade,* which premiered in West Berlin in 1964, and his *Investigation* (*Ermittlung*) of 1965, or Günter Grass's

The Plebeians Rehearse the Uprising (Die Plebejer proben den Aufstand) of 1966, although they were three of the most important political dramas of the 1960s, which shared some of their features with documentary drama. In form and content, Peter Weiss's play *The Persecution and Assassination of Marat as Performed by the Inmates of the Asylum of Charenton Under the Direction of the Marquis de Sade (Die Verfolgung und Ermordung Jean Paul Marats, dargestellt durch die Schauspielgruppe des Hospizes zu Charenton unter Anleitung des Herrn de Sade)*, to give it its full title, introduced the most innovative political drama since Bertolt Brecht's epic or dialectical theater. For Peter Weiss (1916–1982), who had lived in exile in Sweden since 1939, it was a breakthrough on an international level. After the German premiere in West Berlin, the play was produced and directed by Peter Brook in London, Roger Planchon in Paris, Ingmar Bergman in Stockholm, and Hanns Anselm Perten in Rostock in East Germany.

The action takes place on three levels of reality: the murder of Marat in 1793 during the French Revolution; the scenic reproduction of this historical event by the asylum inmates under the direction of de Sade in 1808 during the First French Empire under Napoleon, and the present-day theatrical presentation of this production, addressing the modern audience with numerous allusions to historical parallels. Marat stands for social change and de Sade for the never-changing nature of man; their arguments are being rehearsed for the benefit of the modern audience. The complexities of the arguments offered on different levels of reality made *Marat/Sade* a milestone in the development of political drama.

Weiss's *Investigation,* which was produced in West Berlin in 1965 under the direction of Erwin Piscator, was the first drama to address itself exclusively to the Holocaust. Whereas audience attention in Hochhuth's *Deputy* was directed at the failure of Pope Pius XII, *Investigation* dealt with the actual testimonies of witnesses and of the accused from the Auschwitz trials in Frankfurt in 1963–1965. The documentary material was, however, not rewritten or rearranged for a theatrical purpose, as in documentary drama, but transformed into eleven "Cantos" of an oratorio in memory of the victims. Yet the art form of the cantos, which invoked the model of Dante's *Divine Comedy,* did not exclude the reality of Auschwitz. The titles of the cantos designate the stations and procedures of this modern inferno: "The Platform," "The Camp," "The Black Wall," "Phenol," "Cyclon B," "The Fire Ovens." No attempt is made to present Auschwitz visually on the stage, but its terror is present in the minds of the witnesses who give testimony. Memory becomes the stage and tribunal of reality.

Günter Grass also made use of documentary facts in his play *The Plebeians Rehearse the Uprising* (which premiered in West Berlin in 1966), in which he brought workers of the East Berlin rebellion of June 17, 1953, face to face with a famous playwright and director obviously modeled after Brecht. Such a confrontation never took place, but the facts are assembled for a fictional event to dramatize the conflict between politics and art. The director is shown rehearsing a scene from Shakespeare's *Coriolanus* (one of Brecht's most famous productions in East Berlin), when he is interrupted by workers who appear on his stage, trying to enlist his help in formulating their demands. But instead of engaging in political action, the director tranforms political action into aesthetic material for the benefit of his theatrical production, thereby obstructing the chances for a new revolution. Precious time is wasted, and the workers' rebellion is suppressed by military force.

In its purest form, documentary theater entered the West German stage with Heinar Kipphardt's *In the Matter of J. Robert Oppenheimer* (*In der Sache J. Robert Oppenheimer*), which premiered in 1965 in West Berlin and Munich and was the most successful play of the 1964-1965 season, with 525 performances by twenty-three theaters. Whereas Grass employed documentary facts for a fictional confrontation to indict the artist as a political failure, Heinar Kipphardt (1922-1983) used the transcripts of the 1954 hearings involving the security clearance of J. Robert Oppenheimer, one of the United States's leading nuclear physicists, for his courtroom drama. By confining himself to documentary material, Kipphardt avoided many of the problems Hochhuth and Grass were not able to solve in their montages of fact and fiction. Kipphardt limited his artistic freedom to the selection, arrangement, formulation, and condensation of the documentary material and thus created a form suitable for this particular topic.

The other form of innovative drama introduced in West Germany during the 1960s was the *Sprechstücke,* or "speech plays," of Peter Handke (b. 1942, in Austria). In a note to his *Sprechstücke,* the author explained that this type of experimental drama was written to transform the conventional theater audience: "The *Sprechstücke* have no action. . . . The *Sprechstücke* confine themselves . . . to words. . . . *Sprechstücke* . . . do not want to revolutionize, but to make aware." In his first *Sprechstück,* Handke achieved this effect by insulting his audience, as indicated by the title *Offending the Audience* (*Publikumsbeschimpfung*). After setting the stage for his invectives by way of a long prologue, the playwright had the cast of four speakers exchange insults in beat-rhythm without taking notice of the audience. Under no circumstance was the audience to get the impression that the insults were directed at them. The supreme insult was that as far as the cast was concerned, the audience was totally ignored, after it had been most courteously ushered into the auditorium. The play constituted a deconstruction of conventional audience expectations by means of language. *Offending the Audience,* which premiered in 1966 in Frankfurt, was one of the most successful contemporary plays on the West German stage, running for five years at the Forum Theater in West Berlin.

After three more *Sprechstücke,* Handke wrote *Kaspar,* his first full-length play, which also premiered in Frankfurt (1967). It became the most successful contemporary play of the 1968-1969 season in West Germany, Austria, and Switzerland. Praised as "the play of the decade" and compared in importance to Samuel Beckett's *Waiting for Godot, Kaspar* was performed in New York, London, and Paris, and its author was hailed by the *New York Times* of February 16, 1973, as "one of the most important young playwrights of our time." Employing the story of Kaspar Hauser, an autistic young man who appeared in Nuremberg in 1828 after some sixteen years of solitary confinement and was unable to speak even a single sentence, Handke dramatized the torture of language learning. As he said in his preface: "The play *Kaspar* does not show how IT REALLY IS or REALLY WAS with Kaspar Hauser. It shows what IS POSSIBLE with someone. It shows how someone can be made to speak through speaking. The play could also be called *speech torture.*" As prompters drill standard sentences into Kaspar and he becomes socialized, he loses his individuality. This process is visualized by having Kaspar clones populate the stage in ever-increasing numbers. The play exposes language acquisition as a system of social oppression.

Handke's next two plays, *My Foot My Tutor (Das Mündel will Vormund sein,* 1969) and *The Ride Across Lake Constance (Der Ritt über den Bodensee,* 1970), continued to frustrate and change conventional audience expectations, but they were not as successful as *Kaspar.* In the 1970s Handke returned to the novel. A prominent successor on the West German stage was his fellow Austrian Thomas Bernhard (b. 1931), who continued the typically Austrian preoccupation with language in his plays *A Feast for Boris (Ein Fest für Boris,* 1970), *The Ignoramus and the Madman (Der Ignorant und der Wahnsinnige,* 1972), and *Force of Habit (Die Macht der Gewohnheit,* 1974). Bernhard was called "the Beckett of the Alps" by some of his critics because of his obsession with disease, death, and decay.

The crisis of West German theater coincided on the international level with the Vietnam War, and on the national level with the crisis of the Christian Democratic Union, the political party in government since 1949. A strong extraparliamentary opposition became active in all areas of public life. Consequently, West German theater was also affected by political demonstrations. At the end of a performance of Peter Weiss's *Vietnam-Discourse (Vietnam-Diskurs)* in Munich in 1968, the cast collected voluntary contributions from the audience to support the Viet Cong's war effort, and a performance of Tankred Dorst's *Toller* at Stuttgart in 1968 was interrupted by students distributing leaflets that called for the reorganization of ticket sales. West German dramatists also contributed to the politicization of the theater by writing plays that combined political demonstration with didacticism in the tradition of Bertolt Brecht's *Lehrstücke,* or "teaching plays"—for example, Peter Weiss's *Song of the Lusitanian Bogey (Gesang vom Lusitanischen Popanz,* 1967), *Vietnam-Discourse* (1968), *Trotsky in Exile, (Trotzki im Exil,* 1969), and *Hölderlin* (1971); Hans Magnus Enzensberger's *The Havana Hearing (Das Verhör von Habana,* 1970), and Dieter Forte's *Martin Luther and Thomas Münzer (Martin Luther und Thomas Münzer oder Die Einführung der Buchhaltung,* 1970).

Many theaters attempted to reorganize their administrative structures and to introduce the system of actors' collectives that participate in financial and artistic decision making. Directors created new spaces for theater performances in circus arenas, factories, and soccer stadiums, trying to make the theater environment and the repertory attractive to the working classes. Most of these attempts failed to attract new and more progressive audiences, and the conservatives felt frustrated in their habits and expectations and left the theaters in droves. The total figure for seats occupied in a year went down by 3 million during the theater crises of the late 1960s and has stayed more or less at this level ever since.

The Stein Era: Volksstück and Avantgarde Drama (1967–1983)

With the victory of the Social Democrats at the polls in 1969 and with Willy Brandt as chancellor a new era of intellectual life began in West Germany. This new or "Second Enlightenment," as it was called, also affected West German theater, which during the 1970s tried to turn the stage into a forum of social and political consciousness-raising by means of total theater. This revival of total theater brought the mass exits of audiences to a halt. The representative director of this decade was Peter Stein of the actors' collective of the Schaubühne am Halleschen Ufer (Theater at the Halleschen Ufer) in West Berlin, where he presented highly innovative productions of great verbal and visual expressiveness, sensitizing his audiences against prevailing ideologies. Stein was instrumental in launching the Ödön von Horvath (1901–1938) renaissance, which led to the revival of the *Volksstücke* of the German-speaking

Austro-Hungarian playwright, who had died in exile in Paris. The term *Volksstück,* which is not to be confused with folk drama, designates, according to Horvath's definition, "a play in which problems are dealt with and formulated in as popular a manner as possible, questions of the common people, their simple worries, seen through the eyes of the people" (Patterson, p. 89).

The Horvath renaissance paved the way for the rediscovery of Marieluise Fleisser (1901–1974), a former student of Brecht and an author of *Volksstücke* in her own right, and for the emergence of the new West German *Volksstück,* represented by playwrights such as Martin Sperr (b. 1944), Rainer Werner Fassbinder (1946–1982), who later became internationally known as a film director, and Franz Xaver Kroetz (b. 1946). These young writers considered themselves the sons and heirs of Fleisser. The common themes of the new *Volksstück* were the manipulation of the lower classes by the mass media and consumer capitalism, their inability to articulate their own opinions, and violence as their only escape from financial and social oppression. In *Dairy Farm (Stallerhof,* 1972) by Kroetz, a fifty-eight-year-old farmhand seduces the mentally retarded daughter of his employer. When the farmer realizes that his daughter is pregnant, he fires the farmhand. His wife contemplates an abortion but changes her mind and allows the daughter, who is still a minor, to give birth to the child. The play's minimal dialogue is to be understood as a political statement, demonstrating that the oppression of the lower classes consists of their inability to articulate their needs and to communicate them. The new *Volksstück,* with its depiction of linguistic deprivation, primitive sexuality, and brutality, was the most significant addition to the repertory of West German theater during the 1970s.

The other extreme was represented by Botho Strauss (b. 1944) and his play *Three Acts of Recognition (Trilogie des Wiedersehens),* which premiered in Hamburg in 1977. The setting is an art museum. The action is slight, but the dialogue copious. The museum director and fourteen visitors, some of them his friends, wander through the gallery, noticing the pictures of the exhibition and revealing their tensions, private and societal. The dialogue shows the shallowness of the characters. In spite of the wealth and sophistication of language at their disposal they are unable to express their individuality. Time and again, the sophistication of the language reveals the loss of identity. The dramatic writings by Strauss exemplify and critique the recent turn toward subjectivity in West German literature. His play *Big and Little (Gross und Klein,* 1978) shows a young woman's serious quest for identity, ending in the recognition that there is none to be found.

Kroetz and Strauss were perhaps the most prolific playwrights at the beginning of the 1980s, each representing a different genre of contemporary theater and drama in West Germany. They are joined by Gerlind Reinshagen (b. 1926), who found her own idiom to continue the political drama of the 1970s with plays such as *Sunday Children* (*Sonntagskinder,* 1976) and *Spring Festival* (*Frühlingsfest,* 1980) that deal with the transition from fascist to postfascist society in West Germany as seen through the critical eyes of adolescents. With such talent and institutional support available, the future of West German theater and drama looks promising.

Readings

Demetz, Peter. *Postwar German Literature: A Critical Introduction.* New York: Schocken, 1972.

Esslin, Martin. *The Theatre of the Absurd.* Garden City, N.Y.: Doubleday Anchor Books, 1961.

Garten, Hugh F. *Modern German Drama.* London: Methuen, 1959.

Hayman, Ronald (ed.). *The German Theatre: A Symposium.* New York: Barnes & Noble, 1975.

Innes, C. D. *Modern German Drama: A Study in Form.* Cambridge: Cambridge University Press, 1979.

Kirby, Michael (ed.). "German Theatre Issue," *Drama Review* 24, no. 1 (1980).

Patterson, Michael. *German Theatre Today: Post-war Theatre in West and East Germany, Austria and Northern Switzerland.* London: Pitman, 1976.

Paul, Arno. "The West German Theatre Miracle: A Structural Analysis," *Drama Review* 24, no. 1 (1980): 3–24.

Seidler, Ingo. "The Theater in the Federal Republic of Germany," *Colloquia Germanica* 14 (1981): 193–202.

Thomas, R. Hinton, and Keith Bullivant. *Literature in Upheaval: West German Writers and the Challenge of the 1960s.* New York: Barnes & Noble, 1975.

Writers

Nelly Sachs (1891–1970).
(*Courtesy* text + kritik.)

Elias Canetti (b. 1905).
(*Courtesy Isolde Ohlbaum.*)

Max Frisch (b. 1911).
(*Courtesy Heinz Ludwig Arnold.*)

Peter Weiss (1916–1982).
(*Courtesy Isolde Ohlbaum.*)

Heinrich Böll (b. 1917).
(*Courtesy Isolde Ohlbaum.*)

Paul Celan (1920–1970).
(*Courtesy Wolfgang Oschatz.*)

Friedrich Dürrenmatt (b. 1921).
(*Courtesy Heinz Ludwig Arnold.*)

Ingeborg Bachmann (1926–1973).
(*Courtesy* text + kritik.)

Günter Grass (b. 1927).
(*Courtesy Heinz Ludwig Arnold.*)

Martin Walser (b. 1927).
(*Courtesy Hilde Zemann.*)

Christa Wolf (b. 1929).
(*Courtesy Karin Voight.*)

Thomas Bernhard (b. 1931).
(*Courtesy* text + kritik.)

318

Rolf Dieter Brinkmann (1940–1975).
(*Courtesy Maleen Brinkmann.*)

Peter Handke (b. 1942).
(*Courtesy* text + kritik.)

PETER BEICKEN

——— **13** ———

German Prose After 1945

It is a truism that "all post-war German literature is, naturally enough, one form or another of reaction to Nazism and its disastrous end" (Seymour-Smith, p. 672). However, the division of Germany as a nation due to the development of radically different states in East and West calls for qualification of the historical, geographical, and cultural significance of the term "German." As a consequence, "German" refers to the language that is the common denominator of the four distinctly different literatures in East and West Germany, Austria, and Switzerland. Because of the lingering connotations of territorial oneness suggested by the term "German," critics speak of *deutschsprachige Literatur* (literature in the German language) to avoid nationalistic overtones.

Point Zero

There are parallel indigenous movements in the development of German prose after 1945, in West Germany, Austria, and Switzerland that reveal a high degree of interaction and interrelatedness. Due to a variety of factors, West German prose soon took a leading role. The years right after the war, called *Besatzungszeit* (time of occupation), were characterized by Allied control over West German and Austrian political and cultural affairs. Aiming at *Entnazifizierung* (denazification) and *Umerziehung* (reeducation) the Americans zealously introduced their goals of democratization, supporting the West German economy by their Marshall Plan, which initiated a vigorous *Wiederaufbau* (recon-

---

This chapter does not cover prose from the GDR, which is treated by Frank Trommler in Chapter 15 of this book.

struction) leading to the *Wirtschaftswunder* (economic miracle) of the *Adenauerzeit* (Adenauer era). The prosperous economy helped the book trade to thrive again, and West Germany became a major literary marketplace attracting Austrian and Swiss authors alike. The Austrians Ilse Aichinger (b. 1921), Ingeborg Bachmann (1926–1973), Paul Celan (1920–1970), and the Swiss Max Frisch (b. 1911) are notable examples of writers whose careers have been intrinsically part of the West German literary scene since the early 1950s. In fact, Aichinger and Bachmann were both discovered by the famous Group 47, receiving the prestigious Preis der Gruppe 47 (Group 47 Award), much media attention, and instant stardom.

West Germany, with its powerful influence on publishing, criticism, and the institutions awarding literary prizes, dominated the literary scene throughout the 1950s. It was not until the following decades that the indigenous literary movements in Austria and Switzerland developed a greater sense of identity, fostering distinctly different national and regional literatures that relied more on domestic publishers and support from state and local authorities. In Austria, where there was a unique mix of prewar and postwar writers, the monumental works of the Viennese novelist Heimito von Doderer (1896–1966), *The Strudlhof Steps* (*Die Strudlhofstiege,* 1951) and *The Demons* (*Die Dämonen,* 1956), continued the Austrian novel tradition following the model of Musil. At the same time, movements such as the Wiener Gruppe (Group Vienna, 1952–1956) and Grazer Gruppe (Group Graz, 1960) left traditional modes of writing behind to explore experimental and avant-garde techniques, creating an amalgam of regional concerns and international sensibilities. Likewise there were Swiss groups (Olten, 1972; Solothurn, 1976), signaling a further diversification of the literature in the German language.

After the deluge by the Nazis, the Germans, facing their devastating defeat, came up with totally different rationalizations, in the West referring to the traumatic event as *Zusammenbruch* (collapse) and in the East and to some extent in Austria, where most people felt victims of the *Anschluss* in 1938, as *Befreiung* (liberation), giving the end of Nazi rule a decisively positive note. Young German writers returning from the battlefields and prison camps to a demoralized country and people considered 1945 to be a point of departure, *Nullpunkt* (point zero). Disillusioned and plagued by their consciences, they wanted to start from scratch to create a new world in reality and in literature. Theirs was a disquieting legacy: memories of the war and moral failure. Unlike the authors of *innere Emigration* (interior exile) and exterior exile, they started their task without the legacy of prewar German literature, as most of it had been banned by the Nazis and was still unavailable for quite some time.

A significant example of the new spirit was set by the journal *Der Ruf* (The Call, 1946–1947), edited by the former Communist and Wehrmacht deserter Alfred Andersch (1914–1980), who founded this independent voice of the "young generation" together with Hans Werner Richter (b. 1908), the initiator and leader of Group 47. Hopes for a revolutionary reconstruction of Germany leading to a radical democratization were shattered when the Americans forbade further publication of the critical, left-wing journal. Subsequently, both editors founded with other like-minded writers their Group 47, which almost instantly became the mouthpiece of the younger generation and their *Nachkriegsliteratur* (postwar literature). Simultaneously with the budding of this *Nachkriegsliteratur,* major writers of the literary exile published important works. Hermann Broch's (1886–1951) masterpiece *The Death of Virgil* (*Der Tod des Vergil,* 1945) appeared, albeit in New York, and Thomas Mann's (1875–1955) monumental *Doctor Faustus* (1947), first published in Stockholm, was issued in the occupied zones in 1948. The German book market, controlled and censored by the Allies, for the first time after a long hiatus provided major works by Western authors, who soon were to become models for the young German authors in search of new modes of writing.

While writers of the 1920s and the exile—in the East Johannes R. Becher (1891–1958), Bertolt Brecht (1898–1956), and Anna Seghers (1900-1983); in the West Hermann Broch, Alfred Döblin (1878–1957), Hermann Hesse (1877–1962), Thomas Mann, Heinrich Mann (1871–1950), and Carl Zuckmayer (1896–1977)—continued a literary sensibility and prose style rooted in a totally different historical and aesthetic experience, the younger generation came into its own through *Vergangenheitsbewältigung* (conquering of the past). Of primary importance to these authors was the purification of the German language, which had been bastardized by the ideological contamination of the Nazi period. Considering themselves a "lost generation," writers like Wolfgang Borchert (1921–1947), Heinrich Böll (b. 1917), Alfred Andersch, and Wolfdietrich Schnurre (b. 1920) faced the atrocious consequences of fascist rule.

Borchert in particular, within the relatively short span of two years, became the first postwar literary star in West Germany, a spokesman of the *Nullpunkt* and a unique practitioner of the so-called *Kahlschlag* (clearing of the thickets) and *Trümmerliteratur* (rubble literature). His neoexpressionist play *The Man Outside* (*Draussen vor der Tür,* 1947) is the foremost example of *Heimkehrerliteratur* (homecomer literature). This powerful account of existential despair and angst revived the mood and concern of early Weimar homecoming dramas (e.g., Ernst Toller's

Hinkemann, 1923), but it lacked the hopeful twist of expressionist utopianism. Borchert's unique contributions to German prose were his essentially miniaturist pieces of shorter fiction, plotless, colloquial, and evocative stories of a highly expressive, lyrical quality, exploring in pastichelike configurations of symbolically charged situations the impact of war on the individual and collective psyche. Called brilliant, yet "overrated" (Seymour-Smith, p. 649), Borchert stands out from the many talents because of his artistry in detecting and preserving the human element amid the terrors of a modern, war-created wasteland.

In contrast to Borchert's symbolically charged prose, which is indebted to the traditions of the past, the "new" style of the time is characterized by a distinct sobriety. As pointed out quite often, Hemingway's sober, terse, and often elliptical manner of narration was particularly admired and widely emulated. An example of the affinity with the American's matter-of-fact style can be found in Schnurre's short story "The Funeral" ("Begräbnis Gottes," 1947), which was the first work to be read and criticized by Group 47. It is a piece of *Kahlschlagprosa* representative of its aesthetic principles and moral rigor.

Critiquing The Past and Present

Whereas Borchert's melancholy oscillated between satirical nihilism and sad emotionality, Böll fashioned a style of his own the hallmark of which is a distinct confessional quality interlaced with sobering irony and satirical poignancy. In fact, Böll, a liberal Catholic with sympathies toward the political left, produced some of the most esteemed shorter prose that gave back purpose and dignity to this "lost generation." Fighting the temptation to succumb to disillusioning and demoralizing tendencies, Böll fostered a spirit of defiance in the wake of the rubble-strewn and ruined cities, harboring an unprecedented human misery. Confessing to his sense of individual and collective guilt, Böll searched for new values continuing the traditions of humanism. As spokesman for the ordinary people, he shaped artistically concise and morally engaging reflections of life under fascist oppression, during the war, and after the national catastrophe. Böll's soul-searching tales about the dehumanizing effects of the war, *The Train Was on Time* (*Der Zug war pünktlich,* 1949) and *Adam, Where Art Thou?* (*Wo warst du, Adam?,* 1951), mark the beginning of his remarkable career as a novelist. By far the most celebrated and translated of all postwar German writers, he earned the Nobel Prize in 1972 for his prolific, versatile, and engaging oeuvre, which shows him to be an undogmatic moralist and deeply concerned humanist.

In pursuit of high moral standards, Böll creates in his fiction, time and again, saintly figures whose spirited purity and exceptional individuality nevertheless make them types representing ethical principles of behavior. Criticizing the corrupting influences of the church, state, and society in general, Böll tends to portray his heroes as isolated from the negativity around them. Rather, his main characters are embedded in realistically depicted contexts only to develop extraordinary powers from the ordinary world. This ability to transcend the real and achieve an otherworldly status resembles the topicality and patterns of the legendary *vitae* of martyrs, albeit in secularized form. Böll's worldly-directed religious motivation has its counterpoint in his historical experience, which prevails in his commanding analysis of German time and space. As a member of the "lost and skeptical generation," he is an astute critic of the past and its disfiguration by fascism and the war; he is no less a perceptive analyst of the present and its uncanny restoration. However, because his longer fictional works are at times flawed by sentimentalism and a simplified narrative structure, many consider Böll's shorter prose—the satirical, humorous, masterly crafted stories—his most memorable and greatest achievement.

A more concise critique of postwar Germany came from Wolfgang Koeppen (b. 1906) in his much-acclaimed *Zeitromane* (the novel as critique of an era). Among them are the reportage-like portrayal of one day in bombed-out Munich after 1945, *Doves in the Grass* (*Tauben im Gras,* 1951); the political satire *The Hothouse* (*Das Treibhaus,* 1953), a work scornfully critical of the new German power play in the provisional capital, Bonn; and the novel of perceptive warning against specters of the past, *Death in Rome* (*Der Tod in Rom,* 1954), which detects and exposes the old Nazi leaders who went into hiding in the years of reeducation and reconstruction. It is remarkable that Koeppen, having mastered the Western modernist influences, notably that of Dos Passos, virtually disappeared as a novelist. His *Into the Dust with All Foes of Brandenburg* (*In den Staub mit allen Feinden Brandenburgs*) was supposed to be published in 1975 but never came out, a fate it shared with other much talked about novel projects which Koeppen has yet to deliver. Koeppen has written travel literature and a highly regarded autobiographical story, *Youth* (*Jugend,* 1976), which differentiates itself from the subjective mode of many of the other autobiographies of the 1970s by its reflective stance and historical analysis.

Like Koeppen, other writers of the older generation have their roots in the time before the war. Hans Erich Nossack's (1901–1977) experience dates back to the revolutionary Hamburg of the early Weimar period. However, the turning point of his writing career came in 1943, when he witnessed the horrendous destructiveness of war in the massive bombing of his hometown. The image of the apocalyptic deluge is imprinted in his *The Destruction* (*Der Untergang,* 1943) and also in *Nekyia* (1947) and *Interview with Death* (*Interview mit dem Tod,* 1948). This obsessive theme of a sternly introspective writer, which prevails even in such works as the story of love and adultery in *At Latest in November* (*Spätestens im November,* 1955), finds its surrealist portrayal in the nightmarish, Kafkaesque novel of justification *Spiral* (*Spirale,* 1956) and in the pessimistic account and indictment of the capitalist present in *The Younger Brother* (*Der jüngere Bruder,* 1958). The exigencies of modern life are depicted in *We Know That Already* (*Das kennt man,* 1964), the complex, multilayered narrative of a dying prostitute, who recounts her life and reveals in the act of telling the breakdown of her mind, laying bare the intricacies of existential authenticity. The theme of authenticity is also pursued in Nossack's most accomplished novel, *The d'Arthez Case* (*Der Fall d'Arthez,* 1968), and in his reflection of a variation on the *Doppelgänger* motif (motif of the double) in *A Happy Man* (*Ein glücklicher Mensch,* 1975).

Within the pluralism of postwar German literature Nossack maintained his independence, and his artistic development distinguishes him from most of his peers and predecessors, who continued their writing in a conservative, Christian-humanist, and traditional vein. Gertrud von le Fort (1876–1971), Hans Carossa (1878–1956), Ina Seidel (1885–1974), Ernst Wiechert (1887–1950), Werner Bergengruen (1892–1964), Elisabeth Langgässer (1889–1950), Reinhold Schneider (1903–1958), and Stefan Andres (1906–1970) are the most renowned and prolific of these artists. Their works and views were much revered by the educated middle class. They form an important backdrop against which the younger generation developed its own artistic and ideological identity.

A backdrop and antipode of a different kind was Ernst Jünger (b. 1895), who was suspected of fascist or protofascist tendencies. Outside Germany he is often considered "an interesting, but rather repugnant" writer (Seymour-Smith, p. 611), a judicious evaluation of a cold-blooded intellectual whose *The Glass Bees* (*Gläserne Bienen,* 1957) is at best a satirical revelation of ingenious self-indulgence. Jünger's reverence for the military and war and his elitist views made him unattractive to a generation that rejected the stylish coolness of emotional detachment and human indifference. Nevertheless, a former sympathizer of the Nazi cause, Gottfried Benn (1886–1956), exerted a tremendous influence on the development of German postwar lyric poetry, whereas his prose, notably his only novel, *Novel of the Phenotype* (*Roman des Phänotyps,* 1943), had little impact. Jünger's favorite theme, the war, figures prominently in Gerd Gaiser's (1908–1976) novels, most all of in *The Falling Leaf* (*Die sterbende Jagd,* 1953), which deals in a dense and realistic style with the disillusionment of a fighter squadron based in Norway with its daily business of killing. The book, much acclaimed as one of the best German novels about World War II, tells its story engrossingly without taking sides. Neutrality becomes a fetish of objectivity, resulting in a lack of judiciousness and human involvement. The art of telling engrossing war stories without much critical perspective was perfected by Hans Hellmut Kirst (b. 1914), whose trilogy *08/15* (1954–1955) and subsequent works successfully trivialize narrative themes for a market hungry for bestsellers.

Another backdrop for the emerging new German literature was the increasingly pervasive and powerful writing for *Illustrierte* (magazines) and other branches of the popular press. Against this cheap, conventionalized narrative, called *Trivialliteratur*, high literature saw itself as the conscience of the nation. It is no surprise that by the end of the 1950s the literary developments of the decade after the war culminated in a breakthrough usually dated around 1959, a marker that is considered a point of arrival and departure at the same time. It is the end of the first postwar period and the beginning of the emergence of an indigenous West German literature.

Point of Arrival

The year 1959 marks the publication of three important novels, Böll's *Billiards at Half Past Nine* (*Billard um halbzehn*), Günter Grass's (b. 1927) *The Tin Drum* (*Die Blerchtrommel*), and Uwe Johnson's (1934–1984) *Speculations About Jacob* (*Mutmassungen über Jakob*), three works that exemplified the diversity, liveliness, and artistic accomplishment of the new German literature. In 1960 Martin Walser's (b. 1927) *Half-Time* (*Halbzeit*) followed. These four novels represent individual styles and artistic endeavors as much as they inaugurated the dominant trend in German prose in the 1960s.

Böll aimed in *Billiards at Half Past Nine* at reconciling the traditional genre of the novel as historical narrative with the complex structures of the modernist narrative represented above all by James Joyce's *Ulysses* (1922). Having utilized different narrative modes in his earlier prose, from straightforward storytelling to elaborate techniques of reported thought and highly stylized forms of *monologue intérieur* (interior monologue), Böll now employed the plot line of a family story—its most important model being Thomas Mann's *Buddenbrooks* (1901)— and the modernist strategy of interlaced narrative structures derived from different forms of consciousness. *Billiards at Half Past Nine* tells of a single day (September 6, 1958) in the life of Heinrich Fähmel, a prominent architect who on his eightieth birthday becomes the centerpiece of narrative reflection, which spans the time from the beginnings of his professional career in the Wilhelminian Empire to the present. An intricate use of flashbacks by Fähmel himself and other members of his family, notably his wife, Johanna, pieces together a line of development that encapsulates within the story of his family the history of the German nation from the Kaiserreich through Weimar and fascism to the *Adenauerzeit*. This pastiche of memories resembles a modified synopsis of a modern passion play, since the historical experience it portrays is one of suffering. Yet Böll reflects the crucial forces that victimized the German people. He introduces as a narrative vehicle a secularized biblical element: the use of morally polarized antipodes representing the "lambs" and the "beasts." The latter collectively embody all negative historical and social forces, indicated chiefly by the references to the military, the fascists, and the reactionary and conservative powers that have been responsible for the disastrous events of German history; the former refer to all ethically inspired forces of opposition and resistance that suffered persecution and extinction at the hands of their oppressors. This scheme is at best an oversimplification, and Böll's overuse of leitmotif to hammer out his underlying, yet obvious, division into good and evil strains the reader's willingness to accept the world view presented. Despite its flaws, however, Böll's *Billiards at Half Past Nine* is "one of the most important recent German novels, both from a political and from an aesthetic point of view" (Demetz, p. 187).

Grass, the Danzig-born sculptor, painter, poet, and playwright, "burst upon the literary scene like a sudden thunderstorm" (Demetz, p. 214) and laid to rest all the slogans about the death of the novel that had persistently suggested the obsoleteness of storytelling. His *The Tin Drum* cleverly incorporated elements from the baroque novel to those of Alfred Döblin (1878–1957), Grass's revered master and "teacher," who had been a major mediator of Joycean modernism and Dos Passos's narrative complexities in *Alexanderplatz, Berlin: The Story of Franz Biberkopf* (*Berlin Alexanderplatz*, 1929). Grass drew on his childhood experience in the Baltic town, characterized by ethnic pluralism and animosities between the Germans, Poles, and Kashubes. Ingeniously reclaiming the fabulous element of fiction, Grass combined traditional and modernist structures. He utilizes the *picaro*-aspect by transforming the hero as rogue into a modern madman who is hunchbacked and physically retarded but mentally superbly developed into a ruthlessly cruel and perceptive gnome. Telling his life story from the 1930s through the war into the 1950s, Oskar Matzerath centers his episodic memories around the women he encounters. Yet, the timeless world of the old-fashioned *picaro* is punctuated by the historical experience of German-Polish conflicts escalating into a war that leads to the destruction of Poland by the

Nazis. By refusing to grow up and escaping into a prolonged, yet faked, childhood, Oskar manages to become a weird outsider somewhat reminiscent of the artist in a society of dull burghers.

Being responsible for several deaths himself, Oskar fits perfectly the mold of a negative hero whose account is unreliable and fictitious as well as erratic, ambivalent, and noncommittal. Elevated to the stance of a gifted observer who watches closely a morbid and atrocious world, Oskar is a moral monster himself, a talented counterfeiter of tales that are full of aesthetically veiled anxieties and existential predicaments. Oskar's self-serving narrative, his attempt at justifying his life are adorned with much grotesque detail that suggests, time and again, a world gone mad. Told in a melange of colloquial German and a literary language derivative of traditional, modernist, and trivial models, *The Tin Drum* comes to grips with the collective situation after the lost war, aptly exemplified by the location where Oskar produces his story of fiction and truth: a mental institution where he serves time for his crimes. Grass's most impressive accomplishment in his extraordinary debut as a novelist lies in his artistic ability to employ age-old means of fiction without becoming a mere imitator. Sharply focused, his prose yields maximum contemporary relevance. Unlike Böll, however, Grass distorts the image of the world by rendering it absurd, with the historical material as a stage for timeless human folly.

Johnson's *Speculations About Jacob* follows the example of the French *nouveau roman*. It tells the story of an East German railway dispatcher, whose life and mysterious death (which is never fully clarified) are pieced together by a series of reflectors consisting of the memories and conversations of his comrades, friends, and pursuers. As the title suggests, Johnson embarks on a philosophical inquiry in narrative form into the nature of perception and truth. The novel at the same time reflects on the situation of the two Germanys. Johnson, being from the East, came to the West to be able to publish his works. The style of his prose is dense and, like his main character, pensive. Carefully crafted sentences and a ponderous preoccupation with experiments in fiction characterize what was announced almost immediately after the appearance of the book: "the rise of a new, gifted generation" (Demetz, p. 206) in West German literature.

Another brilliant narrator is Walser in his *Half-Time*. After his Kafka-inspired short stories *A Plane over the House* (*Ein Flugzeug über dem Haus,* 1955) and a much-praised first novel, *Marriage in Philippsburg* (*Ehen in Philippsburg,* 1957), which is a skillful critique of the new German society of the "economic miracle," Walser, an intellectual and masterly virtuoso of narrative techniques and stylized language, presented the Kafkaesque figure of a traveling salesman to explore the changes that had taken place in Germany and the minds of its people. Anselm Kristlein—an evocative name meaning "little Christ"—becomes protagonist and dominating consciousness in the novel *Half Time* (*Halbzeit*, 1960), which compiles a social picture of a nation recovering from the war but marked by its inability to overcome the causes of the moral and historical disaster of a people. Criticizing the ideological nature of consciousness present in his figures, Walser contrasts the uncanny past with present thought, language, and feeling. His novel, employing modernist principles of narration, was to give "an accumulation of everything which an author could articulate at a given time, whether a story, reflections, descriptions, or verbal scraps" (Walser and Demetz, p. 203). Thus, overworked articulation indicates an important flaw in Walser's attempt at creating an impression of totality. The range of perspective here falls short of the omniscience familiar in the traditional novel.

Continued Criticism

The narrative as historical, social, ideological, and epistemological critique—this is the core of the new German prose and fiction of the beginning of the 1960s. And the major figures referred to here continued their critical enterprise in prose. Böll relentlessly fights the heirs of the Nazi era by sharpening the satire in his narratives, such as *The Clown* (*Ansichten eines Clowns*, 1963), *Absent Without Leave* (*Entfernung von der Truppe*, 1964), and *End of a Mission* (*Ende einer Dienstfahrt*, 1966). The latter two stories resume his mockery of the military, employing irony and black humor. Sharply criticized as a sympathizer of the radical left, Böll replied in the 1970s with the saga of an ordinary woman as a saintly figure in *Group Portrait with Lady* (*Gruppenbild mit Dame*, 1971), followed by the angry indictment of the witch-hunt methods of the mass media in *The Lost Honor of Katharina Blum* (*Die verlorene Ehre der Katharina Blum*, 1974), with the pointed subtitle "How violence can originate and where it can lead to." His latest novel, *The Safety Net* (*Fürsorgliche Belagerung*, 1979), represents a fictional inquiry into the changed climate of West German society, haunted by both terrorism and the frighteningly brutal antiterrorist backlash. Böll, while remaining independent politically, supported the left-liberal coalition government of Social Democrats (SPD) and Free Democrats (FDP), setting his hopes on reform and social progressiveness.

Grass, continuing his career as a prominent writer with the novella *Cat and Mouse* (*Katz und Maus*, 1961) as well as the massive novel *Dog Years* (*Hundejahre*, 1963), parts two and three of his *Danzig Trilogy*, engaged more directly than Böll in party politics by campaigning for the SPD in the 1960s and 1970s. His experiences were reflected in detail in his *Diary of a Snail* (*Tagebuch einer Schnecke*, 1972), an astute account of the political activism of a moderate leftist. Grass's novelistic analysis of the years of the student unrest in *Local Anaesthetic* (*Örtlich betäubt*, 1969) failed to repeat his earlier success. His magnum opus of the 1970s, however, *The Flounder* (*Der Butt*, 1977), and to a lesser extent, the homage to the founder of Group 47, Hans Werner Richter, in *The Meeting in Telgte* (*Das Treffen in Telgte*, 1979) left behind the turbulence of political strife to focus on universal themes. *The Flounder* meets the challenge of the women's movement head-on in a controversial narrative depicting the topical subject of women in history and in contemporary society. In this voluminous tale, Grass explores the roles of both men and women throughout the development of humanity, from the mythical times of Stone Age matriarchy to present-day patriarchy. Deriving its basic concept from a fairy tale by the brothers Grimm, "The Fisherman and His Wife," the novel presents an omnipotent narrator who compiles this parabolic tale of the disasters resulting from the masculine domination of history. Women are relegated to being victims or, at best, recorders of male violence, resisting only at times the continual onslaught of patriarchal destruction.

Whereas Grass's writing developed in the same direction as a central theme of the socially changed 1970s, Johnson became silent as a novelist for a long time after he succeeded in expounding his political theme of juxtaposing the two Germanys in *The Third Book About Achim* (*Das dritte Buch über Achim*, 1961) and *Two Views* (*Zwei Ansichten*, 1965), which were followed by his massive account and critique of the Vietnam years in *Anniversaries* (*Jahrestage*; 2 vols., 1970, 1971). Johnson's attempt at interlacing old-world experience—the life of his heroine Gesine Cresspahl in Germany—with her New York years depended greatly for its success on the degree to which her individual story was charged with general significance. Interspersed with the narrative thread are excerpts from *New York Times* dispatches about the war in Vietnam, providing a continual account of the historical present with which Gesine finds herself confronted every day. Although a writing block, compounded by personal problems, settled in, Johnson finished and published the third part of *Anniversaries* before his untimely death in March 1984.

Walser, probably the most prolific and problematic of the four major novelists, completed his *Kristlein Trilogy* with *The Unicorn* (*Das Einhorn*, 1966) and *The Fall* (*Der Sturz*, 1973), concluding his preliminary critique of the consumer society, with its alienating social fabric and dislocated individuals devoid of a true sense of identity. He experimented with narrative modes that were bound to dissolve narration altogether into self-reflection in *Fiction* (*Fiktion,* 1970) and radicalized his critique of the artist as an accomplice of the bourgeoisie in *Gallistl's Sickness* (*Die Gallistl'sche Krankheit,* 1972), only to throw the main character into the arms of communist friends who proclaim a solution to all social evils.

He returned after this excursion into the realm of strict partisanship to more tales of alienation and nonidentity. The life of his next middle-class nonhero, a socially isolated white-collar worker whose personal and professional failure sends him into the realm of unlove, *Beyond Love* (*Jenseits der Liebe,* 1976), resembles a weak imitation of a Kafka story. This work was followed by the masterfully narrated novella *Runaway Horse* (*Ein fliehendes Pferd,* 1978), a powerful, ingenious, and much-acclaimed reflection of Goethe's *Elective Affinities* (*Die Wahlver-wandtschaften,* 1809). Walser's beautifully told encounter of existential confrontation and resolution of conflict juxtaposes *eros* and *thanatos,* old and new, myth and modernity. The figures are presented with enough individuality to give their typicality a singular concreteness rarely achieved in recent literature. The end is hopeful for the hero, another middle-class figure and teacher at a German *Gymnasium,* and his wife, although the open end calls for an effort to meet the challenge of realizing one's full human potential in a relationship that until then had been mediocre. The language, controlled and concise, provides illumination for the reader to embark, like the hero, on the journey to individual uniqueness and authenticity. Walser departed from this use of classical style and contemporary sensibility in his next two novels, *Labor of the Soul* (*Seelenarbeit,* 1979) and *The Swan House* (*Das Schwanenhaus,* 1980), both exploring his familiar theme of the master-servant relationship in an open, industrialized society.

The work of these major novelists is complemented by that of writers like Arno Schmidt (1914–1979), who stood outside the established literary market and public interest for a long time, and Alfred Andersch, who remained independent of the dominant trends. Schmidt's highly experimental and peculiar prose continued to fascinate a small but dedicated following, whereas Andersch espoused a radical political and intellectual critique of the past and present in his novels *Flight to Afar* (*Sansibar oder der letzte Grund,* 1957), *The Redhead* (*Die Rote,* 1960), *Efraim's Book* (*Efraim,* 1967), *Winterspelt* (1974), and *Father of a Murderer* (*Vater eines Mörders,* 1980), the moving account and shrewd analysis of Andersch's years at his Munich school under the direction of the father of the mass murderer Himmler. Also of a critical nature is Siegfried Lenz's (b. 1926) novel *German Lesson* (*Deutschstunde,* 1968), an excruciatingly sinister reflection of the years 1943–1945. Nazi rule then exerted its most oppressive pressure on the people, who were confronted with decisions to join in the service of their country or to resist a morally and politically unacceptable, beastly regime. Utilizing, as Grass did, a youthful central consciousness, Lenz heightens the intensity of compassion and conflict felt by the reader, whose reading is challenged by a complex mode of perspectival narration shifting from one character to another, thus reflecting the inner conflicts of the figures and their difficulties in resolving them.

New Sensibilities

The preoccupation of these German prose writers with depicting the historical, national, and/or social experience of their people reflects the growing uneasiness of the 1960s, which were for the most part a time of experimentation, transition, and unrest. A significant group of West German writers adopted the impulses of concrete poetry and developed an elaborate theory of literature as text. Helmut Heissenbüttel's (b. 1921) *Books of Texts* (*Textbücher,* 1960–1967) and his experimental novel *D'Alembert's End* (*D'Alemberts Ende,* 1970) radicalize aesthetic form and propose a complete dissolution of the narrative to break ground for a new language and communicative process freed of the restrictions of conventional fiction. Jürgen Becker (b. 1932) likewise assembled "texts" in *Fields* (*Felder,* 1964), *Fringes* (*Ränder,* 1968), and *Environments* (*Umgebungen,* 1970). Becker reveals his origin in modernist art, happenings, surrealism, and the formalism of postnaturalist prose, e.g., that of Arno Holz (1863–1929). The distrust of conventional or even modernist modes of narration fostered by a general uneasiness concerning the precarious social consensus in the 1960s led many a young writer to further experimentation or at least to a rejection of accepted narrative conventions. This is true for Reinhard Lettau (b. 1929), Ror Wolf (b. 1932), Ludwig Harig (b. 1927), Hubert Fichte (b. 1935), Herbert Achternbusch (b. 1938), Uwe Brandner (b. 1941), Klaus Stiller (b. 1941), and Peter O. Chotjewitz (b. 1943).

The intensification of experimental forms of writing for the sake of newness in prose and fiction provoked, or was counterbalanced by, more realistic modes of writing, notably the so-called *Kölner Realismus* (Cologne realism) of the group around Dieter Wellershoff (b. 1925), with Nicolas Born (1937–1981), Rolf Dieter Brinkmann (1940–1975), and Günter Herburger (b. 1932) as its main representatives. Brinkmann, since his untimely death in 1975, has been elevated to exceptional prominence due to his successful protest against political and ideological conformity in the years of unrest. Maintaining a radicalized form of individualism in his life style, poetry, and prose, Brinkmann sought the outsiders of history and culture. Rimbaud, the early Benn, as well as American pop and underground literature, all influenced his anarchic concept of a "new sensibility," which he freed from traditional values and political partisanship. Blending the legacies of outsiders in literature with the clichés of everyday life, Brinkmann chose for himself the mold of an angry young man protesting the restrictions hindering his artistic expression. His obsession with the descriptive prose style is exemplified in his only novel, *Nobody Knows More* (*Keiner weiss mehr*, 1968), and the posthumous *The Film in Words* (*Prosa*, 1982).

Quite different were the concerns of several other groups of writers who followed tendencies of the 1920s in developing the operational mode of literature as a tool for social and political change. In 1961 a number of workers who were also writers formed the Group 61 in Dortmund to join their efforts in the portrayal of everyday reality in the age of modern industrialization. Best-known is Max von der Grün (b. 1926), whose novels *Night Light and Fire* (*Irrlicht und Feuer*, 1963) and *Patches of Ice* (*Stellenweise Glatteis*, 1973) depict workers and ordinary people in their milieu. For most of these writing workers literature served as a means of gaining a better self-understanding; at the same time they intended vigorous criticism of a society that still showed remnants of the old class structures. Following in the vein of Egon Erwin Kisch's (1885–1948) masterly models, Günter Wallraff (b. 1942) utilized the genre of inquisitive reportage to criticize the excesses of exploitation by large companies and smaller capitalist ventures. Wallraff has become notorious for his revealing investigations of the practices of the tabloid *Bildzeitung* (Illustrated News) and its manipulative sensationalism.

Modernizing the naturalist fancy for direct realism, Erika Runge (b. 1939) published a collection of interviews with workers in *Bottrop Documents* (*Bottroper Protokolle*, 1968), followed by the anthology *Women: Seventeen Attempts at Emancipation* (*Frauen: Versuche zur Emanzipation*, 1970). This latter volume was a clear indication that the question of women's emancipation was soon to become a major issue. Runge admitted with disappointment that none of the women she had interviewed felt emancipated. She blamed social conditions for this significant lack of freedom for women. Energized by the growing politization in the wake of the student movement, a more radical, Marxist group split from the original formation to found about twenty Literary Workshops of the Working World in 1970. Clearly the aim of this movement was to have a greater impact on workers and the society at large.

A champion of the new critical literature and a post-Brechtian Marxist theater was Peter Weiss (1916–1982), a foremost playwright and practitioner of political and documentary theater in his *Marat/Sade* (1964) and *Investigation* (*Die Ermittlung*, 1965). His auspicious prose beginnings had included the experimental *The Shadow of the Coachman's Body* (*Der Schatten des Körpers des Kutschers*, 1960), as well as the auto-biographical accounts of his youth and emigration from Germany in *Farewell to the Parents* (*Abschied von den Eltern*, 1961) and *Point of Arrival* (*Fluchtpunkt*, 1962). Weiss elevated his blend of fictional and critical documentary writing to a new level in his magnum opus and legacy *The Aesthetics of Resistance* (*Die Ästhetik des Widerstandes;* 3 vols., 1974, 1978, 1981), a major *roman d'essay*. In his reflective narrative Weiss attempts to legitimize the existence and task of the artist in an age of oppression. Confronting the tribulations of world history since the 1930s, Weiss presents a memento to the victims of fascism. At the same time he preserves the legacy of working-class resistance to repressive regimes, a concern shared by Alexander Kluge (b. 1932) in his highly intellectual brand of documentary and fictional literature.

Kluge, a noted filmmaker (*Yesterday's Girl; Abschied von Gestern*, 1966), developed a cool, distanced style that elevates Brechtian didacticism to a highly theoretical level of text-reader relationship. After the decline of the German protest movement Kluge, like many others, remained on a leftist course, continuing his work for an enlightened, critical perspective in opposition to the bogus view of reality created by the commercial media. Although the immediate concerns of the protest movement abated in the 1970s, a variety of politically oriented writers and social critics avoided the sellout to the new trends that came about in the early 1970s, when the slogan *Tendenzwende* (change of sensibilities) was used by the right to discredit leftist holdouts. The new sensibility movement, at the same time, reset priorities that the protesters of the 1968 generation had abandoned in their shortsighted effort to bring about sudden social and political change.

Trends in Austria and Switzerland

An intriguing part of the development of German prose after 1945 is the contribution of Austrian and Swiss literature. Both countries have a long history of developing their own cultural identity and literary traditions. This process of self-definition continues both apart from and in relation to the developments in West Germany. As a matter of fact, many a Swiss and Austrian author became an integral part of the literary scene in the Federal Republic after the war, although simultaneous independent movements arose in Austria and Switzerland.

The complex interrelations of the three literatures in German can best be illustrated by the example of the Austrian writer Franz Kafka

(1883–1924), who had a distinct influence on the prose style of several generations of writers after World War I. Austrians like Ilse Aichinger, Elias Canetti (b. 1905), and much later, Peter Handke (b. 1942); the Swiss Friedrich Dürrenmatt (b. 1921); and Germans such as Hermann Kasack (1896–1966) and Martin Walser are indebted to the German-writing Jewish author from Prague to various significant degrees. Canetti, a Sephardic Jew from Romania who had lived in London since he emigrated in the 1930s, won the Nobel Prize in 1981 for his chiefly essayistic oeuvre investigating mass culture and psychology, as in *Crowds and Power* (*Masse und Macht*, 1960). His only novel so far, *Auto-da-fé* (*Die Blendung*, 1935), has been followed more recently by his perceptive autobiographical writings, *The Tongue Set Free* (*Die gerettete Zunge*, 1977) and *The Torch in My Ear* (*Die Fackel im Ohr*, 1980). Increasingly recognized in Germany and abroad for the scope and depth of his pensive work, Canetti remains an outsider and imaginer who stimulates reflection on the conditions of human nature, the existence of "mass man," and the madness threatening humanity.

More integrated into the West German developments of the 1950s and 1960s were Ilse Aichinger and Ingeborg Bachmann. Aichinger's novel *Herod's Children* (*Die grössere Hoffnung*, 1948), a vivid account of the author's anxiety during the war and a moving plea for the creation of new hopes for the future, was complemented by *The Bound Man and Other Stories* (*Der Gefesselte, Erzählungen*, 1953), which skillfully combine Kafkaesque sensibility with existentialist philosophy. Bachmann, a celebrated poet at first, explored in her stories *The Thirtieth Year* (*Das dreissigste Jahr*, 1961) and *Simultaneous* (*Simultan*, 1972) the fragmenting impact of a social and existential reality that had a paralyzing effect upon her figures. Her many female figures especially experience the disintegration of their personalities under the oppressive rule of patriarchal structures that have infiltrated language and the innermost feelings of hapless victims. This is depicted most impressively in Bachmann's fragmentary trilogy *Modes of Dying* (*Todesarten*) of which the centerpiece, *Malina* (1971), appeared during the artist's lifetime. The novel at first received much negative attention from critics ignorant of its narrative mode of inward self-scrutiny. The topic of the devastating split of the self and the destruction of the female psyche at the hands of a murderous male figure representing the violence of patriarchal powers only recently became a rallying ground for feminist critics, who feel greater kinship with Bachmann's excruciating tale of self-reduction.

Thomas Bernhard (b. 1931), too, emphasizes the absurdity and negativity of human life devoid of meaning. His heroes experience the destructiveness of the world as self-destructive drives of their egos, notably in the novels *Frost* (*Frost*, 1963), *Disturbance* (*Verstörung*, 1967),

The Lime Works (Das Kalkwerk, 1970), and *Correction (Korrektur,* 1975). Bernhard's latest work, *Concrete (Beton,* 1982), however, reveals a greater irony and a lighter hand at depicting the idiosyncrasies of an all-pervasive negativity that is punctured by the author's black humor.

Peter Handke, who started out as a shrewd *raconteur* and *provocateur,* skillfully employed the clichéd slogans of everyday language in his *Sprechstücke* (speech plays) for satirical purposes, offending his audiences in a calculated manner. Handke then moved to a new kind of prose indebted to traditional authors such as Goethe, Stifter, and Kafka, the detective story, and influences stemming from the philosophy of language. His much-acclaimed *The Goalie's Anxiety at the Penalty Kick (Die Angst des Tormanns beim Elfmeter,* 1970) fused the various elements highly successfully. It was followed by a work clearly derivative of the *Bildungsroman* (education novel), *Short Letter, Long Farewell (Der kurze Brief zum langen Abschied,* 1972). Handke's narrative reflection on his mother's suicide, *A Sorrow Beyond Dreams (Wunschloses Unglück,* 1972), defines the narrative process as "an act of memory . . . from enjoyment of horror it produces enjoyment of memory" (p. 67). This self-encounter of the artist as a mourner is also an homage to his mother as a victim of social and mental entrapments. It was hailed as a marker of the "new sensibility" and "new subjectivity" of the 1970s. Handke pursued his narrative mode of relating the inner world in outer events in his *A Moment of True Feeling (Die Stunde der wahren Empfindung,* 1975), a tale along the lines of Kafka's *Metamorphosis (Die Verwandlung,* 1915), permeated, however, with Handke's own brand of magical and mystical realism. *The Left-handed Woman (Die linkshändige Frau,* 1976) follows more closely the pattern of an alienation tale set for a stylized stage, as can be seen in Handke's film version, which is indebted greatly to the work of Japanese filmmaker Yasujiro Ozu (b. 1903). Handke's most recent work, *Through the Villages (Über die Dörfer,* 1981), continues his mystical trend and bestows an almost priestly function on the artist as a spiritual leader.

Austrian writers went through many generational conflicts after the war. Handke's infamous journal entry, "Austria: that which makes me suffocate" (*The Weight of the World: Journal 1975–1977; Das Gewicht der Welt: Journal 1975-1977,* 1977) reveals a hatred for his native country that betrays the ambivalence toward all things Austrian that is shared by many younger Austrian writers. Theirs is a skeptical and critical attitude toward tradition and social and political appeasement. Aichinger's codeword *Misstrauen* (distrust), coined after the war when many were outraged at the Austrian people, who had become accomplices to fascism, is given new poignancy by writers such as Jutta Schutting (b. 1937), Barbara Frischmuth (b. 1941), Michael Scharang (b. 1941), Gerhard

Roth (b. 1942), Peter Turrini (b. 1944), Franz Innerhofer (b. 1944), Elfriede Jelinek (b. 1946), Gert Friedrich Jonke (b. 1946), and Brigitte Schwaiger (b. 1949). Typical of the criticism launched at the stifling atmosphere of Austrian life in the 1950s and 1960s is Konrad Bayer's (1932–1964) postsurrealist experimental writing, *the sixth sense* (*der sechste sinn,* 1966), representative of the style developed by the Group Vienna in cabaret-like manner. The playful experiments of Ernst Jandl (b. 1925) and Friederike Mayröcker (b. 1924) dwell on the Austrian preoccupation with language and its philosophy, whereas Jonke, G. Roth (*Winter Journey; Winterreise,* 1978), and Innerhofer (*Beautiful Days; Schöne Tage,* 1974) explore the no less Austrian topic of alienation and identity crisis.

The Swiss contribution to German prose after 1945 was for a long time dominated by a few writers, above all Friedrich Dürrenmatt and Max Frisch, whose careers are unthinkable without the critical resonance and readership they found in West Germany. Frisch's undisputed stature as an accomplished playwright is complemented by a string of highly successful and significant novels: *I Am Not Stiller* (*Stiller,* 1954), *Homo Faber* (1957), *A Wilderness of Mirrors* (*Mein Name sei Gantenbein,* 1964), *Montauk* (1975), and *Man in the Holocene* (*Der Mensch erscheint im Holozän,* 1979). These works focus on the problem of marriage and identity, which Frisch's heroes encounter in everyday life. Frisch's major theme, which goes far beyond regional or narrowly Swiss concerns, deals with the existential impasses of male heroes who repeatedly come face to face with their failure to live up to expectations.

The appearance of writers such as Peter Bichsel (b. 1935), Otto Friedrich Walter (b. 1928), Adolf Muschg (b. 1934), Hermann Burger (b. 1942), E. Y. Meyer (b. 1946), and Fritz Zorn (1944–1976) indicated a growing concern with regional issues. Although most of these and even younger writers are oriented toward the literary market of the Federal Republic, they concern themselves increasingly with the social and political problems of their country. The emergence of a Swiss youth culture and the protests that erupted on several occasions in 1980 and 1981 became a driving force to politicize the developing Swiss literature, which is striving for self-definition, supported by a growing number of domestic publishers who help in warding off the dominating influence of the West German book trade. This new regionalism enhances the diversity already existing in countries like Austria and Switzerland. At the same time the regionalism is permeated with "international" elements. A good example is Claudia Storz's (b. 1948) novel *Jessica, Ill-constructed* (*Jessica mit Konstruktionsfehlern,* 1977), which gives a vivid picture of the Swiss student scene and is simultaneously concerned with the incurable disease of the heroine. Both the drawbacks and the general aspects of student life have implications representative of the sufferings and conflicts common to the Austrian and German student movements as well.

Representative Women Authors

After the war a number of women writers, such as Elisabeth Langgässer (*The Quest; Märkische Argonautenfahrt,* 1950), Marie Luise Kaschnitz (1901–1974), and Luise Rinser (b. 1911), held their own in a literary marketplace dominated by men and male interests. Kaschnitz's stories (*Long Shadows: Lange Schatten,* 1960) and autobiographical writings are poetically inspired pieces of soul-searching and dwell on the tradition of female self-reflection prominent in the autobiographies of the past. Rinser, a prolific fiction writer and a stout Christian, as shown in *Nina* (*Mitte des Lebens,* 1950) and *Rings of Glass* (*Die gläsernen Ringe,* 1941), more recently has developed into a critic of conservative trends in Germany. Her diaries and her autobiography, *Embracing the Wolf* (*Den Wolf umarmen,* 1981), reveal a fighting spirit that dates back to her imprisonment by the Nazis for political reasons.

Predating the feminist movement of the 1970s are, in addition to Aichinger and Bachmann, the prolific Gabriele Wohmann (b. 1932) and Gisela Elsner (b. 1937). Wohmann's novel *Serious Intention* (*Ernste Absicht,* 1970) is a narrative *tour de force* relating the confused memories of a young woman lying on her sickbed and facing death. In her collection of stories, *Paulinchen Was at Home Alone* (*Paulinchen war allein zu Hause,* 1974), Wohmann is cool, detached and intellectual. Shrewdly reproducing the everyday mentality of her ordinary people, she reveals the hidden motivations, rationalizations, and deceptions of her characters. The sardonic tone betrays a satirical involvement on the part of the author, who rarely shows compassion, as in the analysis of the mother-daughter relationship in *Excursion with Mother* (*Ausflug mit der Mutter,* 1976). Elsner's novels, *The Gigantic Dwarfs* (*Die Riesenzwerge,* 1964) and *The Next Generation* (*Der Nachwuchs,* 1968), present brilliant attacks on a society that produces grotesque monsters through the dullness of everyday life.

The women's movement came into being in the aftermath of the students' movement, and West German literature experienced sudden changes with the advent of feminist writers. It was the Swiss-born Verena Stefan (b. 1947) who created a significant breakthrough with her *Shedding* (*Häutungen*), first published in 1975. The book combines confessional and reflective elements, lyrical passages and sensitive prose of a female in search of her womanhood, alone and with other women, after disappointing relationships with men. Stefan's key text articulated the anxieties and yearnings, the frustrations and hopes of a generation of women who awakened to realize their dilemma in a male-dominated world.

Much of the new subjective mood and female sensibility that was to develop the *Frauenszene* (women's scene) and *Frauenbewegung* (women's movement) was anticipated in Karin Struck's (b. 1947) novel *Class Love* (*Klassenliebe,* 1973), followed by *The Mother* (*Die Mutter,* 1975) and *Loving* (*Lieben,* 1977). Struck was soon to be criticized for her turn to inwardness and a cultish celebration of motherhood and femininity. A reflection of the private experience of social reality can be found in Elisabeth Plessen's (b. 1944) *Such Sad Tidings* (*Mitteilung an den Adel,* 1976), a major document of the literary critique of the generation of fathers and their incapacity to break open the patriarchal structures of power. The politically rebellious mood of the 1960s reappears in these finely tuned and individualized forms of social criticism.

Of note are the works by Christa Reinig (b. 1926), whose novel *Emasculation* (*Entmannung,* 1976) is a vibrant attack on men by an ardent feminist. Social criticism of a similar vein can be found in Renate Rasp's (b. 1935) *A Spoiled Brat* (*Ein ungeratener Sohn,* 1967), a sardonic indictment of traditional methods of child rearing and education. More distinctly autobiographical is Helga M. Novak's (b. 1935) novel *The Ice Saints* (*Die Eisheiligen,* 1979), which depicts a German childhood not unlike Christa Wolf's (b. 1929) *A Model Childhood* (*Kindheitsmuster,* 1976). Hannelies Taschau's (b. 1937) novel *Public Peace* (*Landfriede,* 1978) reflects the complacency of a small town in the Westphalian countryside. Angelika Mechtel (b. 1943) attempts in her novels *Broken Games* (*Kaputte Spiele,* 1970), *Eat, Bird* (*Friss Vogel,* 1972), and the stories in *Dreams of a Female Fox* (*Die Träume der Füchsin,* 1976) to further the critical realism prevalent in the 1960s in order to fashion it into a tool more congenial to the concerns of women in West German society.

Style, tone, and subject matter in the prose writings of these and other women authors have enhanced the diversity of a literature that has undergone much change since the war. West Germany—more so than Austria and Switzerland—is a society continually under stress. Affluent and for the most part stable politically, this society nevertheless has experienced shifting conflicts, at times reaching crisis proportions. Protest, unrest, and terrorism belong as much to the postwar experience as economic progress and rapid expansion of industry and commerce. Because of the recent past, fascism, and the situation of the divided nation, German writers encounter more irritants than their Austrian and Swiss counterparts. These irritants both stimulate and paralyze their literary imagination.

It is, above all, the individual authors who represent the essential developments in the German-speaking countries. Recently writers such as the subtle, intellectual Botho Strauss (b. 1944) and the proletarian, tenacious Ludwig Fels (b. 1946) have shown how far apart authors representative of their generation can be in outlook and personal style. Strauss's much-acclaimed story *Devotion* (*Die Widmung,* 1977) furthered the subjective mode of writing through self-reflection and sophisticated reproduction of his hero's meandering mind as a result of the loss of love and identity. Fels's novel *A Colossus of Love* (*Ein Unding der Liebe,* 1981), however, presents the figure of a grotesque yet sensitive loser, a type familiar from Böll's *The Clown* and Grass's *The Tin Drum.* Through the eccentric view of his hapless and freakishly fat hero a panorama is given of the uncanny continuities underneath the prosperity and collective materialism in Germany. In a world of profit and efficiency those weary of the precarious "miracle" are pushed into loneliness, suffering, and silence.

German prose after 1945 has been characterized by the effort to deal imaginatively with the historical legacies that remain irritating in a society obsessive in its pursuit of material ends at the expense of spiritual integrity. Against the obliviousness and overconfidence of their contemporaries, authors in Austria, Switzerland, and West Germany use their prose writings to further individual and collective goals that help to preserve a sense of dignity.

Readings

Demetz, Peter. *Postwar German Literature: A Critical Introduction.* New York: Pegasus, 1970.

Herrmann, Elizabeth Rütschi, and Edna Huttenmaier Spitz (eds.). *German Women Writers of the Twentieth Century.* Oxford and New York: Pergamon Press, 1978.

McClelland, Charles E., and Steven P. Scher (eds.). *Postwar German Culture: An Anthology.* New York: Dutton & Co., 1974.

Seymour-Smith, Martin. *Funk and Wagnalls' Guide to Modern World Literature.* Vol. 2. New York: Funk and Wagnalls, 1973.

Thomas, R. Hinton, and Wilfried van der Will. *The German Novel and the Affluent Society.* Toronto: University of Toronto Press, 1968.

Waidson, H. M. *The Modern German Novel.* London and New York: Oxford University Press, 1959.

WINFRIED KUDSZUS

—————— **14** ——————

Lyric Poetry in German Since 1945

New Beginning and Old Irrationalism

After the horror of the Nazi years, the question was often asked whether literature, particularly lyrical poetry, could still be written. In 1949, after his return from exile in the United States, the sociologist Theodor W. Adorno wrote in his essay "Cultural Criticism and Society" ("Kulturkritik und Gesellschaft"): "To write poetry after Auschwitz is barbarian." Even though Adorno later modified this verdict and excluded, for example, the poems of Paul Celan, there is truth in his words about German lyrical poetry—and literature—after 1945. A poet who wrote "lyrically," using "beautiful" words and images as if a harmonious reality existed, could be accused of blindness and dishonesty with ample reason. Language itself had become suspect. It had deteriorated into a propaganda tool of a brutal regime and was permeated with clichés, corrupted words, opaque concepts.

At "zero hour" ("Stunde Null") in 1945, the poet Günter Eich (1907–1972) took a survey of the objects and words that had survived. Entitled "Inventory" (*Inventur*), his poem begins:

> This is my cap,
> this is my coat,
> here's my shaving gear
> in a linen sack.

> A can of rations:
> my plate, my cup,
> I've scratched my name
> in the tin.

This chapter does not cover poetry from the German Democratic Republic, which is treated by Frank Trommler in Chapter 15 of this book.

Wolfgang Weyrauch (1907–1980) coined the term *Kahlschlag-Literatur* for this kind of literary reduction and realism in the works of Eich and others. *Kahlschlag* (clearing of the woods) was, however, passé as early as 1950. To be sure, Eich received that year's award of the Group 47 (Gruppe 47), a literary association critical of the past and dedicated to a new beginning. Yet his new poetry included such fanciful departures from reality as the text entitled "Franconian-Tibetan Cherry Garden" ("Fränkisch-tibetischer Kirschgarten"). Eich and most of his fellow writers had begun to avoid the confrontation with their politico-historical heritage.

In Gottfried Benn's (1886–1956) writings, such a confrontation remained almost entirely absent. In 1933 the heightened bathos and the vitalistic irrationalism of his expressionistic works led him to a strong endorsement of the Nazis' rise to power. Around the middle of 1934, he awakened from his intoxication, and he spent the remaining Nazi years in spiritual withdrawal. After the war, however, he published two further volumes of poetry in a decidedly irrational mode, *Static Poems* (*Statische Gedichte,* 1948) and *Intoxicated Flood* (*Trunkene Flut,* 1949). And his lecture "Problems of Lyric Poetry" ("Probleme der Lyrik," 1951) achieved programmatic significance for the strongly ahistorical trends in German poetry of the 1950s. Benn spoke here of poetic "artistry" and of the necessity of "form" while also emphasizing the ecstatic essence of poetic language. The noun, he wrote, is the "phallus of the spirit, centrally rooted." Benn's words and views were clearly unaffected by the skepticism of the *Kahlschlag.*

In his last volumes of poetry, however, Benn himself gained some distance from his deliria. Although these works are permeated by a sentimental mood and by laments about the fading of trance-like states in old age, there is also ironic self-recognition, as in the volume *Distillations* (*Destillationen,* 1953):

> Above all I experience bottles
> and in the evenings a little radio,
> these are the tepid, the languid
> hours of twilight.

In the German original, "radio" and "twilight" rhyme in a deliberately amateurish, self-ridiculing manner: "*Funk*" and "*Dämmerung.*" Unvarnished personal lines also appear in Benn's latest poetry:

> I have often asked myself and found no answer,
> where do tenderness and goodness come from,
> today again I don't know and must now depart.

Reality Experienced and Transformed

Paul Celan (1920–1970), a poet whose style was free of bombast, remained independent of the domestic German discussion about *Kahlschlag* and *Stunde Null*. Born and raised in the southeastern European city of Chernovtsy and persecuted as a Jew by the Germans—his parents fell victim to these persecutions—Celan had experienced his *Stunde Null* before 1945. His poem "Death Fugue" ("Todesfuge"), written in 1945 after years of suffering, includes the words: "Death is a master from Germany." After postwar stays in Bucharest and Vienna, Celan settled permanently in Paris in 1948.

Celan's language and imagery are nourished in such a profound sense by their critical self-reflection that they seem to have been written in opposition to themselves. After relatively melodic and accessible, if somewhat surrealistic, beginnings (*Poppy and Memory; Mohn und Gedächtnis,* 1952), the intricacy of Celan's poetry becomes increasingly apparent. In *Language Grid* (*Sprachgitter,* 1959), the language is dense and resists the casual reader. Even more complex in its associative richness is Celan's latest poetry, which initially appears to be impenetrable. The difficulties begin with the titles of the volumes, which are virtually untranslatable neologisms with multiple connotations: *Lichtzwang* (1970, *Light Compulsion*?) and *Schneepart* (1971, *Snow Segment*?). Various levels of meaning exist simultaneously within the smallest confines. There is, however, another side to Celan's complexity. In its departure from conventional language, Celan's poetry gains a strange familiarity, which the reader can experience by an immediate response to the words and images as if they were living "creatures"—a notion Celan explores in his poetological lecture *The Meridian* (*Der Meridian,* 1960).

Celan created from the intensity of his existential suffering as well as from a growing insistence on a complex and resistant language that, nevertheless, is not fundamentally incomprehensible. His poetry lives up to the *Stunde Null* without joining in the programmatic pronouncements of the *Kahlschlag* generation. His relentless search for meaning generates hope beyond despair in "songs" that surpass the reality we know:

THREAD SUNS
above the grey-black wilderness.
A tree-
high thought
tunes in to light's pitch: there are
still songs to be sung on the other side
of mankind.

Nelly Sachs (1891–1970), who fled Berlin and the Nazis in 1940 and then remained in Stockholm, was related to Paul Celan in being persecuted and trying to find meaning and words in an infinitely abysmal world. The Holocaust dominates *In the Habitations of Death* (*In den Wohnungen des Todes,* 1947) and *Eclipse of the Stars* (*Sternverdunkelung,* 1949). Both titles refer to it, and in both volumes fear and horror merge with the paradoxical possibility of a mystical liberation. A key concept here is "dust," with its connotations of transitoriness and redemption. The poems attempt to unite extreme suffering with rebirth. The hope expressed in them is rooted mainly in Judaic-Chassidic mysticism of the eighteenth and nineteenth centuries. In a further phase of her work, Sachs refers to thirteenth-century Judaic mysticism, particularly the book *Sohar* of the Spanish cabbala. Signifier and signified magically find their way to one another in the first collection of this new phase, *And No One Knows How to Go On* (*Und niemand weiss weiter,* 1957). For Nelly Sachs, this magical interrelation offers another possibility of transcending her suffering in her work.

Although Sachs still strongly referred to Judaic mysticism in her volume *Journey into a Dustless Realm* (*Fahrt ins Staublose,* 1961)— again in order to overcome the disintegration of reality and language— the poems in *Death Still Celebrates Life* (*Noch feiert das Leben,* 1961) reflect the beginning of an extension of her mystical world view into universal dimensions. The horror of a hospital ward pervades this new volume, but the horror is fused with the hope for another, though invisible, world. The collections *Glowing Enigmas* (*Glühende Rätsel,* 1962–1965), *She Who Seeks* (*Die Suchende,* 1966), and *Be Parted, Night* (*Teile dich Nacht,* 1971) further develop the fusion of concreteness and mystical universality while introducing everyday situations into the poetic texts.

The use of mystical conceptions in the works of Nelly Sachs does not include a premature dispensation of solace. She developed a language of transformation, not of a final rest in fulfillment. In her poetological *Frankfurt Lectures* (*Frankfurter Vorlesungen,* 1959–1960), the Austrian Ingeborg Bachmann (1926–1973) points to the "movement originating in suffering" in a poem by Sachs from *Flight and Metamorphosis* (*Flucht und Verwandlung,* 1959). The poem "Without Compass," focuses on a young man who, without a compass, is locked in struggle with all the luminaries:

He thrusts himself off
from the rocking chairs
of domesticated generations

beside himself
with the fire helmet
he wounds the night.

The following lines which Nelly Sachs quoted in her Nobel Prize speech (1966), also came from *Flight and Metamorphosis:* "I hold instead of a homeland / the metamorphoses of the world."

In the works of Ingeborg Bachmann, "an extremely skeptical examination of the relations between word and world" (*Frankfurt Lectures*) is to be found. Like Paul Celan, Bachmann first emerged into prominence in the early 1950s, at a meeting of the Group 47. Similar to Celan and Sachs, she insists on the close proximity of linguistic skepticism and hope, yet her poems are comparatively accessible and melodic. In her volumes *A Respite for Time* (*Die gestundete Zeit,* 1953) and *Invocation of the Great Bear* (*Anrufung des Grossen Bären,* 1956), silence and the difficulty of generating a meaningful language are frequently recurring motifs. Words and reality are separated by an unfathomable distance, as Bachmann had also discovered in Ludwig Wittgenstein's philosophy of language. After 1956 Bachmann rarely wrote lyrical poetry. The final lines of her second and last volume of poetry evoked hope for a "song" beyond "silence":

Only sinking around us of stars. Reflection and silence.
Yet the song above the dust afterwards
will transcend us.

Linguistic Experimentation

The relation between language and the world is subjected to intense scrutiny in other ways by "concrete poetry," which likewise goes back to the 1950s, although it was beleaguered and disregarded at the time. In his influential book *The Structure of Modern Poetry* (*Die Struktur der modernen Lyrik,* 1956), Hugo Friedrich points to the breakdown of traditional forms of lyrical expression and to a mode of "writing poetry from language." Concrete poetry can be seen as a radical extension of such phenomena. Its birth date is generally set in 1953, when the *Constellations* (*Konstellationen*) of the Swiss writer Eugen Gomringer (b. 1925) appeared. Determinedly detached from traditional views of language and with special emphasis on visual elements, Gomringer's poetry was also influenced by commercial art and industrial design. Even silence acquired accessibility:

silence silence silence
silence silence silence
silence   silence
silence silence silence
silence silence silence

Till the end of the 1950s concrete poetry was quite removed from nonpoetic concerns, but it experienced a development in the 1960s toward a greater commitment. Helmut Heissenbüttel's (b. 1921) text "Political Grammar" ("Politische Grammatik") had already caused a stir in 1959. In 1966 Claus Bremer (b. 1924) published his *involving texts* (*engagierende texte*) and in 1968 the socially and politically committed *Texts and Commentaries* (*Texte und Kommentare*), which resist established power. "I have hardly been able to always stand nicely in line," he comments in *Texts* on an earlier piece in which the words "to always stand nicely in line" are repeated fifty-two times. Referring to the sociopolitical movement of that period, Bremer characterizes the structure and intent of this piece ambitiously: "This organization provokes the impulse towards freedom and stimulates the faculty of reason."

Poetry of Madness and Resistance

The undogmatic and ingeniously witty Ernst Jandl (b. 1925) has pursued mainly an expanded mode of concrete writing. He has also been influenced by the linguistic experiments of the Vienna Group (Wiener Gruppe): Friedrich Achleitner, H. C. Artmann, Konrad Bayer, Gerhard Rühm, Oswald Wiener—all of them first active in the 1950s. Jandl has composed "sound poems" (*Lautgedichte*) and "speech poems" (*Sprechgedichte*) as well as visual texts, but he has also written in less experimental, relatively conventional ways.

Jandl is a flexible, many-faceted poet, and his sensibility extends to so-called psychopathological writings. Life's imperfection and fragility is the focus of the volume *the yellow dog* (*der gelbe hund,* 1980). Language here assumes deteriorated and random characteristics. One of the poems is dedicated to a fellow Austrian author, Ernst Herbeck (b. 1920), a chronically schizophrenic poet who lives in an institution and has become known under the pen name Alexander. A few years earlier, another Jandl poem, "horse and rider" ("ross und reiter"), had appeared in the appendix of Herbeck's volume *Alexander's Poetic Texts* (*Alexanders poetische Texte,* 1977). Written "for alexander," it begins:

yesterday on stallions, with wine and jest
shot today through spine and chest
hoppity hoppity rider

father will be your provider
father will spring at time of death
into your mouth as a fresh breath
spread himself into your brain

Jandl's sympathy with those oppressed and pushed to existential peripheries indicates the growing esteem that psychopathological phenomena and works have captured in recent German literature. This includes an admiration for stylistic originality, and thus it is not surprising that Friederike Mayröcker (b. 1924), the virtuoso of an experimental, multilayered, polyphonic style, contributed a poem to *Alexander's Poetic Texts* entitled "MADD (forebear) (forebode) (hereair):/ ALEXANDER-COLLAGE"; "UMNACHT (Ahn) (Ahnung) (hierluft):/ ALEXANDER-COLLAGE." Alexander's own poem "The Squirrel" ("Das Eichkätzchen") begins, similarly to Jandl's "horse and rider," in a seemingly innocent, jolly tone:

In heath and wood,
'twas there I felt good.
The forester felt fright,
as it was on the tree, the squirrel.
It sprang from all to the branch.
and shrivelled from heat. The
forester froze. And his rifle.
The forester saw how it just appened
and stabbed im in the coat and fell
from the tree like snow.
The squirrel had a semi-
pelt of brown czar. The fell was
                          well.
The fox looked now and again and
ate it up. To fetch the meal. The
squirrel was dead. The fox was
long. as the forester his rifle
and shot. He missed it.

It becomes quickly apparent that this poem's opening lines, seemingly normal and joyful, conceal sheer brutality. The merriment of life in the forest mirrors the corruption of so-called normality. "He missed it" is a counterstatement directed at societal hunting rituals. Close textual analysis has shown the intimate connection between the poem's intellectual thrust and its highly complex style, which includes subtly meaningful violations of linguistic rules. Above all, Alexander's text cannot simply be dismissed as "word salad."

Rolf Dieter Brinkmann (1940–1975) created yet another mode of poetry that deviated from the norm. With his aggressively countercultural works, he openly attacked the preoccupations of his contemporaries. The preface to his final volume, *Westwards 1 & 2* (*Westwärts 1 & 2*, 1975), begins: "The story tellers keep telling, the auto industry keeps manufacturing, the workers keep working, the governments keep governing." Often in epic detail, the poems take precise and critical aim at realities that include questions of contemporary politics. In "Political Poem 13 Nov. 74, FRG" ("Politisches Gedicht 13. Nov. 74, BRD"), environmental pollution and inhuman job pressures become poetic themes: "biologically seen: a cancerous society. A heart- / attack society." Destruction of language as a means of public and private communication is characterized in a similar vein: "the 'public language' a fraud . . . & the bodies / their conditions are narrated in the form of advertising spots."

Brinkmann was strongly influenced by American pop art and underground literature, and he developed a heightened sense of the poetical potential as well as the shock value of triviality and everyday events. He was a proponent of the new sensibility of the 1960s, which tried to move away from lifeless abstractions toward a more concrete, physical, and emotionally integrated existence. In the preface to his poetry volume *The Pilots* (*Die Piloten*, 1968), Brinkmann referred in particular to the West German literary scene: "The dead admire the dead!" He soon became aware that the new sensibility in literature and life was being gradually co-opted, commercialized, and consumed by the old society. In his "Poem 'for Frank O'Hara'" ("Gedicht 'für' Frank O'Hara") in the volume *Grass* (*Gras*, 1970) Brinkmann wrote: "I struggle / myself against the noiseless disappearance of tenderness from / my body." In a way, Brinkmann's death in a London traffic accident in 1975 proved to be an affirmation of his views of heartless consumerism. Like a brilliant advertising ploy, the news of his end contributed greatly to the posthumous breakthrough of *Westwards 1 & 2*. Today, Brinkmann remains widely read, as does Wolf Wondratschek (b. 1943), who has been writing in a similar vein since the mid 1970s. His volume *Final Poems* (*Letzte Gedichte*, 1980) is as foreboding as its title indicates. "Black Serenade" ("Schwarze Serenade") envisions the end of humankind:

> . . . imagination is surpassed,
> a comet appears in the evening sky.
> That concerns everyone. Now it's everyone's turn.
> Now only reality keeps imagining.
> Europe—knee-deep in radioactivity!
> Germany—finally of interest! A red-hot rag

sprinkled with dust from the stars.
American skyscrapers—only one story high.
The satellites radio silence.
The bang fades into the universe . . .

The Concerns of the Day

Brinkmann's attention to everyday reality and his growing political awareness reflected changes in German poetry that had announced themselves as early as the 1950s. In the collection *My Poem Is My Knife* (*Mein Gedicht ist mein Messer,* 1955), edited by Hans Bender (b. 1919), Karl Krolow (b. 1915) proposed the "open poem" that could "literally incorporate *everything.*"

Krolow had come a long way from his beginnings, when he wrote somber, metaphorical, naively ahistorical nature poetry (*Naturlyrik*), such as that published in his volumes *Highly Praised, Good Life* (*Hochgelobtes gutes Leben,* 1943) and *Affliction* (*Heimsuchung,* 1948). The chronological sequence of these volumes, unbroken by the year 1945, is not coincidental. *Naturlyrik* was a way of focusing on the realm of nature rather than on human failure and catastrophe. Wilhelm Lehmann (1882–1968), a leading practitioner of the genre and young Krolow's model, wrote deliberately ahistorical poetry before, during, and after the Nazi years. For him and numerous other writers of *Naturlyrik*, there never was a *Kahlschlag.* The woods remained uncleared as a kind of sanctuary for the special use of the deaf and blind in the world of history. Also, this kind of poetry blended easily with the self-satisfied years of the West German "economic miracle" (*Wirtschafts-wunder*) and the concomitant restorative, anticritical—and anti-intellectual—political trends. Throughout the 1950s, such *Naturlyrik* was written in great quantities. A notable exception was Günter Eich's nature poetry. Increasingly, nature appeared in his poems in uncomfortable, even menacing ways. Eich's 1955 volume *Messages of the Rain* (*Botschaften des Regens*), showed a deep distrust of established certainties that presupposed the experience of recent history.

Having proposed the "open poem," Krolow wrote lighter, less ponderous poetry in the 1950s than in his early years. In particular, Krolow's work now showed the influence of modern French and Spanish poetry, for which he played an important mediating role in postwar Germany. This task was an essential one, since German poetry was largely shut off from international developments during the Nazi years. Krolow's writing became more condensed in his *Invisible Hands* (*Unsichtbare Hände*), published in 1962, as did, around the turn of the decade, Celan's and Eich's poetry as well as the poems of Marie Luise Kaschnitz

(1901–1974) in her 1962 volume *Your Silence—My Voice* (*Dein Schweigen—meine Stimme*).

Even Krolow's condensed writing avoided hermeticism. In the later 1960s and 1970s, Krolow focused on the commonplace and, similar to Brinkmann's more committed approach, he pursued a postmodern course characterized by subjectively chosen themes and a somewhat colloquial style. The titles of his later volumes of poetry illustrate this direction: *Everyday Poems* (*Alltägliche Gedichte,* 1968), *Nothing More Than Life* (*Nichts weiter als Leben,* 1970), and *For the Sake of Simplicity* (*Der Einfachheit halber,* 1977). Although often rhymed, the poems in Krolow's volume *Autumn Sonnet with Hegel* (*Herbstsonett mit Hegel,* 1981) retain a closeness to everyday language. Yet there is, as in Wondratschek's *Final Poems,* a new darkness and fear:

Most are fearful,
You shove grass into the cigarette.
You burn. You lie in the bed,
Squeeze the grass into the cigarette.
Most are fearful.

Political reality is only indirectly present in Krolow's poetry of everyday matters; the poems of many of his contemporaries in the late 1960s and early 1970s turned distinctly political. Hans Magnus Enzensberger (b. 1929) was a representative and precursor of this development. In a socially more concrete version of Krolow's demand for the "open" poem, Enzensberger had dealt critically with political questions even in the 1950s. His first volume of poems, *defense of the wolves* (*verteidigung der wölfe,* 1957), presents such concerns as the perverse alliance between the rulers and the ruled, the "wolves" and the "lambs":

you lambs . . .
you are blinding one another . . .
throwing yourselves on the bed
of indolent obedience . . .
. . . you want to be
mutilated. you
won't change the world.

Alongside his political involvement during the acquiescent Adenauer era, Enzensberger revealed a differentiated sense of aesthetics. He proved to be a connoisseur and subtle assimilator of international modern poetry, as became evident also in his volumes *vernacular* (*landessprache,* 1960) and *braille* (*blindenschrift,* 1964). "Revision, not revolution" was his motto until about 1967, when, in the wake of his experiences in the United States and Cuba and of his sympathies for the radical extra-parliamentary opposition in the Federal Republic, he curtailed his lyrical production and committed himself primarily to politics and cultural politics. In 1968 the trend-setting issue 15 of the anthology *Kursbuch* (*Timetable*) appeared. Edited by Enzensberger, it included his observations entitled "Platitudes Concerning the Most Recent Literature." His thoughts about the death of literature and its superfluity in the conflict of social classes were widely assimilated, and a whole host of authors turned out aggressively political texts, such as the pieces in *Agitprop: Poetry, Propositions, Reports* (*Agitprop. Lyrik, Thesen, Berichte*, 1969). Enzensberger himself, who on closer inspection had questioned in his *Kursbuch* essay the actual political significance of literature rather than its right to exist, continued writing. He wrote less, however, and with a distinct preference for a laconic, reflective style on the model of the German (later East German) writer Bertolt Brecht (1898–1956). Brecht's influence on reflective, politically oriented poetry was considerable, and Enzensberger was the most remarkable of his followers.

A different, apocalyptic turn characterizes Enzensberger's epic poem *The Sinking of the Titanic* (*Untergang der Titanic*, 1978). In far-reaching fantasies and reflections, Enzensberger finally bids farewell to utopias, particularly those of the 1960s. His volume *The Fury of Vanishing* (*Die Furie des Verschwindens*, 1980) adds further acrimony to the sense of doom. Its central long poem is entitled "The Tree Frogs of Bikini" ("Die Frösche von Bikini"), the island where early nuclear testing took place:

> . . . He thinks of Bikini often.
> Everything is there again, he muses,
> thirty years after the apocalypse,
> "on the ladder of evolution."
> Tree-frogs, dewy-fresh,
> irresistible. They climb, he muses,
> acrobatically, even the weather
> keeps improving. The white
> beaches, empty of humans—
> As in the starry skies above us
> the hard radiation, the helium flash,
> the unchecked extravagance:
> the same here on earth . . .

Directly political poetry in the style of the *Agitprop* collection has faded since about 1970. Yet, as Enzensberger's writing exemplifies, a concern for pressing issues has remained. Often, to be sure, the concern is all but lost in private indulgence and a mindless fixation on everyday activities, as in many of the poems in the anthologies *Poems for Readers* (*Lyrik für Leser,* 1980) and *Different from the Flower Children: Poems by the Youth of the Seventies* (*Anders als die Blumenkinder. Gedichte der Jugend aus den 70er Jahren,* 1980). For many writers, however, personal styles and themes link intimately and concretely with questions of social significance. Brinkmann, Wondratschek, Krolow, and Enzensberger as well as Jürgen Becker (b. 1932), Günter Herburger (b. 1932), Nicolas Born (1937–1979), and Peter Handke (b. 1942) contributed each in his own way to the new responsible sensibility of the 1970s.

New Impulse

Recent volumes of poetry by two women writers, Ulla Hahn (b. 1946) and Sarah Kirsch (b. 1935), have been widely acclaimed. *Heart over Head* (*Herz über Kopf,* 1981) by Hahn and *Earth* (*Erdreich,* 1982) by Kirsch are both intensely personal and at the same time strongly committed to contemporary reality. Stylistically, they are subtle and multifaceted. Hahn's poetry relates to centuries of literary history, yet her verse treads lightly and transforms tradition with irony and wit. Her poems are equally wide-ranging in the emotional realm. There are moments of happiness in everyday life, and there is the terror of existence and of history. German history in particular is not forgotten. Ulla Hahn's poetry includes the shock of memories dating back beyond her lifetime into the Nazi years.

Sarah Kirsch, who left East Germany for West Berlin in 1977, takes a chilling view of the present in her new volume. To some extent, she shares the apocalyptic sense so widespread in German literature around 1980. Yet she also tries to nourish a sense of hope and resistance against all odds. Her final poem in *Earth* evokes the image of a ship, named not the *Titanic* but the *Nautilus,* a multifaceted name that includes the allusion to the Argonauts and their tireless quest for the Golden Fleece. Kirsch's *Nautilus* moves in uncertain seas, yet it also fosters the growth of "seaweed." There is a sense of isolation and yet of survival throughout the poem. Intertwining allusions to death and growth appear repeatedly. In the opening lines of the poem, the survivor-figure Noah turns from the record of his own journey to the poetry of Friedrich Hölderlin (1770–1843), the great German poet who spent most of his life in the role of a madman:

At night he closes the log-book, and opens
The large Hölderlin edition while
The Nautilus slowly moves her

Old-fashioned superstructures, terraces
Overgrown with seaweed, into the moonlight. It is
Meaningless to wait for the assignment.

Readings

Demetz, Peter. *Postwar German Literature: A Critical Introduction.* New York: Schocken, 1972.
Knörrich, Otto. *Die deutsche Lyrik seit 1945.* 2nd ed. Stuttgart: Kröner, 1978.
McClelland, Charles E., and Steven P. Scher, eds. *Postwar German Culture: An Anthology.* New York: Dutton & Co., 1974.

FRANK TROMMLER

—— 15 ——
Aspects of Literature
in the
German Democratic Republic

The reading public in the United States has not been exposed to a great
deal of East German literature. Authors like Christa Wolf (b. 1929),
Heiner Müller (b. 1929), Reiner Kunze (b. 1933), and Ulrich Plenzdorf
(b. 1934) have had a difficult time reaching the American reader in
spite of some very good translations. They have tended to remain in
the shadow of Bertolt Brecht (1898–1956), who returned from exile to
East Germany in 1949. For a long time, contemporary German literature
has been associated with West German writers like Heinrich Böll (b.
1917) and Günter Grass (b. 1927), the Swiss Max Frisch (b. 1911) and
Friedrich Dürrenmatt (b. 1921), the Austrian Peter Handke (b. 1942).
That noteworthy authors are also at work on the other side of the Berlin
Wall has only very slowly become known in the United States.

Attention has generally been directed toward the phenomenon of a
critical literature in a communist state rather than toward individual
writers. A great deal of the interest in reading East German works has
been motivated by the desire to learn something about conditions on
the other side of the Wall rather than by a curiosity about new aesthetic
impulses. Even if it is true that this literature has only laboriously freed
itself from the limits of socialist realism and is hardly innovative in a
formal sense, it is nevertheless a mistake to view it merely as a
documentation of conditions in the German Democratic Republic (GDR).
It is an artistically independent literature that plays an important role
in the German literary scene.

Writers, Readers, and the Party

East German literature differs in many respects from the literatures of
other communist countries. There is no need, even for the circulation

of politically undesirable texts, for a *samizdat* patterned after the underground press in the Soviet Union. Works that do not translate the official party line into literary language often appear simultaneously in East and West Germany. Works that are expressly critical of political conditions do not remain unpublished but appear in West Germany. From there, they then return to East Germany via television, radio, and other means.

In 1979 the state drastically reduced the possibilities for publication in the West, and a severe penalty was fixed for authors who circumvent the copyright office. The tension between writers and the state reached a high point at the time. This followed a period of temporary improvement during the early 1970s after Erich Honecker had succeeded Walter Ulbricht as chief of state. Wolf Biermann's (b. 1936) forced emigration in 1976 marked a turning point in the process. Although he proclaimed himself a Communist and supporter of the German Democratic Republic, Biermann had greatly annoyed the political establishment with his critical songs and satirical poems. The letter of protest against his forced emigration published by well-known writers like Christa Wolf, Jurek Becker (b. 1937), Sarah Kirsch (b. 1935), Volker Braun (b. 1939), Heiner Müller, Franz Fühmann (b. 1922), Stephan Hermlin (b. 1915), Stefan Heym (b. 1913), Günter Kunert (b. 1929), and Erich Arendt (b. 1903) produced a strong reaction by the party. Some writers were forced to accept serious obstacles to their work. Subsequently, numerous other artists and dramatists fled to West Germany; among them were the prominent poetess Sarah Kirsch, the dramatist Thomas Brasch (b. 1945), and the poet and prose writer Reiner Kunze. Kunze's sensitive criticism of the repressive everyday life in East Germany in *The Wonderful Years* (*Die wunderbaren Jahre,* 1977) has also been published in the United States.

The East German state has at times acted with severity against its critics, as in the cases of the scientist Robert Havemann (1910–1982) (*Dialectics Without Dogma; Dialektik ohne Dogma,* 1964) and the economist and party official Rudolf Bahro (b. 1935) (*The Alternative in Eastern Europe; Die Alternative,* 1977), who shook the foundations of the system. This severity gains plausibility from the unique position of the GDR in the Eastern bloc of nations. Apart from North Korea, it is the only state that must constantly confront the fact that a larger portion of the nation lives in a larger neighboring state that grants more political freedom and boasts a more productive economy. Poland, Hungary, and Czechoslovakia can take their national unity for granted even when liberalizing movements attempt to set in motion a reform of the state or of socialism. By contrast, the government in East Berlin must always keep in mind that every breach in the officially drawn limits between East and West can have unforeseeable consequences for the stability of the state. Thus it must often proceed in a more orthodox manner than its neighbors in the socialist sphere.

This orthodoxy has remained almost unchanged in spite of the intensified economic contacts brought about by the Eastern policies of the Federal Republic under Willy Brandt and Helmut Schmidt. On the contrary, the precondition for such close contacts is the special insulation from the West. Just as before, it is only the old people who are allowed to travel to West Germany and the political controls on all public remarks are very strict. With this repressive attitude, socialism has been as unsuccessful here as in Poland and Czechoslovakia in realizing its goals of a new socialist culture. The consequence of the public control of intellectual life has been an intense withdrawal into private spheres.

There is little of the revolutionary spirit recognizable in this withdrawal. It can be maintained that Lenin grounded his conception of cultural politics firmly on the continuation and reinterpretation of bourgeois traditions, since the revolutionary workers and peasants were still incapable of producing a proletarian culture. Yet he certainly would have rejected the tendency toward private concerns that is evident from East Berlin to Vladivostok. In this regard, there is nothing that the numerous official proclamations about the socialist cultural revolution can change. In the *actual* forms in which it has manifested itself in Eastern Europe, socialism has preserved a remarkable number of cultural traditions that are characteristic of bourgeois, capitalist society. Since World War II, modernization and a consumer mentality have destroyed many of these traditions under capitalism, yet they have retained special significance under communist regimes as the refuge of the individual. The poetic and intellectual value of a literary work, for example, is often more intensely felt in Eastern than in Western society, where market value is decisive. Almost every writer who has moved to the West has regretfully commented that it is much more difficult to genuinely move the reader there.

This difference was cogently summed up by Günter Kunert, a noted poet who had protested Wolf Biermann's forced emigration in 1976 and who then himself went to West Germany in 1979 after a long hesitation. In an article that appeared on November 24, 1979, under the title "I Could Scream, But No Longer Write" ("Ich konnte schreien, aber nicht mehr schreiben") in the *Frankfurter Allgemeine Zeitung*, a leading West German daily newspaper, he wrote:

> An author has a different significance for readers in the GDR and the Federal Republic. There exists in the GDR an interest fixed on literature that does not find a point of fixation anywhere else. The reader seeks for

something in literature that he cannot find elsewhere. This begins with information and extends to the transcendence of his existence—to point out that "something" in lofty language. The reader in the GDR is left to his own devices and thus somewhat helpless. He therefore searches in literature for reference to what has imprecisely been called the sense of existence. A demand is made of literature which it cannot fulfil since literature is not an article of faith nor a religion. Yet due to the circumstances, literature in the GDR is forced into a schizophrenic condition: it must yield something that is not inherent in it. So it too stands somewhat helpless in the face of the enormous expectations placed on it by readers. Yet the significance of literature is so extraordinary there precisely because these expectations are so diverse and so profound. This is one of the reasons that kept me in the GDR.

Kunert stressed that this attention naturally has a particularly beneficial effect for poetry, which in general has difficulty finding a reading public. Kunert also took up the matter of the exaggerated ideas in the West about the income of writers in the GDR, where the writer is also marketed in a certain sense:

There too the writer must do work that is not central to his interests in order to earn money. Thus I had to finance the writing of my poems. I have always had to be productive in another way. I worked in radio and, as long as it went well—that was a long time ago—in television. I have written films and done imitations of poetic works. In sum, a writer in the GDR must also involve himself in literary pandering if he wants to finish certain works that demand more time. Nothing is without a price tag.

It should be added that the breakthrough into the West German market has naturally been of great benefit for those East German writers willing to take the risk. Moreover, these writers have secured for themselves a certain freedom of movement with their earnings in West German currency, even though the state has skimmed off a large portion of it. Today as yesterday, this is still the great trauma of writers and artists as well as much of the population: to be shut in behind the Wall and to be unable to travel to Munich, Rome, or New York, while the news from such places daily flickers across the television screen. Armed with the increasing market value of their products and the resolutions of the Helsinki conference in 1975, writers have been able to obtain exit visas more easily. Yet they have been very careful not to be permanently banned to the West as troublesome critics but to retain their right to a return trip. On the other hand, a few unknown authors have acquired the publicity ensuring their works' success in the

West only by the spectacular circumstances of their emigration to West Germany. Such success, however, has never lasted very long.

This involvement with the West German market and public has been advantageous for Austrian and Swiss writers for many years. In the case of East German writers, it demonstrates how far removed from realization are the hopes of the party for a separate literature and culture. After the construction of the Berlin Wall in 1961, Walter Ulbricht provided enormous support to the program for building a socialist German national literature. In the 1960s, the German Democratic Republic achieved an amazing economic recovery, sometimes referred to as the "other German economic miracle." As the tenth largest economic power at the end of the 1960s, the GDR had won the respect of its own population. With the crises of the 1970s and the growing dependence on the Federal Republic, this image has, however, lost its timeliness. Dependence on the Federal Republic peaked when the West German deutsche mark was unofficially granted the status of a second currency. Among writers and literary critics, it is only official spokesmen who insist on the fundamental difference between the German-language literatures. Yet there are in fact certain distinctions between East and West German literature that stem from different political and social developments. These differences must be kept in mind so that works appearing in East Berlin, Leipzig, or Dresden will not be measured with a false yardstick.

Two Generations of Writers

Writers of the young generation, like Heinrich Böll, who began to write in West Germany after the war, declared the year 1945 to be a "zero point" from which a new German literature was to be reconstructed. In the Soviet occupation zone, on the other hand, the continuity with the leftist literature of the 1920s and 1930s was emphasized. Prominent representatives of the German left like the dramatists Bertolt Brecht and Friedrich Wolf (1888–1953), the poet Johannes R. Becher (1891–1958), and the philosopher Ernst Bloch (1885–1977), as well as the novelists Anna Seghers (1900–1983) and Arnold Zweig (1887–1968), returned to East Germany from exile and tried to pick up the threads of their earlier accomplishments. The preconditions for the development of a socialist literature in Germany seemed to be extremely favorable. Did the young generation of writers have to do anything more than to follow in the tracks of their elders? Were they not in a better position than the West German authors, who concealed their insecurity as debutants with the notion of a "zero point"?

The hopes for a new literary blossoming were not fulfilled. The most gripping and successful account of the Third Reich was by Bruno Apitz (1900–1979), an author who was otherwise silent. In a novel written as a documentary, *Naked Among Wolves* (*Nackt unter Wölfen,* 1958), Apitz reported his experiences as a prisoner in the concentration camp at Buchenwald, where he had belonged to a resistance group. Certain poems by Stephan Hermlin, Peter Huchel (1903–1981), Johannes R. Becher, and Erich Arendt gave impressive witness to the period of fascism, war, and exile. Anna Seghers, the author of momentous novels on Nazi Germany (*The Seventh Cross; Das siebte Kreuz,* 1942) and exile in France (*Transit; Transit,* 1944), was not able to match these early accomplishments with her novel *The Dead Stay Young* (*Die Toten bleiben jung,* 1949) and the works set in East Germany, *The Decision* (*Die Entscheidung,* 1959) and *Trust* (*Das Vertrauen,* 1968).

Several factors were responsible for the disappointing general development. Most prominent of these was Stalinism, which from 1948 on transplanted Soviet cultural policies to Germany. It brought so many restrictions with it for writers and artists that they were unable to develop new forms of expression. Even Brecht, the most famous of the emigrants who returned home, built up his world-renowned Berlin Ensemble in political isolation. It was closely watched by the party and repeatedly censored. Although they were praised outwardly in the interest of public relations, neither Brecht nor other writers were able to influence official cultural politics to any great degree. Brecht's epic theater began to make its impression on younger dramatists only after his untimely death in 1956. It was even longer before his late poetry, with its juxtaposition of encouragement and criticism of the new society, found a broad acceptance. The only writer who was able to influence official cultural policies was the former expressionist poet Johannes R. Becher, who became minister of culture in 1954. Becher had long since replaced the wildly exalted echoes of expressionism in his poetry with a sterile classicism. He nevertheless became aware of the problems of combining a critical poetry with an official post. During the period of thaw after Stalin's death in 1953 and especially at the time of the Hungarian uprising in 1956, Becher proved to be such a critical observer of events that he was subsequently the object of vigorous attacks by the party. He died in 1958.

Another reason for the creative impotence of the authors who returned was the dilemma of adjusting to the everyday realities of a destroyed Germany after their exile in the United States, France, Mexico, or the Soviet Union. It was, moreover, difficult to comprehend the mood of the Germans after the defeat of fascism. The writers' surprised reaction to the construction workers' strike on the Stalinallee on June 17, 1953, shows how little they understood the workers. The strike quickly spread across the entire country and set off tremors in the regime. On the other hand, the writers were among the most vocal critics of Stalinism during the Hungarian uprising in 1956. That revolt, which was brutally suppressed by the Soviets, was supported by the prominent Hungarian Marxist literary critic Georg Lukács (1885–1971). With the renewed callousness of Soviet cultural policies, however, the writers were unable to push through their ideas of a democratic socialism.

A third reason lies in the method by which the Communists settled accounts with fascism. Paradoxically, the problem was precisely the rapid denazification that made no compromises and went far beyond what the Western occupation forces undertook. The accounts of fascist crimes and the dismissal of thousands of teachers, judges, and officials who had served the Nazi regime for twelve years represented a tremendous accomplishment. The party and the occupying power, however, retained control of this purging and declared the end of fascism in East Germany. The economic explanation formulated by the Communist International in 1935 was held to be the definition of fascism: Fascism is the "openly terroristic dictatorship of the most reactionary, the most chauvinistic and the most imperialistic elements of finance capital." The antifascist attitude of the new government was thus established. The question was left entirely unanswered, however, how the Germans who populated the new socialist state could have submitted to Hitler and remained subjects to him for twelve years. Most important, the topic of how the individual had experienced and "mastered" National Socialism and the war remained undiscussed. "We have turned our backs much too soon on the immediate past in our eagerness to turn to the future," Brecht remarked in 1953. "The future will depend, however, on our settlement with the past." Alongside the official settlement of the past, the party left little room for the individual confrontation in literature.

The emancipation of the new literary generation was accordingly less successful than in West Germany, where the Group 47 established itself on the basis of an individual reckoning with the past. For East German writers, socialist reconstruction was the prescribed pursuit. Of the younger generation, only Franz Fühmann was successful in treating the themes of fascism and war from an independent point of view, immune to the demands of socialist realism. His story "The Jews' Auto" ("Das Judenauto," 1962) became well known. It depicts in several episodes the changes of a young man from the Nazi era to his integration into the socialist state. Fühmann is particularly adept at breathing life into the seduction of the petite bourgeoisie by Nazi slogans. His stories also draw upon numerous motifs from fairy tales. Fühmann has become one of the great German prose writers.

Johannes Bobrowski (1917–1965), a slightly older writer who during World War II was already writing poetry, has consistently situated the theme of war and German guilt toward the Eastern populations at the center of his works. His novel *Levin's Mill* (*Levins Mühle,* 1964) became a model for the turning of East German authors away from the clichés of reconstruction to the sensitive depiction of individual experience. In a totally personal tone of apparent self-absorption, Bobrowski develops in these "34 Sentences About My Grandfather" a landscape of provincial culture in West Prussia, enlivened by its German, Jewish, and Polish elements. The author pursues the guilt of the Germans in the relationship of the two protagonists, the rich German mill owner and the Jew Levin. He shows how his grandfather gets rid of his Jewish competitor by unfair methods and continues to play the role of a man of integrity. Bobrowski's depiction is not by means of straight narrative but through dialogue and reflection, including reflection on language itself.

Bobrowski is among the prominent East German poets, along with Becher, Brecht, and Peter Huchel. With his seemingly complicated metaphors and sentence constructions that are permeated by various temporal levels and motifs, he has developed a poetically restrained tone that is commensurate with the oppressive theme of German guilt. The poetry collections *Sarmatian Time* (*Sarmatische Zeit,* 1960) and *Rivers of the Hereafter* (*Schattenland Ströme,* 1962) belong unmistakably to the German lyrical tradition since Hölderlin. As often as Bobrowski's poems give expression to moral admonitions, they are nevertheless radically different from the critically sober admonitory poems of Brecht, which often tend toward the satirical.

Brecht's influence on the younger generation of East German poets cannot be overestimated. These authors, who grew up in the GDR, learned together with him how to avoid the schematism of official agitation as well as the classicism of Becher without giving up the political message. Brecht created a poetic language that made of everyday experience material for timely criticism and future hopes. His *Buckow Elegies* (*Buckower Elegien,* 1953) are apparently very private impressions, yet they point unmistakably to the political changes in Germany. That Brecht was fully aware of the problems of the communist state in Germany is obvious in the often-quoted poem "The Solution" ("Die Lösung," 1953). He commented in the following clever lines on the fact that the workers themselves had rebelled against the workers' government on June 17, 1953:

After the uprising of the 17th June
The Secretary of the Writers' Union
Had leaflets distributed in the Stalinallee

Stating that the people
Had forfeited the confidence of the government
And could win it back only
By redoubled efforts. Would it not be easier
In that case for the government
To dissolve the people
And elect another?

Authors like Günter Kunert, Wolf Biermann, and Karl Mickel (b. 1935) have followed this lead in developing a new poetic vocabulary whose reflective attitude raises questions about the directness and banality of official communications.

This influence reached its peak effect, however, only around the mid-1960s. At first, the younger writers concentrated on the positive aspects of the socialist reconstruction and imitated models of Soviet novels of socialist realism from the 1930s and 1950s. Important stimuli for bringing literature together with the sphere of work came from the "Bitterfeld Way," a program named after Bitterfeld, the site of a decisive conference. Even party chief Walter Ulbricht, alongside cultural politician Alfred Kurella, joined in the discussion. It focused primarily on two goals. The first was to encourage workers themselves to write and lay the foundation for a socialist culture. Secondly, writers were to be sent into the factories in order to familiarize them with the workers' reality and to inspire new works of socialist realism. It was not long before it became clear that a new socialist literature was not going to develop on this basis, even if authors like Erik Neutsch (b. 1931) (*Track of Stones; Spur der Steine,* 1964) did open up the much-discussed access to the workaday world.

There was, however, one novel inspired by the Bitterfeld Way that broke down the world of clichés about the socialist worker-hero. The work kindled the first widespread public discussion of the new literature in which the opinions of the young generation were heard. The novel *The Divided Heaven (Der geteilte Himmel,* 1963) was the first longer prose work by Christa Wolf, who drew on her own work experiences in a factory that produced railroad cars. Wolf portrays her heroine Rita as she completes her internship in the factory and hesitatingly approaches the world of work. The central theme, however, aims well beyond this. It concerns the attitude, pro and con, of a young woman toward the East German Republic at a time before the Berlin Wall had made a freely chosen departure impossible. Rita travels to West Berlin to her fiancé, Manfred, who has left the GDR and now asks her to live in the West with him. She says no—as it turns out, only a few days before the erection of the Wall on August 13, 1961. After her return, Rita attempts to commit suicide between two railroad cars. The book begins when she wakes up in the hospital and recounts her attempt to justify the decision to remain in East Germany without her fiancé.

The critics took particular aim at the relatively positive portrayal of Manfred and the love story superimposed on the political decision. Less attention was paid to the artistic weaknesses of the book. With its trite optimism and romantic images, it was doubtless just a beginning. To some extent it was modeled on short stories in the Soviet Union that depicted the escape of youth from the regimented everyday world of Stalinism at the end of the 1950s. In glorifying youthful individualism, Anatoli Kuznetsov, Vasili Aksenov, Chingiz Aitmatov, and other Soviet writers had, with clamorous public approval, questioned the regimentation of socialist realism. The Soviet poet Evgeny Evtushenko had a comparable effect in the Khrushchev era with his lively public readings that took on the character of mass demonstrations. The "poetry wave" that also affected East Germany at the beginning of the 1960s was accompanied by this simultaneously critical and optimistic tone.

Soon after Christa Wolf's *The Divided Heaven*, Hermann Kant (b. 1926) greatly widened the developmental possibilities of realism in East Germany with his first novel *The Great Hall* (*Die Aula*, 1965). Kant too placed youth at the center of his novel. The narrator of the work, the journalist Robert Iswall, is slated to deliver a speech to his former classmates about their student days in the department for workers and peasants. Here young workers had been trained since 1949 to be teachers, scientists, and engineers. Iswall does not give his speech, but writes the book instead. Ten years earlier, it would have become a socialist heroic epic. Instead of the stereotypical description of the construction of the GDR, Kant produced a humorous depiction, richly episodic and full of allusions, of a group of young people.

Other young authors also liberated themselves from the regimentation of the Stalin era by writing about youth. In the theater, an energetic, high-spirited style came into fashion that increasingly deviated from Brechtian classicism. Peter Hacks (b. 1928) and Heiner Müller, dramatists who had learned from Brecht, experimented with a combination of socialist classicism and irreverent youthfulness. These attempts found little support, however, from the guardians of the existing socialist system. The writers' efforts to ground socialism in the spontaneity of a new generation less encumbered by Stalinism seemed generally suspect to the party. Works by Peter Hacks (*Cares and Power; Die Sorgen und die Macht,* 1958; *Moritz Tassow,* 1961) were dropped from the theatrical repertoire. Those by Müller were not even allowed into production at the time. In *Cares and Power,* Hacks depicts the conflict between two factories. One, a briquette factory, constantly delivers an inferior product in order to achieve the goals of the plan. The other, a glass factory, is dependent on these briquettes. The conflict comes to a head in the relationship of the briquette worker Fidorra to the glass worker Hede Stoll. Although Hacks imitated closely the structure of the problems in the officially produced works, his realistic depiction of workers nevertheless was little appreciated in the ruling party, the Socialist Unity party (SED). Instead of involving themselves wholeheartedly with communism, the workers in the drama are interested mainly in money, food, drink, and sex.

Heiner Müller's examination of attitudes toward reconstruction in the GDR was even more critical. *The Sweatshop Worker* (*Der Lohndrücker,* 1956) portrayed the difficult years after 1945; the theme of *The Building* (*Der Bau,* 1964) was the transition from the centrally planned economy of the 1950s to the less bureaucratic economy of the 1960s. With themes borrowed from Erik Neutsch's novel *Track of Stones, The Building* focuses on the conflicts of an "anarchistically" inclined foreman with the orthodox thinking of a dynamic party secretary.

Achievements and Disillusionment in the 1970s

The fall of Nikita Khrushchev from power in 1964 brought an end to "liberalized" cultural politics everywhere in Eastern Europe. In East Germany, the eleventh plenum of the Central Committee of the SED in December 1965 represented the turning point. Literature has undergone a marked change since the second half of the 1960s, when most of the innovations of the seventies were introduced. Two elements in particular that are closely bound together have characterized this development. In the first place, the party looked on literature much less than before as an ally in its endeavor to effect social change. Literature was considered to an even lesser degree as a "transmission belt" for passing on the ambitious reconstruction program to the population, especially the youth. The scientific and technological revolution—catchwords of the 1960s— had in the meantime developed its own dynamics, which were less dependent on such support. Moreover, television had moved to the center of public interest in East Germany. The party saw in television an instrument more effective than literature for spreading its conception of a socialist society. At the end of the 1960s, during the period of television's greatest popularity, several series were aired on the successful construction of the GDR. The central figure was generally the innovative factory hero who prevails over the resistance of his coworkers. He helps them gain a new confidence in their work and in socialist society. Literature, on the other hand, with its reflection on individual existence, was considered by Ulbricht as a source of disagreeable criticism of the socialist state. Even Hermann Kant, who was anything but an opponent of the government and who became president of the writers' union in the 1970s was unable to publish his novel *The Imprint* (*Das Impressum*) in 1969. The work was to be a stocktaking for the twentieth anniversary of the founding of the GDR, but the ironic reflections of the main character, chief editor David Groth, proved to be too insolent for the authorities.

The second element bound up in the literary change occurring in the mid-1960s had to do with the writers' realization of the restrictive cultural policies under which they worked. They recognized that they had turned into a blind alley with the attempts to project a new, more youthful, more imaginative version of socialism. The suppression of the "Prague spring" in Czechoslovakia in 1968 also drew the attention of the West to the destruction of their hopes. They now turned more emphatically to the problems of the individual in society.

This retreat into introspection can be traced most clearly in the development of Christa Wolf. In 1968 she published the novel *The Quest for Christa T.* (*Nachdenken über Christa T.*). However, so few copies were printed that the novel was not widely available. The book is fundamentally different from the methodical works of socialist realism in its reflective form of sensitive recollections. Its heroine, Christa T., is a young woman who, in a society of heroes and fighters, prefers to be an antiheroine and to seek self-fulfillment in her own way. Before her death from leukemia, Christa T. had been a friend of the author, who now tries to track down the secret of her life's story. It did not escape the party bureaucrats that the resignation expressed here by the author of *The Divided Heaven* was a very critical commentary on the possibilities for individual fulfillment in the East German state. Like Kant's *The Imprint*, this novel was published in a large edition only under Erich Honecker. In the meantime, its sales had soared in the Federal Republic.

Christa Wolf turned to fascism as a theme in her next book, *A Model Childhood* (*Kindheitsmuster*, 1976), and ran up against criticism once more. Again she develops her subject in the very personal form of recollections. On the occasion of a trip to her homeland, she recalls her childhood during the Nazi era, when she grew up well protected and without an awareness of the crimes being committed around her. Her thesis is that the black-white, good-evil paradigm of antifascism is not sufficient for the analysis of what went on in Germany prior to 1945. She shows through her own example how little the experience of fascism and its crimes have been psychologically digested. With her reflections on guilt, Christa Wolf hit upon a delicate problem that the

East Germans have in general avoided by assuming that those guilty of fascism were living in West Germany.

Heiner Müller pursued the same theme on the stage in the 1970s with starkly contrasting images and scenes. The playwright treats the German past as the great trauma of the present in the plays *The Battle* (*Die Schlacht,* 1974), *Germania: Death in Berlin* (*Germania Tod in Berlin,* 1976), and *The Life of Gundling: Friedrich of Prussia Lessing's Sleep Death Scream* (*Leben Gundlings Friedrich von Preussen Lessings Schlaf Tod Schrei,* 1977). In place of Brecht's classicism, he opts for the heavily instinctual, almost psychoanalytic theatrical action of Antonin Artaud. German history is represented as the progressive deformation of the human instinctual structure, as the fateful development from positive creativity to the horrifying production of death. The question intended by the author forces itself into the mind of the audience: What will come from a socialist system that is developing from such rudiments?

Other writers have brought the traumata of recent German history to life in a less shocking way. But this approach cannot veil the reality of the poets' deep involvement in formulating their disappointment about the shortcomings of the socialist experiment in Germany. Among those who stand out are Günter Kunert and Sarah Kirsch, who in the meantime have both emigrated to the West. Kunert, whose poems are often thematic reworkings of recent history, makes no secret of the resignation and growing historical pessimism in his later works. Along with Christa Wolf and Irmtraut Morgner (b. 1933), Sarah Kirsch has become an impressive spokeswoman for the social and literary self-liberation of women in East Germany. Her poems focus with particular intensity on the introspective scrutiny of the self. Included in this scrutiny are the everyday political realities of the GDR that are sifted for possibilities of identification and poetic hopes. The introspective process finally ends in unsettled resignation. It is often impossible to separate erotic and political disappointment. This is the case even in the apparently simple yet difficult poem "Black Beans" ("Schwarze Bohnen") from the volume *Incantations* (*Zaubersprüche,* 1973):

Afternoons I grind coffee
Afternoons I assemble the ground coffee
Backwards pretty
Black beans
Afternoons I undress dress
First make up then I wash
sing am mute

The criticism of conditions in East Germany does not mean, however, that authors like Kunert and Kirsch consider life in the West any less critically. By emigrating they sought conditions of undisturbed literary activity, not the subjection of their writings to yet new political guidelines. Moreover, the alienation of the individual in the achievement-oriented society, a central theme of many writers, is apparent even beyond the borders. East German authors have been successful with this theme in the East and the West, especially after Erich Honecker's succession of Ulbricht in 1971 brought new breathing space for criticism.

The most spectacular success in the East and West German theater was won by a play that depicts a restrained version of the international youth revolt. With his *The New Sorrows of Young W.* (*Die neuen Leiden des jungen W.,* 1972), Ulrich Plenzdorf made obvious reference to Goethe's scandal-filled success *The Sorrows of Young Werther* (*Die Leiden des jungen Werthers,* 1774), at the same time capturing with incredible facility the adolescent jargon of the jeans generation around 1970. The modern play also depicts a love triangle between a couple and an odd-man-out who dies at the end. Unlike the situation in Goethe's work, however, his death, even though it appears to be (almost) inevitable, is accidental, not a suicide. The hero, Edgar Wibeau, dies in the process of testing an apparatus for spray painting that he had built for his work brigade of painters. His death, a theme that had long been taboo in East German literature, comes about in the course of an experiment that was to benefit society. Thus it really presented no challenge to the party line. Controversy was aroused, however, by the impertinent allusions to the "classical literary heritage" the SED so conscientiously cultivates. Another source of offense was criticism of the socialist society by a youthful outsider in jeans who took great pride in *not* complying with approved public norms.

Like Christa Wolf's *The Divided Heaven* ten years earlier, Plenzdorf's work opened up new arguments in the discussion of socialist literature. The center of discussion was the question to what extent the author could neglect the bias advocated in socialist realism in order to ferret out the reality of the situation. This discussion showed just how little relevance the program of socialist realism still had for writers. Arguments Brecht had used against Lukács in the 1930s finally found a broad consensus. Brecht's goal, in contrast to that of the Hungarian Marxist, whose theory was dominant in the GDR for a long time, was not a system of realism representing a part of the systematic thinking of Marxism. Brecht strove for a realism that could be dialectically developed from each actual situation and even included modern forms of montage. He exposed the tension between idea and reality and sought to alienate the familiar and commonplace so that the possibility of change might be apprehended. For orthodox Marxists, however, this procedure opened all too many possibilities for criticism and "deviation." The planned conference on realism, which was to have provided official clarity on these matters, was never held.

Brecht was also a source of important arguments in the discussion of the "classical heritage" that was kindled by Plenzdorf's work. In the leading literary journals *Sinn und Form* (Meaning and Form) and *Weimarer Beiträge* (Contributions from Weimar), critics and proponents of an intensive cultivation of the classical literature of Goethe and Schiller confronted one another. Under Stalin this cultivation had been dogmatically turned against modern aesthetics and granted absolute authority. The departure of Ulbricht in 1971 also played a great role in this debate. He had wanted to create the new culture of the GDR as a new classicism. At the beginning of the 1970s, Brecht's writings dealt crippling blows to this sort of anachronistic thinking. Although he became a self-styled classical writer in his late years, he never intended to obscure his spirit of contradiction in the billowing mists of hallowed incense.

Due to Honecker's liberal cultural policies after 1971, it became possible for the novelist Stefan Heym to receive the recognition he deserved in the GDR. As a former emigrant to the United States, he had written the best-selling novels *Hostages* (*Der Fall Glasenapp*, 1958) and *The Crusaders* (*Kreuzfahrer von Heute*, 1950, GDR; *Bitterer Lorbeer*, 1966, FRG). He was permitted to publish his veiled treatment of the barbaric methods of authoritarianism in *The King David Report* (*Der König David Bericht*, 1972); nor did he hold back in his criticism of the actual state of socialism to which he had voluntarily returned during the McCarthy era. Younger authors like Jurek Becker (*Jakob the Liar; Jakob der Lügner*, 1970) and Volker Braun (*Unfinished Story; Unvollendete Geschichte*, 1975) gained a wide reputation at the time. Others like Karl-Heinz Jakobs (b. 1929) (*The Interviewers; Die Interviewer*, 1973) and Günter de Bruyn (b. 1926) (*Buridan's Ass; Buridans Esel*, 1968; *The Awarding of Prizes; Preisverleihung*, 1972) freed their prose from the clichés of socialist realism and produced detailed depictions of everyday life.

Above all, it was Braun's *Unfinished Story* in *Sinn und Form* that caused a sensation in 1975. When Karin, the heroine of the narrative, picks up Plenzdorf's *The New Sorrows of Young W.*, an interesting comment is made: "Just the word 'sorrows' in the title was horrifying enough. It was in the newspaper, that the author was trying to 'impose' his own sorrows on society. That would be novel, she now thought, that the sorrow of the individual would disturb society." But this is precisely what happens in the events that befall Karin. Frank, the man she loves, does not correspond, as an outsider, to the moral and ideological precepts of her parents and the party. Almost like in Schiller's *Love and Intrigue*

(*Kabale und Liebe,* 1784), the lovers rise up in defiant rebellion against society. Braun leaves the story "unfinished"; i.e., he refuses to reconcile the conflicts at the end where socialist realism prescribes harmonization.

Among the women writers, besides Sarah Kirsch (*The Panther Woman; Die Pantherfrau,* 1974), Brigitte Reimann (1933–1973) (*Franziska Linkerhand,* 1973), and Gerti Tetzner (b. 1936) (*Karen W.,* 1974) have made it plain how dependent the woman still is in socialist society. In opposition to the official demand for the integration of the individual, they are making the private demand of independent self-realization. Irmtraut Morgner has set in motion an entire panorama of fantastic narrative motifs in the voluminous *The Life and Achievements of the Troubador Beatriz According to the Testimony of Her Accompanist Laura* (*Leben und Abenteuer der Troubadora Beatriz nach Zeugnissen ihrer Spielfrau Laura,* 1974) in order to illuminate the often-acclaimed emancipation of the woman under medieval and modern conditions.

Subjectivity, which attained new meaning in the West with the adjective "new" during the 1970s, has become the basis in all of these works of a self-consciously critical literature. Just as in the West, the question is how the individual can find self-realization in a modern society in which everything from morning to evening, including free time, is regulated. It has long been evident that socialism has no better answers here than capitalism. In 1963, during a celebrated conference on Kafka, East German critics still defended the opinion that Kafka's description of loneliness and alienation was valid only for life under capitalism. This assertion is made today only by wholly orthodox Communists.

The relationship of East German writers to the West German public would not, however, have become so close if the party had not pushed authors in the direction of the West even more strongly with its restrictive policies after the Biermann affair in 1976. What at first appeared to be an interesting market for books often became a place of refuge at the end of the 1970s.

Wolf Biermann had been under house arrest for years. In contrast to the poets Karl Mickel, Günter Kunert, Volker Braun, and Sarah Kirsch, who commented on life in East Germany in the sometimes difficult language of the modern poem, Biermann created an easily intelligible and popular song form in the tradition of Heine and the early Brecht. With his witty formulations of the contradictions between the claims and reality of socialism in the GDR, he provoked the enmity of the party even though he called himself a Communist. Characteristically, he reversed the charges that are normally aimed at the individual. His poem "Reckless Abuse" ("Rücksichtslose Schimpferei") in the 1965 volume *The Wire Harp* (*Die Drahtharfe*) is a good example:

I, I, I
Am full of hate
Am full of hardness
My head's been cut in two
My brain has been run over

I don't want to see anyone!
Don't just stand there!
Stop staring!
The Collective is on the wrong track

I am the individual
The Collective has become isolated from me
Don't glare at me so understandingly!
Oh yes, I know very well
You're waiting with earnest certitude
For me to swim
Into the net of self-criticism

But I am the pike!
You'll have to maul me, hack me to bits
Put me through a meat grinder
If you want me on bread!

The party refrained from putting Biermann through the meat grinder. He was simply deprived of his citizenship during a tour in West Germany that had unexpectedly been agreed to. The protest other East German writers raised made enormous waves. It rendered the party momentarily speechless and demonstrated that it had no model for its confrontation with the new literature of socialist writers—at least none that deserved the name "socialist."

Readings

Flores, John. *Poetry in East Germany. Adjustments, Visions, and Provocations, 1945–1970.* New Haven: Yale University Press, 1971.

Gerber, Margy, ed. *Studies in GDR Culture and Society.* Washington, D.C.: University Press of America, Vol. 1 (1981), Vol. 2 (1982).

Hedlin, Irene Artes. *The Individual in a New Society. A Study of Selected "Erzählungen" and "Kurzgeschichten" of the GDR from 1965 to 1972.* Bern: Peter Lang, 1977.

Huebener, Theodore. *The Literature of East Germany.* New York: Frederick Ungar, 1970.

Huettich, H. G. *Theater in the Planned Society. Contemporary Drama in the GDR in Its Historical, Political, and Cultural Context*. Chapel Hill: University of North Carolina Press, 1978.

Hutchinson, Peter. *Literary Presentations of Divided Germany. The Development of a Central Theme in East German Fiction 1945–1970*. Cambridge: Cambridge University Press, 1977.

MANFRED K. WOLFRAM

16

Film in the Federal Republic of Germany

When on April 14, 1980, Hollywood's Academy of Motion Picture Arts and Sciences awarded its prestigious Oscar for the best foreign film to Volker Schlöndorff's *The Tin Drum* (*Die Blechtrommel*, 1979), a remarkable achievement had been spotlighted and internationally acknowledged: the New German Cinema (*Neuer Deutscher Film*).

The evolution of the New German Cinema (NGC) in the Federal Republic of Germany (FRG) has been painful. Uncertain of its direction, many times doubtful of whether it would subsist at all, the troublesome growth began to sprout on February 28, 1962, at the 8th Oberhausen Short Film Festival. The Oberhausen Manifesto evolved during six formative and incisive days, carrying the signatures of twenty-six directors who noisily and provocatively demanded a radical departure from the prevailing film establishment. They announced their desire and right to create an uncompromising new German feature film industry. The established film industry was condemned for being too strongly influenced by predominantly American commercial interest groups and for adhering exclusively to safe, conventional film forms and styles. "The old film is dead, we believe in the new one" became the credo of the Oberhausen Manifesto, and its signatories proclaimed the birth of the Young German Cinema (*Junger Deutscher Film*).

Early Years

Indeed, there was plenty to lament in the 1950s and early 1960s concerning the state of the film industry in the FRG. At the 1961 Berlin International Film Festival there was no prize for a best German film—there simply was no outstanding German film. The West German film industry seemed to have exhausted its artistic and intellectual resources. Surprisingly, since the end of World War II no systematic artistic attempt had been witnessed in the FRG that could have related its emerging film culture to the filmic achievements of German expressionism in the cinema of the Weimar period (1919–1929), milestones in film art and history.

With the creation of the Federal Republic of Germany on May 23, 1949, when the Basic Law went into effect, the era of the German postwar film (*Deutscher Nachkriegsfilm*, 1949–1962) began. The people of the FRG got busy rebuilding their cities and factories, and produced an economic miracle that impressed the industrial world. German industriousness and quality craftsmanship were gradually reaffirmed and accepted by the world community.

In 1955 the FRG feature film industry reached its peak of production. A total of 128 West German films were released during that year. In 1956 over 817 million people visited the movie theaters, and by 1959 a total of 7,085 movie houses existed in the FRG. These figures are indeed impressive, and they generated a tremendous capital return from film investments. Yet, on a qualitative level, the West German film industry released very mediocre products. The genre of the homeland film (*Heimatfilm*) reestablished itself very early. A prototype for this postwar genre is the movie *Green Is the Heath* (*Grün ist die Heide*, 1951), which offers a most unproblematic plot to the movie-going audience. Happy country folks in idyllic surroundings feel sheltered in an ordered world. Ludwig Ganghofer's *Hubertus Castle* (*Schloss Hubertus*, 1954) celebrates Bavaria's tourist trappings, indulging filmically in the proverbially idyllic charm of the Black Forest. Variations of this genre comprise the cycle of "Sissy" films (1955–1957) starring Romy Schneider. Set in imperial Austria, these films evoked a fairy-tale world that was heartily endorsed by the movie-going public's sympathy and support. In succeeding years, detective thrillers and Karl May westerns were added to this type of film. All of them are unproblematic in their themes, soliciting mindless diversion. They were complemented by older and newer Hollywood movies dubbed into German. Artistically and intellectually, this film repertoire was indeed dismal.

The West German public certainly did not need to get engaged politically in or through these films. The thesis has been advanced that, subliminally, the West Germans could not face their immediate past, which had traumatized the civilized world. Questions of guilt and conspiracy, and of the crimes of Nazi Germany, were suppressed by the citizens of the economic-miracle state, judging by their responses to media productions. Yet several exceptions had existed since the immediate postwar years. These films foreshadowed noticeable steps of a people on a path toward new democratic autonomy and maturity.

The fate of Germany in 1945 rested with the United States, Britain, and France in the west and the Soviet Union in the east, dividing Germany, respectively, into the western and eastern occupational zones. The elaborate film production facilities of the former UFA (Universum Film, AG, or Universal Film Company), centralized administrative support facilities, and production studios were under Soviet control. In November 1945, at the request and direction of the Soviets, all UFA production facilities were reorganized and nationalized to become DEFA (Deutsche Film AG, or German Film Company) in May 1946. DEFA productions were released relatively soon and distributed in *all* the occupational zones. Among them one finds Wolfgang Staudte's (b. 1906) *The Murderers Are Among Us* (*Die Mörder sind unter uns,* 1946). The subject of the film is the prosecution and trial of a now decent, honest citizen who had committed crimes during the war years. The Americans recalled Erich Pommer (1889–1966) from the United States to become film commissioner. Pommer had been a distinguished UFA film producer during the height of the German cinema of the Weimar period (1919–1929). He had produced the famous *Cabinet of Dr. Caligari* (*Das Cabinet des Dr. Caligari*) in 1919. One of the first films released in the western zones was Helmut Käutner's (b. 1925) *In Former Days* (*In jenen Tagen,* 1947). The director attempted to illuminate the Nazi years by exemplifying the fate of an old motorcar as it changes hands seven times.

Many films released shortly after the war dealt with Germany's immediate past and present; they are classified as rubble films (*Trümmerfilm,* 1945–1949). Among the distinguished foreign directors who were attracted to shoot a rubble film in Germany was Roberto Rossellini, father of the neorealist film movement in Italy. His *Germany, Year Zero* (1947) recorded some extraordinary footage of life in the ruins of Berlin. For the Germans themselves, rubble films depicted too mimetically their devastated, impoverished lives. Rubble films, therefore, did not draw large audiences when compared to the later homeland films.

The realization of total defeat, unconditional surrender, and the inescapable and at the same time unimaginable truth of the atrocities committed by Germans in the name of Germany had to be faced at a time when day-to-day survival of each individual was uncertain. The German audience clearly preferred movies promising a brief respite from this dreadful existence. The Italian and French movie-going public were not much different in this respect. Neorealism did not find an immediately responsive audience in Italy either. Successful evolution of this filmic movement was due to favorable acceptance in the United States. The majority of the movie-going public there had not experienced directly the total devastation of war as had the Europeans. The American public and its critics hailed neorealist films as honest portrayals of human postwar tragedy and discovered in them the potential of a new filmic form. The French public witnessed its major postwar film development as late as 1958 with the ascendance of the New Wave.

On October 7, 1949, the Soviets founded the German Democratic Republic (GDR), responding to the creation of the Federal Republic of Germany (FRG) by the Western Allies. The premise for the division of Germany into two ideologically incompatible states had thus been established. The two Germanys developed separately, causing an indomitable quest for national identity by the people of this divided country.

From the early 1950s, DEFA film releases in the GDR had to undergo the closest supervision by the ruling Communist party and its leaders. Attempts to deviate from established party guidelines were severely reprimanded. Film productions in the GDR were to serve as didactic devices to educate the public on the inevitable class struggle between communism and capitalism, and the constant threat from the West. Pending the degree of security and public support the East German government imagined to possess among its people, this position was more or less visibly enforced. Brief moments of apparent creative freedom granted to East German filmmaking talents have to be understood as concessions to appease a rebellious public until tight party control could be reestablished. Any classification of GDR films into "antifascism," "socialist realism," "socialist contemporary" (enhanced by a "human approach"), or "documentary realism" (a blend of *cinéma vérité* and neorealism) in order to appraise them in the context of filmic, artistic development in the GDR falls short of accepting their primary purpose: to function as propagandistic art to promote the German Communist party or state. Filmic development in the GDR since its inception has been negligible. The East German cinematic "miracle," debated in the Western world in the early 1970s, remained a mirage. *Jacob the Liar* (*Jakob der Lügner,* 1975), directed by Frank Beyer, was the first East German film production ever presented at the West Berlin International Film Festival (1976). Very few East German releases have since reached movie houses in the West.

In West Germany, an evolving group of intellectuals fought the public's escapism during the postwar era. Setting out to create an honest film culture in the FRG, Hilmar Hoffmann in 1954 created the Oberhausen Short Film Festival. During the following years, this festival became the platform for the nonestablished young experimental filmmakers. In 1959 Haro Senft (b. 1927) and Ferdinand Khittl introduced the workshop DOC '59 at the festival. DOC '59 might be regarded as the initial formative stage of the gathering storm that was to unfold at Oberhausen in 1962. The importance of these professional meetings cannot be overemphasized. The young German filmmakers did not have access to a past they could draw upon, artistically, intellectually, or from the point of view of craftsmanship. Film production in Nazi Germany (1933–1945) was designed to advocate party objectives. Nazi cinema distinguished itself by degrading human beings into faceless, uniform masses of relentlessly marching, monotonous columns. Man blended into machines, ever thrusting forward. Finally, brutality and destruction through war were glorified and mystically embellished as the natural order of things. When this horror came to an end Germany had been reduced to ashes. The new filmmakers grew up in a filmic void. Models for these aspiring young German film directors had to be searched for in foreign countries.

In the interim, older film directors released several films that suggested a more responsible, mature, and pensive plot structure than the staple fare. In 1959 Wolfgang Staudte directed *Roses for the State Prosecutor* (*Rosen für den Staatsanwalt*), and Kurt Hoffmann's (b. 1910) *The Prodigies* (*Wir Wunderkinder*, 1958) was introduced the previous year. Both movies deal with former Nazis who had gained respectability and influence in the court system or the industrial section of the young but frail Federal Republic. In 1960 Staudte was honored with the Federal Film Prize (*Bundesfilmpreis*) for his film, but he refused to accept it. In 1959 Bernhard Wicki (b. 1919) directed *The Bridge* (*Die Brücke*), which can be regarded as West Germany's first contribution to antiwar movies. Although this film was very successful on the national and international markets, it ultimately failed by not addressing itself to the causes of World War II. Herbert Vesely (b. 1931) in 1961 chose Heinrich Böll's postwar novel *The Bread of the Early Years* (*Das Brot der frühen Jahre*) for filmic adaptation. The film was very well received in the FRG and was also commercially successful. It brought Vesely the Federal Film Prize in 1962.

The various attempts by committed film directors, however, did not seriously challenge the mindless entertainment movies produced by the established film industry. This industry, nevertheless, by the end of the 1950s had suffered a different and severe setback. The public began to stay at home. Decline in attendance at movie houses was directly proportional to the increase in the number of television sets purchased and hours spent watching television programs in the homes of West German citizens. By 1967, only 250 million visitors paid admission to see movies, representing a drop of 75 percent when compared to 1956. The industry tried to regain a portion of the movie entertainment market by flooding it with "soft porn flicks." Schoolgirl and housewife stories now seemed to occupy the minds of the average movie-goer. Since television could not broadcast this material into private homes, the sex wave could have turned the tide for the film industry. It did not. Entropy had set in, and only radical treatment could cure the FRG's film production.

Rebellion

Desperation and frustration were voiced at the 8th Oberhausen Short Film Festival on February 28, 1962. The young filmmakers regarded the apparent failure of the FRG's official film industry as proof of moral decay. They attacked the irresponsible, exploitative attitude of private and commercial interest groups. In their stead, they proclaimed the Young German Cinema. The twenty-six signatories of the Oberhausen Manifesto declared their intention to take the initiative in the reconstruction of the German feature film industry. Among them were Alexander Kluge (b. 1932), Edgar Reitz (b. 1932), Herbert Vesely, and Haro Senft. They had come of age through shorts and experimental and feature films. Their oeuvre and its gradual artistic acceptance at national and international film festivals, shown by the film prizes they received, provided these filmmakers with the necessary conviction that they could have a decisive influence upon the future of the German film.

The position of the *Jungfilmer* (first-generation filmmakers), however, was actually precarious. The established film industry, although in severe jeopardy, did not acknowledge defeat. It did not welcome the opportunity for a breath of fresh air. "Grandpa's film" (*Opas Kino*) was not quite dead, and the "kid's film" (*Bubis Kino*) was not yet quite established. The schism between old and new, projected so vividly to the public, left traces of distrust and hostility among the factions involved. In spite of their dynamic rhetoric, the *Jungfilmer* needed role models and direction. In the FRG, where no significant intellectual filmic debate had existed during the years of the German postwar film, there were no models to emulate.

Neighboring France, however, offered the flourishing New Wave (*nouvelle vague*). Movies of Chabrol, Resnais, and Godard found their way into West German movie houses in 1960. Their impact was immediate. Many of these young French directors had worked as film critics for the well-established French journal *Cahiers du Cinéma* before they began to make movies. The chief editor of the journal was the already legendary André Bazin. A closely knit group of prominent intellectuals began to reconstruct the French movie scene, which, up to 1958, had generally been as superficial as that in West Germany. They propagated the notion of the "author's film" (*cinéma d'auteur,* or *Autorenfilm* in German), which was pursued by the directors of the

New Wave. French film critics acknowledged the artistic contribution of various film directors who left a significant imprint (style, signature) upon their oeuvre. Their film camera was equated with the pen (*caméra stylo*), the traditional tool of the literary author. The film director, or "author," was elevated to the position of creator, situated in and drawing upon the cultural life of a given society. The young filmmakers embraced this rich perspective, as voiced by Edgar Reitz at Oberhausen in 1962.

The blending of the creative functions of author and director seemed most provocative, challenging the young German filmmakers to adopt for their filmic heritage such internationally renowned film directors as Renoir, Cocteau, Lang, Hitchcock, Ford, and Fuller.

Another influence upon the *Jungfilmer* came from Brazil. By 1960, young Brazilian film directors were instrumental in reshaping their domestic film scene. A revolt against foreign—especially American—film dominance, led to the *cinema nôvo* movement. The Brazilian director Glauber Rocha advocated that the chance for creating an independent Brazilian cinema lay in expressing itself in terms of its own culture. Themes and language of *cinema nôvo* movies mirror the history and tribulations of the Brazilian people through a rich, often strange and mythical folklore. These movies are not content with simple entertainment but reach far into their cultural heritage.

The actual reality of film production proved difficult for the *Jungfilmer*, however, since a financial support system for such an undertaking hardly existed in 1962. The only school in Germany preparing students for professional careers in the film industry at that time was the German Institute for Film and Television (Deutsches Institut für Film und Fernsehen—DIFF) in Munich. DIFF was founded in the early 1950s. In 1962 this institute was in no position to seize the historical moment and welcome the *Jungfilmer* by providing them with a solid professional, technical, and theoretical basis. An ongoing history of fiscal problems had diminished the institute's effectiveness. To overcome the impasse, Alexander Kluge, a signatory of the Oberhausen Manifesto, and Detten Schleiermacher founded the Institute for Film Design (Institut für Filmgestaltung der Hochschule für Gestaltung) in Ulm in 1962. For several years this small institute was remarkably productive and probably instrumental in shaping the movement of the Young German Cinema. Kluge, himself an innovative and now internationally acclaimed film-maker, was regarded by many of the *Jungfilmer* as their spiritual leader. The lack of adequate production space, however, was painfully felt, and public pressure was brought upon the various ministers of culture of the states of the Federal Republic to rectify the situation.

Finally, in September 1966 the German Film and Television Academy (Deutsche Film und Fernsehakademie), Berlin (DFFB), and in November

1967 the Academy for Television and Film in Munich (Hochschule für Fernsehen und Film—HFF) opened their gates to prospective students. These institutions, it was hoped, would guarantee a stable learning environment that would produce the future generations of film directors in the FRG. Unfortunately, the creation of these institutions had been delayed for too long. When they finally materialized, the television industry had molded the viewing habit of the West German public to such a degree that little desire existed in that audience for experimentation or innovation. In short, the public's early support for the Young German Cinema movement turned into disinterest. In 1965, however, the Board of Curators of the Young German Cinema (Kuratorium Junger Deutscher Film) was formed, based upon a decree of the federal minister of the interior. The existence of this board was crucial to the artistic survival of the Young German Cinema during its formative years. Many of the feature film debuts of *Jungfilmer* could be realized only because of direct sponsorship by the board. Werner Herzog (b. 1942), Peter Fleischmann (b. 1937), Edgar Reitz, Vlado Kristl (b. 1923), and Alexander Kluge were among the first beneficiaries.

The established film industry continued to produce and distribute its mediocre fare throughout the years 1962–1965. Audience attendance declined, while *Jungfilmer* refined their skills by producing movie shorts at home or by going across the border. Volker Schlöndorff (b. 1939) studied in Paris, at the Institut des Hautes Etudes Cinématographiques (IDHEC), and afterward became assistant director to Louis Malle, Jean-Pierre Melville, and Alain Resnais. Peter Fleischmann enrolled at first at the DIFF in Munich. Later he continued his studies in Paris at the IDHEC. He, too, improved his skills further by remaining in France and working as assistant director for Jacques Dewever, Jacques Rozier, and others.

In 1966 the breakthrough of young German filmmakers finally occurred. Four movies created excitement at major national and international film festivals at Cannes (France), Venice (Italy), and Berlin (FRG). Ulrich Schamoni's (b. 1939) *It* (*Es*) and Volker Schlöndorff's *Young Törless* (*Der junge Törless*), based on a novel by Robert Musil, were the official FRG entries at the Cannes Festival. *Young Törless* was awarded the International Critics Prize at this world-renowned international film fair. Alexander Kluge's first feature film, *Yesterday's Girl* (*Abschied von Gestern*), was celebrated at Venice, receiving the prestigious Silver Lion, while Peter Schamoni's (b. 1934) *Closed Season on Fox Hunting* (*Schonzeit für Füchse*) gained a Silver Bear at the Berlinale (a special prize of the international jury at the West Berlin International Film Festival). Oberhausen had prepared the theoretical basis for and had established the moral claim on this success. The international successes in 1966 proved to the *Jungfilmer* that their efforts had been recognized.

New Filmic Form

Alexander Kluge's *Yesterday's Girl* is regarded by many film scholars as the most significant of the early successes. It provided for acceptance of the Young German Cinema by a broad public in the FRG. The script of the film was based on his book *Vitae*, published in 1962. *Yesterday's Girl* demands active participation from its viewing public. The story is discontinuous. There are no predetermined themes supported and developed by successive actions. Beginning and end of this film are not achieved by a linear build of shots, scenes, and sequences. The protagonist, Anita G., is introduced to the audience in episodes. Having come from East Germany, she draws the spectator into her unsuccessful attempts at integration into West German society. Her plight, endless beginnings, is mirrored in a disjunctive montage technique. Each sequence becomes a statement in itself, tied to the next by simple titles, citations, or narration. The intensification of her personal tragedy is developed through the use of microperspective that each episode represents. Anita G. remains the unwanted outsider throughout the film.

Kluge blurred the fictional character of his movie whenever possible to provide it with an air of authenticity. Fictional scenes, for example, include nonactors in their actual professional roles; a real state prosecutor, for example, portrays the film's state prosecutor. Kluge also recognized the importance of locations, functioning as documents. They served Kluge in his concern to strengthen the impression of the real. His script had to remain very flexible to respond to unexpected locational alterations as well as to unrehearsed contributions of his cast. Kluge's technique provides his film with authenticity, which, in turn, comments plausibly upon the perverse situation of his heroine, a Jewish woman. The schizoid existence of two German states and the personal background of the protagonist do not permit her to live a normal life. Her reality provides the context of this tragedy, in which past and present are interwoven and inseparable.

Volker Schlöndorff's *Young Törless* testifies to the director's intelligence and acuteness in dealing with both Germany's immediate past (the emergence of Nazi Germany) and its present. The various interior and exterior locations comment upon the action of the film and foreshadow the development of the human tragedy. The audience witnesses how Törless becomes guilty while a young student at a military academy. Although not personally responsible, a bystander, Törless participates indirectly in the physical abuse and the emotional torment and rape of a young Jewish fellow student. Robert Musil, the author of this novel, anticipated the elements necessary for a fascist state. Schlöndorff, in turn, uses his film as an analogue for the more recent history of the German people. He confirms within the visual form the inevitable acceptance of the Holocaust. The interior of the academy is dark and foreboding. Its exterior is closed in by walls and stone columns. The image suggests imprisonment. Schlöndorff is also very decisive in the use of narrative. The spoken word is void of feelings. Dialogues are short; they suggest indifference and in so doing are disruptive, opposing communication. The system is geared to dehumanize the individual. Schlöndorff learned how to make films during his apprenticeship years in France, and he chose Louis Malle as associate producer for this film.

Although significantly different from the common fare of commercial film releases, the works of the *Jungfilmer* did not succeed in speaking a *radically* new film language, as promised in the Oberhausen Manifesto. Technically, the French New Wave had introduced the elliptical film style and narrative forms that resemble the documentary. What was *new*, however, was the choice of text and its sober treatment. Common people caught in a larger historical and political context they cannot alter became recurring filmic themes. Commonplaces and confrontations seem to be the dialectical methodology underlying these films, functioning on a sociocritical level. Their open-ended form thrusts the unresolved problem onto the viewer, who, when leaving the movie theater, is challenged to seek his own final resolutions. These films are uncomfortable and difficult. Although the audience responded well at first, most were soon persuaded to return to less demanding material. The established commercial film industry interpreted the audience's fatigue as a sign of weakness on the part of the Young German Cinema.

Deviation and Setback

Opas Kino subsequently lobbied for a new film subsidy law. The Film Promotion Law (Filmförderungsgesetz—FFG) materialized in December of 1967. The Film Subsidy Board (Filmförderungsanstalt—FFA) in Berlin was entrusted to collect 15 pfennigs, the *Filmgroschen*, for every ticket sold at the box office. This revenue was to be distributed among film project applicants according to the following criteria. The reference film (*Referenzfilm*), i.e., a film director's most recent film, had to achieve a gross income of DM 500,000 over a period of two years from its initial release. This amount could be reduced to DM 300,000 if the reference film was awarded a film rating of "valuable" or "especially valuable" by the Film Rating Board (Filmbewertungsstelle—FBW) or if the reference film received a prize at a national or international festival.

At first the new Film Promotion Law seemed quite flexible. It began to isolate the established from the nonestablished film directors, however. How could a young and inexperienced film director raise the production budget for his reference film? At the time the Film Promotion Law went into effect, the budget of the Board of Curators of the Young German Cinema had been substantially reduced, rendering it ineffective. Earlier it had been possible to gain financial support from the Board of Curators on the basis of a film script or even an outline for a film treatment. The board had sponsored more than twenty-five film projects during its first three years. Unfortunately, only a few of these films reached the public, and this may have aided in the hurried creation of the Film Promotion Law.

As a result, the experimental filmmaker and the newcomer encountered a very difficult financial situation. The more seasoned directors representing the Young German Cinema faced the same problem. Now everyone had to compete with the established commercial film industry. Movie projects were conceived and implemented on the basis of previous successes, which invited serialization of merely average projects. Slowly, triviality began to set in again. The "authors" went into isolation. While in France the directors of the *cinéma d'auteurs* formed a lively homogeneous group, the German *Autoren* were forced into a fiercely competitive economic struggle. Striving to combine complex production requirements (such as securing funds and film distribution) with the artistic directing demands of the medium drained their creative energy. What little was left of this energy had to be employed for scriptwriting, since adequate scripts were few and far between. While the *Jungfilmer* tried to cope with this situation, the public increasingly withdrew from the movie theaters.

The year 1967 ushered in a new type of director. A remarkable feature of this second generation of young German film directors was their distance from German culture, past or present. The second generation was a typical product of the fantasy world of the movie industry itself, particularly Hollywood. Its filmmakers derived their themes, formed their style, by copying American gangster films. They were fascinated by their movie experience without establishing a critical distance. Into this category belong Klaus Lemke's (b. 1940) *48 Hours Till Acapulco* (*Achtundvierzig Stunden bis Acapulco*, 1967), Rudolf Thome's (b. 1939) *Detectives* (*Detektive*, 1968), Rainer Werner Fassbinder's (1946–1982) first feature film, *Love Is Colder Than Death* (*Liebe ist kälter als der Tod*, 1969), and Roland Klick's (b. 1939) *Deadlock* (1970). The title of Klick's film appears symptomatic of this short-lived genre.

Technically well made, these films were slick yet pale copies of their American models. The depicted human rage resulting in violent death rang false, because it had no credible counterpart within the experience of the West German moviegoer. These movies are a series of unfortunate experiments. They are empty, void of human feelings and emotions. Fassbinder's *The American Soldier* (*Der amerikanische Soldat*, 1970) introduces traces of human suffering and compassion yet remains dominated by a poorly digested mythology of the American gangster world, dabbling in clichés.

The emergence of the second generation "apprenticeship" films was accompanied by the appearance of the left-wing or anti–homeland film (*neuer Heimatfilm*). Its filmmakers took advantage of the privileged position the *Heimatfilme* had occupied in the hearts and minds of the West German movie-going public. These directors situated their stories in provinces like Southern Bavaria. In order to produce "genuine" *Heimatfilme*, regional dialects were introduced into the films. Instrumental in making this genre enticing to others was the director Peter Fleischmann. His film *Hunting Scenes from Lower Bavaria* (*Jagdszenen aus Niederbayern*, 1968) is the prototype of the *neue Heimatfilme*. This type of film did not intend to create an idyllic pastorale of the homeland. On the contrary, it wanted to correct that fantasy by exposing its myth. The brutality of the masses turning against the individual is a major theme of Fleischmann's movie. His film was so unnerving that official FRG film critics unleashed a furor over this production. Fleischmann had dared to blemish the tabernacle.

The 1971 releases in the FRG of Volker Schlöndorff's *The Sudden Wealth of the Poor People of Kombach* (*Der plötzliche Reichtum der armen Leute von Kombach*), Reinhard Hauff's (b. 1939) *Mathias Kneissl*, and Uwe Brandner's (b. 1941) *I Love You, I Kill You* (*Ich liebe dich, ich töte dich*) belong to the *neue Heimatfilme*, dealing with, respectively, the province, the dialect and, as a twist, the past and the immediate future. By placing the action in a different time frame, the directors shielded themselves somewhat from the film critics' immediate wrath.

To probe the fabric of the countryside was these directors' intention, similar to Fleischmann's. Themes varied. The suppressive, exploitative nature of land barons toward their peasants drives individual farmers to break the law by poaching. Unjust levying of taxes creates suffocating burdens for poor country folk. They are forced to turn to crime or fantasy in order to escape their dreadful reality. In Brandner's film, a futuristic, idealistic rural society becomes so barren that it chokes its subjects into delirium. Feelings and sympathies among individuals are regulated in order to maintain a blissful state of conformity, which is ultimately homologous with death. The intent of these *neue Heimatfilme* was to comment metaphorically on the present socioeconomic and political conditions in the FRG.

These films were considered to be box office poison, failures, making distributors reluctant or even hostile to book films representing the Young German Cinema for their domestic movie houses. The strongly negative posture of the exhibitors was compounded by the large market share of foreign distribution companies in the FRG. United Artists, Fox-MGM, Warner-Columbia, and Ciné-International controlled 45 percent of the total distribution, and Music Corporation managed the second largest chain of movie houses in the FRG. The *Jungfilmer* sought the solution of a cooperative. In 1971 the Film Cooperative of Authors (Filmverlag der Autoren) was founded. Thirteen members collectively engaged in the production and distribution of their films. Among them were relatively new names as well as some of the more seasoned *Jungfilmer*, such as Uwe Brandner, Thomas Schamoni (b. 1936), Hark Bohm (b. 1939), Peter Lilienthal (b. 1929), and Wim Wenders (b. 1945). A very busy season began for these enterprising filmmakers. Yet only a few of their productions were well received by the West German audience. Films that stand out are Fassbinder's *Ali: Fear Eats Soul* (*Angst essen Seele auf,* 1973), *Effi Briest* (1973–1974), adapted from the novel by the nineteenth-century writer Theodor Fontane, and Bernhard Sinkel's *Lina Braake* (1974–1975). Increasing financial losses forced the Film Cooperative of Authors to withdraw from any production efforts and to concentrate exclusively on the distribution of its products. As a result, the cooperative had to be reorganized legally by the end of 1974. Seven of the original thirteen members remained, among them Bohm, Fassbinder, Brandner, and Wenders.

Many of the film critics had become tired of defending the *Jungfilmer* and second-generation filmmakers. These critics, however, did not succeed themselves in creating a filmic dialogue in the FRG. No invigorating film journal, such as the French *Cahiers du Cinéma,* had emerged. The film journals that had existed ceased circulation. Among the casualties were the journals *Film* (1970) and *Kino* (1974). The journal *Film-Kritik* was classified as esoteric and was therefore ignored by most of the public. The blame for this gloomy state of affairs also rests with many of the filmmakers themselves. Often they were more egocentric and didactic in their filmic approach than the medium could possibly endure. Many of their films lacked entertainment value. Simple enjoyment was apparently frowned upon and replaced by heavy-handed doses of dialectical theory. Modest production budgets did not improve upon the filmic form, either. Often, hurried shooting produced technical shortcomings. Lack of filmic production technique was a further contributing factor. The Young German Cinema was isolated on the national scene. Yet the early, frustrating years of the 1970s also witnessed the ascendance of several outstanding film-directing talents, among them Rainer Werner Fassbinder and Werner Herzog.

Enduring Talent

Opinion concerning Fassbinder's oeuvre is very divided. Whichever side one takes, Fassbinder remains the most prolific of the young German filmmakers. In 1967 he joined an already established theater group in Munich. He performed and later directed at the "action-theater." The creative environment induced him to try his skill at playwriting. In May 1968 the theater went bankrupt. Most of the stage players stayed together and founded a new theater, the "antiteater." This group had to move around frequently, with varying success, before finding a permanent home. In a back room of the restaurant Witwe Bolte in Schwabing, Munich's university district, one could participate in the activities of these essentially communal performances. At the end of 1969, the owner of this establishment gave notice to the group to leave his premises. These restless years affected Fassbinder's development significantly. In 1969 he directed his first feature film, *Love Is Colder Than Death.* From 1969 to 1970–1971 Fassbinder produced eleven more features, using for all of them as stock acting company the players of the *antiteater.*

Fassbinder's movie *Why Does Mr. R. Run Amok?* (*Warum läuft Herr R. Amok?* 1969/1970), cowritten and codirected with Michael Fengler, marks the beginning of Fassbinder's personal style. The story depicts the daily life of an average petit bourgeois family. Their surface activities suggest a relatively whole world, except for minor blemishes that spoil the tranquil existence. The protagonist's latent yet ever-increasing fury makes him destroy his family in anguish. After a horrible primal scream, he commits suicide. Fassbinder and Fengler had roughly outlined their dialogue and relied on the improvisational skill of their cast to fill in the necessary detail. Consequently, the narrative is painfully slow, as time-consuming as in real life. The stage players' forte in ad-libbing a sketchy situation was the necessary element to provide stark naturalism. The pale colors of this film reminded the spectator further that he is watching lifeless images. In 1971 Fengler and Fassbinder received the Federal Film Prize for this movie.

In the same year, *The Merchant of the Four Seasons* (*Der Händler der vier Jahreszeiten*) was released. This film portrays the intensifying isolation of an average man. His loved ones, mother, wife, sister, see in him only their provider and intend to use him to fulfill their personal ambitions. He attempts to break away from them but is too weak to make it on his own. His environment closes in on him. In despair, he begins to drink and to beat his wife. Ultimately, he knows that there is no escape for his kind. He becomes mute, drowning his sorrow in alcohol. This most average human being is crushed by the cruel life that surrounds him. Finally, he collapses by drinking himself to death publicly, surrounded by his "family" and his "friends." The image structure of this movie is very static. Fassbinder's visual space confines people. Rooms appear to be stuffy and claustrophobic, there is really no action. Many shots look staged, artificial. They resemble *tableaux morts*, frozen images, reminders of impending death. There exists a feeling of clumsiness in the overall perceptional design of this film. However, this ineptness evokes a strong sympathy for the protagonist. The technique of the film director serves as an analogue for the existential fright of the character. In a larger context, Fassbinder exposes the success of the economic miracle state (*Wirtschaftswunderstaat*) and its falsely envied progress as harboring a disease. In 1972, Fassbinder was awarded the Federal Film Prize for this production.

The year 1972 saw another remarkable Fassbinder movie, *The Bitter Tears of Petra von Kant* (*Die bitteren Tränen der Petra von Kant*). The setting, a voluptuously decorated apartment, borders on kitsch and carries a silent, passionately visual language. A relentlessly moving camera suggests the nervous activities of the women, who, engulfed by loneliness and disappointment, engage in a power struggle. Broken pride and ignited jealousy motivate mutual invitations to dependency and submissiveness. The women ultimately experience rejection and humiliation.

Fassbinder's *Ali: Fear Eats Soul* (1973) is another example of this director's empathy with common people. Ali, a Moroccan foreign or "guest" worker (Gastarbeiter), meets Emmi, a cleaning woman by profession. The two fall in love and get married. This public declaration, however, creates problems. Emmi, a sixty-year old widow, is at least twenty years older than Ali. This disparity is aggravated by the fact that Ali is implicitly unwanted, a foreign element in West German society. Emmi's children despise Ali and begin to reject their mother as well. Local merchants refuse to do business with Emmi, an old customer. Her colleagues at work treat her as an outsider. Ali finally collapses, unable to bear any further confrontations. Fassbinder's camera is honest; it plainly and continuously records the unfolding of the tragedy.

In 1974 the Cannes Film Festival awarded its prestigious International Critics' Prize to *Ali*. The international recognition, the first major one since 1966, was proof to foreign critics that the Young German Cinema still existed. Across the borders and abroad its productions were increasingly welcomed and widely distributed and discussed. The international movie audience began to look seriously at the New German Cinema or NGC, as it was known from here on.

Probably the most individualistic of West German filmmakers is Werner Herzog. His reputation is of one at best sublime, at worst bizarre. Unquestionably, Herzog is a filmmaker of extraordinary convictions and fantasy. His work speaks a visual, filmic language of unusual dimensions. He finds images that possess haunting, awesome qualities and leave a deep resonance with the spectator. In his quest to see in a new way, Herzog is prepared to travel far and to accept extreme hardship.

Herzog possesses no formal training as a filmmaker. His burning desire to make films, however, seems to be the only necessary condition to sustain his willpower. His filmic visions make him endure and prevail. *Fata Morgana* (1968–1970), one of his early films, can be described as a visual poem. Shot in East, West, and Central Africa under dreadful production conditions, jeopardizing the property and lives of the production crew, this film stands as an example of the powerful image structure of Herzog's vision. Our eyes interact with unaccustomed landscapes. The camera sweeps across deserts, rests upon villages. Their surface beauty or horridness speaks directly, literally, to the spectator, who seems to discover a new planet. The film is structured into a myth in three parts, "Creation," "Paradise," and "Golden Age." Attempts to interpret the story linguistically, however, are not very fruitful. The essence of the film rests in seeing as an intelligent and primary mode of one's existence in this world.

In 1972 Herzog released *Aguirre, the Wrath of God* (*Aguirre, der Zorn Gottes*). The setting for this picture is again unusual. The cast and production crew found themselves on remote rivers in the jungle of the Upper Amazon in Peru. The overwhelming grandeur of the landscape, with its indifference to man's existence, is the silent protagonist of this movie. The conquistador Lope de Aguirre incites a rebellion among his small band of followers to break away from the Spanish crown. Through intimidation, murder, and the installation of a puppet Emperor of El Dorado, he gains control. However, increasing madness sets in, which is proportional to the futility of his deeds, particularly when seen against the backdrop of the Amazon jungle and rivers. The ever-present, silent nature is gradually encroaching upon the mobility of the conquerors. Nature dictates the confines of this film from the very beginning. The long opening shot reveals a thin silver line descending into the luscious green jungle. On their expedition, the soldiers endure inhuman hardships without making the slightest progress. Finally they decide to build rafts in order to expedite their perilous journey. From there on, the treacherous currents take command. An unending voyage into madness unfolds, finding its resolution in the death of every man.

The closing shot symbolizes the hubris that had taken hold of Aguirre. The camera encircles the conquistador while opening up to a cover shot. The raft spins helplessly in the drift. Aguirre's armor is rusty, the raft in disarray. Dead bodies are strewn around while hundreds of monkeys have taken possession of the raft. The camera zooms out further, the human tragedy comes to rest—an insignificant point in the landscape, swallowed up by an indifferent nature. The opening and closing images of the film invite the metaphor of a circle. There is no beginning and no end. This journey is doomed to failure from its inception. Infinity prevails.

Herzog's *The Enigma of Kaspar Hauser* (*Jeder für sich und Gott gegen alle*) was released in 1974. Hauser, a foundling, experiences nature and the society of man for the first time as an adolescent. After seventeen years of seclusion (he was kept in a dark basement with no direct contact with any other form of life), he is thrown into the world and experiences the extraordinary beauty of nature—a most lyrical pastorale of finely composed visual images. Soon Hauser meets his fellow men. Lacking an adequate ability to speak or to interact within societal norms, this experience creates a trauma for Hauser. The efforts of *Homo sapiens* to enlighten this "savage" prove to be destructive at the end. Slowly, society succeeds in killing all joy in life for Kaspar Hauser, replaces it with fright, and finally murders him. The strength of this film is enhanced by the performance of the protagonist, played by Bruno S. His presentation is as fascinating as it is disturbing, even shocking. The part of Kaspar Hauser resembles to a large degree the personal experience of Bruno S. The film was selected as the official FRG entry in the Cannes Film Festival in 1975. It received the International Critics Award, the Special Jury Prize, and the Ecumenical Prize, bringing the New German Cinema into the limelight.

Uneasy Partnership

At home, throughout the early 1970s, many of the German filmmakers realized their projects in coproductions with regional television corporations. Always in need of programs, the nine independent television corporations (combined in the national broadcast structures of the Standing Committee of Broadcasting Corporations in the FRG [Arbeitsgemeinschaft der Öffentlich-Rechtlichen Rundfunkanstalten—ARD]), Second German Television (Zweites Deutsches Fernsehen—ZDF), and five so-called third channels (Dritte Programme) welcomed such cooperation. Working for the medium of television offered specific aesthetic challenges, but it also imposed political limitations upon the filmmakers. Concessions had to be made to the in-house supervising program editors

(*Fernsehredakteure*) in order to stay within the established guidelines of a particular station. Further, any movie aired on television severely reduced its audience appeal for a subsequent second screening in a public theater. From the start, a potentially major source of income for the young filmmakers was critically jeopardized.

The constraints deriving from the collaboration led to a compromise between the film and television industries. In November 1974 the Film/Television Agreement (*Film/Fernsehen-Abkommen*) went into effect. With this agreement, the combined West German television industry became the largest single employer for young filmmakers. During the next five years, DM 34 million was spent for television-film coproductions, and filmmakers gained several major concessions from the television industry. The agreement, still in effect in the early 1980s, stipulates that no film can be aired on television within the first two years of its existence. After that time, rights to it are transferred to regional television corporations. Particularly appealing film projects may be granted an additional large sum of production money if the television station decides to secure special rights through advance purchase. Through these rights, the film can run a maximum length of five years in movie houses before it is broadcast. The major television corporations also promote the activities of the Film Subsidy Board (Filmförderungsanstalt—FFA), contributing DM 1 million to its funds annually.

Stifling Atmosphere

The encouraging development in the film industry in the FRG was overshadowed and ultimately drastically affected by a politically conservative backlash. The trend toward conservatism (*Tendenzwende*) began to generate a highly restrictive environment for creative filmmakers. From 1974 through 1977, the Western world witnessed a frightening increase of counterproductive violent acts by left-wing terrorist groups. Their crimes aided indirectly in the hurried implementation of the controversial Radical Decree (*Radikalenerlass*) and the professional proscription (*Berufsverbot*) by the governing parties in the FRG. An uneasy feeling spread throughout the land, affecting each and every citizen. Government security measures were felt by many. Intellectuals, particularly if they were thought of as difficult or their political ideology as unreliable (this usually meant a political affinity with the left), were ostracized. The first victims of this defensive posture were soon apparent.

When the regional West German Radio and Television Corporation (Westdeutscher Rundfunk—WDR) withdrew its financial support from the worker's film (*Arbeiterfilm*), the genre soon collapsed. In previous years, the German Film and Television Academy in Berlin had distinguished itself with thought-provoking productions. Christian Ziewer (b. 1941) and Max Willutzki's (b. 1938) *Kinogramm I* and *Kinogramm II* (1969) shorts, which concern themselves with citizens' initiatives (*Bürgerinitiativen*) and renters' concerns (*Mietprobleme*), are exemplary. They were used as constructive communication devices to initiate a positive dialogue among the various opposing parties concerned. These politically motivated shorts paved the way for several feature-length *Arbeiterfilme*. *The Wollands* (*Die Wollands*, 1972), directed by Ingo Kratisch (b. 1945) and Marianne Lüdcke (b. 1943), depicts the life of a welder. The protagonist, Horst Wolland, learns to accept the necessity of solidarity of action within the working class in order to preserve its rights and dignity. The film does not discuss the situation of the worker but confronts its target audience, the working class, with its own reality. This theme is further developed by the same directing team in *Wages and Love* (*Lohn und Liebe*, 1973–1974). Here, workers resolve their individual differences in favor of strengthening the working crew of the factory against management. These *Arbeiterfilme* were not primarily entertainment. Their principal purpose was to invite debate. Within the climate of *Tendenzwende*, however, the tolerance to support this kind of activity did not exist.

Tendenzwende affected other creative individuals as well. The FRG's avant-garde and documentary filmmakers preferred emigration to the suppressive climate. Klaus Wyborny (b. 1945) settled in New York, Peter Nestler (b. 1937) moved to Sweden, and Jean-Marie Straub (b. 1933) and Danièle Huillet left Munich for Rome. Others became silent, i.e., they abandoned their preferred creative medium. Vlado Kristl started painting and Werner Schröter (b. 1945) turned to the theater. The movie that unnervingly depicts these uncertain years is *The Lost Honor of Katharina Blum* (*Die verlorene Ehre der Katharina Blum*, 1975), based on a novel by Heinrich Böll. The film was codirected by Volker Schlöndorff and Margarethe von Trotta. Katharina, a domestic, has become politically suspect to the police because of her accidental acquaintance with an alleged anarchist. The boulevard press exploits her misfortunes unscrupulously, without professional ethics or principles. This film became the most attended feature of all the Young German Cinema releases.

Media distortions of reality continued to escalate in the FRG. The political climate became more intense, while the general public increasingly avoided the movie theaters. By 1976, annual attendance had dropped to 115 million visitors. When in the fall of 1977 the radical Baader-Meinhof gang abducted the leading FRG industrialist Hans-Martin Schleyer and subsequently murdered him, the country suffered a shock. Leading intellectuals saw themselves paralyzed and as potential targets of the ensuing nationwide police dragnets. Werner Herzog hinted at intentions to emigrate to Ireland. Alexander Kluge withdrew to write. At the 1977 West Berlin International Film Festival, Rainer Werner Fassbinder, who had been chosen as Director of the Year in 1976 by the highly respected *International Film Guide*, announced his contemplated departure for New York. Apparently, as in the 1920s, Germany was not capable of providing a permanent home for some of its most instrumental, creative talents.

The artistic restrictions regarding the *Jungfilmer* during the destructive years of 1975–1977 were further compounded by the difficult financial situation experienced by the Film Cooperative of Authors. By the end of 1976, it faced near-bankruptcy. Rudolf Augstein, publisher of the widely circulated weekly magazine *Der Spiegel*, preserved its existence, however, by purchasing 55 percent of its shares. Of the thirteen original founding members, only Bohm, Brandner, Geissendörf (b. 1941), and Wenders remained.

Film production did not cease during this time. On the contrary, the signing of the Film/Television Agreement in 1974 had set the stage for prolific cooperation. However, coproducing with a television corporation became a bitter experience. Every script had to be filtered through numerous committees before it could be accepted. Alterations in the form of seemingly endless rewrites by the in-house supervising program editors became a normative procedure. If a young writer or filmmaker wanted to work within these confines, he had to be most willing to grant liberal concessions to the editors and to comply with their judgment. Texts were "purified" of any potentially political intent. As a result, many noncommittal literary filmic adaptations (*Literaturverfilmungen*) were undertaken. Some of the literary pieces chosen were E.T.A. Hoffmann's *The Devil's Elixirs* (*Die Elixiere des Teufels*, 1976, directed by Manfred Purzer [b. 1931]), Ibsen's *The Wild Duck* (*Die Wildente,* 1976, by Hans Geissendorfer and Theodor Storm's *The Rider of the White Horse* (*Der Schimmelreiter*, 1977, by Alfred Weidenmann [b. 1918]).

An interest in *Literaturverfilmungen* is not inherently negative. The New German Cinema filmmakers—Fassbinder, Schlöndorff, and Wenders, for example—selected as literary models works by Grass, Böll, Handke, Fontane, and Kleist. Writers, in their turn, were attracted to the filmic medium. The long friendship between Peter Handke (b. 1942) and Wim Wenders resulted in the Wenders adaptation of Handke's novel *The Goalie's Anxiety at the Penalty Kick* (*Die Angst des Tormanns beim Elfmeter*, 1971). Several more adaptations originated from the productive Handke-Wenders collaboration. Handke explored his own directing talent in several films, most recently *The Left-handed Woman* (*Die linkshändige Frau*, 1977).

Yet the commitment to literary adaptations of the majority of film releases from 1975 to 1977 is flawed because it focused on cultural values of a period long past. Comparisons with the present were avoided. Critical interpretations of the predominantly nineteenth-century literary creations were generally shunned. Contemporary literature dealing directly with the immediate present was conspicuously absent. Therefore, this period of literary adaptations has been regarded as critically mediocre (*Literaturverfilmungskrise*). Its film productions did not surpass simple literary illustrations. The only purpose seems to have been aesthetically pleasing entertainment.

Turning Point

Had German film directors abandoned their efforts and gains since Oberhausen and before? Did they acquiesce in the atmosphere of political sterility and intellectual stagnation in the FRG? Many film directors who had previously announced plans for emigration changed their minds and acknowledged their artistic obligation. In the late fall of 1977 a large group of intellectuals, consisting of writers (Heinrich Böll and Wolf Biermann) and filmmakers (Alf Brustellin/Bernhard Sinkel, Hans-Peter Closs/Katja Rupé, Rainer Werner Fassbinder, Alexander Kluge/Beate Mainka-Jellinghaus, Maximiliane Mainka/Peter Schubert, Edgar Reitz, Volker Schlöndorff) decided to make their voices heard collectively. They were united in their conviction to take a public stand, addressing the recent political incidents in the FRG. *Germany in Autumn* (*Deutschland im Herbst*) is the filmic result of their efforts. The film is uneven, probably because many people were involved in its making. Central to the complex theme is an administrative council meeting of television program executives and editors who cannot decide whether or not to accept a television version of Sophocles' *Antigone*. There are seemingly endless discussions. The entire situation is ludicrous. The debates are incorporated into a larger frame, the documentary footage of various ceremonies accompanying the state burial of the industrialist Hans-Martin Schleyer, juxtaposed with the burial of the anarchists Raspé, Ensslin, and Baader. The film conveys intensely a profound conviction of tolerance. *Germany in Autumn*, Margarethe von Trotta's (b. 1942) *The Second Awakening of Christa Klages* (*Das zweite Erwachen der Christa Klages*, 1977), and Helke Sander's (b. 1937) *The All-Round Reduced Personality* (*Die allseitig reduzierte Persönlichkeit*, 1977) testified at the 1978 West Berlin International Film Festival that the German filmmakers had regained their strength to engage in a critical, realistic cinema. Creative film scripts were in demand again. Of the eighty-one films produced in 1979, only fifteen were based on literary models. Political sterility and intellectual stagnation had ended.

The city of Munich had proposed a film exhibition in the form of a commercial entertainment festival for the month of July 1979. Many film directors disliked this approach. As a protest, they quickly organized the Hamburg Film Festival of Filmmakers (Das Filmfest der Filmemacher) in September 1979. As in Oberhausen in 1962, a manifesto was drawn up in Hamburg and signed by about a hundred filmmakers. They professed that their strength as filmmakers rested in their diversity, yet they recognized that they pursued the same basic interests. In unison they attacked the limited creative range allowed them by supervisory boards, television program editors, and other interest groups. Imagination cannot be administrated. The German film of the 1980s had to be free. Acknowledging the difficult journey of the past seventeen years since Oberhausen while looking with confidence into the new decade, these German filmmakers brought to the fore the New German Cinema in the FRG after it had already been accepted on the international film scene.

International Acknowledgment

After German film directors had been successful at the International Film Festival at Cannes, France (1974: Fassbinder's *Ali*; 1975: Herzog's *Kaspar Hauser*), the most important film markets became interested in the New German Cinema. The U.S. distributor Dan Talbot of New Yorker Films exhibited *Ali* at his New Yorker theater on upper Broadway in New York in 1974. The first reception of this film was not encouraging, so it was quickly redirected to the university market. However, after Manny Faber of the journal *Film Comment* devoted a perceptive article to Fassbinder in its November/December 1975 issue, the director was discovered and established in the United States. Werner Herzog experienced a similar introduction. *Kaspar Hauser* was acquired by Don Rugoff for his Cinema 5 chain. In October 1976 it opened at New York's East Side Beekman theater and lasted no longer than four days. Critics were again much more positive and reviewed *Kaspar Hauser* and its director with great enthusiasm and support. Jonathan Cott of *Rolling Stone* published a lengthy interview with Herzog in the November issue. Herzog promoted his films at several U.S. film festivals. Eventually, he stayed in San Francisco as director-in-residence and guest of Francis Coppola.

Beginning in March 1977, a Fassbinder Festival lasted twenty weeks at the New Yorker theater. Meanwhile, at the D. W. Griffith theater on the East Side of New York, Herzog's *Aguirre* had its first-run presentation.

It filled the theater for four consecutive weeks, followed by a six-week booking at the Surf theater in San Francisco from May through June of 1977. *Aguirre* also traveled to Boston and Chicago during the same year. When it returned to New York, it was screened at the trend-setting Cinema Studio for an additional six weeks in October and November. Herzog now was an established cult-director in the United States. Dan Talbot acquired Herzog's *Stroszek* (1977) and exhibited it for seven weeks at the New Yorker. The Fassbinder Festival that he had created expanded into the year-long German Film Festival.

In 1977 the NGC was established throughout the United States. The Pacific Film Archive in Berkeley, California, the Surf and Clay theaters in San Francisco, the "Houston International Film Festival and Film Markets" became permanent homes for the NGC. In March 1978, *Time* magazine published a most complimentary column on the NGC. "The new German cinema is the liveliest in Europe . . . as far as foreign films are concerned, the 70's belong to the Germans."

The established German film directors have been courted by major United States film distribution houses and have accepted their invitations for international cooperation. Werner Herzog's *Nosferatu—The Vampyre* (*Nosferatu—Phantom der Nacht*, 1978) was distributed by 20th Century Fox and Fassbinder's *The Marriage of Maria Braun* (*Die Ehe der Maria Braun*, 1978) by New Yorker Films. The latter film opened at the Cinema Studio, and by August 1980 it had run continuously for forty-two weeks, subsequently moving across the country. Volker Schlöndorff's *The Tin Drum* (1979) was released by United Artists. When *The Tin Drum* received the Oscar as best foreign film in 1980, the German cinema had concluded its long, arduous journey toward maturity and acceptance. In February 1982, *Time* magazine stated: "[German film makers are] coming to financial success in their own movie market, to artistic maturity on theater screens around the world, to terms with a painful historical past."

Readings

Clarke, Gerald. "Seeking Planets That Do Not Exist: The New German Cinema Is the Liveliest in Europe." *Time*, March 20, 1978, pp. 51–53.

Corliss, Richard. "Bravado Is Their Passport: Germany Exports a Wave of Taut, Topical Film to the U.S." *Time*, February 22, 1982, pp. 68–69.

Cott, Jonathan. "Sign of Life." *Rolling Stone*, November 18, 1976, pp. 48–56. (Interview with Werner Herzog.)

Faber, Manny, and Patricia Patterson. "R. W. Fassbinder." *Film Comment* 11, 6 (November/December 1975):5–7.

Holloway, Ronald. "A German Breakthrough?" *Kino: German Film* (West Berlin) 1 (October 1979):4–17.

_____."The Long March to the East Side." *Kino: German Film* 2 (Spring 1980):3–10.

_____."Oscar in Amerika: On the Road to Independence?" *Kino: German Film* 3 (Summer 1980):3–10.

Liehm, Mira, and Antonin J. Liehm. *The Most Important Art: Eastern European Film After 1945.* Berkeley: University of California Press, 1977. (Includes several chapters on the development of film in the German Democratic Republic.)

Pflaum, Hans Günther, and Hans Helmut Prinzler. *Film in der Bundesrepublik Deutschland.* Munich: Carl Hanser Verlag, 1979.

Quarterly Review of Film Studies 5, 2 (Spring 1980). (The entire issue is devoted to the NGC.)

Sanford, John. *The New German Cinema.* Totowa, N.J.: Barnes & Noble, 1980.

Film in Germany
(Photographs courtesy Inter Nationes)

Volker Schlöndorff (b. 1932).

A still from *The Tin Drum*, showing Angela Winkler (left) and Gunter Grass (right). Schlöndorff directed this film in 1979.

Margarethe von Trotta (b. 1942).

Werner Herzog (b. 1942). (*Photo courtesy the German Information Center.*)

Rainer Werner Fassbinder (1946–1982).

A scene from the collaborative film *Germany in Autumn,* showing filmmaker Alf Brustellin (left) and writer Wolf Biermann (right), two of the film's creators.

17

Art in Germany,
1945–1982

The Third Reich marked a cultural break of such far-reaching proportions that the young generation of German artists anxious to resume their training or work after its collapse in 1945 found no solid tie to the tradition of the prewar German avant-garde. They began anew amid a desert of bombed cities without academies, museums, or functioning galleries. Starved for new impressions and stimulation, these youthful artists devoured the French conceptions of a nonobjective, freely abstract art that gave expression to spontaneous feelings. These ideas began to work their way sporadically over the borders as early as 1946; the rediscovery of German art from before 1933 followed only gradually in the 1950s.

In the Rhineland as well as in Berlin and Dresden, attempts were made after 1946 to bring together the many emigrant artists of expressionism, the Bauhaus, and critical realism in large exhibits. Such reconstructions of art history had considerable success among the older generation of German artists but found little resonance at first in the younger generation. These twenty- and thirty-year-olds showed an unmistakable preference for the abstract movement from the West, which they saw as a progressive new beginning that contrasted with the reminders of war and its horrors in the art of their German predecessors.

It is scarcely surprising, then, that the key words "German art" are found in art history after 1945 only as a geographical description of local events and as a description of tendencies spawned on the spot by outstanding individual artists like Willi Baumeister (1889–1955) or, later, Joseph Beuys (b. 1921). The label "German art," with an emphasis on national identity, disappeared completely in the Federal Republic of Germany in the 1950s under a supranational confluence of Western European and American art. This entirely new phenomenon of a strongly dominant international style remained unchallenged for a quarter of a century. Euphorically celebrated at the international exhibition Documenta 2 in the city of Kassel in 1959, it was recapitulated in 1981 in the retrospective exhibition "Westkunst" in Cologne. It was called into question only in the second half of the 1970s by a young generation of painters after it had deteriorated into rational, unpictorial, and elitist structural norms. Its place was taken by a labyrinth of isolated explosions of fantasy.

The Connection with the International Style

In 1958 Will Grohmann, one of the significant art critics of the 1950s, stated with regard to the first decade of postwar German art that "the 'Great Abstraction' had dislodged the 'Great Reality.' " Also, Grohmann clearly saw that the real classics of the postwar period were rooted in the avant-garde of the early twentieth century. Willi Baumeister, for example, felt indebted to cubism, E. W. Nay (1902–1968) to expressionism, and Fritz Winter (b. 1905) had been a pupil of Kandinsky (1866–1944) and Klee (1879–1940). Both of the great precursors of spontaneous abstraction, Hans Hartung (b. 1904) and Wols (1913–1951), had been able to maintain their tie with the international avant-garde during the Third Reich by living in France. Willi Baumeister, on the other hand, was one of the very few German painters who, in the seclusion of a forced inner emigration, had formulated an abstract expressive language of subjective signs that paralleled the avant-garde tendencies of the Ecole de Paris or American abstract expressionism.

In Baumeister's *African Images* (1940), the "painting" material itself—a rough sandy sediment—was made accessible as an independent sphere of effect. And in a comparable development, the German painter Julius Bissier (1893–1965), through the medium of his watercolor drawings, had in 1930 pioneered the calligraphic brushstroke as a meditative code and lyrical psychograph of subjective feelings. Surviving the war intact, this creative potential experienced a rapid breakthrough after 1946 even before the first strong impulses of the international *art informel* from France penetrated Germany after 1948 with the help of Hans Hartung and Wols. In Willi Baumeister's works a type of painting emerged that was characterized by archaically suggestive formations of a "metaphysical landscape" and created with a freely invented and lyrical pictorial language (Figure 1). Julius Bissier evoked the works of Hartung and Wols with his swerving, nonobjective brush strokes (Figure 2). While Far Eastern calligraphy in Hartung's works of the 1940s was processed in the form of subjectivistic ciphers (Figure 3), Wols built his graffitilike images from the chaos of spontaneously painted layers of color (Figure 5).

Young painters like K. O. Götz (b. 1914) and K.R.H. Sonderborg (b. 1923) went one step further in the early 1950s and developed automatic improvisation (Figure 6). They were the first to integrate the new postwar German art into the international avant-garde. As early as 1948 Götz was able to find his way around abroad. In Paris he became acquainted with Jackson Pollock (1912–1956) and his impetuous technique of drip painting. In West Germany itself, however, Pollock's painting "explosions" became known only at the time of the first exhibition of American art in Berlin in 1951.

Although in 1948 the first formation of a West German group of young artists in the club "youth west" (*Junger Westen*) rallied disparate forces, subsequent alliances were marked by programmatic leitmotifs. In 1949 in Munich the group called ZEN appeared. The membership included, besides representatives of the older generation, Sonderborg and Emil Schumacher (b. 1912) as well as a few other younger painters. It was mainly through their initiative that the group oriented itself, parallel to the calligraphic direction within American abstract expressionism, toward the strongly expressive, gestic characters in the East Asian languages. What manifested itself in Sonderborg's work as spontaneous notation in the sense of a psychic automatism found a planned integration into partially plastic, crustaceous painting bases in Schumacher's work. In their pastose material presence, they became autonomous as rudimentary metaphors for an archaic bond to nature (Figure 7). Schumacher combined the free rhythms of *art informel* with a mythical system of emblems similar to that in Willi Baumeister's sand images. These were, in turn, a further development of abstract formulation based on Kandinsky and Klee.

Three years later there were further group formations in the Rhineland, mainly of young talent, in the wake of *art informel*. It is not surprising that the former artistic metropolis of Berlin was not able to reassert the international importance it had enjoyed prior to 1933. It had become a divided city, located within East German territory and culturally dominated by the Soviet Union. Artistic activities shifted instead to the western parts of the Federal Republic and particularly to the rapidly prospering regions of the Rhine. The individual members of these groups varied the informal system of emblems and the calligraphic technique of painting. In the second half of the 1950s, under the increasing influence of French tachism and American action painting, the calligraphic element dissolved into a mere spattering technique that soon ran its course.

Certain deliberate designs contrasted refreshingly, however, with the profusion of such spontaneous self-displays. Examples were the spatially extensive relief structures developed by Karl Fred Dahmen (b. 1917) and Bernhard Schultze (b. 1919) on the basis of Baumeister's pastose painting material. In Dahmen's material pictures, the rough color coating evolved into objects with tactile stimuli that evoked direct associations with geological formations and rough walls. In Schultze's works the painting substance grew luxuriantly into labyrinthine, somewhat surrealistic forms of decay and decomposition.

In the course of the 1950s, the exchange of artistic ideas between Europe and the United States rapidly grew into active communication and kindled in West Germany some degree of rediscovery of historical surrealism. The German-born artist Max Ernst (1891–1976) greatly furthered this development. He had risen to world fame in the circle of Parisian surrealists in the 1920s. Through his marriage to the American art collector Peggy Guggenheim, Ernst also played a central role after 1950 in the international politics of art. In particular, the Guggenheim collection had become a mediator between the American and European avant-garde through its exhibitions in Europe.

Far removed from the rather spectacular publicity around Ernst, genuinely surrealistic fantasies were quietly pursued after 1946 by the seclusive Richard Oelze (b. 1900), who was duly appreciated only years later in the wake of pop art. In contrast to Ernst, Oelze drew his subjects exclusively from dark and oppressive spheres; demonic masks or faceless figures emerge in gloomy metamorphoses from tree trunks overgrown with thickets and from junglelike, primordial landscapes. Mac Zimmerman (b. 1912) also painted and drew dream landscapes. His style in the 1950s, however, showed less affinity to Ernst and Oelze than to automatic calligraphy, and it was only a decade later that his figurative manner emerged. Young painters like Horst Janssen (b. 1929) and Paul Wunderlich (b. 1927) built on the erotic surrealism of Hans Bellmer (1902–1975), whose works in Germany, like those of Ernst, received a fitting reception only in the years following the war. In the works of Janssen and Wunderlich, eroticism and morbidity mingled with elements of persiflage, irony, or even bitter satire.

In contrast to the rejuvenation of surrealism, the rediscovery of expressionism occurred more slowly. It was first introduced extensively at the first Documenta exhibition in Kassel (1955), which belatedly stimulated the desire to make up for lost time, particularly with regard to the painters of Die Brücke (The Bridge), and the late Emil Nolde (1867–1956).

In contrast, *Neue Sachlichkeit* (verism) was not even granted a belated rehabilitation in the 1950s; thus the veristic object poetry of such significant painters as Bruno Goller (b. 1901) and Werner Heldt (1904–1954) was registered at the time only at the periphery of the German art scene. It was also a long time before Max Beckmann (1884–1950) was rediscovered in Germany. His myth-making late works found extensive resonance in the painter's new American homeland. In Germany, only HAP Grieshaber (1909–1981) and his pupil Horst Antes (b. 1936) understood their oeuvre in the tradition of Beckmann's figurative expressionism. Antes fused the informal expressiveness of his time with mythical figurations in the prototypical gnomish shape of a cuttlefish. Reminiscent of Beckmann's works, it is struggling for an understanding with its environment (Figure 8). Another expressionist tradition, the formative power of lyrical color cultivated by Kandinsky and the group Der Blaue Reiter (The Blue Rider) found its continuation in the harmonious color tones of E. W. Nay, who organized disk-shaped color forms into rhythmic color chords free of any figural combination (Figure 4).

In view of the dominance of abstraction and *art informel*, neither the critical expressionism of a George Grosz (1893–1959) or Otto Dix (1891–1969) nor the agitatorial, provocative satire of the Berlin dada movement of the 1920s had a chance of being revived. After the long years of the Third Reich and its strategy of regimentation, the need for an intimate pursuit of the private self initially prevailed over socially critical attitudes in postwar German art.

Around the end of the 1950s, however, the psychomotor intoxication of automatic improvisation and the calligraphic notation showed signs of erosion. In the United States as well as in Europe, a reaction set in against action painting, tachism, and *art informel*. These directed attention away from spontaneous artistic acts to a thorough exploration of the chromatic qualities of color itself. This kind of painting was inspired largely by the experience of East Asian art and by the meditative philosophy of Zen Buddhism, to which the group ZEN in Germany had turned earlier. The group SYN, the successor to ZEN in the 1960s, was also grounded in Zen Buddhism. Founded in 1965, the SYN alliance was a kind of reservoir into which flowed the scriptural components of *art informel* as well as the first theoretically based analyses of color. It is therefore not surprising that the outward image of SYN was very heterogeneous and that dialectical characteristics stood out even in the individual works. These characteristics were interpreted by the artists themselves in a cryptically philosophical manner as symbols for the tensions between the organic and the intelligent life of human existence.

More productive than this adaption of the symbolically rich wisdom of the Far East was the kind of abstraction initiated in Europe by the Italian Lucio Fontana (1899–1968). Also inspired by Far Eastern meditation, Fontana had by 1946 laid out plans for dynamic spatial paintings in which color would unfold in conjunction with light, motion, and sound. The first realizations of this program were his slit-open pictures. The spatially extensive monochromy of Fontana's pictures was then brought to a unique perfection by Yves Klein (1928–1962) in the shape of completely monochrome sponge reliefs. The Düsseldorf artists Otto Piene (b. 1928), Heinz Mack (b. 1931), and Günter Uecker (b. 1930) attached themselves particularly to Klein as well as to the pre-1933 Bauhaus experiments with movable light equipment. They made the dynamic relationship among light, color, and space their central theme in spectacular performances and in theoretical analyses. Under the programmatic name Zero, each of these three artists presented the vibrating capacity of light and color with a unique means of expression. Uecker arranged the white nail in diverse patterns as the central form for modulating light refraction on a white surface (Figure 9); Piene organized gigantic smoke and light ballets in order to produce an energized space of colored light. Mack experimented with various light reflections and interferences on raised or lustrously smooth metal surfaces (Figure 10) as well as with rotating cubes, vibrating stelai, and fluorescent plexiglass forms. These experiments earned him a worldwide reputation.

Distinguishing itself from the Zero movement, which concentrated on the spatially agitated luminosity of light and color, so-called concrete abstraction probed the characteristics of the painted color in its specific correspondence to the surrounding space. In contrast to the lyrical abstraction of *informel*, it was concerned with the objectifiable demonstration of the diverse characteristics of color. For this purpose, clearly delineated geometrical forms were used. Concrete abstraction drew its central inspiration from Josef Alber's *Homage to the Square*. With this work, Albers (1888–1976), a former Bauhaus student who lived in the United States, had produced a neutral form for the meditative display of the chromatic characteristics of color. So-called op(tical) art also referred to Albers and wrested dynamic modes of appearance from painted color. For this it used contrasts of black and white as well as irradiation and afterimage effects that stimulate the eye to color perceptions of three-dimensional spaces.

The color series of Victor Vasarely (b. 1908), a Hungarian living in France, also belong in this context. His works were widely imitated and quickly attained broad popularity in Germany as well as in the United States. In conjunction with the influence of American hard-edge painting, they found a reflection during the 1960s in the structured color surfaces of Karl Georg Pfahler (b. 1926). Due to the preferred use of strongly luminous colors, this direction in Germany was called *Signalkunst* (Signal art). The clear association of this term with the colors used in the German traffic system increasingly widened the gap in the course of the 1960s between *Signalkunst* and its American model, systemic painting. The lucid structural analyses of the latter also contrasted with the direction of the German variant toward the effects of pop art.

The lyrical counterpart to this geometric version of hard-edge painting also captured a great deal of attention. Here, however, the influence of Fontana and Klein was more tangible than that, for example, of the Americans Clyfford Still (1904–1980), Mark Rothko (1903–1970), and Morris Louis (1912–1962). In general, the unobtrusive language of this freer hard-edge painting remained in the background. The euphoria of the German art scene over the dazzling spectrum of objects and colors of the rapidly ascending pop art was the major reason for this neglect. Thus it was only in the 1970s that the sensitive chromatic presence in the pillow pictures of Gotthard Graubner (b. 1930), their objects drawn into the emanation of color, received a fair assessment. In these pictures, numerous layers of nylon meticulously stretched over the pictorial surface create fine nuances of subtle color tonalities. Instead of flat surfaces, these soft pillowlike curvatures produce colors that modulate with the light. They literally reach out from the wall into space (Figure 17).

In the Wake of America

Under the influence of the pop art boom, a system of emblems alluding to technology and the metropolitan environment developed from *Signalkunst*. These emblems fluctuated between schematic figuration and geometric construction. Although there was no pure pop art in Germany, the adulterated German form of pop colorfulness, geometric surfaces, and emblematic themes was carried along by the successes of the American and English pop waves. Lacking significance in its own right, however, it was quickly forgotten. Among German artists, the enthusiasm for the modernistic iconography of pop art was less active than receptive, because nearly five years passed between the Anglo-American birth of pop art and its perception on the German art scene. When in the mid-1960s the German art market was eagerly consuming Warhol's (b. 1928) and Lichtenstein's (b. 1923) icons of the American way of life, the countermovement of minimal art, with its cool aesthetics, was already in fashion in the United States. Due to the constantly increasing contacts between the United States and Europe, this countermovement was perceived simultaneously with the pop boom by German artists and critics. Thus pop art in Germany was actually embedded in a conglomeration of stylistic influences.

The German return to figuration in the 1960s was not limited to pop art. It came about in close conjunction with neosurrealistic and neodadaistic tendencies. Because the war had prevented the exhaustive development of their creative possibilities in Germany, both tendencies clearly demanded an intensive elaboration. The neodadaistic component became highly significant in German new realism as well as in the "happening" and Fluxus movements, and the neosurrealistic current of the 1960s culminated in the so-called fantastic realism. The latter became known on the international art scene as a typically German phenomenon and presented dreamlike fantasy worlds with realistic figurations. Gerhard Altenbourg (b. 1926), an East German individualist untouched by the socialist realism around him, transformed his poetic fantasies into finely limbed figural compositions and landscapes with calligraphic lineation and subtle specks of color. Beyond this, fantastic realism produced an abundance of erotic images alternating between aesthetic harmony and chaotic disintegration. It was not unusual for these to slip into a trendy, calculated routine.

No such routine developed in the other manifestations of the increasingly abundant figuration in German painting and sculpture. Impulses from neosurrealism and pop art blended with the first artistic ties to the tradition of *Neue Sachlichkeit*. Konrad Klapheck (b. 1935), a student of Goller in Düsseldorf, was the most significant talent in the discovery of veristic images. In his images of magically isolated machines, he was able to make technical, everyday tools like the typewriter, sewing machine, cash register, calculating machine, telephone, and shoe tree into statements of human characteristics. By their lack of perspective and cold construction, Klapheck's photographically realistic devices avoided becoming mere *trompe l'oeils*. To an extreme degree, they formulated the figurative reaction to the vague gesture of *informel* as well as the antithesis of the advertising typology of pop art. Klapheck's *Typewriter* (1955), painted without shadows against an empty background, is a metaphor for man's isolation in an environment marked by technology and anonymity (Figure 11). Painters like Fritz Köthe (b. 1916) and Peter Klasen (b. 1935), on the other hand, referred openly and directly to pop art and its repertoire of urbane advertising motifs. Through this pointed bias, they exposed the iconography of advertising to an ambiguity wavering between acclamation and ironic antagonism.

Sigmar Polke (b. 1942) and Gerhard Richter (b. 1932) have been particularly instrumental in creating new perspectives for the 1970s and early 1980s. In humorous picture puzzles, Polke has played an ironic game with clichés of consumer society and stylistic conventions from past and present. They represent an important point of departure for the bold gestures of young German painters in the early 1980s (Figure 20). Gerhard Richter has made a central contribution to the self-scrutiny of painting with purely formal means of expression. After his training at the Academy of Art in Dresden, Richter left the GDR. In 1963, together with Sigmar Polke and Konrad Fischer-Lueg (b. 1939), he demonstratively opposed the catch-phrase "capitalist realism" to the political regimentation of socialist realism in his former homeland. Under this banner he proposed a total renunciation of pictures with meaningful content and of an illusionistic style. In an apparent paradox, he realized this goal by means of photo painting. His pictures were done with the help of entire series of photographs in which crowds of strangers, newspaper articles, landscapes, or irrelevant cloud formations were captured. The content of the single picture became absolutely unimportant through the arbitrariness in the selection of the subject. The pictorial statement concentrated instead entirely on the "how" of painting and on the quality of the colors. Richter exploited the tints and hues in illusionary color compositions as well as in nuanced gradations of gray (Figure 12). With this individually manipulated photo painting—far removed from any hyperrealism—Richter made a highly original contribution to the systematic investigation of painting fundamentals that had developed at the end of the 1960s on the international art scene as a consequence of conceptual tendencies.

There was actually no genuine concept art at all in Germany. Only the barest rudiments of a conceptual art could be found in the work of Peter Roehr (1944–1968), an artist who died at the age of twenty-four. In the late 1960s, he concentrated on a severely serial principle of montage and built his "additions without composition" out of typographic and textual elements as well as film sequences, advertising jingles, objects, and photographic materials (Figure 16). Hans Haacke (b. 1936) and Hanne Darboven (b. 1941), two German artists who live mainly in New York, took part in the systematic and severely formal countermovement to pop art that became known in the United States as minimal and concept art. Their biographies call to mind that New York was the center of the international style at the time and the Mecca for most German avant-garde artists.

The situation at home, to be sure, was less encouraging. It was principally the representatives of tachism who had attained teaching positions in the academies. After 1965, moreover, pop art fever hit the German art market with such blind force in relation to alternative forms of expression that the resulting lack of attention paid to the German avant-garde gave these artists good reason to move to New York. Here they quickly found agreement with their ideas on an objectified language of art from artists like Carl Andre (b. 1935), Donald Judd (b. 1928), and Sol LeWitt (b. 1928). Thus the works of Hans Haacke with their biological, physical, and sociological contents, which transferred the scientific manner of thinking in systems and models to art, were noticed in Germany only some years after their origins. American art critics, galleries, and museums had long recognized their quality. The same was true of Hanne Darboven's additions of numbers according to certain indices. With the help of mathematical formulas and series of numbers, Darboven conceals a personal register in these additions. It is accessible only to those who can decode the index of the various diagrams.

The time displacement that has generally marked the German reception of the international avant-garde since the 1950s was neutralized only once in the 1960s, with happenings and Fluxus events. At the time, Wolf Vostell (b. 1932) was successful in spontaneously transporting to Germany the happening concept that had been developed by Robert Rauschenberg (b. 1925), John Cage (b. 1912), Claes Oldenburg (b. 1929), and Allan Kaprow (b. 1927). Together with other German artists he was also able to tie into the international movement of new realism. As a kind of collage made up of incidents and series of events related to elementary forms of the theater, the happening proved to be an attractive instrument of expression, with its possibilities for improvisation and with its inclusion of everyday banalities. It was an excellent medium for reactivating and bringing up to date the conceptual potential of dada. Through the concept of "decollage-happening," moreover, Vostell endowed the German neodadaist action art with a satirical and provocative component. It emphasized consciousness-raising and the sociopolitical decoding of absurd and destructive environmental conditions. It took over the act of poster shredding from the parallel movement of the French *nouveau réalisme*, mocking the glamour and consumption of modern society.

In the face of real events like the Vietnam War, politically involved sculptors like Siegfried Neuenhausen (b. 1931) used pop art, neosurrealism, or neodada according to need in order to give their object art the impelling effect of shock or violent emotion. Neuenhausen's torture dolls affected observers just as directly as Vostell's *Miss America* of 1968 striding over a captured Vietcong soldier or Klaus Staeck's (b. 1938) biting political satires on the German political landscape, modeled after John Heartfield's (1891–1968) dadaist poster montages of the 1920s.

No other German artist pursued the mediation of art and life with such extreme consequence as Joseph Beuys, who began with happenings in 1962. Scarcely one year later, he formally incorporated his events into the Fluxus movement. For his own ritualistic productions, the happening concept of free improvisation and the inclusion of the public was less acceptable than the Fluxus events, which moved according to fixed scores. For Beuys, one of the most important acts was the declaration of his biography as an art work and the consistent citation of his life (in the form of personal relics) as the material of his artistic constructions. Beuys made use of a large body of forms of expression, partly traditional and partly contemporary. He lent them an axiomatic symbolism, using them in conjunction with contrasts like felt and fat and drawing upon potential mythological meanings. Particularly in the object ensembles of the 1960s, felt and fat appear again and again as pictorial images for energy accumulators. Felt has the capacity for storing heat; fat can change from solid to liquid form, emanating warmth (Figure 14). Thus Beuys projected the experience of life's diversity—the fluctuation of forces between chaos and form, between the "organic" and the "crystalline" principle, between nature and spirit—into palpable images more striking than mere abstract concepts.

With the extension of his artistic activity into practical politics, Beuys made the link between past and present culture. He merged elements of the sociopolitical thought of 1968 with Rudolf Steiner's anthroposophy as well as with German classicism and romanticism into the leitmotif of a "social sculpture, an art of social building." His remarkable pedagogical capacity for recognizing and inspiring the creative potential of his academy students in Düsseldorf has made Beuys the most significant university teacher on the German art scene since 1945, a fact unchanged by his temporary removal from office. The large group of former Beuys students that extends from Blinky Palermo to Reiner Ruthenbeck, Anselm Kiefer, Ulrike Rosenbach, and Katharina Sieverding constitutes a representative cross-section of the internationally respected German avant-garde of the 1960s. And for the first time, renowned foreign artists point with pride to the fact that they have been either students or collaborators of this German professor of art.

Isolation Within the Pluralistic Labyrinth of Styles

Beuys's ability to make methodical functional and situational relationships visible is one of the most important stimuli that he has provided the younger generation. Productive impulses for a reaction to the perfectly geometrical structures of form-conscious Minimal Art have emanated from the impressive "poverty" and the immediately perceptible corporeal quality that are peculiar to Beuys's objects and installations. These impulses are expressed in Reiner Ruthenbeck's (b. 1937) apparently formless scattering of paper balls, in the accumulation of coal dust, or in the unusual bonding together of glass and dark material. The trained stonemason Ulrich Rückriem (b. 1938) has similar aims with scrap iron or unhewn rock fragments, which he manipulates in ways appropriate to the material. This material art, which shows a peculiar ambivalence between form and antiform, is basically a direction of art initiated in Europe, and its Italian designation *arte povera* has also been accepted in Germany as a general stylistic denotation. Since *arte povera* emphasizes the originating or utilization process more strongly than the end product, this manipulation of difficult organic and inorganic materials not normally used in art has also been called process art in Germany.

During an extended stay in New York in the 1960s, Franz Erhard Walther (b. 1939) worked on another form of German process art oriented more toward functional analysis. By proposing a certain perception or action that acquaints the attentive viewer exactly and in detail with the functional factors at play, this process art has a strongly involving character. In Walther's so-called blueprints, didactically structured operating instructions include specific proposals for use along with explanatory drawings and instruments sewn by the artist (Figure 15 a, b).

In the course of the 1970s, the German art scene increasingly branched out into an almost bewildering multiplicity of creative experiments. The individual artist's growing renunciation of an allegiance to an international style indicates not a decline, but rather a strengthening and a liberation from the adoring gaze cast until now at New York models. The gradual dissolution of what had internationally crystallized in the two preceding decades is an indirect result of the political upheaval of American self-consciousness in the wake of the Vietnam and Watergate fiascos. There has also been a tendency toward moderation in Western Europe and the United States due to the growing economic crisis. On both sides of the Atlantic the consequences included a retreat into past cultural values and a concentration on private matters. Exhibitionistic gestures appeared, traces from individual lives were quietly gathered, personal symbols found their expression. With concepts like "individual mythology" (for Michael Buthe [b. 1944]), "trace protection" (for Dorothee von Windheim [b. 1945]), and "narrative art" (for Fritz Schwegler [b. 1935]), the search for private refuges was paraphrased. At Documenta 5 in 1972, Michael Buthe exhibited a spatial structure, *Homage to the Sun*, which he erected for himself alone as a cultic refuge far removed from the grayness of the everyday world. Buthe unites the most diverse symbols—from archaic and non-European cultures as well as from hippy life styles—into an alchemistic labyrinth of myths that consciously evades a direct interpretation (Figure 19).

Even in action art, with its ties to the happening, hermetic performances limited to the artist alone were put on behind closed doors and recorded only by film or video camera. Performance artists like Luciano Castelli (b. 1951) emphatically acknowledged their homosexuality in such events, while Jürgen Klauke (b. 1943) and the photo-artist Katharina Sieverding (b. 1944) questioned the fixation on normal behavioral patterns and cliché-ridden sexual roles in partially aggressive gestures of sexual transformation. The visual dramatization of homosexuality is often tied to feminist declarations, which also play a role in the alternative political scene outside official parties and institutions. On film and in live performances, an artist such as Ulrike Rosenbach (b. 1943) ventures to define women's liberation in ways that try to push beyond the economic forefront far into unconscious scenes of the primordial battle between the sexes.

These pluralistic expressions of the self can be most interestingly observed in painting and drawing, in which a turbulent revival is occurring. This rebirth stems from the particular suitability of these media for the fixation of spontaneous visions. Common to all the pictorial scripts is the dynamic juxtaposition of contrary elements, statements, and styles. In spite of his early death in 1977, Blinky Palermo (Peter Heisterberg [1943–1977]), the pupil of the mystic Beuys, has become along with his mentor one of the most important forces behind this development. He rejected a specific stylistic tie even in the late 1960s when minimal art and concept art controlled the international image of avant-garde art. He succeeded in seeing beyond his day and in creating a sensitively balanced formal context that produces an identity between the color and its object. The identity is all the more intensely experienced in that it is a sentient truth, not comprehensible in words. With colored objects like the *Blue Disc and Stick* (1968) as well as with wall paintings, Palermo creates a balanced and exacting scrutinized spatial structure involving colors, proportions, and material contents (Figure 18).

Intense gestures and a joy in myth-making are intrinsic to another direction of the new painting that achieves a "Germanic" demeanor in the works of Georg Baselitz (b. 1938), Markus Lüpertz (b. 1941), and Anselm Kiefer (b. 1945) by manipulation of Teutonic legend and national history. The quotation of German symbols represents a direct parallel to Syberberg's colossal films on Richard Wagner, Karl May, and Hitler, which aspire to create a typology of the "German" soul. A. R. Penck (b. 1939), the former outsider in the German Democratic Republic (GDR) who now lives in the Federal Republic, cultivated a mythological profundity in the 1960s. In his works, similar to prehistoric cave painting, he reduced human existence to coded functional traces in a kind of suggestive invocation in order to preserve only the essentials of experience in memory.

Rigorous subjectivity is currently to be found among the very young representatives of a German neoexpressionism, who have also been called the "young wild men." The references in form and content back to the harsh metropolitan subjects of Dix and Grosz are striking in the works of the Berlin adherents of this free style. The atmospheric temper of underground provocation and the exhibitionism of punk are also resonant in their lavish use of color. Particularly the works of K. H. Hödicke (b. 1938), Salome (Wolfgang Cilarz [b. 1954]) and Rainer Fetting (b. 1949) possess a willful spontaneity. These artists have linked expressionistic figuration and a zeal for calligraphy in the style of abstract expressionism. Although intensely involved with the self, the Berlin artists by no means take themselves very seriously but consider their wild style more an ironically impudent protest against all cultural conventions than a profound statement of the soul. The impression arises that the young wild men are bent on the stormy rediscovery of the joy of painting that had all but disappeared in the frugality of minimal art. Precisely because of its unsystematic egocentricity, it is obvious that such an art without morality and design cannot long remain unchallenged. The attack comes mainly from the socially and politically involved realistic figuration that has increasingly established itself in Berlin.

Through the active promotion of culture by the Federal Republic, Berlin has become attractive for a growing number of artists in the last few years as a place to live and work. Also, as the residence of the German Academic Exchange Service (DAAD), the former German art capital makes studios available every year to internationally renowned stipendiaries. The far-reaching dependence of the divided city on the international political situation has made the Berlin artists as well as the students at the Free University more sensitive than elsewhere to political and social problems. It is therefore not surprising that a critical realism based on neodadaist impulses has been developing here since the later 1960s. With wit, irony, and sometimes also a soberly objective style of reporting, this critical art closely examines the realities of the Federal Republic and sporadically casts a glance over the border between the two Germanies, which is nowhere else as directly observable as in Berlin.

A Look over the Wall

In spite of the division of Germany after the war into two states with entirely different philosophical assumptions and cultural aims, East and West Germans possess a common basis in their cultural tradition before 1933 that has prevented a total dissolution of the sense of a national culture. Both sides have learned to respect the other's distinct sociopolicical fundamentals and not merely to defame them, and there have been signs of a dialogue between East and West German art in recent years.

Since the first, spectacular East German participation in the Documenta exhibition of 1977, it has become increasingly possible for East German art to venture across the borders onto the Western art scene it had observed so long. The growing representation of East German art in West German institutions and galleries has led to a widespread interest among critics and collectors for this art and its socialist characteristics, particularly for the paintings of Wolfgang Mattheuer (b. 1927), Werner Tübke (b. 1929), Willi Sitte (b. 1921), and Bernhard Heisig (b. 1925).

The path that led to these recent successes was a long one. In the later 1940s, the expressive realism in East Germany, with its reference to pre-1933 critical realism, should certainly have earned greater resonance than it actually did. Among the communist painters of this style were those of the prewar generation, such as Otto Nagel (1894–1967), Hans Grundig (1901–1958), Curt Querner (1904–1976), and Wilhelm Lachnit (1899–1962). But because of its fascination with American and French subjectivism, the West had little interest in those artists who had come out of the ASSO (German Association of Revolutionary Artists, founded in 1926) and who acknowledged "social realism" in the tradition of Heinrich Zille (1859–1929), Käthe Kollwitz (1867–1945), and Ernst Barlach (1870–1938).

Beginning in 1951, however, cultural policies required a stylistic alignment with the Soviet model of socialist realism. A younger generation carried through a program in painting and sculpture under the motto "the New Man needs a new portrayal." This program propagated the political goals of the SED (Socialist Unity party), namely the "active and productive effort" in the reconstruction of heavy industry and in the pursuit of agricultural collectivization. In most of the pictures exhibited in Dresden in March 1953 at the Third German Art Exhibition, it was evident what was understood by a simple, exemplary hero-worker in the GDR. An imposing number of worker portraits (Figure 21), demonstration pictures, industrial landscapes, and scenes depicting work processes described the new image of man in a realistic style that had copied its posed arrangements of figures from nineteenth-century representational painting.

In the course of the 1950s, the genre of landscape painting entered fully into the service of economic production propaganda by depicting only such subjects as industrial landscapes, mining scenes, or collective farms with tractors tilling the soil. Historical painting had but one subject: the history of class warfare. The self-portrait, a popular genre in the 1940s, as well as the family portrait, had disappeared almost completely from the art scene.

Paintings of workers and work brigades in the "service of the proletariat" became the most strongly encouraged and central pictorial genres in the 1950s. Stylistically, these paintings were modeled on the representational posing of bourgeois portraits and group pictures of the nineteenth century that stressed external status symbols. Through the symbols, the people depicted acquired a kind of monumental pose with symbolic amplification. For the most part they were not given individually characteristic facial expressions; on the contrary, they were dominated by an expression of herculean power. With this pictorial conception, the conformity with Soviet models was complete. Acquiescent to Lenin's demand that art had to be "popular and partisan," these models blocked every progressive stylistic experiment in the Soviet Union after 1927.

Works by East German artists of the younger generation who dared to vary the pattern of the realistic concept with willful formal experiments invited the party's reproach of Western decadence and were largely pushed aside. When in the 1960s, however, the insight circulated among artists as well as cultural bureaucrats in the GDR that the herculean type of poster-worker was no longer an adequate representation of the socialist world of work, the party leaders of the SED instigated a change in the concept of socialist realism with a summons to stylistic experimentation. Just as in the 1950s, the reason for the change was a specific program in GDR politics. In the second half of the 1960s an economic policy based on a belief in progress and science established itself. It held that socialism, with the help of the most advanced technology, could surpass capitalism. The new socialist image of humans in art was now the worker comprehensively educated in technology and ideology, who had some similarity with the image of humans in the Renaissance. Besides Willi Sitte, artists such as Bernhard Heisig, Werner Tübke, and Wolfgang Mattheuer now became stylistically representative of the altered image of painting. The new style initially aroused only a cautious interest on the part of Western art criticism. This interest, however, has grown steadily.

Both of the central genres of GDR painting bear the stamp of this so-called middle generation of painters. The scenes with workers (Figure 21) and the historical picture (Figure 24) represent the public image of socialist realism up to the 1970s and even to today. The scenes of workers are basically an individualized extension of the portraits of workers and work brigades already described. The new historical picture has a more complex conception, with its goals of delving into the socialist aspects of all cultural history and of confronting capitalism with the communist ideology. The essential new elements of painting in the 1960s are less in content than in the turn to a pluralistic concept of style and in the individual, even psychological, characterization of the figures portrayed.

The Long Farewell to Socialist Realism
in the GDR

Painting in the GDR underwent its most decisive change at the beginning of the 1970s, when the growth of stylistic quality and the elaboration of unique painting techniques combined with a growing orientation toward problematic subject matter. In 1971 the SED officially sanctioned structural experiments in art. However, the room granted by the party for experimentation was not used by stylistic innovators only. There emerged in individual works a more differentiated realism and a multileveled sense of problems. This initiated an increasing demand for the expression of individual emotions in a decidedly personal way.

There are basically two tendencies in the art of the GDR in the 1970s. First, there is the broad spectrum of a socialist, realistic painting that builds on the style and contents of the painter-professors Tübke, Heisig, Mattheuer, and Sitte. This direction is a specific product of the GDR. It has cautiously freed itself step by step from the traditional norms of a dogmatic socialist realism and is today an independent representation of socialist consciousness. The subject matter includes a growing number of statements involving concrete situations of conflict within the socialist order. This critical view of real problems is, however, never meant destructively. As an involved socialist, the artist aims for an improvement of the actual socialist system by pointing to its insufficiencies. The most numerous themes of this kind are the growing need for private space, a narrow-minded bureaucracy, and the danger of anonymity in the communication between the state and the individual.

Other artists raise issues of environmental protection or present conflicts growing out of the escalating gap between the generations and their different demands. Of particular significance is the series of symbolic pictures laden with conflicts painted since 1969 by Wolfgang Mattheuer (Figure 22). The stylistic repertory for this type of subject matter is broad. Willi Sitte erects his cellular, collagelike structures based on influences from futurism to modern montage techniques. Conscious connections to expressionism, to Léger (1881–1955), and the *Neue Sachlichkeit* as well as to the critical realism of the ASSO or Renato Guttuso (b. 1912) can be observed in the works of many other painters.

In the genre of historical painting, the allegorical works by Werner Tübke have aroused the greatest interest. With an almost somnambulistic assurance, Tübke feels at home in the styles of the old masters like Rubens and Altdorfer. And with a refined sense for the symbolical and mythical treasures of all of cultural history, he always produces that quotation that seems appropriate to a fantasy fusing past and present for the interpretation of life from the socialist viewpoint (Figure 23). This tie to the so-called cultural heritage is an essential characteristic of contemporary art in the GDR. To the art observer from the West accustomed to constantly new and original discoveries of images, it is a characteristic difficult to comprehend and hard to follow. If, however, the specific form of the historical painting is to be adequately judged, this "heritage reception," as it is called by art critics in the East, must be taken into account. This is especially true because it also conceals political statements in its stylistic quotations as, for example, in Bernhard Heisig's crudely colored depictions of a murdering, plundering soldiery with their borrowing of veristic modes of expression from George Grosz and Otto Dix (Figure 24).

In the works of some of the younger painters, the scale of stylistic loans from the West extends from dada reminiscences to Salvador Dali (b. 1904) and Max Ernst. There is also something like a second tendency of painting in the GDR within this group of young painters. It is a search for new, still unspent means of expression, not necessarily figurative ones, to symbolize individual experiential horizons. In the 1960s an abstract imagerial language of high quality existed only in the very personal notations of Gerhard Altenbourg (b. 1926) and Carlfriedrich Claus (b. 1930), which were actually better known in the West than in the GDR; the 1970s offer numerous stylistic experiments with abstract painting, as well as with the collage, the photographic montage, and even with action art.

Beyond that, a self-willed avant-garde has been emerging since 1979 in Dresden as well as in Karl-Marx-Stadt that, with its psychographic recording of entirely personal experiences, consciously distances itself from the realism of other GDR painters. Besides Penck, who now lives in the Federal Republic, the intellectual founder is Jürgen Böttcher (b. 1931), who has become known for his work in documentary films. After a few years of inactivity as a painter, in 1978 he found his way back to drawing in combination with a technique of painting over photographs. From this synthesis of media, he developed a manner of expression both fresh and individual that directly corresponds to the explosive codes of the contemporary artistic avant-garde of Western Europe.

In many other non-figurative, dadaistic, and actionistic means of expression, there is presently some persistence of eclecticism. It would be false to equate such activities with their Western parallels. For the East German artists, these experiments are above all conquests of new expressive media that they are discovering, testing, and evaluating.

Glossary of Terms

Abstract expressionism. The most significant international current in art during the late 1940s and 1950s. The concept was at first limited to American abstract painting called *action painting*, which emphasized emotion and improvisation. It later became a collective designation for the parallel European currents, *tachism* and *informel.*

Action painting. A painting technique involving the artist in physical activity. Initiated by the abstract expressionist Jackson Pollock in 1947, it found numerous imitators in Europe. Colors were splashed onto a gigantic canvas spread out on the ground so that the spontaneous physical movements could be deciphered from the tracks of color on the canvas.

Arte povera. A stylistic direction of *object art* initiated in the early 1970s by Italian artists that stresses the use of flimsy natural materials, both organic and inorganic, as well as of the synthetic materials of modern technology.

Automatism. Conversion of dream states into a spontaneous manner of presentation that is not rationally controlled. This somnambulistic process of painting was developed by *surrealism* and after 1947 brought to its peak of refinement by *action painting* in the form of rhythmic painting activities.

Bauhaus. A school founded in 1919 by Walter Gropius in Weimar for the fine arts, architecture, and the skilled crafts. Constructivist and scientific tendencies predominated, and all artistic disciplines strove for clarity, objectivity, and functionalism. In 1928 the Bauhaus was relocated in Dessau. In 1933 it was closed by the National Socialists. Josef Albers, a teacher at the Bauhaus, founded a "New Bauhaus" in Chicago in 1937.

Calligraphy. The flowing and energetic linearization with pen or brush, especially as it was developed in Far Eastern brush techniques.

Capitalist realism. A term developed in analogy to *socialist realism* by Gerhard Richter in 1963 for his own works as well as those of other artists. These works dealt with the trivialities of the everyday world of the consumer mentality and the ideals of taste of the petite bourgeoisie during the early 1960s.

Concept art. A designation for artistic attempts in the mid-1960s issuing from *minimal art* that seek the clearly defined and objective establishment of systematic relationships and methodical processes. Textual paraphrases, photographs, and diagrams almost entirely replace the painted picture as the forms of representation.

Concrete abstraction. A nonrepresentational artistic form that generally excludes references to nature, lyricisms, and symbolic compositions.

It uses instead precise pictorial elements like geometrically structured fields of color as its structural means. This countermovement to *abstract expressionism* received a first theoretical framework in 1930 in the famous, only issue of the journal *Art Concret*.

Constructivism. Designation for an abstract direction in art initiated in Russia in 1912. It constructed paintings and sculpture from geometrical and stereometrical elements and considered these works to be the aesthetic reflection of a modern world dominated by mathematics and technology. Constructivist ideas also formed an important basis of the *Bauhaus*.

Critical realism (social realism). A socially involved direction of realistic figuration in Germany that has become particularly prominent in West Berlin since the 1960s. It finds its ties to tradition in the works of Käthe Kollwitz and the *Neue Sachlichkeit* as well as in *pop art* and *photographic realism*. Politically critical realism is understood as a reaction to the *socialist realism* of the GDR.

Cubism. A stylistic creation of Picasso and Braque originating between 1909 and 1912 that was derived from the late impressionism of Cézanne. Cubism gave up every manner of painting that created a spatial illusion and instead constructed the painted objects on the canvas with geometrical elements like cubes and rhombuses. Using this technique, several partial views of each object are simultaneously represented. Cubism thus became the forerunner of an abstract art.

Dada. An international artistic movement initiated in 1916 that has no specific program and no fixed theory. Its one object and goal is to destroy bourgeois artistic and social values through a manner of expression that is provocative, paradoxical, ironical, and comic.

Ecole de Paris. A collective designation for all artistic directions since impressionism (i.e., since around 1900) that have originated on the Parisian art scene. More specifically, the Ecole de Paris designates that loosely bound group of painters in Paris from 1945 to 1960 who individually followed various currents of abstract painting (*tachism, informel*).

Expressionism. An artistic movement spread across all of Europe from 1900 to 1915 and represented in Germany by the two groups Die Brücke (the Bridge) and Der Blaue Reiter (the Blue Rider). The strongly accented colors of expressionist works gave passionate expression to emotions, religious ecstasy, social involvement, and psychoanalytic exploration. The painters of the Bridge were more inclined to figural representation, those of the Blue Rider to abstract compositions as an expression of their feelings.

Fantastic realism. A German and Austrian style that developed in the 1950s from *surrealism*. Reverting to the techniques of the old masters, fantastic realism created a mode of expression that is imaginatively erotic, ironically disorienting, and at times, intensified to manneristic grotesqueries.

Futurism. An artistic movement originating in Italy in 1909 that strove for an artistic realization of the modern technological age. Dynamism, simultaneity of movement, and color rhythms were its central expressive principles.

Happening and Fluxus. An action art developed at the end of the 1950s and the beginning of the 1960s by the American *new realists.* It combined tendencies of dadaist improvisation with the automatic representational gestures of *action painting.* The goal was a sensitization of the capacity for experience by means of unusual theatrical performances in which the public could participate.

Hard edge. The exact delimitation of color tones in hard edge painting by means of rigorously separated geometrical planes.

Hard edge painting. Initially an American, then also a European, style of the 1950s and 1960s that derived from *concrete abstraction* and aimed at the presentation of color tonalities. In contrast to the lack of emotion in *concrete abstraction,* the effects of color in hard edge painting are decidedly lyrical.

Individual mythologies. Pictorial and, to some extent, hermetically encoded representation of subjective world views, archaeological inclinations, narrative self-exploration, and documentations from cultural history. These mythologies are understood as a reaction of European art in the 1970s to the lapidary objectivity of *minimal art* and *concept art.*

Informel. Designation for a European direction in abstract art that originated in Paris around 1945. It set itself apart from *concrete abstraction* by the rejection of an organized formal structure and by freely invented rhythmical symbols.

Material picture. Designation for works of art that place a special emphasis on the sense stimulations of materials like sand, coal, cement, or straw. These raw materials are in part mixed with colored substances to produce a rough pictorial base.

Minimal art. A tendency in sculptural construction that first appeared in the United States in the 1960s. As a reaction to the emotions of *abstract expressionism,* it aims at lapidary, logical, and simple basic structures of formal expression. The serial display of similar elements plays an important role.

Monochromy. The use of only one color, in contrast to polychromy.

New realism. An artistic style at the end of the 1950s and in the early 1960s that united the various progressive movements in America and Europe against the predominance of *abstract expressionism.* It aspired to be a renewal of *dada* ideas. The action forms of art, the *happening and Fluxus* and *pop art* emerged from American new realism.

Object art. Since *cubism* and the use of unconventional materials in plastic construction, modern sculpture has been subdivided into an object art, in which every raw material is artistically respectable, and traditional sculpture, which continues to work with conventional materials like bronze and wood.

Op art. An American and European direction in art in the 1950s and 1960s that emerged from *constructivist* abstraction. It concentrated on a systematic analysis of light refraction, light reflection, color interferences, and moiré effects.

Pop art. An artistic direction that developed independently in both the United States and England in the late 1950s. Its pictorial themes were derived from the industrial culture of the modern metropolis. In its forms of representation, pop art absorbed impulses from advertising and the media.

Process art. A stylistic direction of the 1970s that focuses more sharply on the process of a work's production—i.e., the measurements and the treatment of the material—than on the end product. Process art thus not only has close ties to *concept art*, but also to *arte povera*.

Sharp-focus realism (hyperrealism). A monumental and realistic mode of painting in America and Europe during the 1970s. It depends on certain perspectives and manipulative possibilities of photographic optics to slightly distort the objectivity of the realistic picture.

Socialist realism. A Marxist-Leninist theory of art formulated at the first Writers' Congress of the Soviet Union in 1934, which gradually became obligatory for all communist-bloc states after World War II. The norm demanded of the artist is a concrete historical depiction of reality in its revolutionary development. For graphic art, socialist realism prescribes realistic figuration as the only suitable method for the reflection of reality and demands that its content be partisan and rooted in the national soil.

Surrealism. A movement founded in 1924 in Paris by André Breton that later extended across the international art scene. In its continuance of *dada*'s anarchistic ideas, it exchanged the normal constraints of logic for the unconscious and the absurd. With *automatism*, it invented a technique of representation for psychic experiences that was not rationally controlled.

Systemic painting. A current in painting parallel to *minimal art*, which is embodied mainly in sculptural works. An exhibition organized in New York's Guggenheim Museum in 1966 gave the designation "systemic painting" to this analytic and formal direction of painting.

Tachism. The term coined in France for a spontaneous and abstract manner of painting since the latter 1940s. Color is brought onto the canvas in a speckling fashion as an automatic abreaction of psychic impulses. A style parallel to American *action painting.*

Verism (Neue Sachlichkeit). A realistic tendency in German painting from 1918 through the 1920s. In contrast to the eruptions of feelings in *expressionism* and the abstractions of *constructivism, Neue Sachlichkeit* seeks the inherent order of the phenomenal world and strives for a pictorial acuity free of emotion.

Young Wild Men. Reference to painting in America and Europe since the latter 1970s that is characterized by strongly expressive colors and cryptic personal symbols.

Readings

Celant, Germano. *Arte Povera.* New York: Praeger, 1969.

Fox, Milton S. (ed.). *Art Since 1945.* New York 1958.

Gachnang, Johannes. *New German Painting.* Milan: Giancarlo Politi Editore, 1982.

Grohmann, Will. "Germany, Austria, Switzerland," in Marcel Brion et al., *Art Since 1945.* New York: Thames and Hudson, 1962, pp. 155–220.

Jappe, Georg. "Young Artists in Germany." *Studio International.* No. 941, February 1972.

Katalog: Berlin, A Critical View. Ugly Realism 20s–70s. London: Institute of Contemporary Arts, and Berlin: Berliner Festspiele, 1978.

Lippard, Lucy R. *Six Years. The Dematerialization of the Art Object from 1966 to 1972.* New York: Praeger, 1973.

Naylor, Colin, and Orridge, Genesis P. *Contemporary Artists.* London: St. James Press, and New York: St. Martin's Press, 1977.

German Art
(All artwork reproduced by permission)

1. Willi Baumeister, Metaphysical Landscape with a Yellow Center, 1949. Oil and plastic wood on cardboard, 81 × 100 cm. Former collection of Karl Swoher, Hessian State Museum, Darmstadt.
2. Julius Bissier, 8 Oct. 58 Ascona, 1958. Egg-oil tempera on linen, 17.5 × 26.8 cm. Art collection of North, Rhine Westphalia, Düsseldorf.
3. Hans Hartung, T. 49-9, 1949. Oil on canvas, 89 × 162 cm. Art collection of North-Rhine Westphalia, Düsseldorf.
4. Ernst Wilhelm Nay, Circle Signs, 1961. Oil on canvas, 200 × 120 cm. Art collection of North-Rhine Westphalia, Düsseldorf.
5. Wols, Ultima composizione, 1951. Oil on canvas, 70 × 63 cm. Collection of Jacques Ulmann, Paris.
6. K.R.H. Sonderborg, 16.37–17.13, 1956/57. Tempera on cardboard, 70 × 92 cm. Kunsthalle, Hamburg.
7. Emil Schumacher, Cadmium, 1958. Oil on canvas, 170 × 131.5 cm. Kunsthalle, Hamburg.
8. Horst Antes, Masked Figure on Yellow, 1965. Oil on canvas, 120.4 × 100.5 cm. Kunsthalle, Hamburg.
9. Günter Uecker, White Picture, 1959. Wooden plate with nails, covered with linen and sprayed white, 55.5 × 60 cm. Kaiser Wilhelm Museum, Krefeld.
10. Heinz Mack, Light Dynamo, 1960. Wooden box, aluminum plate, corrugated glass plate and electric motor, 57 × 56 × 22 cm. Kaiser Wilhelm Museum, Krefeld.
11. Konrad Klapheck, Typewriter, 1955. Oil on canvas, 68 × 74 cm. Private collection of the artist, Düsseldorf.
12. Gerhard Richter, Pedestrian, 1963. Oil on canvas, 140 × 176 cm. Former collection of Karl Swoher, Hessian State Museum, Darmstadt.
13. Wolf Vostell, Miss America, 1968. Canvas photo, glaze and silkscreen on canvas, 200 × 120 cm. Museum Ludwig, Cologne.
14. Joseph Beuys, Snowfall, 1965. Felt plates over fir branches, 23 × 120 × 363 cm. Public art collection, Basel (E. Hoffmann Endowment).
15a. Franz Erhard Walther, Semicircle II: Outside, 1972. Strong canvas material, radius: 6.00 m; 20 cm wide. (From: Franz Erhard Walther, *Arbeiten 1969–1976*, 2nd type set, Biennale Sao Paulo, 1977).
15b. Franz Erhard Walther, Progressions by Sections I, 1973. Strong canvas material, each section: 11.78 m; 26 cm wide.

16. Peter Roehr, Untitled, 1965. Paper in Plastic, 49.5 x 48.5 cm. Paul Maenz Gallery, Cologne.
17. Gotthard Graubner, Spatialized Color: Dharma I, 1977. Oil, acetone, and turpentine on canvas, 280 × 280 cm. Gallery in Bochum. (See catalogue of Documenta 6.)
18. Blinky Palermo (Peter Heisterberg), Blue Disc and Stick, 1968. Two-part object leaning against the wall consisting of a plywood disc and stick covered with blue linen tape. Collection of Dr. Speck, Cologne.
19. Michael Buthe, Homage to the Sun (part of a room-size installation at Documenta 5), 1972. Colored cloths, wood. Photo by Karl Heinz Krugs, Hamburg.
20. Sigmar Polke, Landscape, 1966. Plastic on canvas, 100 × 90 cm. Gallery M. Werner, Cologne.
21. Willi Sitte, Figures in the Shower, 1978. Pencil/watercolor on paper, 100 × 75.5 cm. Ludwig collection, New Gallery, Aachen.
22. Wolfgang Mattheuer, Burning Guitar, 1975. Silkscreen in 12 colors, 78 × 59 cm. Ludwig collection, New Gallery, Aachen.
23. Werner Tübke, Large Beach, 1968/69. Mixed technique on canvas, 200 × 135 cm. Ludwig collection, New Gallery, Aachen.
24. Bernhard Heisig, Prussian Museum, 1976/77. Oil on canvas. Diptych, 150 × 165 cm, 150 × 60 cm. Ludwig collection, New Gallery, Aachen.

1

2

3

4

5

6

7

8

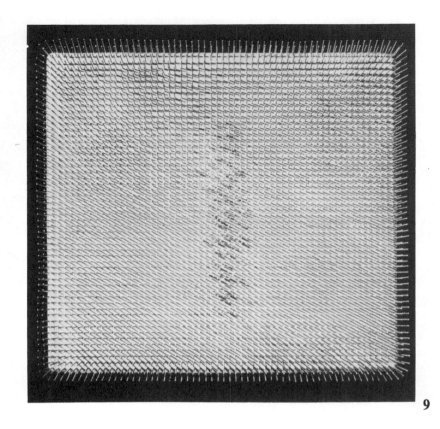

9

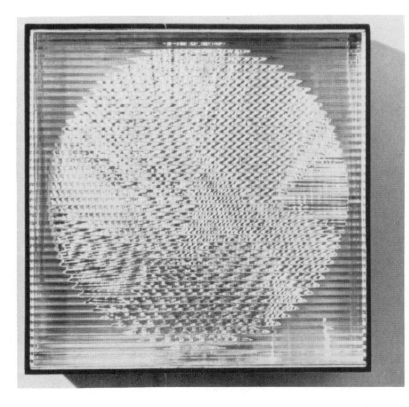

10

14

13

16

15a

15b

15a The user walks slowly along the semicircle, beginning at either end. The inside form remains negative behind him, the surroundings slowly unroll before his eyes. Arrival at the end point—with the starting point directly behind him—makes the user very conscious of the negative interior semicircle; nevertheless, his atteniton—directed forwards—hardly extends beyond the prolongation of the base.

15b Neither participant can see the segmentations of the other side; only by observing the other person's relative position can the sections be distinguished. When one changes position, the act of lifting the canvas to enter the construction also helps the observer perceive the segments.

17

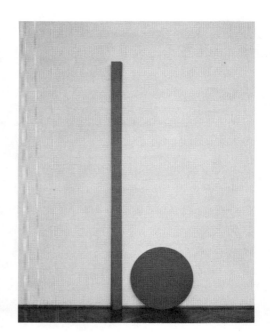

18

19

20

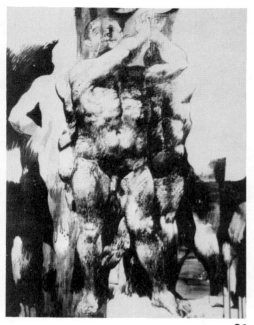

21

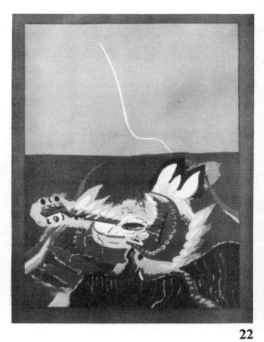

22

24

23

Index of Proper Names